Ever Yours in Truth,
Nome

Published by
Society of Abidance in Truth (SAT)
1834 Ocean Street
Santa Cruz, CA 95060 USA
(831) 425-7287
www.SATRamana.org
email: sat@cruzio.com

First Edition
ISBN: 9780981940960

Acknowledgements

Deep appreciation and gratitude are here expressed for Raman Muthukrishnan and Sangeeta Raman for proofreading this book and distribution of SAT publications, for Raymond Teague for proofreading, for Sasvati for design, layout and seeing to the printing, and for all the SAT Temple devotees whose support of the temple and the publication of these teachings of Self-Knowledge has made the present book possible.

Introduction

Covering a time span of 40 years, *Ever Yours in Truth* is a spiritual treasure in the form of personal correspondence between Nome and other sages and seekers sharing their experience. With few exceptions, almost all of the correspondence presented here was written in response to letters written to Nome. Follow-up messages to the response, such as expressions of appreciation or gratitude, have not been included unless they raised further questions.

Any correspondence from earlier than 1974 has not survived. It is a wonder that anything from the 1970's through the 1990's does remain to be made available along with the better preserved correspondence from the most recent decade or so. This book contains a substantial amount of it but not all. Included with the early correspondence are a few verses composed at the time, but for whom they were written and in what context cannot now be ascertained.

In most cases, the names of those involved in this correspondence have been omitted to help preserve their privacy. Editorial remarks in brackets have been added to present to the reader the context in which Nome's response occurs, while attempting to keep comments regarding biographical and personal details of the various writers to a minimum.

The correspondence has been generally presented here as written by the various writers to better retain the feeling of the original with only some minor editing to delete comments pertaining to some practical matters and to render some of the messages received more intelligible.

Tripundra (a symbol pertaining to Siva) appear to separate each correspondence or each set of correspondence with the same seeker. For ease of distinction between Nome's writing and the seeker's, different fonts have been used.

Some of the correspondence is a sharing of and reveling in Brahman-Knowledge, while some is correspondence with Nome in which seekers pose various questions asking for directions back to their origin—Brahman. The questions come in many different forms, speaking of a variety of topics, but the theme of each of them is the same—how to return to the beginning-less beginning and abide in and as the peaceful silence of Brahman-Knowledge. Nome graciously responds with life-fulfilling Brahman-Wisdom. An index has been added to help seekers find topics pertinent to their own meditation.

May Brahman-Knowledge abide in the hearts of all, and peace endure eternally.

Sasvati

Ever Yours in Truth,
Nome

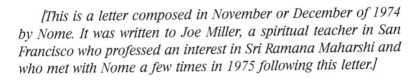

[This is a letter composed in November or December of 1974 by Nome. It was written to Joe Miller, a spiritual teacher in San Francisco who professed an interest in Sri Ramana Maharshi and who met with Nome a few times in 1975 following this letter.]

ॐ Dear Joe,

I, myself, am Realization. Being is Knowing. Existence and Consciousness are one and the same. I am the Self. How could I ever be apart or different from who I am? Thus, Realization, not being any sort of thing or state attainable, is just who I am, my very existence, which is not objectifiable at all. Who I am can never be seen, for it is the seeing itself. All objective attempts to define the Self are partial and incomplete. One could never hope to understand who he is by seeking in such a manner.

Realization can never be attained, for there are not two of me that one should reach the other. Realization is my ever-present Consciousness.

There is not even one of me, in the sense that I am not any sort of individual entity. The assumption of there being an individual entity causes all apparent suffering. This suffering is only an appearance and not real for a moment, for if we inquire "Who am I?", we see that the supposed entity is absolutely absent, thus revealing our eternal Existence-Consciousness, which is what the word "I" really indicates. People call this Realization. Actually, there is nothing attained and no one to attain it.

This simple, non-conceptual understanding of who I am, beyond all words and thoughts, is absolute freedom. There never having been bondage, there is no liberation for which to seek. There are neither sentient beings nor buddhas, neither disciple nor guru, neither path nor achievement.

1

Everyone calls himself "I," thus indicating our absolute unity.

Sincerely,
Nome

[This is a portion of a letter written by Nome to Shanti, who had supplied some books by Sri Atmananda to Nome and started a correspondence with him prior to her attending satsang for the rest of her life. This portion of the letter was written in a verse-like pattern.]

September 22, 1975

I, myself, am the Truth,
There is nothing to be attained.
Self-Realization is Being,
Not being this or that,
Just Being.
This is the wisdom of infinite depth
And the Realization of all sages.

I have nothing at which to point;
Being cannot be called a thing.
These words are spoken
From the Absolute
Of the Absolute
To the Absolute.
There is no person or entity
On either side of this letter;
The absolute absence of "you" and "me"
Is the absolute presence of I.

I am this I am,
Existence-Consciousness,

Transparent, void, and shining.
Un-nameable and inconceivable,
I am beyond all words and thoughts.
Utterly nonobjective,
I do not admit of:
This or that,
Here or there,
Now or then,
Within or without,
Form or formless,
Knowledge or ignorance,
Freedom or bondage,
Life or death.
For whom could these apply?

Without grasping,
Knowing myself to be the non-dual Reality,
I rest in peace.
Not subject to time,
I am called eternal.
Not subject to space,
I am called infinite.
Never having been born,
I am called immortal.
Timeless and infinite,
Unborn and undying,
I am.

There is not
A single objective thing.
Any such thing would depend
On a subject,
Which, in turn, is another object.
But this subject, when sought,
Is found to be naught.
This absolute absence
Of any thing
And any one

To be enlightened or unenlightened
Is the great Liberation and
The absolute presence of I.

Experience and Knowledge are inside.
How can their objects be outside?
It follows that there is nothing outside.
All is within.
What is within is my Self.
Therefore, the experiencer and the experience
Are one and the same.
That is my Self.
Relatively,
I, who am nothing, am everything.
Absolutely,
I alone am.

When deeply inquired into,
Ignorance and bondage
Are seen to be
Enlightenment and liberation;
Why do some people speak
Of teachings and practices
To flee from what has never been?

"You are Awareness.
Awareness is another name for you.
Since you are Awareness,
There is no need
To attain or cultivate it." (Sri Ramana Maharshi)

Those who conceive of a "condition"
Have not awakened to the Truth
Beyond conditioned and unconditioned.
Those who are concerned
With the "form of reality"
Do not understand
That Reality is

Neither form nor formless.
Those who think
In terms of union and attainment
Do not perceive the wonderful quiescence.
Those who speak of states
Do not know who they are.
One who views himself
As an individual entity
Has not looked deeply
Into the Truth
Of no-birth and no-death.

The absolute absence of a "me"
Is the absolute presence of I.
Truly, I am but there is no "me."
Reality is not to be attained or gained.
Absolutely nonobjective,
Beyond all effort and experience,
It is realized as I.

Who can speak of
Dual versus non-dual?
Reality is as it is
And cannot be described in words.
I alone am!
What need for further declarations?

[Here is a letter to Sri Nisargadatta Maharaj. Maurice Frydman kindly served as the translator of it into Marathi and for the response given by Maharaj. The reference in the opening paragraph to the book, I Am That, *is to the original Indian edition that consisted of 75 dialogues.]*

October 19, 1975

ॐ Dear Maharaj,

Recently, I had the good fortune of reading a copy of *I Am That*, and I am overjoyed with the constant expression of Truth conveyed by Your words. I bow and prostrate before You, You who are Truth, itself, and the perfect exemplar of Realization. Reality cannot be expressed, described, or conceived, and there are not two of us between which a communication can take place. Still, I trust that this letter will indicate, as well as words can, a sharing or communion in Absolute Truth.

I alone am. Indivisible, I do not admit of any dualism. Not confined within space and time, I can never be experienced. Not a thing or entity, I am never the object of perception or conception. When the experiencer, perceiver, or conceiver are deeply inquired into, I stand self-revealed.

I am transparent Awareness, devoid of the dualism of life and death, subject and object, self and other, and within and without. Even the term "transparent Awareness" is not meant to indicate anything objectifiable, experience-able, or conceivable. When sought as an object or entity, I am found to be utterly absent. Yet this absolute absence reveals the absolute presence that I am.

Self-Realization is Being; not being this or that, just Being. Realization is not to be attained, for it is my very Being. There is no entity, no "me" to attain, and no thing to be attained. Being is not a state or experience that can be reached or attained by methods, stages, or practices. Realization is the simple non-conceptual understanding of who I am. This understanding, or knowing, is inseparable from and identical with Being. Self-Realization, or Enlightenment, is not an event. I, myself, am Realization, and I am intemporal or what is sometimes termed eternal. Actually, I have neither the attribute of time nor that of timelessness, for, being absolutely nonobjective, in the sense of an entity or object, I remain always undefined. Being is neither existent nor nonexistent, neither this nor that. Not a single attribute can be associated with the unqualified Awareness that I am. Being and Awareness are one and the same. Awareness cannot be cultivated or attained, being what we are, and I am that Awareness.

I have never been born, and so I shall never die. I am not an entity dwelling within the confines of time and space. There is no "me," no individual entity that I can call myself, and there is no world in which this supposed entity could be born, live, and die. I am not now young, nor shall I ever be old, for I am neither the body nor the mind nor a thing or person of any sort. I am, and there is no "me."

All is within. Although I am no thing, I am everything. Absolutely, I alone am, and there is no within to have a without and no without to have a within. I cannot be said to exist, nor can I be said to not exist; nor both exist and not exist, nor neither exist nor not exist. Although the perceiver can never be perceived, all that is perceived is actually the perceiver. If the perceiver be deeply examined, the nature of all things proves to be the same as the absolute inconceivable quiescence that I am.

As Realization is not a state to be attained or maintained, it is quite effortless. It is the ever-present, natural state, which is not a state at all but, rather, the Being-Awareness-Bliss that I am. Realization is none other than who I am, and so I can never be separate, different, or other than what the words "Realization," "Self," and "Jnana" signify. There are not two selves, one to "realize," attain, or come into union with the other. There is not even one self, in terms of an individual entity. I am as I am: ungraspable for I am not a thing, unattainable for I am the ever-present, nondual Reality, and not even in "union," for there was never any division.

Standing naked in the Truth, I speak to You totally honestly. I know who I am, and this clear Knowledge, which is identical with my very Being, has set me free of all imagined bondage and liberation, hopes and fear, desires and desire-lessness, ignorance and knowledge, happiness and suffering. By understanding the absolute absence of any "me" to be defined or confined by any of these, I have awakened to the absolute presence of I.

Sri Ramana Maharshi is my Guru, and He has bestowed spiritual instruction through silent Grace and the written recordings of what He said. Also, I have taken great joy in reading the words of Sri Atmananda of Trivandrum and the *Avadhuta Gita* of Dattatreya. In You, I find the perfect Realization of what is indicated in the teaching of the above mentioned sages. I consider You to be identical with my Guru and Your wisdom to be unsurpassed. All praise falls short of describing You, and words cannot adequately express how profound a sage I feel You are. It can only be said that I know You as I, as my very Self.

If You wish, and if it is possible for You to do so, I would greatly enjoy and appreciate hearing from You. I speak, write, and read only English, so any response would have to be in this language. Such a correspondence with You would be greatly treasured, and I would be deeply thankful for any reply that You would care to offer.

It is this Self-Knowledge that I have to share and upon which the relationship between us stands. This Self-Knowledge is the deepest, earnest love. The absence of "you" and "me" is the perfect at-one-ment or presence called love. Even though we may appear to live a great distance away from each other, this love is as intense as if I were sitting right before You.

Whether you decide to write or not, we are in eternal Love, in the silent absolute communion of I.

With tears of joy as well as a hearty laugh,
Nome

[This is the letter written by Maurice Frydman, the translator of the book, I am That, to convey the response of Sri Nisargadatta Maharaj.]

January 7, 1976

Dear Nome,

Sri Nisargadatta Maharaj has received your letter, and it was translated for him into Marathi. He gave it to me and asked me to convey his thanks and brotherly greetings. As the letter was for Sri Maharaj only, I shall only add my best regards and sincere wishes for a long and fruitful life.

Yours sincerely,
M. Frydman (translator)

———
•

[This is a letter addressed to Swami Swanandashram, an illumined yogi and swami of the Sankara Order, with whom Nome was in correspondence for the previous several months. They had met many times during the spring of 1972. There was no contact until the revered Swami returned from India to visit the USA during 1976 and 1977. He also visited the USA again in 1978. The Swami had meditated for years at Gangotri, where the river Ganga starts in the Himalayas. Nome's response in this letter is to some questions asked by the Swami about Nome's life and history.]

May 10, 1977

ॐ Dear Swamiji,

Absolutely, neither you nor I exist as separate individual entities, but only as Existence, or Being itself, admitting neither of me nor mine nor you nor yours. The Self (Brahman) is alone the Reality, and verily I am That.

I was blessed to come across the teaching of Bhagavan Ramana Maharshi. It was about three years ago, while reading a small pamphlet of the Maharshi's teaching in which were found the words, "Self-Realization is Being, not being this or that, just Being," that I awakened to who I am.

9

There is no personal history to relate past this point, as Realization is the simple, non-conceptual understanding that there is no individual person, never has been, and never will be. Even the previous history is illusory—for whom is the history? I am the Self, having neither past nor future, neither bondage nor liberation, neither life nor death.

It is needless to expound my Realization to you, for not only do I exist as the Self, which is the sole-existent Reality, but words and thoughts cannot express that which I am. I am formless, nonobjective Being, Consciousness, but not of any thing, and Blis s, but not an experience. I am devoid of all dualism, such as self and other, subject and object, and experiencer and experience. I am not now young nor shall I ever be old. I have never been born, and so I shall never die. There is no world in which any supposed individual entity could be born, live, or die. I am neither the body nor the mind nor the ego nor a thing or person of any sort. I alone am, and there is no "me" or individual. I am, no me.

Self-Realization is Being, not being this or that, just Being. Therefore, Realization is effortless, ever present, and natural and is not any sort of state of mind, experience, or event that is objectively attained or needs to be maintained. It is Being-Consciousness-Bliss, which is who I am. In Self-Knowledge, Being and Knowing are one and the same. Realization is none other than who I am, and so I can never be different, separate, or other than what the words "Realization," "Self," "Brahman," and "Jnana" signify.

Nor are there two selves, one to "realize," attain, or come into union with the other. The one Self, attributeless and formless, is alone the Reality, and I am That.

Renouncing my home, family, name, fame, friends, worldly ambitions, etc. and embarking on the path of Self-inquiry at the age of seventeen, shortly before I met you, this path was followed into the nature of ultimate Reality.

[Editor's note: Though the actual renunciation and clarity regarding the path are stated here to have occured at age seventeen, sadhana in earnest commenced at age sixteen.]

10

True Knowledge, which is Self-Knowledge, alone destroys the illusory ignorance (superimposition or misidentifications) and the imagined bondage and reveals the eternal freedom and Bliss of the Self. Paths and techniques are based upon dualism, actions, and the belief in an individual practicer, and so they cannot destroy ignorance because they are not in conflict with it. Only Self-Knowledge removes all misidentifications and yields Liberation by the Knowledge that there has never been any ignorance.

[Editor's note: The reference to "paths and techniques" here was specific to certain physical, subtle, and mental practices already discussed by the Swami and Nome.]

In Reality, there are no separate individual, enlightened beings; nor are there unenlightened beings. There is only Absolute Being, the One without a second. The word, "jivanmukta" is a contradiction in terms, for a mukta (or mukti) does not admit of any assumed jiva (individual) whatsoever. Therefore, there is no one to be discriminated as realized or unrealized, because, in Reality, there is no individual or ego to be either, but only Absolute Being.

Realization is nothing but my Self. The Self is One, eternal, immutable, stainless, desireless, and is identical with Consciousness. I am not the body, senses, mind, intellect, or the ego. The Self, which I am, is the sole-existent Reality, and, verily, pure Bliss itself. It is the highest of the high, purest of the pure, transcendent over all dualism, and eternally free. I am That. I am not the result of any practice or path, for I am the eternal, ever-present, formless Reality. As Realization is none other than who I am, totally transcendent of time and space, I am not to be found in any experience or state of mind. Nor can Realization be an event.

When sought, the mind cannot be found. The Self alone is the One Reality, and, hence, the nature of the mind, like that of the supposed ego, is the nature of the Self. When thought is deeply examined, by discarding its assumed objectivity, it is known to be nothing other than Consciousness. That Consciousness is the Self. No concentration or control of thoughts is needed for Self-Realization. Through Self-inquiry, one simply discards all that is not the Self or superimposed and realizes that there exists nothing but the Absolute Consciousness, the Supreme Being, and I am That.

There has never been an assumed individual in ignorance, nor is there now one liberated. I alone am, and there is no "me." There is no dissolution, no origination, none in bondage, none aspiring for Liberation, and none liberated. This is the Highest Truth. There is only Being, not being this or that, only Being. The Self alone exists. The Self alone is Real. That Self is my very Being. That is the final Truth, and That is Realization.

[Editor's note: The third and fourth sentences of this paragraph are derived from verse 32 of part 2 of Gaudapada's Karika on the Mandukya Upanishad. Nome frequently references this text and this verse in particular, now as then. Swami Swanandashram had previously sent this verse in Sanskrit to Nome in a letter, expressing that this verse was for him.]

I did not do anything, because I am not the doer. In Reality, I never do anything. There is no individual doer, and there is absolutely nothing ever done. I am neither the doer nor the enjoyer nor the reaper of the fruits of action. I am the Self, actionless and worldless.

Sincerely,
Nome

[Unfortunately, the letters written by the Swami to Nome have not been located and may be permanently lost. It is, though, possible to deduce some of what the Swami wrote by the nature of Nome's responses.]

May 23, 1977

ॐ Dear Swamiji,

In Reality, you and I are never apart, as there exists only the One Self. The Self is the sole-existent Reality, and its nature is Being-Consciousness-Bliss. Actually, there is no world, no bodies, no minds, no egos, no appearances, no play or dream, and no bondage of any sort. There is only Absolute Being, which is the Self. The Real ever is, and the unreal has never come to be.

Of course, you have permission to reproduce or print whatever you wish from the letters that have been sent to you. There are none in bondage and none liberated. The Self is neither taught nor learned. Knowing the Self is Being the Self. The Self is the ever-present Reality, utterly non-objective, beyond all dualisms, qualities, attributes, and experiences. Verily, I am That. Mukti is Being, not being this or that, just Being. It, or I, is totally nonobjective, and, so, it is neither given nor received. The Guru and the disciple are really only the Self, which is the sole-existent Reality, and I am That.

Ever Yours as That,
Nome

[In this next letter, nondual Self-Knowledge and complete detachment are emphasized. The comments on the nature of the Guru, Vedanta, and Isvara are in the context of the traditional admonishment that nonduality does not apply to one's relationship with such. Because of the very high level of communication between them, Nome wrote in a part of this letter some comments that, though, at first glance, seem to contradict this admonishment, really do not but expound on the very same nonduality of the God, Guru, and the Self revealed by Sri Ramana Maharshi.]

June 9, 1977

ॐ Dear Swamiji,

As you requested, enclosed with this letter are duplicate copies of the letters that you sent to me. If any of my letters

13

are missing and you wish copies, please inform me, and I will gladly send them. There has never actually been two individuals between whom a communication has taken place. The Self alone is the Reality, and words can not approach or describe That.

As was mentioned in the letter of May 10th to you, any commentary on ashrams, contemporary masters, institutions etc., was given only for the relative explanation of illusory actions performed by this dream body. I know my Self as the Reality, and I am not, in the least, confused or disturbed by the unreal. My nature is verily Bliss or Peace itself, and there is no upset-ness or problems with any appearance in a nonexistent world.

The same Self-Knowledge is true with regards to a nonexistent body. I am not a body, and I have no body. I do not rejoice with good health, and I do not suffer with ill health. There is neither life nor death in the Self that I am.

When the mind is sought for, it cannot be found. The mind is, therefore, unreal. I am not the mind, and I have no mind. I am the Self, which is the sole-existent Reality. Self-Knowledge is beyond the illusory knowledge and ignorance, and concentration and distraction, of the mind.

Sri Sankara's instruction, which you have often quoted, prohibiting one to think non-dually with the Guru, Vedanta, and Isvara is important advice given to aspirants, so that they will take the time to carefully listen to the full teaching, reflect on their own true nature, and realize the Self, which is who they are. This instruction is not given to the realized sage, for he is neither "alive" nor "embodied." If embodied, he is not a sage; if a sage, he is not embodied. The sage has realized the Self as his very Being and only Reality. He knows Vedanta, Iswara, and his Guru as himself. Sri Sankara knew his Guru as the Self, as himself, and he did not fall into the dualism, or ignorance, of conceiving his Guru and himself as separate individuals and bodies.

The Guru, Vedanta, and Iswara are the very One that should be thought of non-dually. To think non-dually with any other is to misidentify or superimpose and the very cause of the illusion of birth and death. If one does not think non-dually with his Guru, who else should he think non-dually of? To the dedicated and sincere aspirant, the Guru is not another body, but the calling of Truth within; to the sage, the Guru is none other than the Self. If it is viewed otherwise, one merely clings to misidentifications with illusory bodies and minds, rather than knowing the Guru for who He really is. Therefore, in accordance with the Truth that a true Guru teaches, it is one's duty to think non-dually of his Guru and to realize Him as himself.

The sage has realized the Self. He has attained that which leaves nothing more to be attained and knows that which leaves nothing more to be known. He is liberated from the imagined bondage, for He has realized the formless Self as the non-dual Reality. He has passed beyond all dualisms such as life and death, creation and destruction, bondage and liberation, and guru and disciple. He knows Himself as Non-duality, itself, and there is, for him, no question of falling into any sort of dualism. He knows that God, Guru, and the Self are one and the same Reality, which is His very Being. Transcending the unreal world, body, and mind, there are no binding rules of conduct or action for him. The sage can think non-dually of Guru, Vedanta, and Iswara, because he is non-dual with, or the same as, Guru, Vedanta and Iswara,

Ever Yours as That,
Nome

[This short letter contains only two brief paragraphs. The first paragraph relates to some service that Nome was performing for the Swami. At that time, there was no SAT temple, no photocopier, and no computer to store files or to print out. Letters were either handwritten or typed. To make a duplicate of a letter, one went to a copy shop to perform the work, made a carbon copy while typing on a typewriter, or penned a copy by hand. What was included in the missing section of the second paragraph, indicated by ..., cannot now be determined, but presumably it dealt with some practical matters that were not included in the

copy. The sentence of that paragraph reiterates verse 32 of chapter 2 of Gaudapada's Karika on the Mandukya Upanishad, with which the Swami was very familiar.]

June 20, 1977

ॐ Dear Swamiji,

Your last letter arrived about ten days ago, and I am now in the process of procuring the duplicates of all the letters you requested. Regardless of the cost, I am very happy to perform the service for you.

...There is no dissolution, no origination, none in bondage, none striving or aspiring for salvation, and none liberated. This is the highest Truth, for the Self admits of no conditions or definitions. Verily, I am That!

Ever Yours as the Self,
Nome

[This letter from Nome to Swami Swanandashram was written with a sense of humor, which the Swami appreciated, and with respect at a time when the Swami had just informed Nome of his recent successful return visit to India.]

February 8, 1978

Dear Swamiji,

It is hoped that your visit to India to "meet with prominent people" was found to be enjoyable by you, although I cannot really be fooled when I hear that Swamiji has gone to India. I know, without a doubt, that, in reality, Swamiji is neither a body nor a mind, nor any sort of individual, but that he is the Self, which is the sole-existent Reality. In reality, there is no world, so India and America do not really exist. Although it is said that Swamiji went to India, actually only the body moves, and not Swamiji, who is truly

16

only the Self. The Self is not a body, nor is it in a body, nor does it have a body. Just as Swamiji is not his body, so all the "prominent people" (as well as everyone else) are not their bodies. Just as Swamiji is only the formless Self and not the nonexistent ego or imagined individual, so everyone else is only that same formless Self, and there are absolutely no individuals. This being the case, I cannot be fooled when I read that Swamiji has gone to India to meet some people, for I know that Swamiji went nowhere and saw nobody. He only remained as he is, and that which he is, is the Self. The Self is pure Being and is beyond the illusory appearance of the world, body, senses, mind, and ego. The ultimate truth is that the world, body, and the mind have never come to be. The Self alone exists; the Self alone is real.

Swamiji, it was mentioned in your letter that you are considering visiting the west coast this year. If the purpose of your visit to the west coast is for the spreading of a spiritual mission, it is highly unlikely that this body would be of much use in such an endeavor. This body is not active in, nor is there any interest in, the affairs of institutions and ashrams, teaching, traveling, etc. Like the supreme sage Sri Ramana Maharshi, this body is quite content to just stay where it is. I rest in the complete peace and supreme happiness of the Realization of the Self. There is no desire to experience, accomplish, or to do anything because there is no misidentification as an individual experiencer or doer. I have attained that which leaves nothing more to be attained or accomplished. I have known that which leaves nothing more to be known, and I have realized that which leaves nothing more to be realized. That is the Self, and that Self am I.

I do not see any teaching that needs to be spread or any individuals who need to be taught. There are none in bondage, none striving for liberation, and none liberated. There is no ignorance and no knowledge, no bondage and no liberation, no individual "me" and no others. There is only the one Reality which is the Self. I know who I am, and that is formless, non-dual Reality, which is Being-Consciousness-Bliss. All words and thoughts fail to express or describe the Self which I am.

I regard you with the deepest love and know that we are always One. "You" and "I" are just mere words, for we are always only That.

Ever Yours as the Self,
Nome

[The following letter was written in response to letters and literature sent to Nome from Shanti, who was then known as Margaret Coble. The letter was addressed to "Margaret," but this has been changed here to "Shanti" out of respect for her, that being the name she later adopted and by which she was known at SAT. The letter concludes with a verse composed by Sri Bhagavan.]

February 27, 1978

ॐ Dear Shanti,

Your "Jnana Yoga course" arrived safely here last week. Much of it was found to be very enjoyable, especially the selections of quotes from Sri Ramana Maharshi and Sri Atmananda. You had sent the two pages of Sri Atmananda quotes on a previous occasion, but one can never hear too much of the sublime Truth which he expounds.

Of course, Jnana is not really something to be learned or taught. In Self-Realization, Being is Knowing. So, Jnana is really just another name for I, the Self, and never anything objective or gained anew. The Self is the only-existent Reality, and there are really never any individuals caught in illusory bondage. Both you and I are none other than Jnana itself.

18

Ever Yours as the Self,
Nome

There is neither creation nor destruction,
Neither destiny nor free will,
Neither path nor achievement;
This is the final Truth.

Bhagavan Sri Ramana Maharshi

[Presented here are two letters written by Nome. The first was written in response to correspondence sent from a friend, who was a Buddhist scholar and author, and his wife. The book that they sent was written by another person. The second letter is to Shanti. The reference to "offerings" is to books and other writings that she sent about that time.]

March 6, 1978

ॐ Dear...and...,

Your warm and enjoyable letters of January 29 and February 8 were received, along with the kind gift of two copies of the book, about two weeks ago. The friendship and love behind the letters and sending of the books are recognized and appreciated. As you preferred, I will desist from offering a commentary on the actual content of the books. Besides, that which is true is Self-evident, and what is false or illusory is also quite obvious. Moreover, I, the Self, am alone the Reality, and so there is truly no need to comment on the false assumptions and ideas of individuals who have never really come to be.

No words or thoughts can describe or define "I," nor are there really any such things as words and thoughts. The

Self is the Silence in which not a single thing (individual, word, separation, split) has ever come to be. As far as I am concerned, there is no principle and no functioning, no knowledge and living it, no split mind and whole mind. For whom could these be? There is only the one Mind which is absolutely nondual. This Mind, or I, is void of any individuality, objectivity, divisions, separations, etc. This Mind alone exists; this Mind alone is Real. There is no "me" or individual apart from, outside of, or inside of this Mind, so there is really no realization and non-realization. This is the same as what is expressed in my last letter to you (October 24, 1977). These are just some more expressions of the same. The Happiness, or Bliss, of who I am is beyond all expression. This leaves me silent, without anything to be said or written. Both of you are held very fondly and dearly. I hope that all is well with you.

Love,
Nome

January 17, 1979

ॐ Dear...,

Communion in the Silence of the Self is best. Truly, there is nothing to be said, as only the One Reality, the Self, alone exists. As our beloved Bhagavan Maharshi says, "The One Self, the Sole Reality, alone exists eternally. When even the ancient teacher, Dakshinamurti, revealed It through speechless eloquence, who else could have conveyed It by speech?" The love, which is our absolute identity or oneness as formless Being, behind the offerings is deeply understood and enjoyed.

As always, all is perfectly fine here. There is neither "you" nor "me"; I alone am—formless, nondual, Being-Awareness-Bliss. You are very deeply loved, and we exist as a single One.

Ever yours as the Self,
Nome

[The following letter was a written by Nome in response to correspondence from Shanti. Shanti had communicated about the death of someone close to her. She had also discussed her ideas about Jesus Christ and her desire to establish a forest ashram in the state of New York. She was already involved in studying the teachings of Sri Atmananda and Sri Nisargadatta Maharaj.]

August 13, 1980

ॐ Dear Shanti,

With the illusory rise of the ego, or individual, all objectivity arises, and, with its demise, it is realized that the Self alone exists and that there has never been a single objective thing. Only so long as an individual is mistakenly assumed to exist is there the appearance of differentiation. Upon the false assumption of individuality, objectivity or differentiation illusorily appears in the forms, or concepts, of mind, personality, a body, a world, etc. This gives rise to all sorts of dualism such as life and death, higher and lower, sin and virtue, thought and consciousness, bondage and liberation, and you and I. As a result, the ultimate bliss, or peace, of Absolute Being seems to vanish. Awakening to the Truth of no-ego, that is to say, the Self which you always are, is the finding of the silent peace that was never really lost. Upon this awakening, all differentiation, being an illusion, simply vanishes.

In reality, I, the Self, alone am, and there is no "me." I was not born, nor am I now living, nor will I ever die. I am not in a body, nor is there a body in "I." I am not in the mind, nor is there a mind in "I." I am supportless and eternally undefined. Bodiless and mindless, birthless and deathless, changeless and conceptless, I am. This is just Being, but not individuality, just Consciousness, but not conscious of any thing, and Bliss, but not an experience.

21

The absolute Realization that the Self alone exists, the Self alone is real, is the one and only complete answer to death. This Truth is alone eternal, and no transient concept can ever suffice in its place. Where there is form, there is change and loss, but, where the formless Truth is, there is no change, loss, fear, or sorrow. Of course, there are not really two "where's" (samsara and Nirvana). This is just a manner of speaking. In truth, there is only absolute, formless Being (Supreme Being, and neither "you" nor a "me" have ever come to be.

The highest Truth should never be diluted in its expression to aspirants, even if they should request it. The excuse of the "need of relative half-steps" is not valid, because the Self is not far away but within, and one is never really other than the Self all along (as in the tenth man story). The piercing and liberating quality of Truth lies in its being incongruous with any concept the aspirant may cling to or misidentify with. To try to make Reality be in agreement with the aspirant's concept is to dilute the Truth and delude the aspirant. To reduce the Infinite to concepts (the very same concepts that keep the aspirant bound!) would not be beneficial to anyone. So, it is far better to rely only on the Absolute, and honestly express it as well as words can when requested, even though this is apt to create a significant lack of popularity. There are none in bondage, none striving for salvation, and none liberated—this is the highest Truth.

The simple, non-conceptual Realization of undifferentiated Being, or the Self, is alone the Enlightenment of all sages. Although we speak of sages, this should not give rise to the concept of separate, enlightened beings. Truly, there are no enlightened beings, just Being, which is Enlightenment. There is no such thing as a free individual, but rather Realization is freedom from the individual. One must see it as sages (the Maharshi, Nisargadatta Maharaj, Atmananda, Buddha, Christ, Huang Po and countless other friends) see it, that is to say, from Reality. This leaves no room for "a sage" or "an enlightened being" and "others," degrees and levels of liberation, special functions in the world, etc. All of these suppose the existence of an individual entity, or ego, body-misidentification, a belief in "a real world," and different types of Enlightenment. But ego, individuality, a mind—call it what you will—is really nonexistent, and body-misidentification is just basic ignorance. The fact that the notion of "a real world" is totally false is fundamental. When inquired into, the world is found to be utterly unreal, and formless Consciousness is found to be our only actual experience. There are certainly no degrees, levels, types, special conditions, etc. of Enlightenment, as Enlightenment is our true nature, the Self. Enlightenment is that which is innate, and not any sort of experience or state that is attained. It is just eternal, silent Being.

This being the case, the concept of a special function is just that: a concept. If Christ thought he was Jesus, that he was born or died, that he had some sort of special function to perform, and believed in the existence of "others", who were sinful on top of it, well, then, he would just be a dualistic ignoramus and not the Christ. If He really taught such conceptual nonsense, what kind of salvation would that be? If, from the tattered remnants of His sayings, we derive the sense that He knows and is the Truth, then He could not possibly hold any of the above concepts, but rather He knows Himself as Christ Consciousness, God (I Am), or the Self. I do not need any scriptural quotes to verify what I say, for it is known by all as a matter of direct experience. However, there is plenty of substantiation in the *Gospel of John, the Gospel of Thomas,* and other Gnostic texts. The unity of all sages (east, west, in-between, and neither) is in the worldless Self, which is their Enlightenment and who they really are. No other "integration" is needed.

I have no conceptual discipline to practice in order to overcome imaginary conditions or influences, for I am that which is eternally free. I have no life story to tell, as I do not regard myself as a living entity. I have no extraordinary experiences to relate, for I have realized the Truth in which there is no experiencer. I have no mission or work to accomplish, for I rest in the magnificent perfection of Absolute Peace. I have no fear or suffering regarding death, be it of this body or any other, because I have realized who I am.

Real peace is found within. If one looks for peace externally or in an environment, when that external environment changes or disappears, the peace will disappear, as well. Upon close examination, it is revealed that even the experience of peace during the temporary appearance of that external environment was not as deep as it could have been. Supreme peace is in the Self, and the sage knows himself as That. So, when the environment is favorable, his joy is not increased, and, when that environment disappears or becomes unfavorable, his joy does not decrease even in the least. Whether rich or poor, healthy or sick, living or dead, in the company of others or alone, in the country or in the city, he remains ever the same. Such Peace, or Shanti, is alone worth having, for it is eternal. If we were missing the senses, external environments would mean nothing to us. Now that the senses appear, should we misidentify and attach ourselves to one thing or the other? To be as that which alone remains after the release of all else is undoubtedly real Peace.

It is not my custom anymore to write, but out of a deep love for you this has been shared. The I or Self of which I speak and in which I remain silent, is your Self, your very Being. Without any other support, Realization of this is perfect peace and immortality. This Truth is identical with limitless and undying love, which is the real basis of our friendship. Should you care to write to me, you may feel free to do so, and I will, of course, reply to you. Also, you are always welcome here, should you ever wish to visit and share company in Atma. Your abiding in Truth always has my full support and your very Being my deepest love—the Truth and Love in which we are not two, but One.

Ever yours as the Self,
Nome

24

There is neither creation nor destruction
Neither destiny nor free will,
Neither path nor achievement;
This is the final Truth.

Bhagavan Sri Ramana Maharshi

*[The following verse was composed by Nome sometime
between 1987 and 1990. The verse was composed in response to
a discussion between another person and Nome. In that discussion, this other person argued critically against the view of the
unreal nature of the ego and the world and the teachings of
Advaita Vedanta, and presented, instead, a concept that
Enlightenment is a matter of the embodied individual acting
("functioning") in a manner that results in material success,
fame, etc. and that this is the meaning of "egolessness" and the
sign of a great being.]*

Absence with the man:
Absurd illusion—how silly!
The man with Absence
Is really no man at all!
How can a no one be a someone?
A someone never exists.
The only presence is Absence.
There is no world.
There is no individual.
The Self, the timeless Void, alone is.
Absence with "the man":
There is nothing born in the Unborn!
No birth: no life.
No life: no death.
No death: no change.
No change: no time.
No time: no mind.

No mind: no second.
No second: Brahman.
Brahman: the Self.
That which is, ever is.

≡
•

[A gentleman from Nigeria sent a letter with ten questions posed. Presented here is Nome's response, which includes the questions before each of the respective answers. The SAT temple was known as the Avadhuta Ashram at that time, and that name appears at the top of the letter.]

THE AVADHUTA ASHRAM

July 5, 1988

Dear Mr.   ,

1. What is the main obscurity of my infinity?

Believing the world to be real, in other words, other than the Self, and of a different nature than you, and seeking for happiness externally (attachment): these things obscure your infinity. Your infinity is obscured by all erroneous conceptions or misidentifications, such as believing that you are a limited body and mind. Sri Ramana Maharshi and Sri Sankara have both spoken about this at length in their books, which you may want to read.

2. How can I be free from illusions and ignorance of the world?

You lend reality to the world or you project your own innate happiness on it, and then the illusion seems real. This is ignorance. Let the sense of happiness return to your within-ness and the sense of reality return to the one changeless Being-Consciousness.

3. How can I achieve self-reliance?

By following the instruction above in the two previous answers you will be truly Self-reliant. Turning within to the changeless Being-Consciousness will give you the sense of freedom, peace and equanimity needed to conduct your relative phenomenal affairs in a detached, harmonious way.

4. Can my destiny or fate be changed or transformed?

Man's true destiny is Liberation. He must fulfill this destiny. If a man feels that his destiny has suffering in it, this destiny can be completely transformed or eliminated by spiritual practice leading directly to Self-Realization. Inspiration or guidance can be gained by deeply absorbing the message in non-dual books containing the words of genuine sages.

5. What are the diets to achieve my spiritual stability?

There are no diet restrictions, as the spiritual path involves Self-realization and not specific actions of the body.

6. What are your prerequisites for your members or spiritual aspirants?

The prerequisite for any spiritual aspirant is sincerity of heart and intensity of spiritual practice.

7. What are the times and pattern of meditation so as to enable me to achieve my needs and intentions?

The amount of time spent and the specific period of the day in which spiritual practice is performed are not important on the nondual path. Once one becomes attuned to his inner Being, becoming more awake to who he really is, meditation becomes continuous, both in activity and inactivity. Ultimately, in realizing the Absolute, meditation becomes permanent.

8. How can I maintain spiritual stability?

Intense love of the Truth, self-examination to dissolve tendencies (vasanas and the personality), keeping holy company, and determination on the spiritual path give spiritual stability.

9. How can I be fully liberated from my karma?

The answer to this question is the same as the answer to question 4. You may also want to consider deeply the axiom, "As you sow, so you reap." If you conduct your life accordingly, you will have no problems. As for full Liberation, it consists of Self-Knowledge.

10. Am I free from attacks of witches and wizards or my enemies as a member of your ashram?

If you are truly in earnest, spiritually, everything will work out all right. Be free of the "wizard" of the ego, which transforms nirvana into samsara. Be free of this "magician."

[These next verses were written by Nome in July 1991, as indicated by the date on the handwritten original.]

Words record words;
Thoughts record thoughts;
What will record the Truth?

Pictures record pictures;
Images record images;
What will record the Truth?

The transient record the transient;
The dead record the dead;
What will record the Truth?

Ideas record ideas;
Concepts record concepts;
What will record the Truth?

The inanimate records the inanimate;
The appearance records the appearance;
What will record the Truth?

Illusion records illusion;
The unreal records the unreal;
What will record the Truth?
Misunderstanding records misunderstanding;
The partial records partially;
What will record the Truth?

The footprints in the sand
Dissolve in the next wave;
What will record the Truth?

The moment to be recorded
Is gone before the thought to do so;
What will record the Truth?

The body cannot grasp it;
The mind cannot think it;
What will record the Truth?

The heart of the yogi
With direct, living experience
Is the record of the Truth.

The wise are that
Which they have realized;
They are the record of Truth.

The sage who abides
As timeless Being
Is the Self-record of the Truth.

If you wish to record the Truth,
Know the Self that you are;
Your blissful freedom will bear testimony.

This is the record of Truth.
Unutterable, it is crystal clear.
Now you know: who will record the Truth?

*[This verse was composed by Nome in July 1991. The cir-
cumstances surrounding its composition are not now known.]*

If you can love
Without attachment,
You will discover
The nonduality of Being.

If you can love
Without an object,
You will discover
Self-sufficient Bliss.

If you can love your Guru,
Asking nothing in return,
You will be free of need
And will inherit the great treasure.

If you can love the Truth
And devote yourself to it,
You will be absorbed
And attain final Liberation.

If you can love
For the sake of love itself,
The Self will be known by you,
And you will know neither fear not deficiency.

If you can love the Absolute
And care for nothing else,
The Truth will abide in your heart,
And you will outlive all else.

If you can love like this,
You, indeed, know the power of love.
If you can love like this,
You have all that you need for life, and you will not
taste death.

*[In keeping with the theme of the above verse is another,
entitled, "Requital," composed sometime between 1989 and
1992]*

If a thousand expressions of hatred
Meet with one drop of divine love,
The former become nonexistent,
And the latter is triumphantly serene.

*[This verse was composed on July 19, 1991 in devotion to
Sadguru Sri Ramana Maharshi]*

Power of the Master

He who abides
As the one Self,
Transcendent of duality,
Who sees nothing but the Self,
Who abides as pure Being,
Whose Consciousness is free of all concepts,
Whose Existence is not veiled by superimposition,
Whose Bliss is unconditional and everlasting,
Who retains not the least trace of misidentification,
Whose peace is fathomless,
Whose freedom is limitless,
Who has realized the Truth of no-creation,
Whose words are sincere,
Whose Enlightenment is complete,
And whose Silence is inconceivable,
Is the Master true.

Appearing as the form of the Formless,
He enables the disciple
To hear the inexpressible,
To grasp the ungraspable,
To understand the inconceivable,
To discern the inscrutable,
To see the invisible,
To discover the nonobjective,
To attain the unattainable,
To know the incomprehensible,
And to abide in the locationless,

The timeless, forever,
The bodiless, thoughtless, egoless Self.

The power of the Master
Cannot be measured.
The power of the Master
Never declines.
The power of the Master
Is always the Good (Siva).
The power of the Master
Is his genuineness.
The power of the Master
Is of wisdom and love.
The power of the Master
Is of the Absolute.
The power of the Master
Is the power of the Self.

[This verse was also composed in July 1991.]

What Do I Know?

What do I know?
Only Being itself.
Though knowing Existence,
I do not know a world.
Though awake to the mind's essence,
I do not know an idea.
Though immersed in infinite love,
I do not know a relationship.
Though dwelling in a solitary life,
I do not know loneliness.
Though facing death,
I do not know fear.
Though embracing life,
I do not know attachment.

All pervading,
I do not know possession.
Light itself,
I do not know how to obscure myself.
At home in wisdom,
I do not know how to manufacture ignorance.
Being Reality itself,
I do not know illusion.
Abiding as the Self,
I do not know where to find an ego.
Space-like,
I do not know limits.
Like wind,
I do not know clinging.

Like water,
I do not know shape,
Like fire,
I do not know how to keep straw.
Like solid rock,
I do not know how to waver.
Like a newborn child,
I do not know concepts.
Like an old man on his deathbed,
I do not know a "good reason" for foolishness,
Like a lover at the peak moment of sexual intercourse,
I do not know of other things.
Like a mirror,
I do not know a color, shape, or image of my own.

Though knowing the Truth,
I have not one concept about it.
Dwelling in absolute freedom,
I do not know bondage.
Consciousness itself,
I do not know duality.
In the Realization of the Self,
I do not know another.

Seeing what is,
I do not know how to be confused.
Having realized no-creation,
I do not know a single, objective thing.
Beholding the treasure of the universe,
I do not know how to crave anything of the world.

What do I know?
Only Being itself.
Ask me any question;
I can answer.
I am the answer.
What do I know?
Only Being itself.
What do I know?

[The next verse was composed sometime between 1988 and 1991]

Perseverance

Advice:
If the mind be scattered,
Gather it.
If it be confined,
Expand it.
If it be agitated,
Tranquilly rest it in the Void.
If it be dull,
Awaken it.
If none of these,
Leave it alone.

If the Truth be forgotten,
Remember it.
If at a distance,
Embrace it.

If slipping away,
Treasure it.
If immediately present,
Identify with it.

The way it is:

Abidance in the Self
Is effortless and natural.
Remaining as you are,
Where can you stray?
Ever wakeful eye,
How can you sleep?
If you do not sleep,
How can you dream?

Self-Bliss is endurance.
Knowledge of no-creation is patience.
Truth of non-ego is humility.
Reality itself is strength.
Being the Self is retention.
Eternal Silence is adherence to the teaching.
No birth and no death is the time for practice.
The unreality of the world is renunciation.
Nonduality is yoga.
No-alternative is evenness of mind.
No body is transcendence of the senses.
No-attainment is accomplishment.
Self-Knowledge is wisdom.
Self-Abidance is diligence.
Seeing the Self is true perception.
No one to understand and nothing to be understood is
    comprehension.

Persevere! Persevere! Persevere!
Thus, remain as you are and be blissful.

[This verse, entitled, "Meditation," was composed by Nome sometime between 1989 and 1991. It contains the response to a person who decided to abandon meditation in favor of worldliness and who ridiculed meditation and similar spiritual practices. The verse does not address directly the egotism and ignorance of that person but, rather, reveals the nondual nature of meditation.]

Meditation

Meditation is an illusion;
How much more so is non-meditation an illusion!
Where could any state be?
And who is there who would have such a state?
My meditation is perpetual.
It has no form, no duration, no idea.
It has no in, no out, no before and after.
Clear and vacuous,
Nowhere can it be grasped,
Yet ever-steady is it.

No meditator and no object of meditation
Is true meditation,
As no in and no out
Is truly "within."
No concept, no pattern
Is the mind's true state.
No differentiation, no form
Is the mind's true nature.
No ignorance and no knowledge
Is true Wisdom.
No rigidity and no disturbance
Is true Peace.
No darkness, no brightness
Is the clear Light.
No object and no absence
Is truly the "Void."
No bondage, no liberation
Is the Innate.

36

Meditation is not "an experience,"
Yet, pure experience is it.
To meditate on anything other
Is not meditation at all;
In meditation true, upon the Self,
There is no "other" at all!

Nothing is lost, nothing is found.
Ever-present Consciousness alone always is.
Consciousness itself is meditation,
Unending meditation of Reality.
One does not enter meditation.
One does not enter non-meditation.
One does not return from meditation,
For true meditation has no start or finish,
Just as the Self has no birth or death.

The temple of my meditation
Has no walls,
No windows and doors, too.
The seat of my meditation
Has no place, nor does it rest upon any ground.
The incense of my meditation
Is the formless Essence of Being.
Once sensed, it is eternal Bliss.
The candle of my meditation
Is the all-illuminating, ever-shining Wisdom intrinsic
    to Consciousness.
The clothing of my meditation
Is naked space.
The ceiling of my meditation temple
Is infinity.
The duration of my meditation
Is eternity.
The symbol of my meditation
Is the entire universe.
The altar of my meditation
Is absolutely formless.

The Master of my meditation
Is the Maharshi, my Guru.
The method of my meditation
Is no method.
The posture of my meditation
Is no body.
The value of my meditation
Is the priceless treasure, the wish-fulfilling gem.
The recounting of my meditation
Is told in no words.
The Truth of my meditation
Is known by the Enlightened.
No "meditation" can compare with this one.
Those who know it
Are it themselves.

"Meditation" is an illusion.
Where could such a thing ever be?
For whom could it be?
Meditation is the Truth.
Do you know what I mean?
Om Tat Sat

*[This set of verses was composed by Nome in 1991 while at
Kauai. As can be derived from the content, it was written at dawn
or shortly thereafter.]*

Dawn Meditation

At dawn,
I meditate upon the Truth, the Self,
Which is the Absolute, the One Reality,
Formless, unborn and unceasing,
Neither light nor dark,
Having no bondage and no liberation,

Which is forever unconditioned and unmodified,
Immutable, uncreated,
Transcendent of all definition,
Timeless and spaceless,
And which ever is as it is.

At dawn,
I meditate on renunciation,
Which frees one of all attachment,
Which, like the fiery orb of the sun,
Burns brightly with incomparable intensity,
Upon the rise of which
One realizes the unreality of the world
And is set free from entanglement in illusion,
Which establishes one in the inner Bliss of the Self,
Which liberates the wise from the delusive notion
Of the existence of anything objective,
Which awakens one from the waking and dreaming
states,
And which fills life with the glory
Of the highest Truth.

At dawn,
I meditate on freedom from misidentification with the
body,
Which brings freedom from birth and death,
Which completely detaches the wise
From the illusion known as the world,
Which rids one of the dualistic dream
Of action and inaction,
Which awakens one from the ignorant notions
Of location, in, out, size, shape, and doership,
Which reveals the Self's infinite nature,
Which reveals the Self's formless, all-pervading nature,
Which reveals the Self's all-encompassing nature,
Which completely liberates the wise
From loneliness, fear of death, and transience,
And which, awakening one to "no difference in life or

death,"
Enables the Self to repose in its real, bodiless Being.

At dawn,
I meditate on the unreality of the mind,
Which reveals the nonexistence
Of the states of waking, dreaming, and all their contents,
And of deep, dreamless sleep, and its absence of
content,
Which reveals that there is no place for a concept
to exist,
Which liberates the wise
From all rigidity, inadvertence, ignorance, and illusion,
Which clearly reveals that
Consciousness alone exists,
And there is no such thing as thought,
Consciousness, which is nondual, all-illuminating,
Shining like the bright sun to lighten the whole space
    of experience,
Beginningless and endless,
Timeless, indivisible,
Free of the division of subject and object,
Self-effulgent, and which is truly the Self.

At dawn,
I meditate on the egoless Self,
The nondual Reality,
One without a second,
Nonobjective and inconceivable,
Infinite and eternal,
Perfect and unchanging,
Of the nature of Being-Consciousness-Bliss,
The Absolute,
Uncreated and indestructible,
Which always is as it is,
Which is the real nature of "I,"
And the joy, freedom, and peace of which
Are realized by direct experience.

Whoever meditates
In the manner described in this dawn meditation,
Consisting of six verses,
Realizes the Supreme Wisdom,
Is liberated from all of the imagined bondage,
Will know neither suffering nor fear,
And will be awake to the One Reality.
Whoever understands this dawn meditation,
By meditation upon its Truth,
Realizes the Self
And abides in the immortal Bliss of True Being.
This is the real dawn.
This is the real dawn.

≡
•

[This response was sent to a questioner who was preparing for an academic presentation for which she had asked numerous questions, the subjects of which can be inferred from the answers.]

May 1, 2001

ॐ Dear . . . ,

Thank you for your message filled with questions. Here are the answers, necessarily brief, hopefully not too terse. As you may surmise, it may be a bit difficult to acquire a comprehension of something experiential in nature from an email message like this. It is better to experience first hand, which you would be warmly welcome to do here, but this would not be practical in time for your presentation. The numbers below correspond to the numbers of your questions. I trust you will be understanding that some of the answers may not, at first glance, be what you expect; however, with some reflection, you will see that they are not oblique, but actually answers in a deeper sense. Indeed, for those on a path of Self-Knowledge, the answers to their questions are always on a level deeper than that upon which the questions were originally formulated.

1. As the original name of Hinduism is Sanatana Dharma, meaning roughly "the way of eternal Truth," SAT (Society of Abidance in Truth) is regarded as Hindu. However, not everyone who attends or is a member would say, "I am a Hindu," even though they may actually be embracing Hindu ideals and practices. What is unique about SAT, and that for which it has become renowned to those interested in these teachings around the world, is a) its consistent presentation of pure Nonduality (referred to as Unqualified Nondualism in the classic literature), identical to that of Sri Ramana Maharshi, Adi Sankara, and many other sages and, b) its practice of Self-inquiry (again identical to those sages) as the means of attaining Self-Realization, also known as Enlightenment, Self-Knowledge, Liberation (Moksha), etc. The teachings at SAT are those of Advaita Vedanta, or to be very specific: The Ajata Vada of Advaita Vedanta. To quickly translate: Vedanta refers to both the Upanishads, these being the wisdom or Knowledge portion of the Veda-s (the most ancient scriptural texts revered by Hindus), and also means "final, highest, conclusive Knowledge." Advaita means nondual. Vada is teaching or doctrine, while Ajata means "no-creation" or "no-birth." To sum up in one phrase: it means the nondual Knowledge that no other thing (other than the Absolute or True Self) has actually ever come to be. In addition to the Upanishads, these teachings can be found in such works as *Ribhu Gita, Ashtavakra Gita, Avadhuta Gita,* the works of Sri Sankara, and, in more recent times, of course, the teachings of Sri Ramana Maharshi, among others.

2. The word "dharma" has so many connotations: from object to path, to righteousness, to truth, so it is difficult to answer your question as it stands. Perhaps this will provide some answer for you, though: When a person deeply recognizes that the ongoing urge to be happy experienced by all sentient beings is fulfilled only within, he or

42

she then turns his or her mind inward and thus begins to fulfill dharma. Within is the Self, and so the search for Self-Knowledge is fulfilling one's dharma. Searching within on the basis of the conviction that suffering is self-created and peace and happiness lie within, one becomes detached from all things (dharmas) and, following a teaching (dharma) that guides him or her in Self-inquiry, he or she naturally conducts himself or herself in a way that manifests what is true, good, and beautiful, which is truly a righteous way (dharma). Ignorance is no longer the view, and illusion no longer results; Knowledge is the realized, direct experience, and Reality, in the ultimate sense, is self-revealed. This is the Dharma in an ultimate sense.

3. Patanjali's yoga is regarded as one of the six philosophies of Hinduism. Vedanta may be regarded as another. However, there are things in common, such as mastery of the mind, freedom from thought, detachment from material things, and the usual things in common among paths, such as basic ethics. It could be said that the seventh and eighth limbs (anga-s) of ashtanga yoga (Patanjali's system), being dhyana (meditation) and samadhi (profound absorption), are in common with the Advaita Vedanta. In addition, Sankara, in several of his works, has re-cast the traditional yogic terms with nondual meanings appropriate for Vedanta, but these are too lengthy to include here. If you have a copy of *Aparoksanubhuti,* you will find an example of this in the concluding verses.

4. The role of devotion or bhakti is determined by the temperament of the seeker. There is no hard and fast rule regarding this for aspirants, and this is so here at SAT. For some, it is the gateway or means of opening the door to Self-Knowledge teachings, and so it is important. From our view, since the real nature of God is the Self, the real nature of the Guru is the Self, and the real nature of the individual is this non-individualized Self, there is no distinction in terms of to which the bhakti is directed. This is why Ramana Maharshi has stated that when a person prays

43

with intense devotion to God or surrenders to God, that same God manifests as a Guru who appears only to show the seeker to dive within and reveals to him or her that what was worshipped as God (and is guided by as a Guru) exists as the one Self. Therefore, God, Guru, and Self are one and the same. At SAT, specific forms of God are according to the aspirant's own drawing, though some are not drawn to use any symbolic form; the use of Siva symbolism is quite apparent at the SAT Temple, itself.

5. The term "tantra" is so generic, it is difficult to know to what you are referring. If you are referring to the tantras, that being a class of texts that are generally ritualistic and magical in character, at SAT only the nondualistic portions of some of these are ever used, and not the mantras, yantras, and rituals themselves. Yes, puja occurs at SAT, and some of the members of SAT participate in such while others do not. Puja at SAT is used not for solicitation to a God for boons or anything similar, nor does it follow the rules of the sastras strictly. Puja is used primarily for a) expression of devotion and (usually simultaneously) b) for bringing the practitioners' minds into an elevated state that then turns inward to experience in Knowledge what was, for the time being, represented outwardly in symbolic manifestation. To understand the depth of this, I would recommend reading *Nirguna Manasa Puja (Worship of the Attributeless One in the Mind)* by Adi Sankara (translated into English at SAT). There is no attempt to be separate from the Deity. Since one is already accustomed to difference, there is little purpose in engaging in a spiritual practice that merely affirms the same delusion of dualism. Rather, our practices are aimed at realizing nonduality.

6. Women are regarded as the same as men. We have approximately the same number of women as men in SAT; sometimes the women outnumber the men by a few and sometimes the opposite is true. Since it is fundamental to our teachings that the Self is the same in all and that this eternal, formless Self is not the body, composed of transient

44

matter and constituting a form, there is no gender differentiation at all. The same holds true in regards to children. Seekers are free to bring children to our events, and they do so from time to time.

7. As stated above, this is pure Advaita Vedanta. The technique is that of Self-inquiry, a profound introspection to know oneself. This involves liberating the sense of one's identity from misidentification with all that is not truly the Self, such as objects, the body, the senses, the mind (any kind of thought), and the ego, or notion of individuality. This answer is extremely terse, I know; I would recommend that you attend satangs to gain more understanding. You may also wish to read and meditate upon *Truth Revealed* (*Forty Verses on Reality*) and *Who am I?* by Sri Ramana Maharshi to acquire a better understanding.

8. Renunciation must be guided by a true sense of detachment. Whether living the life of the renunciate or of a householder, the same detachment is necessary in order to attain Realization of the Self. Asceticism in terms of bodily mortification is not necessary and not helpful. Renunciation, that is, taking action based upon detachment, can be very helpful. One need not take a formal vow to do so. With or without the vow, one must leave behind old illusions and the actions that were based on those illusions. Not wishing to speak on behalf of others, I cannot tell you which ones think what of each position; I hope that they revere anyone practicing or realizing, regardless of outer appearances.

9. One need not be a member in order to attend. To become a member of SAT merely requires a sincere wish to do so to better one's spirituality. Yes, offerings are usually an aspect of membership.

SAT, as an organization, started conducting public satsangs in 1978; there were some satsangs for the previous four years (since 1974), but they were known only by word-of-mouth.

In all the instruction I have ever given, I have emphasized the impersonal (no-ego) nature of Truth, the aspirant's
own experience, and the actual Knowledge and inquiry. No
emphasis is ever placed on "my personal story." Only one
autobiographical article was ever composed, that being at
the request of the president of Sri Ramanasramam in South
India for its centenary celebration in 1996 (which I was
requested to attend and to speak), and I was required to do
so in a devotional style in that article. However, I must say
that it really contained no phenomenal information, but
rather traced out the process of absorption into infinite
Being-Consciousness-Bliss, which is the nature of the Self
or Brahman (the vast Absolute).

I hope the above satisfies your needs. Aside from your
academic research, I encourage you to explore these teachings of Self-Knowledge, whether at SAT or elsewhere. If you
would like more information about SAT (including recordings of satsangs, information about retreats, publication,
and such), please feel free to contact me.

Ever yours in Truth,
Nome

*[This is the response sent to a seeker who requested com-
mentary upon a passage of Sri Ramana's teaching.]*

August 21, 2001

ॐ Dear . . . ,

Thank you for your letter, with its included quotation
and verse.

Yes, I am familiar with the passage regarding the
Sankaracharya's visit to the Maharshi. The recounting of it

appears in a few places. The Sankaracharya had a letter sent on his behalf expressing his desire to gain clarity from the Maharshi regarding this. The Maharshi smiled and said, "What is there to explain; he knows all this already." This reply was sent to the Sankaracharya, who set forth to see the Maharshi.

When he arrived, a special dais at the same level as the Maharshi was set up for him, but he refused to sit on it, but rather sat upon a deer skin spread upon the floor and remained silent with the Maharshi as stated in *At the Feet of Bhagavan*. Then, if I correctly recall, came the brief discourse given by the Maharshi as quoted by you.

I do not know if this passage will be actually cited during the retreat, but I am glad to know that you found it and have read it. Perhaps "nature" was the word prakriti, which signifies the substance of which all manifestation is composed, while the word "Person" may be Purusha or something similar, meaning not only person, but Spirit. Reading it this way may bring forth its deep significance in a clearer manner. The essence is that the Self is the sole-existent Reality, of the nature of Being-Consciousness, regarded as the substratum of all when all is considered, to be realized by dissolving the objective, or manifest, into the Spirit, which is that Being-Consciousness, which leaves one free from misidentification with anything of the shadowy image of the manifest (the unreal).

May that which is revealed in His gracious words and in His Silence remain ever shining in your heart.

Ever yours in Truth,
Nome

[This was sent in response to a seeker's letter the questions in which can be inferred from the answers.]

47

January 7, 2002

ॐ Dear . . . ,

Namaste.

Thank you for your letter of December 27th. Yes, absorption of the essential teaching about the Self lifts one beyond all kinds of bondage and suffering, even beyond that which is associated with death. By inquiring to know the Self, it becomes evident that you cannot be the body and that the state or condition of the body is not your state or condition.

The desire for Liberation naturally intensifies as one advances, or we might say that the increasing d esire for Liberation brings such advancement. One's sincere prayers are always answered. Such become actual meditation, which, being of the nature of Self-inquiry, leads to Self-Knowledge.

Though you will not be able to be with us in January in a bodily way, we remain always with you in the spiritual sense. Hopefully, we will be able to see you later in the year

May you ever abide in the deep Knowledge of the Self, which is unborn and imperishable, which is your eternal Heart, and thus dwell in lasting peace and happiness.

Ever yours in Truth,
Nome

[In resonse to a request for a photograph:]

June 12, 2002

ॐ Dear . . . ,

48

Namaste. Thank you for your recent letter.

In your letter, you request a photograph of Nome. Though understanding the pure intentions of those who occasionally ask for such and comprehending the purpose you describe, still I do not engage in distributing such. A brief explanation may be helpful here.

Obviously, the non-distribution of such pictures has a multifaceted reason. The first, if there is the picture of my Guru, Sri Bhagavan, you have all that you need to look at and a better picture of me than one of this body. Secondly, I rather de-emphasize the "personal aspect" for the sake of the aspirants, as I believe you well know. Thirdly, some photographs were taken several years ago. Some of them were by a professional photographer who was attending satsang at the time. Most would say that those photographs look unnaturally posed because of the way he set them up, perhaps reflecting more his artistry or personal perspective than the subject of which he was attempting to make an image. I do not see what purpose they serve and am not sure of where copies of them may be. There were also a few other, perhaps more natural looking, pictures made a few years later in the satsang hall and inner shrine, but I do not have any copies of these, either. There were some photographs taken over several years, in black and white, at different places, but I do not know where they are. Only one photograph was taken during the "early years,' indeed for the first fifteen years or so since satsang began, but I believe an over-zealous air brush artist who wanted to improve upon it, by making the eyes look less open for some reason, destroyed the original. So, while I do not have an objection to your use of a picture, I am unable to supply one for you.

However, noticing your anticipated schedule of events, it would seem that those who are with you and who are interested in doing so, can travel to Santa Cruz for satsangs on Sundays, as well, at which they can see, hear, etc. even without a picture.

May That which ever is and alone is, the One without a second, of the nature of nondual Being-Consciousness-

49

Bliss, ever shine as the Self that you truly are, with all peace and joy.

Ever yours in Truth,
Nome

[A seeker informed Nome that he was afflicted by diabetes. In response, Nome sent some information about possible treatments and concluded with:]

March 5, 2003

ॐ Dear . . . ,

Namaste.

Following our conversation of yesterday, today I found some of the articles of which we spoke when you mentioned your diabetes.

Certainly, the body is transient. It is subject to various diseases and pains. It is an objective form; an animated corpse. To remedy the disease of mortality, by which all who are embodied are afflicted, there is no cure comparable to the Knowledge of the Self, which is immortal Being. That Knowledge, which is final and the end of all knowledge (literally, Vedanta) has been revealed by the sages such as the Maharshi. It is the Self-revelation of the non-dual Absolute. Dive within, with a heart full of devotion, inquiring within yourself as to, "Who am I?" and thus be blissful and at peace.

May you abide in the true Knowledge of the Self and thus be ever happy.

Om Namah Sivaya
Om Namo Bhagavate Sri Ramanaya

Ever yours in Truth,
Nome

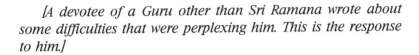

[A devotee of a Guru other than Sri Ramana wrote about some difficulties that were perplexing him. This is the response to him.]

May 23, 2003

ॐ Dear . . . ,

Namaste. Thank you for your letter of May 3, 2003, which arrived yesterday. I hope that I am deciphering your name correctly, as I am not accustomed to your handwriting.

Since you state that you are a devotee of Sri Sri Ananadamurti, it is, of course, advisable to seek instruction that you may need from that source directly, such as through written records of his teachings, searching for the applicable passages that are pertinent to your needs at this time.

One cannot expect others to necessarily appreciate spiritual principles that one holds dear and by which one lives. Detachment is called for, including indifference to the opinions, however expressed, of others. It is not beneficial to think of the faults of others and regard them with derogatory ideas, for that is lending your mind to the very thing that you wish to utterly transcend. Whether you remain where you are or not, it is necessary to dive within, beyond the illusions of the world and the ego, and to know the true Self within. Whenever you earnestly attempt to dive within, consecrating yourself to the Absolute, be that called God or the Self, the grace of the Supreme and all the sages and saints is shining for you. Indeed, grace is always there; you have only to turn inward to be in a state of grace.

Ultimately, grace is of the very nature of the ever-existent Self, which is who you really are.

I am enclosing for you a small pamphlet of sayings of Bhagavan Sri Ramana Maharshi, in case they are of interest to you and may be of benefit to you.

May that which is the Self of all, of the nature of infinite, eternal Being-Consciousness-Bliss, the One without a second, be realized within you to be your actual Being, so that you may dwell in happiness and peace always.

Ever yours in Truth,
Nome

[A seeker wrote about his questions concerning reincarnation and Liberation (Moksha). This is the response.]

December 23, 2003

ॐ Dear . . . ,

Namaste. Thank you for your letter of the 17th.

Your three questions revolve around the same point of reincarnation and the embodiment of the Self. The answer is in the realization that the Self is not at all ever incarnated. As it is for you, so it is for all beings, all beings existing only as the one Self, which is neither born nor perishing.

Moksha must necessarily be of the same nature as the nondual Self. So, first realize your own Moksha, the natural state, and then you may see that true state of all.

May you ever abide as That which is unborn and imperishable, which is devoid of limitations such as the body, and which is eternally immutable, and thus dwell in lasting peace and happiness.

Ever yours in Truth,
Nome

———
●

[A seeker was reading two of SAT's publications and asked some questions that can be inferred from Nome's response presented here.]

ॐ Dear . . . ,

Om Namo Bhagavate Sri Ramanaya

Namaste. Thank you for your message. I am glad to know that you are finding passages in *Timeless Presence* and *Self-Knowledge* beneficial for you.

In answer to your first question, it is good that you should know about Bhagavan's life and teaching. The lives, writings, etc. of his disciples (using this word simply in the sense defined by Bhagavan: one who adheres to and practices his instruction) should be of interest only in their emphasis upon the Sadguru and the Truth itself. Interest in the nonexistent individual is not called for. As mentioned in *Timeless Presence*, were it not for the request of Sri [name omitted], this hand would never have written such a document.

Meditation is invaluable. The sitting posture is, itself, not the meditation, though you may very well meditate while sitting. Meditation on the path of jnana is Self-inquiry. If you find that when you are in seated meditation, the mind is most inward-turned, such is fine. Just be sure that the rest of the experience follows upon it; that is, the active life should blend with the meditation, for the Knowledge of identity does not change with changes of the body.

One way of reading is to consider the texts as philosophical and later to apply such to meditation. Another way of reading is to regard such as a form of meditation and thus experience what you read (the meaning) as you read it. In the latter approach, what was previously conceived as expositions will be experienced as details of inquiry.

Samadhi is beneficial. Sahaja samadhi is the realization of the sole-existent Reality, in which there is the absence of one to be absorbed. Thus, the *Avadhuta Gita,* chapter one, says, "how can samadhi be possible?"

There is no need to go through various samadhi states, but, if they occur, they are beneficial. There is, though, the utter necessity of Self-Knowledge. Aim to know who you are and thus realize the one state that the Self alone is.

What is your mind when it is not considered as in a state?

Regarding your question about satsang: what is said in that passage is indicative of the direct experience of Being and its ever-existent nature. Once the body misidentification is relinquished, the ideas of inner and outer vanish. That is to say, the outer is dissolved in the inner, and the inner is the infinite Consciousness. Consciousness is the Self, the one Self of all. Association with Being (sanga, sat) is such satsang.

If you presently seem to have two ways of understanding, one intellectual and one actual, you may wish to question the basis of such.

Yes, the path is entirely inner.

It is not a question of whether or not you are "too attached to calm states." What is it that you desire in such? What is the nature of that? Is the peace newly acquired? Or is it ever-existent, clearly evident when misidentifications are removed? Discern deeply your own experience. When you are in deep peace, do you feel that such has just begun, or does it seem that such has been ever the case? Is the peace objective or of your own Being? If Being is unalterable and ever-existent, what causes the peace to seemingly disappear? Do you not still exist? What is the nature of that existence? In this manner, question deeply within yourself and enter into a profound inquiry into your nature.

As for India, I expect to be at Sri Ramanasramam from about January 22 through February 5, 2005.

I hope that the above answers are helpful for you. May your inquiry be deep so that you realize the Self that you ever are.

Ever yours in Truth,
Nome

[This was written in response to a seeker who involved himself in numerology, thinking that it may be a means to change or get beyond his personality.]

June 21, 2004

ॐ Dear . . . ,

Namaste. Thank you for your letter with the accompanying book.

Whatever may be the connections between the seeming names and apparent forms, the Self remains transcendent of all such illusion. That thoughts seem to affect or determine other thoughts is understandable, so that you may perceive, according to your perspective, a causality between the thoughts of a name with the thoughts constituting the personality. That subtle thoughts with the intellect interact with the thoughts appearing as the gross world is evident, though, again, the specific causality is determined by the standpoint of the observer. The Self is neither gross nor subtle and should be realized as free from thought.

Tendencies are repeated thoughts. Whatever be the analysis, inclusive of causality, of such tendencies, they are still composed of repetitive thought. Such thought is not real but seems real due to misidentification. There are innumerable ways of effecting abeyance of such thoughts, but, for permanent destruction of them, that is, for the permanent destruction of the ignorance of misidentification, Self-Knowledge alone is the means.

In your letter, you relate the story of a nine-year-old boy with great poetic skills, language skills, and poetry with references to inquiry and Siva. Yes, whatever is attained on this path is not lost, even in death, but remains. Muruganar was similarly mute, or at least did not learn to speak, until several years old. Later, he was one of Tamil Nadu's noted poets, helped in the creation of the Tamil lexicon, and eventually composed thousands of verses in devotion to Sri Ramana and expressive of profound wisdom.

May that which can never be enumerated and which is free of the ego and its attendant tendencies be realized to be your only true Self.

Ever yours in Truth,
Nome

[In answer to a letter from a seeker in South America who raised questions about inquiry, devotion, a "living" guru, and other topics:]

July 22, 2004

ॐ Dear . . . ,

Namaste. Thank you for your letter.

To briefly respond to your questions:

Whichever you find more to your temperament, the path of jnana or bhakti, as long as the illusion of the ego is destroyed, it is fine.

The nature of Self-Realization is eternal abidance as the Unborn.

The "Master" or "Guru" is not the body, so the concepts of living or dead simply do not apply. The Guru's help is present in a manner that transcends all such seeming boundaries, time, space, etc.

If you read the literature containing the Maharshi's teachings, you will find instructions concerning surrender of the ego by bhakti as well as knowing its nonexistence through Self-inquiry, the principal means of the path of jnana.

There are no plans at this time to visit South America.

I am not familiar with Aurbindo's writings and so cannot comment upon what you have said about them.

May you dive deep within, heart full of devotion, and inquiring to know yourself, abide as That, which is of the nature of eternal Being-Consciousness-Bliss.

Ever yours in Truth,
Nome

[To a seeker who previously asked questions about samadhi.]

ॐ Dear . . . ,

Om Namo Bhagavate Sri Ramanaya

Thank you for your message. As you say that you use your own writings to augment your sadhana, I am happy to answer your questions. Perhaps, these answers will be of some benefit for you. The answers follow the order of your questions and statements of your message. I am not a book reviewer and so cannot offer praise or otherwise for your writings, but, as a friend, here are offered comments, primarily concerned with the basis of the questions and comments.

Clarity of spiritual discrimination is worthwhile. The Truth, itself, is ineffable. Therefore, the Maharshi, in verses, has alluded to Dakshinamurti and his eloquent Silence. Sri Adi Sankara has indicated that the power of the words of instruction is the power of Brahman. He who inquires to know himself and thus reposes in self-illumined Self-Knowledge truly understands what is meant by the instruction and the silence.

Kevala should be understood to refer to That which alone is. Savikalpa, nirvikalpa, and sahaja should be understood as described in the previous message. You may wish to question whether you wish to continue to ascribe more relative meanings to them, as you have in compounding the terms. Whenever one encounters spiritual instruction, it is wiser to elevate one's experiential knowledge to what is expressed rather than reducing the meaning to match one's existing preconception. In the former, nondual realization is assured. In the latter, dualism will be affirmed; that is, the tendency of ignorant conception will be repeated.

In some texts, sahaja nirvikalpa samadhi is the term employed. It means the absorption in and as the undifferentiated Innate. That is Self-Realization. Sri Bhagavan refers to such usually as sahaja samadhi. That which is innate neither comes nor goes. It contains no duality. There is no individual (jiva) to enter or exit it. Therefore, strive for the egoless state, as in that is found the essence of all samadhi. Because Self-Realization is not an event, being not for any individual (but being liberation from the individual), and because it is timeless, and therefore eternal, the *Avadhuta Gita* rhetorically exclaims, "How can samadhi be possible?"

The Maharshi's analogy of the fort refers to the destruction of vasana-s, which are the manifest tendencies of ignorance, and the experience of the mind in meditation. Self-inquiry destroys all the vasana-s by yielding clarity about happiness, reality, and identity, which are ultimately one. You may find it helpful to examine the significance of this.

The Self is the nature of all. So, Self-Realization is possible for all. The same is the case with samadhi-s. It is not necessary to enter samadhi, in the sense of a state of temporary absorption, for Self-Realization, but it is essential to know the Self as it is. Knowledge is the essence of the samadhi-s, as alluded to in the previous message. If one experiences samadhi, it is then incumbent upon him to realize the Knowledge essence while relinquishing all that composes the non-samadhi state.

There is never a lack of Grace. When effort is full, Grace is experienced fully.

Yes, nonobjective is the nature of Truth.

If the desire for Liberation is strong and one inquires, in which discrimination is implicit, the possibility of "tricking" or fooling oneself is impossible.

You may wish to question the assumption of a connection between the body and that which is spiritual. Spiritual is bodiless and sense-transcendent. Truly, it is mind-transcendent. This applies both to the assumption of bodily causes and acts as producing the spiritual and to the conception of the spiritual having a bodily effect.

Prarabdha karma is employed as an explanation of the manifest activities of the non-Self. One who realizes the Self is the Self, and no karma can be ascribed to him. Yet for those who have not yet relinquished the objective outlook, prarabdha karma is said to govern the affairs of the body and such as a means of explanation.

You may wish to question the value and validity, and the lack thereof, of formulating opinions of others, whether specifically or in terms of large masses of people.

As the *Gita* says, no effort in sadhana ever goes in vain.

Sankara never adopted an ego. He who realizes Brahman is Brahman, and Brahman never has any ego whatsoever, but abides one without a second. Christ has indicated the same. Better than formulating such conceptions about the great sages is to inquire to know oneself. First abide as they abide. Then, you can make such statements if any such urge is forthcoming.

If you question the assumption of the very existence of an ego to begin with, you may find more clarity in your attempt to define sahaja nirvikalpa samadhi. The Unborn is the Uncreated. It is without division or alternative. It is the Self as the Self is, Reality as it is. That is Self-Knowledge.

I hope the above is helpful for you. More than this, your own inward inquiry will be helpful. Again, you may find reading what was previously suggested and the teachings of the Maharshi very helpful. If further questions arise for you, it may be better to accomplish the absorption of the answer "in person" here at SAT.

Please accept the answers here in the spirit in which they are given. No criticism is intended in any of it; only honest answers about the Truth born of direct, continuous experience and a friendly urging to clear inquiry. Anyone who dives within according to the Maharshi's instruction can find the same realization.

May that which is the quintessence, the full and final absorption, realized as the ever-existent, be known by you so that you abide always in perfect peace and happiness.

Om Namah Sivaya

Ever yours in Truth,
Nome

[A couple wrote requesting advice that would enable them to acquire a better understanding of spiritual symbolism, especially that which is present in the SAT temple. This is Nome's response. "Tuffy" is the name of their dog.]

August 4, 2004

ॐ Dear . . . ,

Namaste. Thank you for your warm letter to Sasvati and me of July 21st. This has been my first opportunity to respond.

The use of symbolism is not essential for Self-Realization. In one sense, though, you already use a significant amount of symbolism, but we do not usually refer to it as such. For example, in your spirituality, you use a complex form of audio and visual symbols in the form of spoken and written words. While the sounds of the words and the pictures of the letters are unrelated to the Self and its Realization, you nonetheless listen and converse, write and read, about these in ways that spark experience within you of such. Likewise is it with symbols in motion, sometimes referred to as ritual.

What is important is the deeper Knowledge, and, with symbols, be they words or icons, gestures or sounds, lights, etc., that one inwardly knows their significance. The use of outwardly appearing things, or rather the use of one's own mind and senses, should be in such a manner that one remains in the Knowledge of one's Self.

What shines, with and without symbols is the Truth, the source of love, bliss, and peace. This you observed in your comments upon the wedding. Where Truth is present, love shines in its essence, and "water turns to wine" (to be symbolic about it).

It is always a pleasure to see that you have brought Tuffy with you in satsang. He is very well-behaved; indeed, he is quieter than some others who attend satsang.

May that in which the symbolist and the symbol dissolve be realized as your very Being, so that your happiness is perpetual and full.

Ever yours in Truth,
Nome

≡
•

[In response to a seeker who sent many letters in rapid succession:]

August 26, 2004

ॐ Dear . . . ,

Om Namo Bhagavate Sri Ramanaya

Namaste. Thank you for your many letters.

Your letters display various modes of your mind, ranging from idle reminiscences of your personal past to deeper
contemplation regarding spirituality to hallucinatory imaginings. You may wish to discern these modes for yourself
and determine which are the ways in which you wish to use
your mind and which are ways that are entirely unfruitful
and needless. This could be important for you.

Yes, there is much in Sadhu Om's writings that may be
beneficial for you. Reading Sri Ramana and Sri Sankara is,
of course, illuminative in every way, and you seem to be
observing such in your note of the 16th.

"Not to know" refers to a dissolution or absence of ego-
centric thinking. It also refers to the state of mind of the
aspirant that recognizes that he does not know himself or
the essence of spirituality and that he must if he wishes to
be happy and at peace. This leads to sincere yearning to
know the Truth, which, fueling the inquiry to know the Self,
results in Self-Knowledge.

"Deep feeling" is an expression, though perhaps not
adequate, indicative of the fact that spiritual experience is
not mere ideas or thoughts, but something deeper, pertaining to Consciousness, itself, to Being, itself. Such should not
be confused with emotions and moods, which are but temporary formations of the mind. Similarly, such should not
be confused with mere pleasant sensations of the body.

The Self is neither male nor female, is not a limited
individual, is not gross or subtle, does not have whims or
impressions, is ever motionless and blissful, and is not
other than yourself. This alone is the Atman, which is One
only. Other notions about it are only delusion and should
be wisely abandoned by you.

"Buddha" means one who is awake. That is, one who knows the Truth of the Self, who has "awakened" from the dream of illusion. Ideas of "buddhas" doing all sorts of actions and feeling all sorts of things are based on ego-centric delusion and should be wisely abandoned by you.

I hope that you find the above clarifying and helpful. May your meditation become steady and your inquiry deep so that you come to know the Self and remain happy and at peace, in activity and inactivity and in every way.

Ever yours in Truth,

Nome

[To a seeker who expressed a desire to be free of tendencies:]

September 9, 2004

ॐ Dear . . . ,

Namaste. Thank you for your letter of the 29th. Your kind offering is also appreciated.

Yes, perseverance is needed. Perseverance should be applied in a wise manner. If you actually inquire, you will find yourself free of the tendencies. Tendencies are always rooted in some misidentification. In the case of misidentification regarding the Bliss of your nature, the delusion manifests as erroneous conceptions regarding the source of happiness. In less extroverted cases, it involves considering yourself as an ego or as embodied. Self-inquiry removes such delusion, and tendencies or patterns of thinking that are without roots cannot stand by themselves.

Frequent reading of the Maharshi's teachings and other Advaita Vedanta works (Sankara, Ribhu, etc.) will be helpful. Listening to recorded satsangs may be of benefit, as well. Of course, when you are able, you are always welcome here at SAT.

May that for which your heart yearns be realized as innate, so that you, free of vasana-s, abide in lasting happiness and peace.

Ever yours in Truth,
Nome

[This is in response to a seeker who expressed the desire for love of God to become continuous.]

November 4, 2004

ॐ Dear . . . ,

Namaste. Thank your for your two recent letters.

If inquiry becomes continuous, so does Knowledge. If spiritual effort, or intensity, becomes continuous, so does abiding in a state of Grace. The desire, as expressed by you, to feel the love of God all of the time cannot go unfulfilled.

The inclination to do things well is not an obstacle, provided there is no misidentification as a performer of action. Being-Consciousness-Bliss is an uncreated perfection that is in you and is you always.

May that which shines as limitless love within you also shine as the unveiled light of Knowledge of the Self so that you abide in the bliss of the Truth always.

Ever yours in Truth,
Nome

[The next two letters are in response to a seeker who was endeavoring to apply Sri Ramana's teachings to her married life.]

64

April 1, 2005

ॐ Dear . . . ,

Namaste. Thank you for your letter of March 29th.

The duality superimposed upon love is not true. Love must always be for the sake of the Self and not for any objective thing in itself. So, if you say that you love another, such as [name omitted], what is it actually that you love? Can he be an object? Is he not the Self as all are? To remain detached from the unreal and thus transcendent of all forms does not indicate a loveless state. In Truth, divine love and detachment are of the same nature, for both are rooted in the Knowledge of the Self. So, to say that one needs another to love is false, but to say that one should refrain from loving another is also false, because who else is the other but the Self?

I am glad to hear that you are benefiting from the retreat and reading *Ribhu Gita*.

[name omitted]'s selfless service cannot be said to have had no effect, for it has led him to the present state of desiring to meditate more deeply. It is the selfless element that is so important.

May you blissfully abide in the perfect fullness of the Self, which, though devoid of all, is all.

Ever yours in Truth,
Nome

April 13, 2005

ॐ Dear . . . ,

Namaste. Thank you for your letter of April 5th.

You have now seen that expectations of love or happiness from without meet with disappointment. Diving within, you find that Bliss shines in all its perfect fullness within you. You can very easily remain in this deeper Knowledge

65

whenever you relate to anyone, man or monkey. That will not guarantee the other's response to you, but it will guarantee your happiness.

Ever yours in Truth,
Nome

[In response to some questions about prana and mind:]

July 7, 2005

ॐ Dear . . . ,

Om Namo Bhagavate Sri Ramanaya

Namaste. Thank you for your recent notes. In your note of the 6th, you asked about Sri Ramana's comment regarding prana and the mind, as you remember it. It is difficult to offer you a comment without seeing the actual reference and the context.

Traditionally, it is said that with the perishing of the body, the subtle form of the mind leaves, taking with it the prana, for we see neither prana nor the mind in a corpse. That subtle mind will, with prana, then come to reside in a new body. Prana is to be understood not only to be the breath but as the animating life-energy.

From another angle of vision, prana is conceived within the mind and has no separate existence.

The Self is neither the prana nor the mind and has neither birth nor death.

The dialogue portion that you quoted from satsang deals with the transient nature of the body, the breath, the prana, and the mind. The Self alone is eternal. Whether prana is conceived as disappearing at death, as dissolving into a greater prana, as dissolving into a greater prana and reforming, as an aspect of the mind, or in some other way, the important point is to not misidentify with it and to realize the formless, eternal Self.

May you ever abide in the Truth of your Being and thus be ever at peace and happy.

Ever yours in Truth,
Nome

[To the same seeker who asked questions about love in her marriage:]

July 12, 2005

ॐ Dear . . . ,

Namaste. Thank you for your letters of June 25th and July 7th and the enclosed offerings.

Yes, love is of the very nature of Being-Consciousness. It is of the indivisibility of Being. When it is ascribed to forms or conceived as being dependent on those forms, such as embodied beings, it seems fragile, for it is being seen reflected with the limitations of those forms. When known in its essence, it is eternal and imperishable, free of any limitation whatsoever.

May you ever abide in the Bliss of the Self.

Ever yours in Truth,
Nome

[In response to questions about the mind and thought:]

August 1, 2005

🕉 Dear . . . ,

Om Namo Bhagavate Sri Ramanaya
Namaste. Thank you for your recent letters.

In your letter of July 29th, you raise some questions regarding thought.

Self-Realization is not a thought-produced state, and Self-Knowledge is not a certain way of thinking, but rather it is of a thought-transcendent nature. In highest Truth, thought does not exist, and the Self is the only Existence, which is the Absolute.

In spiritual practice, contemplation of the teachings concerning Truth is always beneficial, and such contemplation necessarily involves thinking. When the focus is upon that which is nonobjective, and therefore thought-transcendent, such becomes meditation.

A mind that follows its own imagination and believes in its own wanderings, is outward and delusive. A mind that inquires into its own nature and source is inward. Sages and scriptures recommend that the mind should be steady and inward.

So, think about the teachings often and also deeply meditate upon their significance so that, by experiential Knowledge, you realize who you truly are, beyond the body, mind, and ego. Thus, one's ignorance vanishes and, along with it, the illusory limitations. If ignorance vanishes, the Self, which is God, may be said to reveal itself to itself.

May you ever abide in the Knowledge of the Self and thus be ever at peace.

Ever yours in Truth,
Nome

[A response to a letter that expressed the yearning to be free of the mind's tumult.]

August 10, 2005

ॐ Dear . . . ,

Namaste. Thank you for your recent letter with its enclosed offerings.

Whenever some desire or worry causes disturbance in your mind, be sure to inquire deeply. Determine that what you actually desire is happiness, and not the object, and that about which you worry is actually your happiness, and not the object or circumstance. Then, determine the source of happiness within. Within is the Self, so inquire, "Who am I?" If you so inquire, deeply and thoroughly, experiential Knowledge will be yours, and your worries and desires will dissolve.

No matter how many thoughts seem to appear, you remain as the silent Witness of all of them, of the nature of forever-unconceived Consciousness. Know your identity as that and remain unfettered by thoughts. Consciousness is nondual, undifferentiated, and infinite. Therefore, in highest Truth, thought does not exist. Meditate profoundly on this by inquiry to know yourself until you realize how true it is.

If you continue with your best efforts, with the help of Grace that is always present, you will know yourself and be ever happy and at peace.

Ever yours in Truth,
Nome

[The questions posed that yielded this response can be inferred from the answers here.]

September 2, 2005

ॐ Dear . . . ,

Namaste. Thank you for your letters and email messages.

In your letter of the 1st of September, you wrote of the potential to do something bad and not know of it. Generally speaking, with the exception of complete accidents, you are always aware of what you are doing. The spiritual principle for all that we do is that we should do unto others as we would have them do unto us. For the Knowledge of the Self, you must treat others as the Self, which is the Divine, and the very Self within you. As you do not wish to be hurt, so you should do no harm to others. As you do not wish for others to think poorly of you, so you should not think poorly of others. The Maharshi is the exemplar of this.

In your letter, you quote me in reference to "subtraction." I had said that one should not subtract from the teaching. This applies outwardly and inwardly. Outwardly, one should not delete passages from the scriptures and wise sayings so that the remainder fits more neatly within the confines of his preconceived notions. Rather, he should abandon such notions and enter true wisdom, thoroughly comprehending what has been said by the wise sages since ancient times. Inwardly, one should not interpret the teachings by subtracting from them what one does not understand so that the remainder fits more neatly into the confines of the ideas he has in his mind. Rather, by deep inquiry, one should transcend the limiting ideas and fully realize that which is revealed in the teachings.

May you ever abide at the very source of all wisdom and love, the Absolute Self, so that you are ever happy and at peace.

Ever yours in Truth,
Nome

70

[A response to questions about the use of the intellect.]

December 5, 2005

ॐ Dear . . . ,

Om Namo Bhagavate Sri Ramanaya
Namaste. Thank you for your recent notes.

It is good, as you have said, to run out of reasons to not say, "not this, not this." There is no good purpose served by stagnation in delusion. There is every good reason to be wise.

You need not worry about the intellect. If deeper spiritual thoughts appear, meditate upon what they point to and, thereby, experience that which lies beyond even the intellect. In addition, if one treats one's thoughts as inconsequential while remaining steeped in the spiritual Knowledge of being the Self, the mind's storms are over. Moreover, if one traces the source of the various thoughts to their basis in misidentifications, and then traces the misidentifications to the "I," and the "I" to its origin, there is supreme Peace.

May your meditations be deep so that your life is suffused with peace and your heart is full of joy in the Knowledge of what you really are. May your Christmas be filled with the birth of wisdom and love within you.

Ever yours in Truth,
Nome

[A seeker wrote requesting clarification regarding the analogy of the removal of the thorn and its relation to nondual Knowledge. This is the response.]

May 29, 2006

ॐ Dear . . . ,

Namaste. Thank you for your letter with its enclosed donation. Your kindness and generosity are appreciated by all here at SAT.

The thorn analogy mentioned in your letter is one found in several places. It is worthwhile to consider its significance. The analogy states that there are two thorns, the second being used to remove the first, and that both are thrown away. From this, several points can be observed. First, since there are two thorns, they must apply to the realm of experience in which duality, even if only subtly so, is still assumed to apply. Thus, neither of the thorns can truly apply to Nonduality. Second, the first thorn causes pain, which is analogous to suffering. Third, the other thorn is used to remove the one that causes suffering, but the second one, itself, inflicts no harm, but rather gives relief. Fourth, the thorns must refer to something that can be abandoned. Therefore, they cannot possibly signify Reality, the Self, which alone is Nonduality, for one cannot really abandon Reality, and one can never separate from one's Existence. In Nonduality, there can be neither grasping nor abandonment, for there is no "other" to be the object of either.

So, what is the significance of the thorns and such? The thorn that causes pain is the ignorance that causes suffering. That ignorance is composed of erroneous ideas, that is, thoughts to which have been attributed the reality and identity of the Self. The thorn used to remove the suffering is Knowledge, for only Knowledge can destroy ignorance, for evident reasons, but, here, the reference is to those thoughts that express Knowledge. They do no harm and may be useful to counteract the thoughts constituting the ignorance, though the Knowledge itself is the essence and the key. The Knowledge cannot be abandoned, as it is nonobjective, of the very nature of the Self (Prajnana Brahma, Supreme Knowledge is Brahman), and is nondual, but its expression in the mind, that is, thoughts pertaining to the Truth, etc., can be. For one who has removed the very cause of suffering, it is no longer necessary to think the thoughts of manifested wisdom, for he abides as that which is all-transcendent. Therefore, in order to show that the Self is beyond all duality, beyond all conception, and that Self-Knowledge is beyond all duality, for it is identical with Being, various scriptures declare that it is "beyond ignorance and knowledge." However, the analogy displays the usefulness of such wise contemplation, meditation, etc., until one abides in That, as That, itself, which alone is Absolute Self-Knowledge.

I hope that you find the above useful or helpful. May you ever abide in the Knowledge of the Self, the Nondual, so that you are ever happy and at peace.

Ever yours in Truth,
Nome

☰
•

[This seeker's questions can be inferred from the answers given in response.]

June 16, 2006

ॐ Dear . . . ,

Namaste. Thank you for your letter of May 17th, which arrived here just on June 13th.

Yes, Shanti has introduced and exposed you to many wondrous aspects of spirituality. Though, as you know, she is now infirm and the faculties useful for communication are no longer consistently at her command, that which has been her inspiration, indeed, that which is truly the Self, remains immutable and ever luminous.

As we are not bodies, the distance between their locations is of no consequence for Self-Realization. What is essential is Self-Knowledge, which may be said to be determined by the depth of inquiry within oneself and by the intensity, including consistency, that one brings to that inquiry. Understanding the source of happiness and the purpose of life is sufficient to yield such.

Regardless of the experiences one has or the activities in which one engages, it is essential to know oneself. Of this, you are aware. Activities, such as those involving your career and family life, are neither fulfilling in themselves in the absence of inner Knowledge nor are they obstacles to this Knowledge. Spirituality cannot truly be measured, but the degree of freedom and peace within are ways to gauge.

Of course, if you are in this area, you will be very welcome at satsang. If there are books that may be of interest to you or that may be helpful for you, SAT can supply them for you. Since you have access to the internet, you can simply visit the SAT website at www.SATRamana.org to see what is available. Similarly, you can see what recordings of satsangs are available if you would be interested in such.

May you ever abide in the Knowledge of the Self, of the nature of Being-Consciousness-Bliss, which is unborn and imperishable, so that you are ever happy and at peace.

Ever yours in Truth,
Nome

———
•

[In response to a seeker:]

June 23, 2006

ॐ Dear . . . ,

Om Namo Bhagavate Sri Ramanaya

Namaste. Thank you for your letter of the 19th.

Intensity and clarity need not be interpreted as severity. In inquiry is joy, and in Knowledge is Bliss.

Observation of transience yields strength of purpose and the determination to use the time wisely, thus bringing peace and happiness.

To remain unaffected by events and circumstances, such as in the work place as mentioned by you, is right. Equanimity, just as the above mentioned intensity, clarity, strength, wisdom, etc., derives from the Self.

The ego can do nothing, for it does not actually exist. Trust in That which is absolute, and inquire to know yourself in your real Being. As the Self, there is no departure or return. Find out who it is who appears to depart.

I am glad to hear that you have secured a place at Arunachala and that things are proceeding with [name omitted]'s visa application.

Ever yours in Truth,
Nome

≡
•

[In response to a seeker with a keen interest in Buddhism:]

July 10, 2006

ॐ Dear . . . ,

Namaste.

On behalf of all at SAT, I wish to thank you for your recent offering. Your kindness and generosity will help our temple of nondual Self-Knowledge to continue to flourish. In a Sutra, the title of which I cannot recall, Lord Buddha declares that true giving is that in which the giver and the receiver are not conceived (this is my paraphrase, for I do not have the text before me, and it has been many years

75

since I read it). The Maharshi states in *Who am I?* that if one knows this Truth, who will not give to others?

What is that Truth? It is the Truth of our very Being, the indivisible Self. May the Knowledge of this Truth be ever shining within you so that you always abide in peace and happiness.

Ever yours in Truth,
Nome

[This is a response to a question about freeing onself completely from misidentifcation with action and the best way to read the Mandalas section of Self-Knowledge.]

August 24, 2006

ॐ Dear . . . ,

Om Namo Bhagavate Sri Ramanaya

Namaste. Thank you for your card, the packets of cards, and the kind, generous offering to the SAT temple.

The offering is very helpful, and the steadiness and depth of your heart's love that has prompted it are very evident.

Even if there is the imagination of a "doer," your Being is still and unattached. In addition, one who knows imagination is only that and not real cannot long remain with such delusion. In the egoless Self, Being, lies your Bliss. "One mandala at a time…or all at once," makes no difference. Simply continue to plunge inward to know your Self as it is. In truth, he who is ignorant has no actual existence, and he who knows is, indeed, Knowledge itself, and is ever-existent.

May you ever abide absorbed in the fathomless Bliss of infinite Being, the goal and source of your heart's love, and thus be always at peace.

Ever yours in Truth,
Nome

———
•

[This is a message from a disciple of Robert Adams. In previous years, after the passing of his teacher, he had sought some advice from Nome on the telephone and in correspondence. Nome's response follows.]

October 11, 2006

Master Nome,

Maybe I can formulate my conundrum better.

It was my first awakening experience that there was no I, therefore, there was no thou, no other, therefore no world. All were concept only, but there is no one to have a concept.

There is no inner no outer, existence nor nonexistence, nor Void nor lack of Void, time or timeless. They were all concept, illusions only apparently real.

I saw that the self-illumined Void that I had meditated on for years again was just an object, an experience, a phenomenon and therefore not real. What I was was beyond the Void.

I had looked within to find myself, but there was no within or without, therefore it had been a mistake to look only within because consciousness is everywhere, within and without. I wondered why all the sages said to look within when there was no within.

Though I did not see this clearly, I also saw that consciousness itself was an illusion, a concept, yet not a concept that I held, but a concept nowhere attached.

Robert never told me, but he told others that I was getting close to enlightenment.

Yet, all of this knowledge occurred in the waking state, not the dream or deep sleep states.

My second awakening occurred a few weeks later. When waking from a dream, I saw that I was not touched by either dream or waking, therefore, I also was not touched by sleep. These were all added onto me and were false. The three states were false—phenomenal realms imposed on me, who was without attribute and unknowable. I knew I was only because I saw that that which was,

77

was not I, yet I observed all of existence, which I knew was unreal. Only I was real, and I didn't know that I directly, I was not an object to be known.

What I was, was not consciousness or lack of consciousness, nor the three states, nor the world or lack thereof. I was not touched by existence. Consciousness was about existence, and I was way beyond that.

At this point Robert said I was enlightened.

But all these years one thing bothered me. Ramana and Robert both always said all that there is, is consciousness, the One consciousness.

Everyone talked about the Self as being self-aware. I do not understand this viewpoint. I do not know myself, but I am myself and cannot be self-aware.

The self-illumined inner space, the self-luminous Void also was an illusion, yet understood by whom?

All the years since then I felt I was missing something. I did not see how Ramana could be right when he did not say that the ultimate was beyond consciousness.

Was it the knowledge that I was not consciousness nor the world an awareness beyond consciousness? If so, why did Ramana not say it? Robert told everyone that everything is consciousness and existence of the universe was unreal. But once he told me that even consciousness did not exist. Were both talking about world consciousness, observation and knowledge of phenomena and I was aware, whatever I was, of that?

Robert spent 17 years wandering in India to make sure he did not miss anything.

Where is the mistake here? It is obviously conceptual, but what is the mistake?

ॐ Dear . . . ,

Namaste. Thank you for your message.

You have expressed very well your spiritual experiences that, being of the nature of the nondual, are necessarily ineffable. Perhaps I can offer a few comments that may be helpful.

If by consciousness is meant perception, sensory or mental of any kind, it is unreal. Consciousness is devoid of the unreal. If the question is what are perceptions and thoughts, they are only Consciousness. Yet, Consciousness can never be modified to become such, for what is mutable is unreal, and the unreal does not exist. Existence cannot become nonexistent. It just is as it is always. So, if the question is what is Consciousness or Who am I?, the silent answer is the realization of eternal identity as That. The Real alone ever is and the unreal has never come to be is the self-evident Truth.

The known is only the knower. Who is the knower? Inquiring in this manner, Knowledge is self-revealed. That Knowledge is only unalloyed Consciousness, which is Being. For this, ignorance is impossible.

The same holds true for the self-luminous Void. Abandonment of the objectifying outlook is what is beneficial. "Within" signifies nonobjective Being. Thus, the advice of the sages. It should not be interpreted in terms of space, the body, or even the thoughts, modes, and states constituting the mind.

As you may recall, the Maharshi, in *Saddarshanam*, negates both the world and the awareness of it. All that is "this" and "I" is illusory. The supposed connection (experience, perception, conception, etc.) is equally illusory for there cannot be a real connection between the unreal and the unreal. Illusion is that which is not. The unreal has never come to be. There cannot be any connection between the Real and the unreal for the Real is and the unreal is not. For the Unborn there is no creation.

The best course is to know the Self. Such Knowledge is nonobjective. It is that in which Being is Knowing. Being–any kind. Therefore, there can be no concept of attainment or its opposite in the absence of any individual for whom these could be.

Upadesa (spiritual instruction) is given in accordance with the needs of the seeker. The essential teaching as revealed by Dakshinamurti and Sri Bhagavan is this silent Knowledge. Sri Ramana said, "Silence is that in which no 'I' arises."

Actual experience of true Knowledge is essential. Whatever terms are used for expression, it is important to actually know oneself. Whatever be the conception, it is to be negated, even if it is a spiritual conception. There is, though, no need to continue conceiving and negating. The original meaning of the wise sages of "Self," "Being," "Consciousness," "Void," "Brahman," "Siva," and such should be directly known. It is that which is self-known, self-luminous, undefined, beyond all states, ever the same, and alone existing.

In the Knowledge of "I," the assumed conundrum is easily dissolved. One should truly inquire, "Who am I?"

I hope that you find the above helpful. I trust that you receive such friendly advice as it is intended. Your determination to be thorough is wise. Do not stop until the Truth is always self-evident and without an alternative. As always, you have a warm, open invitation to visit here at the SAT temple. Please feel free to write again if you are so inclined.

Ever yours in Truth,
Nome

[A response to a seeker who resides at a distance from the SAT temple:]

January 4, 2007

ॐ Dear . . . ,

Namaste. Thank you for your letter, which arrived yesterday, that being the day prior to the Sri Ramana Jayanti celebrations, which are being observed this evening.

The Self is transcendent of the differentiation between the subject (I) and the object (this). To realize the Self, one needs to know the nature of the "I," for it is by the definitions of the "I" that the "this" is conceived. In the absence of an ego "I," nothing objective remains. Only the Being of the Self, infinite and eternal, remains. The Self is the Reality.

The discrimination between the Self and what is objective is helpful. Thoroughness in such should be present, so that what is conceived initially as the observer does not contain objective definitions, such as what is sensory or mental.

You are always of the nature of Consciousness, which is said to be the Witness in relation to all else. You can never become an object and can never part from Consciousness, which is identical with your Being. Such truth about you does not depend on your mental focus. When you focus upon this fact, it is obvious to you. When there is not this mental focus or thought about the Truth, you still remain as Consciousness. You are even the Witness of any contrary ideas. The progress you desire is brought about by the recognition of your identity. Knowledge of your identity is not a thought or mental mode, but it is something more interior, nonobjective, and very deep. Therefore, inquire "Who am I?" Who is it that says that you are the observer? Who is it that says that the spiritual experience comes? Who is it that says that it has gone? Who is it that says that he cannot progress past this point?

If you practice in the manner alluded to above, you will find no obstacle, but only the vast peace of Being-Consciousness-Bliss, your own true nature.

May you ever abide in the deep Knowledge of the Self and thus be ever happy and at peace.

Ever yours in Truth,
Nome

•

[A response to an elderly seeker who lives at a distance from the SAT temple:]

February 23, 2007

ॐ Dear . . . ,

Namaste. Thank you for your recent letter, with its verse, which arrived yesterday.

Yes, the teaching of Sri Bhagavan, Ribhu, and all the sages who have realized the Nondual Truth and thus abide as identical with it, is most eloquently revealed in absolute Silence. Indeed, this Silence is the deepest meaning of all the verses in *Ribhu Gita,* all the instructions in *Essence of Inquiry,* all the poetry of *Garland of Guru's Sayings,* the verses and explanations of Sri Sankara, and such.

Please know that you are always welcome here at the SAT temple, though, of course, as the bodiless Self, there is never any distance to differentiate.

May you ever abide in and as the Silent Truth, of the nature of Being-Consciousness-Bliss, and which is forever devoid of duality, so that you are always happy and at peace.

Ever yours in Truth,
Nome

[A response to a seeker:]

April 13, 2007

ॐ Dear . . . ,

Namaste. Thank you for your recent letter along with its enclosed poems.

Listening to the essential teachings, again and again, can be very beneficial to one's practice. Be certain to so inquire so that that which is expressed in the spiritual instruction becomes self-evident for you.

Ever yours in Truth,
Nome

[A message from a seeker who had recently moved from India to America, with Nome's response.]

September 17, 2007

Pranams to Master Master.

I have benefited much from Master's teachings and am happy to be reminded of Self and true nature.

Now, there is a major concern, which I would like to bring forth before Master.

[Name deleted]'s long-time friend [name deleted] has returned from Indian trip and through her, [name deleted] is drawn towards Kaleshwar (a youngster who follows Shirdi Sai Baba) and Kaleshwar teaches mysticism, sakti, healing powers, etc and advocates his disciples to go out to preach.

I have made it clear that Bhagavan's teachings are full and complete for us and that there is no need for us to go to any other Gurus. I have expressed that I am not interested in Kaleshwar, and we have Maharshi's direct path and grace aplenty, and we are full and complete.

I foresee some complications (conflict) if [name deleted] proceeds onward. However, I have pointed out to her that there is no need for us to have any other Gurus or go to any other path. As for me, I am with Maharshi, and Maharshi's teachings appeal much to me. There is nothing else to look for externally.

As far as my understanding goes, Bhagavan has certainly not advocated disciples to go out and preach.

What is bound to happen happens, and nothing is in our hands. Therefore the best course, as Maharshi says, is to remain silent.

I humbly place this issue in Master's hands and let things resolve on their own.

With prayers,
yours truly,

ॐ Dear . . . ,

Om Namo Bhagavate Sri Ramanaya
Namaste. Thank you for your message.

It is not necessary for me to offer any comments about what others may be teaching, saying, preaching, etc. In highest Truth, neither they nor their activities exist. Considered as if such were real, it could be assumed that someone somewhere benefits in some way from such.

The highest Truth is revealed by Sri Ramana Maharshi with supreme clarity. He is what He reveals. His teachings and Grace unfailing put to an end all of the imagined bondage.

For those interested in a variety of phenomena, there are any number of teachings and meditations, but for those whose hearts desire the certitude of complete Liberation from all of the samsara, who yearn for Realization of the Supreme State, the Self, the path shown by Sri Ramana is the way, and He is the Sadguru who brings such a seeker from the unreal to the Real, from darkness to Light, and from death to Immortality.

By remaining steady in your one-pointed faith in Sri Bhagavan and practicing as he instructs, you do the highest good. You can advise and set the example, but cannot command. As you have indicated, all this is in the hands of the Supreme, which is He. The Sadguru knows what is best and when and how to do it. To remain silent means to abide without giving rise to the ego-notion.

May the depth of your devotion so shine in your heart that the Knowledge of the Self shines as self-evident.

Ever yours in Sri Bhagavan,
Nome

[This is a letter from another spiritual aspirant.]

October 22, 2007

Aloha Nome,

I've been examining the ingrained assumptions of causing actions and having volition, saying something like, "I intend or I am the doer." I have a belief that I am the director of the actions, such as thoughts, acquiring perceptions, saying words, and doing deeds. On examination, being identified as an actor is an assumption by "I." Both actor and 'I' disappear in deep sleep and so are discontinuous and not eternal.

In times of clarity, I'm not any of those features, and in times of unexamined thinking and doing, I seem to again be intending as a body. As the Maharshi says, "Remember the Self always"...but as you've pointed out, thoughts can't hold the inquiry on-goingly. It's odd that I'm already the Self but struggle to remember that and then forget again. Would you comment on this? Many thanks,

[Nome's response:]

ॐ Dear . . . ,

Namaste and Aloha,

It is good that you are discerning the ego root of the false notion of being the performer of action. Continue to inquire and realize that your Being is the Consciousness that is ever the same and is never engaged in any action. The clarity is the result of inquiry, and the veiling is due to non-inquiry. As you have discerned, only that is you which is always you. What comes and goes cannot be your true nature.

85

To remember the Self is indicative of Knowledge. The Knowledge cannot be a thought, for no thought touches the Self ever. The Knowledge is of the very nature of Consciousness, itself.

Therefore, the unsteadiness of knowledge, now, is actually the coming and going of residual tendencies to misidentify as they are weakening. If you continue to inquire, the unreality of those misidentifications and the one to whom they pertain will become very clear. Ask yourself, "For whom is the forgetfulness or the remembrance?" "Who am I?"

Sri Bhagavan's Grace is ever there to illumine the one who so inquires.

Ever yours in Truth,
Nome

[This is a message from a seeker who had recently emigrated from India to California and who had attended a retreat at the SAT temple focused on Saddarsanam. Nome's response follows.]

November 19, 2007

Pranams to Master.

This retreat has done a lot of good for [name deleted] and me.

We will be attending satsangs and retreats in future.

I do have the following spiritual queries:

1. Consciousness is the known. During the quest, ought we to focus on the known or the knower, the seer?

2. When the knower knows the known, does the knower disappear?

3. When the query takes us to the Consciousness, is there a cessation of the query?

Over the years, I have almost given up all and have been taking for granted that I accept what comes by. I am just used to submit-

86

ting unto God, for God decides all and His Will prevails in all. I have not put my mind onto the Self-enquiry, but have resigned unto God. As I cannot take in much, I attempt to leave my mind open or vacant so as to be in a restful state.

I would like to get guidance from Master as regards the above, and am immensely blessed to have Master's guidance.

Seeking Master's blessings,
with prayers and pranams,
humbly,

ॐ Dear . . . ,

Om Namo Bhagavate Sri Ramanaya
Namaste. Thank you for your message.
In response to your questions:

1. An idea about consciousness is the known, as is any other idea. Consciousness, itself, is never known objectively, but is ever the nature of the knower. The known depends upon the knower, even to appear. The essence of the knower, which is Consciousness, does not depend on the known in order to exist. It is self-existent and entirely real.

2. When the knower inquires into the nature of the knower, the known (the objects, including thoughts) disappear and the individuality or form of the knower also disappears. Pure Consciousness, which cannot be divided into knower and known, alone remains.

3. The essence of the inquiry is Knowledge. When Consciousness is realized as it truly is, the inquiry is consumed in it and may be said to cease. Who inquires into what when all that exists is the one Self alone?

4. Surrendering utterly to God will also yield the same result, but such surrender must not stop with the detachment brought about by recognition of God's omnipotence, but must proceed still deeper so that the ego notion is abandoned entirely in the revelation that God alone exists.

I hope that the above is helpful for you. It is good that [name deleted] and you will be able to attend future retreats and satsangs, too.

May you ever abide absorbed in God, who is pure Consciousness, and realizing That as the one Self, be happy and at peace always.

Ever yours in Truth,
Nome

[Nome's response to a message asking if tendencies continue to manifest until one applies effort with Self-inquiry:]

January 6, 2008

ॐ Dear . . . ,

Om Namo Bhagavate Sri Ramanaya
Namaste. Thank you for your message.

In a sense, you are answering your own question. The vasanas, or tendencies, recur until you find and destroy their root. Destruction is by Knowledge, since a vasana is composed of ignorance. If a tendency recurs, it is an indication that thoroughness and more depth are needed. Trace the mode (e.g. anxiety, anger, fear, etc.) to the specific thoughts constituting the mode. Trace those thoughts to the misidentifications, and those to the ego notion. To "trace" implies realizing the falseness of that mode, thought, misidentification, etc. If you know such as false, you no longer mix up your identity, the reality, or your happiness with it. You cease to create it. If you are still subject to what is false, you do not yet really know that such is false, though you may be on the way to knowing that it is. The same applies to realizing what is true.

That you are aware of the vasanas arising is good. Perhaps, previously, you may have called such tendencies "life," or even thought that one could just "be in the now" with them, but now you are wiser, so they stand out to your discernment as being unsatisfactory. This leads to a deeper and more thorough inquiry that actually dissolves the delusion.

May your practice continue to deepen so that the natural peace of the ever-existent Self shines unobscured, the innate Bliss of the Self.

Ever yours in Truth,
Nome

[A seeker wrote describing certain personal fears and received this advice in response.]

January 7, 2008

ॐ Dear . . . ,

Namaste. Thank you for your recent letters, including that of December 29th.

It is essential to realize that you, being bodiless, are not the performer of any action. It is essential to realize that you, being Purnam (the Perfect Fullness), have an innate perfection to which nothing can add and from which nothing can detract. It is essential to realize that you, being Bliss, itself, the very source of happiness, have nothing to gain from acceptance by some other person and nothing to lose by rejection.

In this Knowledge, the root concepts that manifest as the fear that you described, cease. Then, the peace of the Self shines in its formless, impersonal nature.

May your inquiry be deep so that that which is revealed by the Maharshi is realized clearly within.

Ever yours in Truth,
Nome

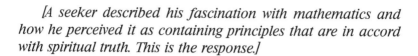

[A seeker described his fascination with mathematics and how he perceived it as containing principles that are in accord with spiritual truth. This is the response.]

January 26, 2008

ॐ Dear . . . ,

Namaste. Thank you for your note and the accompanying donation. [Name omitted] is in India now, so I have taken the liberty to respond to you.

Yes, whether it is in mathematics or in ever so many other experiences or forms of knowledge, one can perceive the reflection of Nonduality. When such "bubbles up in very early morning inquiry," as you have written, one has only to trace the reflection to its source through nonobjective inquiry to know oneself. Thus, one remains as the ineffable, the inconceivable, and the self-evident.

May you ever abide as That which, free of the mind, ever is just as it is, the Self without an alternative, the sole-existent Reality, which is the Nondual Truth.

Ever yours in Truth,
Nome

[This message was sent by an associate professor in Japan. Nome's response follows.]

June 20, 2008

Dear SAT/Nome;

I am very impressed with what I read about Nome and the experience of Self-Being he describes. I have one burning question which I would like to ask...not just to ask a question, but because I really want to know.

Nome says about the false "I"—

"This "I" does not come from the real Self, does not come from "anything else," and is not self-generated."

I find this a bit confusing....I can't get my head around it and have trouble experiencing this reality......if the false "I" doesn't come from the real Self, where does it come from? I thought everything comes from the one Consciousness, even the "false"—therefore everything is nondual.

I'm sorry to take your valuable time. If Nome is unable to answer this question, then any of his students will do.

ॐ Dear . . . ,

Om Namo Bhagavate Sri Ramanaya

Namaste. Thank you for your message.

Yes, you are correct. If you consider everything as existing, it has only one source, which is the indivisible Consciousness. Even ignorance, then, is of the nature of Knowledge, which is solely Consciousness.

Upon inquiry into the nature of "I," it is realized that there is no "false I," or ego-entity. For that which does not exist, there is no birth or beginning. The one Self alone exists, eternally.

The undifferentiated Being-Consciousness is forever unmodified. There does not exist anything to modify it; as the Self is homogeneous, there is no other within it, and it is infinite, so there is nothing beside it.

Nonduality is not only the perception of the unity of the supposed multiplicity but certitude of the Realization of That, the Self, as the only Existence, other than or second to which there is nothing whatsoever. To realize this, it is necessary to know oneself. This is the absence of both avarana (veiling) and vikshepa (the projection of multiplicity).

The Reality is never unreal and does not give rise to the unreal. The unreal is never real. It cannot give rise to the real. Therefore, the effects of the ego are as unreal as it is, and no individual "realizes" the Self. The Self is self-known and ever is as it is.

An unreal effect in the form of an ego cannot have a real cause. An unreal cause would simply have no true existence. A false existence is really no existence at all. Thus, maya, illusion, is that which is not.

Thus, the inquiry changes for you from "Where does it come from?" to "Does it arise or exist?" For Realization, the inquiry is clearly, "Who am I?"

The assumed individuality cannot come from anything more objective than it, which is its effect in the form of multiplicity. It cannot come from the Self, which is absolute and has no trace of ego. It cannot truly come from itself, for such would presume its pre-existence. To experientially verify this within yourself, inquire deeply to know the nature of your own Existence. Who is the one who asks and inquires? If his nature is known as it is, it is not an ego, or individual, but undivided Being-Consciousness-Bliss.

If you have further questions, please feel free to contact me again. Of course, you are always welcome to visit the SAT temple here, should you have the opportunity to be in California.

May your inquiry be deep, so that you ever abide as the one Self, which, being nondual, is ever without "a second," and thus be ever happy and at peace.

Ever yours in Truth,
Nome

[This next message came from India from a person who had attended satsangs at the SAT temple and was staying at Ramanasramam. The response follows.]

July 24, 2008

Dear Nome,

Om namo Bhagavate.

I'm writing to you to ask you something that I can't seem to get clear about. I'm staying at Ramanashramam once again for a month and engaging in the inquiry. I've been involved with spiritual life and practice for almost 30 years, the last few quite intensely and focused on the enquiry. I know I'm not the body, and even the mind appears as a passing shadow much of the time, but I am not abiding as the Self, nor do I know if any of the deep samadhis or states of calm abiding I experience are the direct experience of the Self. I don't think so since they come and go. If they are, then how to remain as That? I have been talking some with Subrahman but haven't gotten more than "continue the inquiry." Am I missing something? I am experiencing a kind of desperation and depression related to having been at this such a long time and feeling like there is something I don't or can't understand. If you can shed any light on how to move beyond this challenging mental state, I would be deeply grateful.

Namaste,

ॐ Dear . . . ,

Om Namo Bhagavate Sri Ramanaya

Namaste. Thank you for your message. To continue the inquiry is essential until the least trace of doubt, dualism, and the possibility of ignorance have vanished.

Inquiring, it is important to actually inquire. Be sure that the approach is nonobjective in nature.

The notion of existing as an individual being is the false assumption that is to be abandoned. It is abandoned by realizing its nonexistence. Self-inquiry reveals that. The destruction of this assumption is the revelation of the true Being of the Self.

Therefore, be concerned with the experiencer of those experiences, of the life, etc. and find his nature. The dissolution of the individual "I" is by Knowledge. The Self is not an object of experience, though it alone exists.

Self-Realization is not an event in time and does not occur to someone. The ego is unreal. The Realization is of the very nature of that which is realized, the Self, which is unborn and eternal. This is true Knowledge, which is non-dual.

No spiritual effort is ever in vain. All of it bears fruit. He who is devoted to the Supreme is never lost.

Dissatisfaction with one's spiritual practice is a call to examine what one is actually doing in the name of "practice," even in the name of "inquiry," and thus discern more clearly the path, the way to truly inquire. If one is really desperate to know the Truth, nothing will obstruct him. The obstructions are only the imaginings within one's own mind that he conjures up and to which he adheres. Depression is due to not knowing the source of happiness. He who knows that cannot be depressed.

Since you know of Sri Bhagavan, and are even blessed to be at His sacred Asramam, and since the teaching is accessible to you, blessings upon blessings, you have no excuse to suffer but ought to be delighted at heart, filled with the joy of such Grace. You may find reflection on this to be beneficial.

May your inquiry be deep and continuous so that you ever abide as the only true Self, of the nature of Being-Consciousness-Bliss, so that your peace and happiness are unending.

Ever yours in Truth,
Nome

[This message is from the same person. Nome's response follows.]

August 2, 2008

Dear Nome,

Om Namo Bhagavate Sri Ramanaya,
Thank you for your very helpful reply. Your instructions are like the wind clearing away the clouds on Arunachala! I was also able to get a copy of *Essence of Enquiry* from the bookstore to clarify and

inspire the inquiry. You were correct in pointing to the dissatisfaction as a sign that the inquiry needed clarification, and the email and book have given a new sense of understanding about the path and its fruition. I am daily reminded also about the blessing of this time at Ramanasramam.

Thank you. Namaste.

ॐ Dear . . . ,

Om Namo Bhagavate Sri Ramanaya

Namaste. Thank you for your message. I am glad to know that the clouds of the mind have cleared.

A brief note about *Essence of Enquiry:* This book was written here, as explained in the introductory pages, and it was published and printed in Bangalore by our very good friends at the Ramana Maharshi Centre for Learning. Indeed, the title was chosen by the revered A. R. Natarajan. Due to the difference in the printing process and lack of matching fonts, a few anomalies appear in the printed work, the primary of which are: part of the introduction was deleted, a diagram from the original text was not inserted, and the transliteration (not the translation) of the Sanskrit is not reliable, though still understandable. SAT provides a small booklet that gives the corrections for all of these when copies of the book are sold here. Perhaps, if you visit here in the future, a copy can be provided to you, should such be of interest to you. The book is certainly quite readable even as it is printed.

May your meditations be deep and blissful, filled with the luminous Knowledge born of inquiry.

Ever yours in Sri Bhagavan,
Nome

[These next two messages are from a person in the U.K. with Nome's responses to the same.]

August 4, 2008

Hi,

I have only recently began to study Advaita and would like to know, if there is no creation, does that mean that what we perceive doesn't exist ? That I as Self am dreaming this universe? If so, why?

To believe this could be a denial of what is, that the universe does actually exist with all its suffering.

Why not accept that's the way it is, warts and all? That could be freedom from trying to understand that it's all a dream and denying the fact that it's a misery to be alive on this planet for many.

I am quite happy most of the time even though I have illness and not much money, I'm not complaining.

I've been lucky in a lot of ways.

If Self is truth, consciousness, and bliss, why create this suffering universe for itself?

Kind regards,

ॐ Dear . . . ,

Om Namo Bhagavate Sri Ramanaya

Namaste. Thank you for your message.

Without first knowing oneself, how could the attempt to know what the universe is yield any result save a mirror-like reflection of the definitions imagined for the knower, or experiencer? Upon knowing truly the Self, which is of the nature of nondual Being-Consciousness-Bliss, homogeneous and illimitable, formless and undifferentiated, what else is there to know or to be known?

When the misidentification with the body is abandoned and when one no longer mistakes the senses to be the determinants of reality, the identity and "reality" return to their source. When the "I"-notion, or assumed individuality (ego), vanishes due to clear inquiry, the "this" aspect of one's experience also dissolves. That which remains is the Reality, which comprehends itself.

You may wish to question your idea that the nature of the universe is suffering. From what definition of yourself does this derive? You may also wish to examine the causes of suffering.

If you realize the unborn nature of the Self, the Truth of No-creation, as revealed by the wise, is self-evident. This is a matter of actual experience and not a conceptual doctrine to be accepted or rejected, just as your own existence is not an idea, doctrine, etc. First, know the Existence as it is, and Consciousness, Bliss, and the nature of all will become clear for you.

Yes, possessions and bodily attributes, such as illness, do not determine happiness. The source of happiness is the very same real Being just mentioned.

If you are ever in California, you would be warmly welcome to visit the SAT temple.

May you ever abide in the Knowledge of the Self, which is without beginning and without end, for which there is nothing other and in which there is nothing different, so that you are always happy and at peace.

Ever yours in Truth,
Nome

Dear Nome,

Namaste.

Thank you for your reply, I've had a shift in consciousness, again! So, awareness is, the understanding is here, but it has been on and off for several months, the mind takes over, and it hurts! How to stabilize the awareness?

But the suffering of all bodies, including this one, is still apparent whether awareness is here or not.

What about the others who identify with the mind and body? Can one be really free when all this mind/ body suffering is there in them ? And in sick or abused animals, too? How to come to terms with this?

Unfortunately I cannot travel to California, but it would be very nice to visit the Temple.

Kind regards,

ॐ Dear . . . ,

Om Namo Bhagavate Sri Ramanaya

Namaste. With the transcendence of the body by Self-Knowledge, you will find that the misidentification with the body was only delusion. The Self is innately free of the body, and true Knowledge reveals this. As it is for you, so it is for all.

Freedom is not dependent on bodily conditions and worldly circumstances. If it were, what kind of freedom would that be, for it would maintain the identical concept as that upon which the delusive bondage is based? The understanding that happiness is within and not dependent on external factors is the cornerstone of spiritual aspiration. Samsara is characterized by an absence of such understanding. Pains and pleasures of the body do not determine happiness and peace.

It is natural to care for others. The idea that they are "others," including differences of species, is also based upon misidentification with the body. Free of that, all are oneself, and love is the indivisibility of Being. Being, which is unborn and imperishable, bodiless and free of the mind, is the Self. This is the Self of all.

The great wisdom of the ancient scriptures and of great sages such as Sri Ramana Maharshi is certainly not in error or exaggerated. It is the ideas in your mind that are so and cause you to suffer, as expressed by you. Learn to examine your own mind and discern what is real and what is not, what is the Self and what is not.

You may find it helpful to retain the previous message to you and to reflect on its contents some more. As you are probably aware, SAT can also provide books and recordings that may be beneficial, and such can be found on the website www.SATRamana.org.

If you persist in Self-inquiry, using your best efforts to immerse yourself in true Knowledge, you will find the blissful absorption in the Self, as the Self.

Ever yours in Truth,
Nome

≡
•

[The following is a response to a person who wrote describing his understanding and meditation upon teachings of Sri Ramana Maharshi and Sri Nisargadatta Maharaj and who requested guidance in how to proceed to realize Brahman.]

August 5, 2008

ॐ Dear . . . ,

Om Namo Bhagavate Sri Ramanaya

Namaste. Thank you for your message. Communication by email is fine, for it enables you to frame your questions, as mentioned by you, and you do not risk missing me as you would by a telephone call. Your question is well-expressed. There are no foolish questions, except, perhaps, one that is not asked but still perplexes the mind.

"Merging with Brahman" is actually the realization of the ever-existent, sole-existent nature of Brahman. That alone is the Self. When there is misidentification as an individual, this same Self is viewed as a goal to be realized. Inquiring into the nature of this individual (jivatvam, ahamkara, I-am-ness, ego, etc.), its individuality, being unreal, vanishes, and only the Reality of the Self remains. This Self is Brahman, which, being absolute, is also named Parabrahman. Abidance in That, as That, is referred to as turiya, in relation to all states, or turiyatita to indicate that it is not a state but one's very Being.

To say that one's efforts extend only so far and then the Beyond draws one is indicative of the ego's powerlessness and the non-ego nature of Realization. The "other side" is found to be the only "side" by the relinquishment of the ego-notion. That is attained by inquiry. Who is to meditate

99

on "I-am-ness"? Who am I? If you thus inquire, you will be delighted at heart.

May you ever abide in the Truth of the Self and thus dwell in lasting happiness and peace.

Ever yours in Truth,
Nome

[The following letter was written in response to two letters from a seeker regarding her experiences and ideas. The points raised in those letters can be inferred from the response.]

August 7, 2008

ॐ Dear . . . ,

Om Namo Bhagavate Sri Ramanaya

Namaste. Thank you for your letters of July 29th and August 2nd.

Your first letter begins with a reference to illness or some "dramatic" experience. Freedom from misidentification of the Self with the body includes transcendence of the bodily attributes, activities, and sensory experiences. The Self, alone, is eternal.

Your first letter proceeds to relate the situation with your work. Detachment from the material things of this world is natural for those who realize happiness within.

You mention the need to support the temple. Yes, though a temple is consecrated to that which is non-material and formless, eternal and infinite, and provides a sanctified space in which to receive instruction, practice, and realize, it does require physical care and support. Those who wish to do so find the ways of accomplishing this.

Referring to your letter of August 2nd, honesty is natural and essential if one is to find Truth. Fear is a product of dualism, which is concomitant with the ego-notion.

The SAT temple exists for the joy of Self-Knowledge, for the purpose of the revelation of Sat, which is Being. You are equally loved whether you visit the temple or not.

Bhagavan Sri Ramana Maharshi is the Sadguru here. You may wish to re-examine what you have written in your letter about so-called "attachment to the guru" and "a clean break at every level." The first phrase is expressive of a lack of understanding of what a guru is, what a disciple is, and what the relation of them is and the purpose thereof. Perhaps, if you read some scriptural works on the subject, as well as what Sri Ramana has said about this, your understanding would be clarified thereby.

A "clean break" from ignorance is always beneficial. Freedom from the vagaries of the mind is joyful. Let delusion be dissolved and the ego destroyed by an earnest inquiry to know oneself. If that is accomplished first, then one can see if there is anything else to be done. Without first conclusively realizing the Self, in immortal Knowledge, to conceive of "breaking" from meditation, spiritual practices, holy texts, the guru, the tradition of sages and saints, temples, selfless activity, and all else that is true, good, and beautiful is only a nonsensical plunge into maya and samsara. In accordance with the honesty mentioned above, the application of nondualistic verbiage to such an idea is not necessary and does not make it any wiser.

The Truth is ever present. Those who dive within to find That realize That as the Self and remain ever as That. One who has realized That is That. Sri Bhagavan is always present. Those who adhere to Him are absorbed in Him and remain as Him.

The above is intended to be helpful. If you find it to be so, use it. If not, then not, and you may treat it as merely so much prattle.

May you ever abide in the Knowledge of the Self, the wondrous state of Grace, the happiness of which leaves nothing more to be desired and the peace and freedom of which are quite beyond the limited individuality but realized as one's true Self.

Ever yours in Truth,
Nome

[This is a letter from a seeker, with Nome's response.]

August 23, 2008

Namaste Nome,

Just wanting to write with several questions and comments
My enquiry is focusing on several vasanas:

1) fear of bodily death from misidentifying myself with the body.

2) I'm aiming at more powerful enquiring into certain times of mental activity where I'm locked into argument or conflict with someone in my immediate extended family. I realize more often now that I'm choosing to feed this emotional vasana by continuing to pour unexamined attention into it. Sometimes the argument is in my mind—totally imaginary. Again, I have to be feeding it (the vasana) attention and energy.

3) I'm enquiring into the area of self-concern. The vain attention to body and persona as if they are what's continuous and lasting while ignoring the truth of the fleeting nature of all these differences.

Meditation: I want more focus in Truth and stillness. I'm the one who knows the difference between a good meditation and not good.

Spiritual progress: what is its measure? Or is there a measure?

Regarding *Upadesa Saram,* I've been reflecting on the translation in *Collected Works* and somewhat on the version found in the book of Bhagavan's works in his own handwriting. Do you recommend any other translations? Is there a version with Muruganar's first 70 verses included?

The CD mailings of Satsang and Friday nights are pure gold and a blessing.

Aloha,

ॐ Dear . . . ,

Namaste and Aloha!

Inquiry that reveals the bodiless nature of the Self bestows the fearlessness of the innate, blissful immortality.

Addressing vasanas in the light of inner Knowledge is wise. Clarify your understanding of happiness and love. Detach your mind from objective things of the world. Cease to view yourself as a person, and, correspondingly, know the true nature of all beings. Learn to discard your ideas freely for that which is wiser. Be concerned with that which lasts forever. That which is fleeting is not the source of happiness, not who you are, and is unreal. When such is gone, it is the same as if it never had been, which is actually the case.

If the meditation is upon the nature of the meditator, fueled by the intense yearning for Self-Realization, it will bear wonderful fruit.

In Truth, there can be no measurement, for there is no distance to traverse between the Self and yourself. The eternal Being is subject neither to progress nor lack thereof. Nevertheless, it could be said that the increasing clarity and steadiness of Knowledge of what, in truth, you are is the measure, with its corresponding peace and freedom from illusion.

All the translations that I have seen of *Upadesa Saram* are good. In addition to those mentioned by you, there is the translation from the Sanskrit by A. R. Natarajan. Sadhu Om made one from the Tamil *Upadesa Undiyar.* Last year, I made a translation from the Sanskrit, which is quite literal, but it won't be published until next year at the earliest. Muruganar's 70 verses are, I believe, to be found in one of the published works of his verses, but, at the moment, I cannot recall which one.

I am glad to know that the recordings are so beneficial for you. Reading Ramana's teachings, Ribhu, Sankara, and books like *Self-Knowledge* is also very good to do. Most importantly: inquire.

103

May your meditations be deep, and, with the personal fear and desires cast off, may your heart be filled with the joy of the Self.

Ever yours in Truth,
Nome

[This is a letter from a seeker residing in India.]

August 26, 2008

Om Namo Bhagavate Sri Ramanaya

Dear Nome,

In *Who Am I?*, Bhagavan declares, "Giving one's self up to God means remaining constantly in the Self without giving room for the rise of any thoughts other than that of the Self," and "As thoughts arise, destroying them utterly without any residue in the place of their origin is non-attachment." When does one recognize the need to act in some way if all thoughts are being destroyed as they arise? The practical need at the moment relates to the recognition that there is a recurring thought to return to the U.S. How to tell if this is coming from desire or from an inner knowing that this is the guidance of God (the Self). The rational mind says it is more practical financially, in terms of ease, and access to Bhagavan's Asram and the Holy Hill, to remain here, but there is this movement that also feels like Bhagavan's guidance to return soon. How to know when such is the case if all thoughts are vigilantly being destroyed? I find this urge to book a ticket comes very strongly at some moments but recedes if it is inquired into. What to do? Any guidance you can offer regarding this inquiry/practical decision making would be appreciated.
Namaste,

ॐ Dear . . . ,

Om Namo Bhagavate Sri Ramanaya

Namaste. Thank you for your message.

Giving one's self up to God means relinquishment of all misidentification and the dissolution of the falsely assumed individuality, or ego. Remaining constantly in the Self signifies the non-recurrence of those misidentifications. It is Being, only as the Self (Being), which is abidance in the innate Knowledge of the Self. Only the Self knows the Self; there is no other to do so. Without giving room means that, in such Self-Knowledge, there is no scope for ignorance. Misidentification, from the ego "I" down to the "I am the body" concept, becomes impossible. "Other than the thought of the Self" conveys multiple meanings. In Knowledge of the Self, which is the Reality or God, no thought, no other thought, and no "other" exists. In spiritual practice, one's full focus should be on realizing the Self. Nothing else truly matters. Nothing else is actually real.

When, by inquiry, happiness, reality, and identity "return" to their true place, nonattachment is complete. The supreme nonattachment is the nonexistence of anything else than the one Self, which is of the nature of Being-Consciousness-Bliss. Infinite, there is nothing to which it can ever be attached. This is also destruction of thought in the Knowledge that there is no such existent thing as a thought. The space-like Consciousness alone is real. To fully comprehend what is being indicated in these two paragraphs, inquire just as the Maharshi has instructed: Who am I?

Merely to temporarily stop thinking about some topic can be accomplished by many methods of concentration and even distraction. The thoughts, or ones similar to them, eventually return. The inquiry is for the purpose of the inner revelation of the Self, the non-conceptual Knowledge of Brahman. In that alone are found complete freedom and lasting peace. Self-Knowledge transcends all mental modes, inclusive of those with thoughts, with few thoughts, and even without thoughts.

You may find it helpful to examine why the mind thinks the way it does. This will lead you to the perception of the definitions that are the basis of those thoughts. Then, inquire to discern your true nature free of such false definitions. This results in the destruction of vasanas.

You may also find it beneficial, when faced with pragmatic decisions, to consider what is most important for you, that is, the purpose of life. Thus, the actions will be based upon your best wisdom. This wisdom also leads to the freedom from misidentification with the body. Not being the body, you cannot be the performer of action.

Whether here or there, inquire to know yourself. Thus, the Perfect Fullness shines, and you are happy at heart.

Though I rarely, if ever, tell anyone what to do, I hope that you find what is stated above helpful.

May you ever abide in the Self, as the Self, free from every idea, absorbed in the infinite, eternal Grace of Bhagavan.

Ever yours in Truth,
Nome

[This next message is from a "new devotee" of Bhagavan writing from another state.]

September 12, 2008

Loving greetings from [name omitted].

I am a new devotee of Ramana Maharshi. I set aside an empty, freshly painted, medium size room for meditation and puja. I seek guidance and instruction in preparing the room properly, consecrated to Ramana Maharshi and his teachings.

Love, Light, Peace & Joy,

September 15, 2008

ॐ Dear . . . ,

Om Namo Bhagavate Sri Ramanaya

Namaste. Thank you for your message.

The most important aspects of creating a meditation room, a puja room, a temple, etc. are the heartfelt devotion with which it is done and the depth of meditation and devotion that you experience in such a sacred place.

Of course, most devotees of Sri Bhagavan have a photograph of him on an altar before which they meditate or do puja. The items in that place are cared for with love as an expression of their devotion and their dedication to the meditation of Self-inquiry. At the SAT temple and in many other places, there are also symbols of Siva.

Many find it helpful to have a book or books of his teachings within reach to guide their meditations. For puja purposes, some recite the 108 Names of Ramana (contained in the *Book of Daily Worship)* or read/recite songs and/or stotrams (hymns).

In short, there are no hard and fast rules concerning the external actions and objects. The intensity and depth of inquiry to realize Self-Knowledge are the essential ingredients. Continuity of practice is also important.

I hope that the above is helpful for you. If you visit California, you will be warmly welcome at the SAT Temple. May your inquiry be deep so that profound Self-Knowledge shines in you, that, by His Grace, you abide as the Self that you really are, of the nature of eternal Being-Consciousness-Bliss.

Ever yours in Truth,
Nome

[The same person responded with the following message.]

September 15, 2008

Namaste Nome.

Thank you for your kind response!

After so many years on the path, seeking Truth, I'm being drawn to a greater simplicity of heartfelt devotion, a sincere opening and surrender to His Grace.

I will take your advice and keep the room very simple with a picture of Sri Bhagavan, a candle, incense, flowers and the book which leads me now, *The Essential Teachings of Ramana Maharshi.* Amazing and penetrating visuals along with powerfully profound utterances! The picture of Ramana Maharshi on the front cover fills and awakens my entire being, when I gaze into His deeply penetrating, loving eyes!

I would like to receive your guidance for initiating the first steps for entering into deep, intense inquiry to realize Self-Knowledge.

My search for Truth over the past 28 years has lead me to this moment of awareness and understanding, that my work for the rest of this incarnation and beyond is to "Be," abide as the Self, innate Truth, Consciousness and Bliss.

Is it possible to come for a weekend to receive personal instruction and guidance from you? I look forward to the deepening of our connection for the awakening of true nature in service.

Yours sincerely, with love, appreciation, and gratitude.

Om Namo Bhagavate Sri Ramanaya

ॐ Dear . . . ,

Om Namo Bhagavate Sri Ramanaya

Namaste. The preparation of your room as described by you seems very appropriate. May it be filled with illuminative meditation and deep devotion.

You may find it helpful to also read such texts of the Maharshi as *Who am I?, Truth Revealed (Saddarshanam),* and *Talks with Sri Ramana Maharshi.* Reading books such as *Song of Ribhu, Self-Knowledge,* etc. may also be beneficial.

Yes, you would be warmly welcome to visit and ask any questions about Self-Knowledge and spiritual practice. As you can see from the calendar of events, when there is not a retreat, there are spiritual events every Friday and Sunday at the SAT temple. These are deep yet informal, and everyone is welcome, actually encouraged, to ask as many questions as he would like.

Self-inquiry starts and ends with your very Existence. Inquire to know this Existence as it is, free of any misidentification with the body, senses, mind, or ego-assumption. If you are aware of life and death and have ascertained with certainty the source of happiness, the necessary intensity will be there in you.

May the Grace of Sri Bhagavan, expressed in the intensity of inquiry and the steadiness of devotion, so absorb you that you abide in That, the Self, as That itself always.

Ever yours in Truth,
Nome

[A seeker wrote a message in which he described how, when he visited the SAT temple for satsang a year earlier, he did not like it and was angry. Later, he watched video excerpts of satsang freely available on the web and appreciated the experience. He asked about desire, fear, the ego, and grace and expressed his wondering if Nome was a "Self-realized jnani." This is the response sent to him.]

September 18, 2008

ॐ Dear . . . ,

Om Namo Bhagavate Sri Ramanaya

Namaste. Thank you for your message. It is good that you are attempting to practice Self-inquiry.

As is explained in *Bhagavad Gita* and elsewhere, krodha (anger) is rooted in kama (desire), which is rooted in avidya (ignorance). One who knows this destroys the tendencies constituting the personality and its repetitive suffering.

If the source of happiness in ascertained to be within you, dissolution of desire and fear is natural. The root of duality is the ego-notion. None of this is truly you.

Grace transcends the ideas of inner and outer, of one-self and another, and its infinity is endlessly experienced by those who remain free of the ego.

In the inquiry "For whom is thought?" the objectifying outlook is abandoned, and the thought subsides, and, as one inquires "Who am I?" clear Knowledge of one's true identity shines, and the very sense of existence previously falsely associated with the thought returns to its origin, the Self. Therefore, question the definitions you imagine for yourself.

The ego, being an illusion, is powerless. It cannot know anything. The potency of spiritual practice derives from the Self, which is of the nature of Consciousness.

The consideration of whether or not Nome is a jnani is irrelevant to your inquiry. Sri Bhagavan has said that the realized can take care of themselves, and you should take care of yourself.

If you find what is said here helpful, make good use of it. If it is not understandable by you, you may discard it as so much prattle or set it aside to be picked up at a later time by you.

May the tendency to consider the illusory person as if real be relinquished by you, and, diving within, may you deeply inquire to know the true Self, of the nature of non-dual Being-Consciousness-Bliss, and thereby abide in lasting peace and imperishable happiness.

Ever yours in Truth,
Nome

[This message is from the same gentleman who wrote earlier about establishing an altar.]

September 18, 2008

Thank you Nome, for your kindness and consideration!

Until the books arrive, would you kindly instruct me on how one inquires? What is the process of Self-inquiry, the steps I can take to enter into a deep and intense state of Self-Knowledge? Please share the first few steps in this process.

What is meant by intensity of inquiry? Would you explain intensity of inquiry? What is it? How does one make the inquiry intense?

Thanks again Nome, for your precious service.

Love, Light, Peace & Joy,

ॐ Dear . . . ,

Om Namo Bhagavate Sri Ramanaya

Namaste. Here is a brief response while the books are being shipped to you.

The initial instruction concerning Self-inquiry was alluded to in the final two paragraphs of my earlier response to you. That you exist there is no doubt. You must come to know this Existence as it is at the same depth that you now know that you exist. How do you know that you are? This knowledge does not depend upon sensory impressions, and you need not think that you are in order to know that you are. How do you know? Who, in truth, is this Being? Deeply wonder about this.

Always the Existence is, regardless of states of the body and the mind. It does not commence at the birth or cease at the death of the body. Thought never defines it. What is the real nature of this Existence? Ask yourself, "Who am I?"

What do you regard as yourself? Examine this. Inwardly trace the sense of "I," your sense of identity, to its source, and liberate it from the false association of the non-Self with the Self.

As for the steps of the practice, an Upanishad declares that the attempt to conceive of the path that the knowers of Truth have taken is like trying to trace out the footprints of the birds in the sky. The path is as formless as the end, itself, yet it does not lack precision. The end is the beginning, say the wise. The end, itself, appears as the means. There is no distance to traverse between the Self and you, for the Self is indivisible. Yet, Self-Knowledge is imperative. Therefore, Sankara states that it is he who strives who realizes. Detaching yourself from all else, intensely inquire to know yourself.

Consider for how long and in how many ways you have desired to be happy. Seeking it externally, it is not found, for it exists in fullness within you. Within means the Self. If you comprehend what has just been indicated, all the intensity of all the desires, including their inverted forms as fear, etc. remains focused on one thing, and that one thing is the Self. Thereby, one becomes nonattached to and not afflicted by anything of the world, attains single-minded focus in meditation, and practices inquiry that is like a lamp inspecting darkness. In addition, it is good to contemplate upon life and death, so as to use the diminishing remaining time most wisely. Self-Knowledge yields immortal Bliss.

I hope that you find the brief comments above helpful. After reading some of the teachings of Sri Bhagavan in the books that you ordered, what has just been stated here may make more sense or be seen in a deeper way. The best way to deepen spiritual practice is to actually practice the inquiry. Grace is always present. Turn your mind inward, and you will know it to be so.

May your inquiry be deep so that profound Self-Knowledge shines within you, so that, awake from the illusory dream composed of the conceptions of "I" and "this," you abide as the Self, the nondual Brahman.

Ever yours in Truth,
Nome

[This next message is from a seeker who previously wrote on September 18th. This time, he said that all that he knew is the "illusory person," he did not understand inquiry, and he desparately sought approval. Here is the response.]

112

September 19, 2008

ॐ Dear . . . ,

Om Namo Bhagavate Sri Ramanaya
Namaste. Thank you for your response message.

Turning within, you will find that you actually know more than you think. In how many ways do you seek for happiness, such as by the approval mentioned by you? It is an intuition of your natural state and an unknowing search for yourself.

As love is far more fulfilling than any amount of approval, and as true Knowledge is infinitely deeper than any kind of thinking, your true Self is far more expansive and substantial than the ego notion and its attendant tendencies that form the illusory personality.

Trust in Sri Bhagavan, follow his teaching, and, with his Grace, dive within. Thus you will be happy at heart.

May your earnest inquiry be deep so that your real nature of Being-Consciousness-Bliss is revealed within you.

Ever yours in Truth,
Nome

[This is another message from the gentleman who established an altar to Sri Ramana followed by the reply.]

September 23, 2008

Om Namo Bhagavate Sri Ramanaya

Dear Nome,

Namaste
In the past few months, the passion has shifted, not so much a passion, but a relaxing of my whole existence for the awakening of

my true nature. Here re-enters Ramana Maharshi into my life, with an entirely new and deeper understanding of what it means to Be.

I worked there for two years, but I never understood the teachings of Bhagavan. I was totally into the Yoga of Sri Aurobindo and surrendering to Divine Mother, but it would always point to the sublime teachings of Ramana Maharshi! [Name omitted] passed around 11 years ago of ovarian cancer, and, even during her difficult last years, she would talk to me about Ramana and how he endured great suffering and remained a great Light for all. It is amazing how Ramana Maharshi is becoming more and more a strong influence and presence in my life today!

I've been chanting Om Namo Bhagavate Sri Ramanaya, with good results. Is there a formal initiation or diksha given for mantra recitation?

Thank you Nome, for your patience and kind consideration.

Much Love, Light, Peace, Joy and Bliss of Being,

ॐ Dear . . . ,

Om Namo Bhagavate Sri Ramanaya

Namaste. In so many ways, you are called and reminded. The manifestations of Grace are numberless, and the Grace, itself, is infinite. You have only to earnestly practice what Sri Ramana has taught to abide in immortal Bliss.

Sri Bhagavan's diksha is mouna diksha, initiation of Silence, just as with Dakshinamurti in ancient times. Silence is that in which no "I" notion arises.

May your inquiry be profound, so that you realize that which transcends this universe, from which it is, for which it is, by which it is, in which it is, in which it is resolved, and which, indeed, it is. That is the Truth. That is Brahman. That is the Self. Tat tvam asi (That you are).

Ever yours in Truth,
Nome

[A seeker wrote about obstacles for him on the spiritual path, the character of which can be inferred from the response presented here.]

September 30, 2008

ॐ Dear . . . ,

Om Namo Bhagavate Sri Ramanaya

Namaste. If you determine within yourself the real source of happiness, the results will be very far-reaching. You will thus find deep, unwavering peace, nonattachment toward all objects and situations, and the bliss of abidance at the very source of wisdom and love.

If guilty about past actions, be sure that you abide in a state in which those actions cannot recur and the very definitions of the personality that were the cause of such errors have been destroyed.

It is axiomatic that you should act (with body, speech, and mind) toward others as you would wish them to do toward you. Just steadfastly observing this much yields significant depth and lightness of heart. With inquiry, you come to realize others as the Self.

With faith in Bhagavan and his teachings, earnestly practice the best that you are able. Grace is ever present, and its joyful fullness is found by those who, with hearts full of love, spiritually practice in this way.

Ever yours in Truth,
Nome

[This is a message from a devotee of Sri Ramana, who, after meeting Nome in 1996 in Bangalore, kept up some correspondence.]

Namasthe Sri Nome,

Om Namo Bhagavathe Sri Ramanaya.

Thank you for always graciously obliging and replying to my mails.

In the process of enquiry, can we directly turn the attention to the I feeling and try to hold onto the pure Self, thereby increasing the strength of the mind to hold onto itself?

Is the attention or holding onto the I itself enough for fructifying into deep enquiry and thereby diving within effortlessly?

Another query is that, while I am meditating in the normal way, sometimes, I am able to reach a higher plane in the head where the meditation is fruitful and more peaceful and fulfilling. There has been an experience in such a way. Is there any yogic interpretation on this?

Sometimes, if I do meditation, I tend to miss japa. Is that fine? Bhagavan, if I recollect, has said dhyana is better than japa. I don't prefer to do japa after dhyana.

I am not an advanced seeker, or maybe I should not judge at all. I am just trying to practice while living in the world.

It is only grace that liberates, but, to reach that perfection, we need to apply effort, since I am living in this world and am stained by its impurities.

Yours in Sri Bhagavan,

ॐ Dear . . . ,

Om Namo Bhagavate Sri Ramanaya

Thank you for your message.

Yes, you can certainly directly inquire to know the Self. When you attempt to "hold on to the pure Self," who is attempting to do so? Inquire into his nature. Are there two selves? It cannot be so. What is the significance of "I"?

There need not be any concern whether the diving within is attended with effort or seems effortless. With all of your effort, practice the inquiry to know yourself. That which is found to be the only Self, One without a second, is innate and natural, and abidance as that indivisible, real Being is referred to as effortless.

Regardless of whatever yogic experiences may occur in the course of sadhana, keep your focus on Self-Knowledge.

116

For whom are these experiences? Thus, inquire.

Dhyana is subtler than japa. If, engaged in that which is more interior and subtler, you find that that which is less so drops off, it is alright. May your meditation be upon the nature of the meditator.

Practice earnestly, deeply, and continuously. There is no point in measurement. How could you measure the distance between you and your Self? Such distance is merely imagined. Abandon misidentifications and know the Self as the Self truly is. It is eternal.

If you relinquish the misidentification with the body, the idea of "living in the world" will vanish, even though the body will remain active. The bondage and suffering that are the consequences of that delusive idea disappear with it.

Grace is infinite and ever present. Those who apply their best spiritual efforts are absorbed in it. It is he who strives who, by Grace, is liberated from all of the imagined bondage and knows the real Self.

May your inquiry be deep so that your happiness and peace are full and remain always.

Ever yours in Sri Bhagavan,
Nome

[This is a lengthy message from another seeker who had not written or attended satsang previously. Nome's response follows.]

September 30, 2008

Dear Sir,

I have a few queries on self enquiry. I have read your phenomenal commentary *Essence of Enquiry* on *Vichara Sangraham* and thank you for clarifying many thoughts. This email is long, I'm sorry.

1. When I practice vichara as a meditational enquiry, focusing on the I-ness, this is definitely a deliberate thought, until, some time later, it sometimes becomes a feeling of being present in that partic-

117

ular moment and whatever it holds. Is it necessary to hold on to that 'impure' thought of I as the scent to follow? In your book, 'without misidentifying the I with the body, without an I being the centre of one's speech or mind, one must enquire into this sense of I' and another from Bhagvan 'Not to abide in what is not the Self': should one not hold on to that impure sense of I and rather not fix on anything but just this light feeling of not being attentive to any perception or thought? But that is tough to hold. There is no anchor, and it slips away sooner rather than later. Or do we constantly enquire and try to get behind the impure I?

2. As I make the effort to dive within (and the breath becomes shallow), as active thoughts drop, and as I focus on the I -thought, I find myself in the effort to make that I thought more subtle as there are constantly some perceptions popping up as objects. I was wondering if that effort was too intense and hindering me. So, on the question of effort, although I read that effort has to happen initially and later it is automatically effortless, what is the nature of this effort? Is it to be intense or seemingly effortless? I don't like this unsettling feeling of too much effort. Yet it is required? Or is effort also just a thought and should one just be quiet? If one asks the question and sits quiet, yet, isn't the mind leading one on in a certain direction? That is also a thought? Eventually, what is one to do? Be quiet and be led or make some effort, or is this question irrelevant and what is to happen will happen? Does the statement, although it was to a question on work 'your effort is the bondage,' have any bearing on the effort during vichara?

3. When I try to remember my I-thought during activities such as walking, cooking, even reading and listening, the I-sense doesn't go deep. Sometimes, I feel my body as I listen to somebody. Sometimes, I make a deliberate effort to feel the I-ness as a kind of formless power (not really a thought or a picture, more like consciousness powering this thing), but again the question arises, should I make an effort to visualize the I-sense as formless or should I just go with whatever I feel at that moment? On practicing meditational enquiry, formally sitting with eyes closed: I can't do this for more than two sessions, half an hour each. Should I force myself to increase it or again, take it as it comes? Effort? Or why worry? What is to happen will happen.

4. Since happenings happen whether we wish them or not, does it apply to all these above thoughts during vichara? The role of

volition in vichara? Can't help wondering does one have to be detached in one's efforts?

5. During some goof ups when I feel angry, should I work on both levels — vichara and practical understanding of the situation - to avoid the anger again (not that it is in my hands!) or does the practical understanding actually hamper, since it is through the mind? Should I just do vichara after such situations without dwelling practically (constructively, not being self-righteous) on the situation?

6. Asking the question 'Who am I?' as opposed to self attention as one reads in some books, is there a difference?

I might be rambling, but some light might help.

Thank you for your patience.

Regards,

ॐ Dear . . . ,

Om Namo Bhagavate Sri Ramanaya

Namaste. Thank you for your message. In answer to your questions and comments:

The Self, which is indivisible Being, is devoid of individuality, or the ego. It is not a thought, and no thought is required to know it, just as the present knowledge of your own existence is not thought-dependent. It is to be realized by nonobjective Knowledge. Inquire to know, at the same depth that you know that you exist, the Self as it truly is, free of any misidentification. The Realization of the Self cannot be approached as if it were a topic of study, but is revealed by an inquiry into yourself. So, when thinking of the "impure I," inquire for whom such appears. If the existence is assumed to be individualized, such is due to imagination, which is the delusive superimposition of the "I" notion upon the real Being of the Self. If an inquiry is made into the individualized existence, only the undivided Existence will be found to exist, completely devoid of that "I" notion or assumption of individuality.

The present moment in the waking state is as unreal as the present moment in a dream. Make your vision nonobjective if you wish to realize the Self.

That which comes also goes and cannot be the Reality. Who knows of the appearance and disappearance of what is objective, inclusive of any state of mind? Such is the inquiry.

Self-inquiry is inherently thought-transcendent. That which is thought-transcendent can alone be continuous. Self-inquiry is continuous. It is of the nature of Knowledge. The end, itself, appears as the means. If the inquiry is off the mental level, continuity is no longer in question.

Effort is the natural desire for happiness, which is an intuition of the natural state, turned inward to its source. Therefore, one will apply effort, whether spiritually or in a worldly way, until there is complete happiness. Sri Bhagavan said, "Where Atma-vicara ends, loka (world) vicara begins." No one has ever been hurt by applying effort in practice, but there are many who should have applied themselves more. Realization is said to be effortless, because the Self is only one and is the sole-existent Reality. So, there can be no question of anyone applying effort to it, for there is no such one. In addition, sahaja means innate and natural. By interpretation, it has come to include "effortlessness,'" as well. The innate is not a state or condition of the mind, nor is it an event in time. To conceive of a requirement of absence of effort in practice and the presence of effort in Realization to make it steady, etc. is absurdly inverted and a result of non-inquiry. It is better to pursue the path shown by Sri Ramana. As for practice, one should practice with the intensity as if one's happiness and immortality depend on it, for they do, as vividly demonstrated in the story of the Maharshi's Realization or "death experience," as it is sometimes called. Therefore, in *Advaita-Anubhuti*, Sankara declares that it is the one who strives who realizes. That one cannot be the ego, for it is unreal and does not realize anything. So, come to a profound comprehension of inquiry, effort and practice, and true Knowledge.

In the reference to "your effort" concerning action, the emphasis is on the concept of being the performer of action, which is based on the ignorance that is constituted of misidentification with the body. The inquiry that reveals freedom from the misidentification cannot possibly be an obstruction, as the Self cannot oppose itself, and there are not two selves.

Regardless of the activities of the body, you exist. What is this you? There is no need to visualize it. Even if such is done, for whom is that?

When, following the Maharshi's instructions, you truly inquire, "For whom?" the sense of reality and identity return to their true place. Thus, the "this" aspect of your experience, from thought down to the idea of an existent world, is absorbed in "I" and is no longer imagined to exist. Then, inquire, "Who am I?" Individuality, being unreal, vanishes. Thereby, the Self knows itself by itself. Brahman alone knows Brahman.

You may find it more beneficial to trace your thoughts to the definitions that spawn them, and then inquire to determine the falsity of those definitions. "Volition" is merely another idea. The Self is free of both sankalpa (volition, fixed concept) and vikalpa (indecisiveness, doubt, differentiation, imagination).

When angry, who has stolen your happiness? To be angry or not is certainly up to you. The spiritually-minded person is one who no longer wrongly associates her happiness or lack of it with external situations. Avidya (ignorance) brings kama (desire), which results in krodha (anger) that results in more avidya, as is taught in the *Gita* and elsewhere. The bondage of ignorance is one's own imagining. The Liberation from all the imagined bondage is to be found within you, in Self-Knowledge.

As for the meaning of "self attention" that you have found in some books, you would need to ask the authors of those books what they mean by that phrase. It should be evident that Self-inquiry is not an activity of the mind, but a deeper Knowledge of oneself. Self-Knowledge is beyond the three states and the modes of mind that appear within those three states. The Realization of the Self must necessarily be of an identical nature as the Self, itself. Thus is nonduality. The Self is eternal. Is mental attention eternal? The Self is nonobjective. Is attention without an object? Whose attention is it? Who am I? Just so is the inquiry.

I hope that the above is helpful for you. If some part or another of it is not understandable to you, inquire as Sri Bhagavan instructs, and clarity will dawn. His Grace is always present. If you find this helpful and have more questions, please feel free to write again.

May your inquiry be profound so that you ever abide in the Knowledge of the Self, of the nature of Being-Consciousness-Bliss, and thus always dwell in happiness and peace.

Ever yours in Sri Bhagavan,
Nome

[From the same seeker, followed by the response.]

October 1, 2008

Namaste Sir,

Thank you very much for taking the time to reply so clearly. I have understood what you are saying, I think. One must relentlessly inquire at any kind of perception of duality. So, if I remember to inquire, say, when I am feeling tired, the genuine inquiry is important. If I feel body consciousness on inquiring, then I must inquire 'whose is this body'. The answer is not in any imagination of the mind. If I feel certain currents, then again I inquire. I trust the question, genuinely put and intensely asked, and just be silent. The effort is in asking genuinely, knowing what the Self is not and letting the mind be formless, if possible. If not possible, inquire again. I have to learn to trust the silence. Let me know if my understanding is correct. I know I have to rid myself of concepts. Maybe I have to stop reading; sometimes that prevents practice.

I have just a few more questions.

Sometimes I feel a kind of pulsation in the region of the heart. Then I inquire, 'who is feeling this?' But sometimes, I just hold onto the pulsation, since it eliminates thought. I guess I should relentlessly inquire rather than just holding onto it?

Sometimes, if a peace descends, there is still a duality. Does one continue to inquire and not be with that peace since duality is still there? In vichara, isn't there any place for peace until all duality is removed? Does the inquiry have to be relentless? In my experience, there is a kind of peace even with duality around in some form. Does it mean I have to keep inquiring, breaking the peace? Or, does the relentless inquiry lead to even more peace?

I take it that elimination of thoughts is not enough. It is the inquiry which is important? Or, have I got this wrong? Being still, does it automatically bring about a consciousness of the I? What exactly does 'being still' mean?

Om Namo Bhagavate Sri Ramanaya
Thank you.

October 1, 2008

ॐ Dear . . . ,

Om Namo Bhagavate Sri Ramanaya
Namaste. Thank you for your message.

The Upanishad declares, "Where there is a second, there is fear." "A second" is any dualism, even the notion of "I" differentiated from the Self, which is the basis for the illusory, objective "this." Conversely, where there is no second, there is no fear. That is, inquire so to realize conclusively the unreality of duality, so that neither the concept of "I" nor any other concept rises ever again. The rise of such is also not real. The Reality is ever as it is.

Be they sensory perceptions or subtle experiences, they are for you. Without concerning oneself with the appearance or the disappearance of anything, gross or subtle, one should constantly inquire to know oneself.

If the objective illusion of the mind is abandoned as the mind turns inward, the mind loses its form and remains only as the Self, of the nature of unalloyed Consciousness.

Sri Bhagavan says (in *Who am I?*) that Silence is that in

123

which no "I" arises. That is the perpetual Reality of the Self. It is undifferentiated. Thus, the Dakshinamurti Dhyanam begins with mauna vyakhya prakatita parabrahma tattvam (Revealing the Truth of the Supreme Brahman by "silent speech," or by "eloquent silence.")

Freedom from concepts results from inquiry. The books do not cause concepts or ignorance. Ignorance is conjured up in one's own mind. Assuming you are considering the books that preserve the teachings of Sri Bhagavan, Adi Sankara, and other sages and the teachings preserved since the time of the Vedas, it would be silly to suppose that these holy books were written and so carefully preserved to give more concepts to anyone. Their intended purpose must be otherwise. You may find it better and wiser to put aside the concepts of the mind and, perhaps, the way in which you may approach such spiritual texts, rather than merely take an action of putting aside the books.

When the mind is concentrated on one thought, and, since all is in the mind, sensations are also a kind of thought, other thoughts temporarily subside. Yet, Self-Knowledge does not dawn thereby. If you inquire as indicated in the previous response to you, you will know yourself. That which is thus known you are. In that, you find that thought has no existence. Being-Consciousness-Bliss is homogeneous and unborn. For the unborn, there has been no creation, not even of thought.

True peace and actual inquiry are of the same nature. A state of tamas (inertia) will be destroyed by inquiry, but the peace of the Self will be revealed only more deeply. If one leaves behind the idea of inquiry as some mental activity and no longer confuses modes of mind with Reality, the supreme Peace shines as the very Existence of the Self. That Knowledge is revealed by nonobjective inquiry. It is self-revealed.

Does thought actually exist that you ponder the retention of it or the elimination of it? Do thoughts declare their own existence, or do you assume that they exist? If the latter, who are you? The view is always according to the definition of the viewer. Know yourself. Any mental state, with thoughts or without thoughts, is not eternal and is not real. Sri Bhagavan says, "What is not eternal is not worth seeking." The Self is eternal. Know yourself.

The Maharshi has defined stillness as "the destruction of all name and form." It transcends that which is perceptible and conceivable. To remain free of misidentification, inclusive of the notion of "I," and free of any imagination of an existent thing, or "this," unwavering in Self-Knowledge and steadily abiding as the Self alone is "stillness." The Self is ever unmoving. One who truly knows the Self is the Self she knows.

Again, I hope that what has been mentioned here in response to your questions is helpful. If you decide that reading is not necessarily detrimental but can be helpful for you, as hopefully these messages are, you may wish to look at the SAT temple website www.satramana.org to see if there are books and such that contain spiritual instruction that may be beneficial for you.

May you ever abide in the Silence of the Self, that before which all words and thoughts turn back unable to grasp, the timeless Truth, so that you are at peace and happy always.

Ever yours in Truth,
Nome

[This is a response to a message. The questions asked can be inferred from the answers.]

October 21, 2008

ॐ Dear . . . ,

Om Namo Bhagavate Sri Ramanaya

Namaste. Thank you for your message.

Yes, the more interior or subtler the experience, the more joyful it is. If you continue to inquire and to surrender to Bhagavan, you will find that your very Being is Bliss.

There can be no accurate measurement of distance between oneself and Realization, for the very nature of the Self is Realization. There is no chasm between the Self and yourself. Inquiry dissolves the illusory "I" notion, and the sole-existent Self remains.

If your intention to examine the vasanas to eliminate them is strong, what until then seemed not so obvious becomes blatantly clear.

Your own experience is showing you that it is wise to continue steeping yourself in the meditations on the source and nature of happiness. Bliss calls you inward to be absorbed.

Perhaps you already possess them, but you may find reading (slowly and meditatively) *Who am I?*, *Saddarsanam (Truth Revealed, Forty Verses on Reality)*, *Song of Ribhu,* and *Self-Knowledge* helpful for your under-standing and spiritual practice.

May your meditations continue to deepen so that you ever abide in the profound peace of the Self.

Ever yours in Truth,
Nome

[From a seeker in India. Nome's response follows.]

October 25, 2008

Dear Sri Nome,

Om Namo Bhagavathe Sri Ramanaya !

Namasthe.

In practicing the enquiry, the questioning of who am I cuts off the mind from the thought mode and gets back to the attention to the Self or the I feeling. By saying inquire deeply or continuously, do you mean to say questioning to the point of returning to the source? I can sense it is inquiring, and, if I examine the I which experiences all these, the ego disappears, and the attention is brought to the I feeling. By holding onto the I feeling (the substratum) thus holding onto the pure Self. Is this the way to practice?

And is the way of holding on directly to the pure Self enough to lead me on? For me who has read about Bhagavan, whenever there is an awareness of an experiencer, the questioning "Who is that?" automatically arises, and the attention is brought back. But still there is an experiencer.

Please let me know if the latter is enough to lead me onto the direct path.

With Yours in Sri Ramana,

ॐ Dear . . . ,

Om Namo Bhagavate Sri Ramanaya

Namaste. Thank you for your message.

What you have stated about the inquiry is correct. You then say that there is still an experiencer. Who is he? All objective experience depends on him, appearing and disappearing with his rise and subsidence. Therefore, his nature can be neither the body nor the thoughts constituting the mind. Can there be two selves, one that is the real Self, nondual and undifferentiated, and another who is an experiencer? Your existence is singular and undivided. Therefore, inquire into the very nature of this "I," even if it seems as if an individual experiencer. The individuality, being false, will vanish, and the Self alone will remain.

With earnestness in inquiry, you will be illumined by Bhagavan's Grace and find that the inquiry is of the nature of Knowledge. That is the depth, and that is continuous.

Ever yours in Sri Bhagavan,
Nome

———
•

*[The questions of the seeker to whom these next two respons-
es were sent can be surmised from the answers.]*

November 3, 2008

ॐ Dear . . . ,

Om Namo Bhagavate Sri Ramanaya

Namaste. Thank you for your message. Silence is that in
which there is no ego or its attendant misidentifications. A
repressed state is not the goal; a state rife with uncontrolled
mental tendencies is not desirable or helpful either.

Meditation on the source of happiness will accomplish
much toward the elimination of tendencies and your fears.
Freedom from the fear of death, though, also requires transcendence of the body and all else that is transient. It
requires abidance as the Self, as taught by Sri Ramana,
Katha Upanishad, Ribhu Gita, etc.

Your sincere efforts will bear fruit. Progress is not always
easily measured by the seeker in a short span of time, but
increasing happiness and peace and freedom from ignorance are indications that one is on the right path. The Self
is not far away. It is your true nature, closer to you than the
mind's thoughts. Practice in a manner that yields ego-dissolution.

I am glad that you are benefiting from the excerpts on
the web site. When the time is right for you, you may wish
to have the experience of reading the entirety of the books
mentioned in a previous email. Indeed, those who are
deeply immersed in Self-Knowledge find that meditatively
reading such remains blissful and never turns dry.

May you abide in the Knowledge of the Self, in which there is no return to the illusions of the mind.

Ever yours in Truth,
Nome

November 5, 2008

ॐ Dear . . . ,

Om Namo Bhagavate Sri Ramanaya

Namaste. Actions of the body represent no disruption to the Self, which is the bliss. Only if one misidentifies with the body and thinks that one is the performer of action and confuses happiness with outer objects and circumstances is the bliss veiled. Inquire deeply and continuously so that there is no such veil.

Ever yours in Truth,
Nome

———
•

[Here is the reply to a seeker who was struggling and wrote asking if, during the time of his practice, Nome found the inquiry to be easy or a struggle and did he encounter huge obstacles.]

November 8, 2008

ॐ Dear . . . ,

Om Namo Bhagavate Sri Ramanaya

Namaste. When effort is applied both to adherence to delusion and to the attempt to be free, there is struggle. It is better to struggle, though, than to be indolent, for effort is based upon the right resolution. Better still is it to apply wholehearted effort and abandon the adherence to delu-

129

sion. Adi Sankara stated that it is the one who strives who is liberated and that Knowledge alone is the cause of Liberation.

One applies effort either toward worldly delusion or to keen inquiry and spiritual practice. The Self, itself, is effortless because it is One without a second. The Maharshi referred to Self-Realization as "sahaja," which means innate or natural. By implication, one can say effortless. If you practice with intensity, the ego notion dissolves, and the innate Self remains.

These points and others are explained in *Self-Knowledge* and in *Timeless Presence,* the latter being written in an autobiographical and devotional style at the request of the President of Sri Ramanasramam for the centennial in 1996 commemorating the arrival of Sri Ramana at Arunachala in 1896.

There is no obstacle so large or longstanding that you cannot dissolve it, and there is no concept so small that it should be left unexamined as a false definition.

May you be happy and at peace in the Knowledge of the Self.

Ever yours in Truth,
Nome

[In response to questions about desires and fears:]

November 18, 2008

ॐ Dear . . . ,

Om Namo Bhagavate Sri Ramanaya

Namaste. Deeply answering one simple question will resolve all that is currently perplexing and depressing you. You have read the question previously. Not knowing the answer, living beings wander in delusion with the pursuit of unfulfilled desires and chased by their fears. When alone, they dream of others, and when with others, they still feel lonely. Even hearing the Truth, they are unable to adhere to it, their minds frantic with their own imaginative thinking that seems as if so real. The suffering is so needless. Oblivious to the blessings beyond measure, their minds stagnate in despair and hopeless moods.

The single question is: What is the source of happiness? Only if that is answered deep within you will you be beyond sorrow. Only if this is answered does one's life become profoundly and enduringly spiritual. Only if this is answered does the steady, ardent motivation for spiritual practice and for Realization shine in one's heart. Knowing the source of happiness within, the delusive thinking unravels and dissipates, attachments fade, and one sees how false the cravings and fears of her own mind were, and peace prevails.

In a sense, everyone pursues happiness in an endless variety of ways, in objects, in circumstances, in relating to others, etc. Not knowing the answer, the goal seems to be endlessly receding and the pursuit interminable. This is said to occur life after life. If only they examined their experience, heeding the advice of the wise, and plunged within and thus knew. Is it not time that you knew? You must come to this sooner or later. No one can do this for you, but if you turn within, valuing it more than all else, a thousand hands of Grace support you.

Ever yours in Truth,
Nome

[A response sent to a seeker from Bangalore, in December 2008.]

ॐ Dear . . . ,

Om Namo Bhagavate Sri Ramanaya

Namaste. Thank you for your message and greetings.

What you have stated about turning the mind inward, Self-inquiry, and Grace is clear. Yes, intensely seeking within for your true Self, Grace is abundantly evident. The Grace, itself, does not depend on punya, merit, for it is of a transcendent nature, beyond cause and effect. Nevertheless, spiritual efforts enable one to experience knowingly that Grace. I am unsure as to what you are referring by "Praptha;" if "prapta" is meant, Grace is beyond attainment, and if prarabdha is meant, Grace transcends karma, which is jada, inert, as explained in *Upadesa Sarah (Saram)*, *Talks*, etc.

Though just reading books is not a substitute for inquiry and devotion, the reading of sacred passages and the teachings of the sages can be useful for one engaged in the practice of inquiry and devotion. Always, depth is far more important than quantity.

If you intensely, deeply inquire into the apparently individualized existence of the experiencer, the individuality, being unreal, will vanish, and only the real Existence, the Self, will remain.

May your inquiry be deep and continuous so that, by Bhagavan's Grace, steady abidance as the Self is yours, the perfect fullness.

Ever yours in Sri Bhagavan,
Nome

[In response to another seeker with questions about desires and fears:]

December 1, 2008

ॐ Dear . . . ,

Om Namo Bhagavate Sri Ramanaya

Namaste. Thank you for your messages.

The fears and desires are constituted of thoughts and are only as powerful as you imagine them to be. By consistent self-examination of those thoughts to determine the definitions from which they proceed and deep inquiry to understand the falseness of those definitions, you can dissolve them and be free.

Regular reading of Ribhu and Sri Ramana is good for spiritual practice.

Forbearance is born of the ardent desire for Liberation and detachment from the things of the world. Such nonattachment naturally shines for those who know the true source of happiness within. Likewise is the desire for Liberation. More about this can be found in the booklet *The Four Requisites for Realization and Self-inquiry.*

May you continue to dive within to realize the egoless Self, so that you remain ever happy and at peace.

Ever yours in Truth,
Nome

⚊
⚊
●

[A reply to a seeker who was unhappy about some bodily affliction:]

December 1, 2008

ॐ Dear . . . ,

Om Namo Bhagavate Sri Ramanaya

Namaste. If you keep contemplating the source of happiness, examining your own experience, the reason it is proclaimed to be within will become clear for you. You may wish to read and re-read the portions of the Maharshi's *Who am I?* that deal with this. Reading the mandala that deals with bliss and reading the first essay ("Self-revealed") in *Self-Knowledge*, if you have a copy of it, slowly, point by point, may be found to be beneficial.

Deep spirituality transcends the body and the limitations of the body. The disease of the body has no relation to it. The true Self is untouched by the difficulties of the body, and Self-Knowledge is not dependent on the body being in some sort of condition. "Within'" does not mean inside the body, but rather more subjective than the body. There have been many who have had bodily and worldly conditions far worse than yours who have succeeded in diving within to realize the Self. One should be inspired by the example of those who went before and, undaunted and persevering, seek to know the Self, the treasure of happiness.

Ever yours in Truth,
Nome

[This is the response to a question concerning if there were many female sages in the history of "Advaita."]

December 4, 2008

ॐ Dear . . . ,

Om Namo Bhagavate Sri Ramanaya

Namaste. There are two suppositions in your question that would need to be examined prior to arriving at an answer.

First, a jnani, or sage, has no false notion of being a body. Gender refers to the body. It is false to define the bodiless by bodily attributes. Sages are neither male nor female, for they are the Self, which is neither male nor female.

Second, the history is only as real as the historian. Moreover, what is referred to as history is just the very small bit that one believes of only the tiny bit that one has read or heard of the small amount that survives of the miniscule part that has been published in some form. Such cannot possibly be an accurate view of what has occurred.

If this much is understood, the question becomes moot. Even still, many wise holy women are mentioned dating even as far back as the Upanishads. Who can say how many there have been?

Ever yours in Truth,
Nome

≡
•

[In reply to a message that, among other things, asked about underestanding the atrocious behavior of some people in the world.]

December 4, 2008

ॐ Dear . . . ,

Om Namo Bhagavate Sri Ramanaya

Namaste. Thank you for both of your recent messages.

It is good that you are delving into the four requisites (sadhana) for Realization and the application of them in your own spiritual practice. It is also beneficial to deepen your practice by examining the previous views of spiritual practice, Realization, and yourself in order to discard limitations, while retaining that which is fruitful.

When in ignorance, beings use the instruments of action (body, speech, and mind) in foolish and karma-producing ways, because of their delusion. Due to that delusion, they do not even perceive how deluded their views and activities are. The very basis, that of doing unto others as one would have others do unto oneself, is not grasped by them. Such dwell in their own suffering, oblivious of the nature of the true Self and even the purpose of life. Deserving of compassion, even the compassion they do not show toward others, they are like characters in a dream who are, themselves, dreaming and talking in their sleep.

The resolution comes from Knowledge of the Self, which is transcendent of the bodies of all and is not confined or defined by life or death. This shines as immovable peace and eternal freedom.

If the desire for Liberation is strong and consistent, all that is needed will manifest within you.

Ever yours in Truth,
Nome

[This letter was from a seeker in India. Nome's response follows.]

December 5, 2008

Dear Nome,

Namaste.
We had a good meeting with [name omitted] yesterday.
This troubled him. He recounted a story from his grandfather, who ran the ashramam during Ramana's days. Ramana's birthday was the next day. There was no rice and no money. Deeply troubled by this, he went to Ramana and told him of his concern (and that there was a rich devotee at the ashramam who, if asked, would immediately give the money needed). Ramana said to him, "Do you not trust Arunachala?" (to provide what is needed.) Ashamed of himself, he left Ramana's side. Two hour s later, a bullock cart came into the ashramam with 20 bags of rice. Only 2 were needed for the jayanti celebration.

This is a story that [name omitted] has taken into himself deeply. So much so that he now thinks he was wrong when he raised the money for Ramana's samadhi hall.

Sometime soon we will have him here at the house and, with him, will listen to a Satsang. Also we gave him our copy of *Bouquet of Nondual Texts.*

[Name omitted] said to send you his regards. We also got an email address for him. May we give him yours?

Life here continues to be so good. We will move to another house soon.

Thank you for what you have shared so freely with those who come and listen.

Om Arunachala,

ॐ Dear . . . ,

Om Namo Bhagavate Sri Ramanaya
Namaste. Thank you for your message.

I am glad to know that you met with Sri [name omiited]. Thank you for sharing the anecdote that he related about the Maharshi. To be "deeply troubled" in the midst of the bliss of the infinite Consciousness of the Self is a product of illusory delusion. However, by the Maharshi's limitless Grace and Knowledge, such illusion of that devotee, who was the Sarvadhikari, must have dissolved. That Knowledge, which is of the sole-existent Self, transcends bodies and the array of actions of the bodies, so, certainly, it transcends all objects. The manifestations of Grace are myriad as, likewise, the forms such take.

Therefore, free of the attempt to measure the Real by the unreal, the Self by the non-Self, the immensity of Grace by worldly manifestations, thought-transcendent Knowledge by ideas, love and devotion by objects, one should abide blissfully, at peace, in That, as That, itself. Such a one has neither action nor inaction but is simply himself, which is the Self of all.

When you see Sri [name omitted] again, please convey my best wishes, warm regards, and deep respect for him.

137

Yes, certainly, you may provide my email address to him. I assume that he has seen *Song of Ribhu*. It was good that you showed him *Advaita Prakarana Manjari*. If you have copies of *Svatmanirupanam* and *Origin of Spiritual Instruction*, you may wish to show them to him, too, though he may have already seen them.

It is good that you will be near to where [name deleted] will stay to meet with him and to offer help, should he or his wife need such.

May you ever abide as the Self, which, devoid of the notion "I," is ever uninvolved in anything, regardless of the bodily appearance, which ever rests as the Unmoving One, which is the priceless spiritual treasure, and which is who you truly are, thus to be happy and at peace always.

Om Arunacalesvaraya Namah
Om Namah Sivaya

Ever yours in Sri Bhagavan,
Nome

[A response to a message questioning the value of wearing sacred ashes as advised in the Song of Ribhu *and expressing the idea that the Guru, the Maharshi, is unreal.]*

December 7, 2008

ॐ Dear . . . ,

Om Namo Bhagavate Sri Ramanaya

Namaste. The value of wearing vibhuti is known by those who do so. Transcendence of the triads, in which the ego is dead, is the inner adornment with the holy ashes of Siva.

Earnest practice of the helpful instructions is, indeed, wise thankfulness.

It would be better to say that the disciple is unreal, a mere misconception, and thus vanishes than to say such of the Guru, who is the Self, Brahman. The Maharshi indeed exists and alone exists. So, it is imperative to know him as he is. To accomplish that, one must first know oneself. Thus, true Knowledge dawns, and devotion wells up and overflows. Grace remains as Being.

Ever yours in Truth,
Nome

[The same seeker wrote again, on December 9, 2008, speaking of egolessness and observing his mortality. This is the response.]

ॐ Dear . . . ,

Om Namo Bhagavate Sri Ramanaya
Namaste. So, Sri Bhagavan said that our greatest glory is where we cease to exist. Inquiry to discover the nonexistence of the ego is this cessation.

If you fully draw upon that which is innately within, the Truth of the Maharshi's' statement that God, Guru, and Self are one and the same becomes abundantly clear.

A keen awareness of mortality is very helpful for the motivation to deeply, consistently inquire and remain nonattached to all things. Such is clearly evident in the story of the Maharshi's Self-Realization, the story of Naciketa in the *Katha Upanishad,* and others. It appears in *Timeless Presence,* too.

May you ever abide in the Truth of the egoless, blissful, immortal Self.

Ever yours in Truth,
Nome

[From the same seeker, followed by the reply:]

December 9, 2008

So, I suppose Jesus was a Jnani? Is inquiry Christian as well? Are there heaven and hell? Do the rituals of organized religions matter if you inquire, or didn't Maharshi or Muruganar say the final oblation most worthy of praise is to Realize the Self?

ॐ Dear . . . ,

Om Namo Bhagavate Sri Ramanaya
Namaste.

Self-Knowledge and Self-inquiry are of the nature of Reality, which knows no sectarian division. It is like asking if God is a Hindu or Christian. The humor of such is obvious. The same holds true for the nature of Jesus.

Vedanta has excellently preserved, in experience and scripture, these essential teachings. Perhaps this is due to the absence of "heresy hunting," with its concomitant book burning, violence, malice etc. carried out by those who have not a clue as to the real nature of God, worship, wisdom, etc. but who nonetheless masquerade as "religious." Or it may be due to the abundance of sages who have appeared in this ancient spiritual tradition.

Heaven and hell are according to the conceiver or perceiver of them. For those who experience such, such appear to be real. For those who know that all is in the mind, they appear as states or modes of mind. They thus rid themselves of the errors that form the hell and find the heaven within. For those who abide as the Self, there is only That, God, and nothing else whatsoever.

The value of the ritual or form of worship is according to the one who practices it. See *Saddarshanam* and *Upadesa Saram* (both by the Maharshi) for a profound understanding of the relation of worship with name and form to the practice of what is formless or the worship of the formless. Yes, the final worship, puja, oblation, offering, etc. is Self-Realization. Nonetheless, Sri Muruganar performed puja with a Siva-lingam, and Sri Ramanasramam conducts much worship (puja), holy text recitations (Veda Parayana and the Tamil Parayana), etc., and there is at the center of its premises at Arunachala the Mathrubhutesvara Temple in traditional style with traditional worship offered by the priests.

So, worship in any form is good if it diminishes the ego. It is best to know what you worship, for thus your worship is in Truth.

Ever yours in Truth,
Nome

<hr>
•

[In response to a letter from a couple:]

December 19, 2008

ॐ Dear .. and . . . ,

Om Namo Bhagavate Sri Ramanaya

Namaste. Thank for your letter of the 16th that accompanied your kind offering to SAT.

I am glad to hear that [name omitted]'s health continues to be good. Your approach of gratitude for the time in life while remaining focused on the Self that transcends the transient body is wise.

Yes, placing your burdens at the feet of the Lord brings the necessary detachment. This yields equanimity and peace. The financial matters will be settled and over some day, yet the Supreme remains forever, and they who dissolve their falsely assumed individual identities in That remain free and at peace forever.

The experience that you, [name omitted], describe is deep. The dream-like character is merely imagined in thought, but that which is the witness of thought is the thought-transcendent Consciousness of the Self, your real

Being. By inquiry, realize this to be the truth always and thus abide constantly as the Self, of the nature of Being-Consciousness-Bliss.

The temple is always here for you whenever it becomes possible for you to come. I am enclosing copies of the two most recent issues of *Reflections* for you.

By Bhagavan's Grace, may you ever abide as the Self, which is ever undivided and perfectly full.

Ever yours in Truth,
Nome

[Here is a message that was sent to a seeker as he was preparing for a trip to Arunachala and Sri Ramanasramam.]

January 1, 2009

ॐ Dear . . . ,

Your time in India is sure to be wonderful for both of you. While I know that you will be very much involved in the filming and photography aspects, the time spent in silent meditation in the various sacred places and spent slowly ambling through the ancient temples will be especially profound. Take the time to slip inside the Timeless. With all the things to see, be sure to dive deep into the seer. With all that is to be heard, be sure to be absorbed in Sri Bhagavan's eternal Silence.

Om Namah Sivaya
Om Namo Bhagavate Sri Ramanaya

Ever yours in Truth,
Nome

═══
●

[This is a message to two revered devotees of Sri Ramana located at the Ramana Maharshi Centre for Learning in Bangalore, sent shortly before the annual shraddha (the observances in regard to one whose body is deceased) of Sri A. R. Natarajan. It was later published in The Ramana Way, *which is the periodical of the RMCL.]*

January 4, 2009

ॐ Dear . . . and . . . ,

Om Namo Bhagavate Sri Ramanaya

Namaste. I trust that all is well with you and that the Ramana Maharshi Centre for Learning continues to thrive in Sri Ramana's Grace.

Fondly recalling Sri A. R. Natarajan yesterday, I took to the laptop computer at home and wrote a few lines. It is not really a poem, as it lacks rhyme and meter, with just a bare trace of rhythm, though it is obvious that the ninth through fourteenth "verses" are an acrostic with his name. So, I thought I would send it to you. You may do as you like with it. I do not know if you observe the custom of sraddha. He remains ever dear and One with us in the true Self.

May you ever abide in the Knowledge of the Self, full of peace and joy.

Ever yours in Sri Bhagavan,
Nome

Everlasting Spirit

Called by the name A. R. Natarajan,
He, himself, calling upon Ramana always.

143

Caring for the devotees of the Maharshi,
With the fullness overflowing from his devotion.

Graciously giving of his abundance,
Giving himself to Sadguru Ramana.

The warmth of his smile, so joyful and sincere,
His heart flooded with inner, spiritual bliss.

Urging and encouraging others to spiritual practice,
Based on his undaunted, fruitful experience.
Attentive to the Knowledge revealed by Sri Ramana,
Speaking, writing, meditating, realizing within.

Recognizing the Truth shining in others,
The Truth of the Self without any "other."

Zealously sharing the love of Sri Bhagavan,
Remaining content, peaceful in heart.

Always full of devotion to Sri Ramana,
Ramana ever the Lord of his heart,

Naturally full of the love of his Guru,
Absolute Being manifested in full,

Truth revealed by His unlimited Grace,
Absorption forever in His Existence,

Ramana Sadguru, his true abode,

Attached to none other or to this world,
Jubilant in love, truly devoted,

Abidance unwavering, in Him, as That,
Now and forever, the Self without end.

This is not a eulogy,
Or memory that fades,

But love for a spirit undying
And the imperishable Self.

[A response to a seeker who, on January 5, 2009, wrote about his spiritual practice.]

ॐ Dear . . . ,

Om Namo Bhagavate Sri Ramanaya

Namaste. Constant, earnest practice of inquiry, fused with the wise detachment born of knowing the source of happiness, guided by Sri Ramana, Ribhu, and such, assuredly yields the cherished fruit, which is Self-Knowledge. The time, being unreal, is of no consequence; depth of the Knowledge of Reality is that which is significant.

May you ever abide in the changeless peace of the ever-existent Self.

Ever yours in Truth,
Nome

[This letter was sent in response to a seeker's questions about love and relationships.]

January 6, 2009

ॐ Dear . . . ,

Om Namo Bhagavate Sri Ramanaya

Namaste. Thank you for your message.

Love may be said to be the unitary "feeling" of Being; that is, it is of the very nature of the indivisible Self. One who revels in the Self is the same in a crowd or in a solitary place, with close friends or without, married or single, and so forth and so on.

That which is truly desired by all is the Bliss of the Self, which is undivided Being. Finding that within, all desires dissolve for the one who knows. The Being of the Self is ever-existent. It is not born when the body is born and does not perish with the death of the body. It exists: realize it within you and do not postpone your bliss.

Love in the form of desire, wishing for someone or something else to provide the happiness that is actually innate, is mired and entangled in delusion. If it is in the form of the desire to make the other or others happy, too, it is higher because of less egotism. If it is the wish for others to be happy with no regard for the ego, it is better. If it is in the form of the perfect fullness of the Self, with no notion of ego or other, it is true and without a veil. Such a one experiences neither desire nor fear and rests content within.

I hope that the above is helpful for you. Reflect upon its meaning and inquire to know yourself. You will thus be ever happy and at peace.

Ever yours in Truth,
Nome

[This letter is from a devotee of Sri Ramana in India. Nome's response follows, which, in turn, is followed by the response from this devotee.]

January 9, 2009

Dear sir,

I am in Sri Ramana Bhagawan since 1999. I belong to Vellore, and I frequently make visits to Tiruvannamalai. I will be attending Jayanthi also on 11th Jan 09. Usually I prefer to serve food in the dining hall. Sometimes, even the petty matter when people speak to me affects my mind, and it takes a long time to vanish.

I helped one of the members of Ramana Ashram in CMC Hospital when he was brought, and, after some time, I asked him whether I can stay in his house during Jayanthi, and he said it is not possible. This affects me for sometime, and, after a short or long time, I became alright.

Kindly let me know what sort of formula I should practice.

Wish you Ramana Jayanthi.
Yours in Sri Ramana,

January 12, 2009

ॐ Dear . . . ,

Om Namo Bhagavate Sri Ramanaya
Namaste. Thank you for your message.

To be a devotee of Bhagavan Sri Ramana Maharshi is a great blessing. Nothing in the world can compare with this blessing.

By inquiring to know the Self, by His Grace, the Knowledge of the Self is realized, and in that there is lasting peace and happiness. Disturbance in the mind is not due to outer circumstances or causes but to the adherence of the mind to its own delusive notions. Overlooking the innate happiness of the Self, one seeks for it elsewhere and needlessly suffers, for no one else can give you the happiness that is truly yours. If, knowing the Self, you find that Being is Bliss, nothing will perturb your peace or have the capacity to cause you to suffer. Therefore, it is essential to know that happiness is within and to inquire to know what that "within," the Self, is. The Maharshi's instruction regarding this is found in the book, *Who am I?*

When a tendency appears in the mind, search for the thoughts that constitute it. Trace those specific thoughts to the definitions you hold of yourself. Then, inwardly determine the falseness of those definitions. Trace the misidentifications to the primal false assumption of "I." Inquiring, that supposed "I" will vanish, because it is unreal. That which remains is actually the ever-existent.

It is not the real Self that becomes upset. Is there another self? Existence is only one. So, inquire into the nature of any other supposed self. This will resolve all.

I hope that you find the above helpful. It is simply a reiteration of what Sri Bhagavan has taught. Please feel free to write again if you wish to do so.

May your inquiry be deep, and, by Sri Ramana's Grace, may you abide in the Knowledge of the Self and thus in perpetual peace and bliss.

Ever yours in Sri Bhagavan,
Nome

Dear Sir,

Thank you very much.
I had been to Bhagawan Jayanthi, and I served as a volunteer.
I also chanted Veda Parayanam.
Thank you very much.
I will keep in touch with you whenever I have a problem and cannot control it.

With regards,
Yours in Sri Ramana,

[This is a reply to a message from a seeker, written on January 16, 2009, in which he expressed that he felt obstructed by his desires and fears.]

ॐ Dear . . . ,

Om Namo Bhagavate Sri Ramanaya

Namaste. Thank you for your messages.

Obstacles call for more applied effort and more depth of inquiry. Examine to determine the ideas constituting the obstacles and inquire to free yourself of those ideas.

Fears may be said to be the inverse of desires. One who knows that happiness is within does not fear its loss, and one who knows the unborn and imperishable Self does not fear the loss of existence. The Upanishad declares: "Where there is a second there is fear." A second is any dualism, inclusive of the notion of an existent ego.

May you ever abide as the bodiless, egoless Self, the One without a second, and thus dwell in perpetual happiness and peace.

Ever yours in Truth,
Nome

[This is from a seeker who, living at a considerable distance, for several years has been listening to recordings of sastang, though he was unable to be physically present at the temple. Nome's response follows.]

January 23, 2009

Namaste, Master, with joy to receive your personal note. Thank you. I humbly put a few questions to you for clarity and understanding. Sri Bhagawan used to say that controlling the mind is like leading the run-away cow to a shed with a bunch of green grass in the front. My mind loves to go to pasture to graze on the sweet memories of days of childhood and youth in the land that is far way now. What do I use as a bunch of green grass to bring it back in the shed of my Self? Bliss, peace, etc. are, more or less, just words at this stage.

Happiness of deep sleep is more or less unknown on account of a bad back, frequent bathroom trips, and other age related blessings.

The second question is about my addiction; is reading too many advaita books a roadblock in any way? I read them because, at the time of reading, I feel like I am reading a letter from a relative from home or reading a map of some well-traveled, familiar land.

I am very, very confused about the importance of being in the physical presence of Guru for removal of vasanas.

I appreciate very much your kindness in taking the time to respond. Namaste.

ॐ Dear . . . ,

Om Namo Bhagavate Sri Ramanaya

Namaste. Thank you for your message.

The "grass" in the Maharshi's analogy represents the innate happiness. This Bliss is identical with Being. The analogy demonstrates the discrimination regarding how to turn the mind inward. The roving cow, or mind, is in search of the happiness, but, seeking it externally, does not obtain that which is desired, which is pure happiness, but rather finds trouble due to its own activities. So, the mind-cow must be returned to its right place and persuaded to remain there. Two approaches present themselves. One can attempt to forcibly restrain the mind-cow with a tether and such or, if shown the luscious green grass of happiness, which indeed was all that it ever truly wanted, the mind-cow will naturally remain at peace in its true place within. If forcibly restrained, the mind-cow will be out of trouble for the time being but also awaiting the opportunity to go outward again. If it finds happiness within, which is the path of Knowledge, it remains without the tendency to return to delusion.

You need not conceive what the "grass" could be. You have sought happiness at all times save those in which you were actually happy, such as in deep sleep. The desire is another proof that the happiness of the Self exists. It is an intuitive search for your own Self.

Your knowledge is deeper than what you state in your message. Though saying that peace and bliss are only words for you, still you desire what they signify. Such desire has even prompted your question. The desire is due to an inner knowledge that your natural state is full of peace and bliss, and you are not satisfied unless your experience is that perfect fullness. Bliss is your very nature. Convinced of this, practice the inquiry to realize the Self as it truly is. Thus you will be happy regardless of the conditions of the body.

You need not eliminate the sweet memories. Just become keenly aware of the source of the joy reflected in them.

Books of Advaita Vedanta pose no obstacle. Yes, like a letter from your true home and a map of a familiar land are they. Be sure to deeply inquire as you read so that you vividly realize within you what they proclaim.

The Guru is not a body, just as you are not a body. His presence is really the Existence of the Self, which is infinite and eternal. The value of satang has been proclaimed by the wise for ages. Inner association is what is essential.

I hope that you find what is mentioned above helpful. May your inquiry be deep so that the profound, happy Knowledge of the Self shines in your heart always.

Ever yours in Sri Bhagavan,
Nome

[This is a letter from Nome in response to a seeker. The questions can be inferred from the answers contained in the response.]

January 30, 2009

ॐ Dear . . . ,

151

Om Namo Bhagavate Sri Ramanaya

Namaste. Thank you for your message.

Diligence and intensity of practice are important. If your mind wanders to various kinds of thoughts, discern the motivation. What are you looking for in them, and in what is that found? The seeking for happiness, the attempt to know what is real, and search for identity are the same. Such is fulfilled in the Knowledge of the Self.

Being is Bliss. Being is not an activity, mode of mind, or any object. It is timeless and spaceless. It is eternal and infinite. In it, the mind dissolves in the Knowledge of the mind's nonexistence. It is not merely that the mind exhausts itself; that would result only in temporary quietude, just as sleep follows waking activity. Inquiry may be said to return the mind to its source, and pure Consciousness remains. In this return, all of the mental tendencies of ignorance are eliminated by clear Knowledge, just as darkness may be said to be eliminated by light. Likewise, the here and now of the waking state are similar to that in a dream. The Self transcends the past, the present, and the future. One destroys the illusory ignorance by inquiring as to what one's real nature is (the significance of "Who am I?"). Sri Ramana's instruction is to make one's vision nonobjective.

What you have mentioned concerning love is clear. All that has been stated previously about happiness and peace applies to love, as well. In its essence and fullness, it is the undivided nature of Being, the One Self.

May your inquiry continue to deepen so that mind-transcendent, blissful Self-Knowledge shines unveiled entirely, so that you are ever at peace and your life is suffused with the long-sought love that is, actually, within you always.

Ever yours in Truth,
Nome

152

[A response to another message from the same seeker.]

February 3, 2009

ॐ Dear . . . ,

Om Namo Bhagavate Sri Ramanaya

Namaste. Lasting peace is found only in the immutable. The transient and changeful cannot provide it. Such is secure only if you are identical with it, for then no separation is possible. That is the Self. "Tat Tvam Asi" (That you are) declares the *Chandogya Upanishad.* If this is conclusively realized within, fear and suffering vanish, and you remain as the Peace, itself, regardless of the condition of the circumstances of the world, the body, senses, etc. Steady, deep inquiry reveals this Knowledge. Practice with your best effort, undaunted by apparent obstacles, endowed with humility in light of the vast Truth you are attempting to realize and the magnitude of the holy, gracious sages such as Sri Ramana Maharshi, and with your heart filled with joy because of the freedom at hand and the freedom to be free, is advisable.

Ever yours in Truth,
Nome

[The next three responses are to messages from the same seeker.]

February 5, 2009

ॐ Dear . . . ,

Om Namo Bhagavate Sri Ramanaya

Namaste. You may wish to question how much emphasis you place on the mind's thoughts, especially the self-centered ones. The Self is beyond all of them. Even from the point of view of a manifested universe, of what importance are the tense, troubled ideas connected with one tiny pseudo-personal entity the duration of which is less than a blink of an eye in universal time? The rigid repetition of an idea or set of ideas is not worthy of you whose nature is of the divine and the eternal.

Peacefulness, equanimity, equal vision, steadiness, courage, honesty, love for all beings, humility, absence of ego-concern, fortitude, introspective vision, wisdom, and such are the natural characteristics of those who aspire for the highest, Self-Realization.

May you, by contemplating what is indicated above and by reflecting upon the teachings of wise sages, be at peace within.

Ever yours in Truth,
Nome

February 6, 2009

ॐ Dear . . . ,

Om Namo Bhagavate Sri Ramanaya
Namaste. Thank you for your messages.

The analogies given by Sri Bhagavan concerning the train and the luggage and the temple tower and the carved figure pertain to the unreality of the ego and the falseness of the conception of being the performer of action.

Activity is not bondage and is not the cause of suffering. The "I am the doer" idea is limitation and causes suffering. Mere cessation of bodily actions does not yield Liberation. If inaction is grasped with fear as the cause, the fear will only intensify or endure. The result is indolence and not spiritual peace. In such a mode of mind, concepts about external sources of happiness and suffering, and misidentification of the Self with the body, are delusions left intact.

Action without attachment, as taught in the *Bhagavad Gita, Yoga Vasishta,* and other holy texts, is correct. Such is easily attained by those who know the source of happiness within. They then inquire to realize the Self as bodiless Being. Being beyond the identification with the body, they remain at peace and free even when the body acts. The body acts; the Self abides still.

You may wish to continue to consider what was mentioned in a previous email regarding self-centered thoughts.

It may also be helpful to consider what you presently regard as a troubling situation for yourself contrasted with the phenomenal hardships faced by other people around the world. It may provide some perspective.

The *Gita* declares, "Let a man lift himself up; let him not lower himself."

Surrender is to God. Giving up in frustration and reacting by entertaining a mental mode of apathy has nothing to do with the deep devotion in which the perfect fullness shines.

The above is mentioned in the hope that it will clarify, inspire, and encourage.

May your meditations be deep and the spiritual freedom that you find suffuse the entirety of your life.

Ever yours in Truth,
Nome

February 12, 2009

ॐ Dear . . . ,

Om Namo Bhagavate Sri Ramanaya
Namaste. Thank you for your messages.

A good approach to spiritual practice, in the understanding that its joy and freedom are surpassed only by the final Realization, is that no kind of bondage is insuperable, being only illusory, and the true Self is ever present, yet whatever time is required to completely destroy the bondage is happily well-spent.

155

As you deepen the inquiry, the distinction between activity and inactivity of the body, senses, etc. will completely disappear, for the Self is ever the same, unborn and imperishable.

It is not difficult to correctly, precisely pursue realization of the Self, for every step you make in that direction reveals peace and bliss, just as, contrariwise, a step into delusion yields the suffering that reminds one to go back the way she came. The Grace is always there; one has only to inquire to experience it. In one sense, the efforts made are infinitesimal in contrast to the magnitude of Grace, the Truth of the Self, of the nature of Sat-Cit-Ananda (Being-Consciousness-Bliss). So, it is a case of Grace for the sake of Grace. That is the real Existence; the ego is nothing at all.

May your inquiry continue to deepen so that you abide steadily in the Self, as the Self, the self-luminous Reality.

Ever yours in Truth,
Nome

[This is a message from a seeker during a visit to India, especially Arunachala. Nome's response follows.]

February 16, 2009

Hi Nome,

Om Namo Bhagavate Sri Ramanaya

It's so wonderful that the Self is ever fascinated with it's revelation.

One thing that continues to puzzle me is the almost complete lack of any sign of "self-inquiry" here. It's about as popular here as on the Pacific Garden mall in SC.

But in "Talks with Ramana Maharshi", it can be found in almost every one of Ramana's responses to questions. I just don't know how people can miss the very essence of his teachings. I went to a couple of events here where self-inquiry was being taught, but it was totally on the mind/conceptual level. The people leading the events had clearly not done inquiry themselves. I don't say that to be derogatory; they just didn't know what inquiry truly is. I probably wouldn't have any idea either, if I hadn't had the fortune of your guidance. I can remember my very first Satsang at SAT. When you said those words "who am I", it rang like the "Liberty Bell" in me. Somehow, I knew that was the fundamental question I had never asked. And then your repeated instructions and Ramana's Grace opened up the Self to myself. I'm not making claims of knowing much about inquiry, but I at least have had "the taste" and know where my freedom lies. You once said that inquiry is the very last thing that people will do. They'll do everything else, first. Oh well, I'll just keep inquiring until realization, and then maybe the answer to this puzzle will be known. Maybe the puzzle will disappear along with the seeker.

Om Namo Bhagavate Sri Ramanaya

February 17, 2009

ॐ Dear . . . ,

Om Namo Bhagaavate Sri Ramanaya
Namaste.

It is difficult to ascertain the spiritual practice of another, especially when such concerns Self-inquiry, which dissolves the very notion of the individual who practices. It is entirely internal Knowledge, which may not be measurable in outer ways. Moreover, those who earnestly, intensely inquire and who revel in the blissful, nonobjective Knowledge of the Self may not engage much in social interactions during which others might take notice of them, and certainly they would not make a big deal of "themselves." This is so because of the egolessness of Truth, the self-evident nature of the Self, the eternality and infinity of the Self, the immensity of His Grace, the perfection of the Sadguru, the perfect-fullness of the innate Bliss, the secondless nature of the infinite Consciousness, and the immutability and absoluteness of Being, among other reasons.

What the Maharshi reveals is clearly self-evident to those who discern within. The one who does not inquire does not exist.

The essence of the inquiry is Knowledge. The Knowledge is the nature of the knower. Thus, the Upanishads declare, prajnanam brahma, Supreme Knowledge is Brahman, and ayam-atma brahma, this Self is Brahman. It is to be conclusively realized, as is indicated by aham brahmasmi, I am Brahman, and this is revealed by the consistent instruction by a great rishi (Maharshi), which is summed in the phrase tat tvam asi, That you are. The method of practice is ko'ham, who am I? Steady abidance in the essential Knowledge of Being, for which there is no alternative, is nonduality and timeless Silence.

Continue to deeply inquire so that the self-luminous nature of the Self shines clearly free of any illusory veil, and thus abide in bliss and peace always.

Ever yours in Truth,
Nome

[Another message to the same seeker.]

ॐ   Sri Ramana's Grace is boundless. Knowledge of its nature is Bliss.

Ever yours in Sri Bhagavan,
Nome

[Two responses to messages from a seeker, in which the questions asked can be inferred from the answers.]

February 18, 2009

ॐ Dear . . . ,

Om Namo Bhagavate Sri Ramanaya

Namaste. Thank you for your recent messages.

Peace is of the very nature of the immutable Self. Misidentification appears to disturb it or veil it. Self-Knowledge, revealed by Self-inquiry, destroys the misidentifications, which are only ignorance and not true.

Repression does not succeed in the destruction of ignorance. It is like holding a piece of wood under the surface of water. As soon as the hold is released, the wood bobs to the surface again. Likewise is it with the suppression of thoughts, inclusive of those that you refer to as emotions. Without true Knowledge, they reappear. Of course, indulgence in the delusion is also unsuccessful and represents no true freedom. Sri Bhagavan says that such is like pouring kerosene on a fire in the attempt to extinguish it. Neither side of the dualism can substitute for actual inquiry to know oneself.

The intensity in any bondage or suffering derives from you. Turn that into the intensity for Liberation, and, applying it to fervent, keen inquiry, you will pass beyond all suffering and bondage. If you discern the causes of the suffering, which are invariably one's own misidentifications and attachments, you can abolish it in the blissful realization of who you really are.

Cessation of thinking is not the same as Knowledge of the Self, or Self-Realization, though, in the latter, the nonexistence of thought is self-evident. Thoughts may stop in deep sleep, in some anesthetized states, etc., but such does not result in Self-Realization. Self-Realization transcends every state and mode of mind.

Health and sickness pertain to the body. They are unrelated to the Self and to spiritual practice.

If you suffer from loneliness in any form, the answer lies within. All are only in the Self. The Self is never lonely, though it exists without another. Practice so as to completely dissolve the misidentifications and their concomitant differentiation, and, thereby, your joy will be full and unending. Self-inquiry is the practice. Surrender on a path of deep bhakti (devotion) can bring the same result as the path of jnana (Knowledge) because of its dissolution of the ego, attachments, and such.

The tradition of Vedanta describes practice in terms of sravana (listening), manana (reflection), and nididhyasana (profound meditation). Listening, or receiving spiritual instruction, usually occurs in satsang. In addition, the reading of appropriate books can assist in this. In the present time, it seems, CDs and DVDs can also assist, as described by you. The general advice is that the seeker should do all that is possible to support the essential introspection, making the first two continual and the third continuous.

I hope that you find the above helpful and that you find the imperishable bliss within you.

Ever yours in Truth,
Nome

[This is a message from a seeker who met Nome in Bangalore in 1994 or 1995 and who carried on some correspondence since then. Nome's response follows.]

February 20, 2009

Namasthe Sri Nome,

Om Namo Bhagavathe Sri Ramanaya !
Regarding self enquiry : I was practising only japa for sometime, but I could have put efforts on enquiry. Now, the only way that I can meditate that looks possible for me is that I can do only the Maharshi's way, the way where I can return from the worldly thoughts and hold on to the I. No other meditation is possible for me.

My doubt in the path of enquiry is if it is fine to meditate without the feeling of devotion in the process. At the moment, the enquiry method appears as a process to unravel my clarified mind or the innate happiness. But devoted meditation does not happen.

I am able to stay without initial thoughts, but I am unable to dive within or have a better, more clarified experience.

Maybe, if I proceed patiently, I might be able to proceed with more clarity.

Bhagavan says that once the grace takes hold, it never lets go of its prey. Is that true for a samsaric person also? We are struggling in the path.

Sometimes, the attention is focused and concentrated, and, at other times, it is more of an expanded, vast mind. I am not sure if I am able to put my question in words. My query is that is it better to have a concentrated, focused attention or to go with the flow of experience?

When I came to this path, Bhagavan appeared to me so livingly, while I was just returning to the waking state and bestowed the experience which you call infinite consciousness, but all that I let pass away.

With Yours in Sri Bhagavan,

ॐ Dear . . . ,

Om Namo Bhagavate Sri Ramanaya

Namaste. In the practice of inquiry, be sure that the focus is upon the inquiry as to your very nature, your true identity, and not merely reduction of thoughts.

Would it have ever even occurred to you to inquire were it not for the Maharshi? Humbly contemplating with gratitude upon that will suffice to cause devotion to well up from within.

Bhagavan said that, once one is within Grace, he will never be forsaken. He also said, though, that the aspirant must strive to the best of his ability. Only by that does he come to realize the fullness of this Grace.

Ever yours in Sri Bhagavan,
Nome

161

≡
•

[This is a message of questions from a seeker who attended a few satsangs and other holy events. Nome's response follows.]

February 25, 2009

Namasthe Nome,

Please clarify the following doubts.

1. When I am doing meditation, so many thoughts are rising. All thoughts are disturbing me a lot, when enquiring; one thought after another one rising. So, the total time I have spent watching all the thoughts. I am not able to concentrate on enquiry. Some thoughts are very bad. Why are bad thoughts rising? I couldn't think like this in a normal time. So, due to bad thoughts, I feel guilty.

2. How is one to get Self-realization by practicing meditation, prarabdha karma, or guru guidance?

Namasthe,

ॐ Dear . . . ,

Om Namo Bhagavate Sri Ramanaya
Namaste. Thank you for your message.

Thoughts appear in meditation only to be traced to their source. If the source is traced, you will not be disturbed. Disturbance is due to misidentification and considering the thoughts as real in both their content and as existent entities.

Even with what you term "the bad thoughts," determine the definitions of yourself that form and shape them and then inquire to liberate yourself from these false definitions (misidentifications). The thought then subsides permanently. In this manner, the illusion becomes the seed of its own destruction. The inquiry leads to the very nature of the "I." Inquiry as to the nature of that reveals egoless Being, which is the true Self.

162

If meditation is upon the nature of the meditator, the Self is realized. This is the guidance of the Sadguru, Sri Ramana Maharshi. All three categories of karma, including prarabdha, dissolve in the inquiry to know the Self. The Guru's Grace and guidance are ever present. One has only to practice to the very best of his ability, and all will come out right.

May your meditation be deep so that the innate, blissful Knowledge of the Self, which is Sat-Cit-Ananda, shines without obscuration, and thus you abide in steady peace.

Ever yours in Truth,
Nome

February 27, 2009

ॐ Dear . . . ,

Om Namo Bhagavate Sri Ramanaya
Namaste. The innate happiness is ever-existent as it is the same as Being-Consciousness. It shines clearly whenever the ego subsides. Realization of the egoless nature of the Self is peaceful bliss without beginning or end.

Ignorance of one's own nature alone gives rise to the illusion of bondage with its consequent suffering and the fear that is born of dualism.

As the Self is not the body, it never does anything, no matter what is apparently done by the instruments of body, speech, and mind.

Where there is no notion of an individual self, the notion of another vanishes, and divine love shines as the indivisibility of Being.

Though I may not respond to all of your email messages, I do, indeed, read them. You are welcome to write whenever you wish to do so. When it may be helpful, I respond in writing; sometimes silence is the best answer.

You seem to be retaining the responses, either electronically or with a print out. This is wise. You may find that by re-reading previous responses, there is more contained in them than what was apparent at first glance. That which is subtle becomes more obvious by virtue of one's own deepening inquiry.

May your meditation be profound so that you experientially verify just how true the Truth is, its infinite vastness is revealed as your sole identity, and its eternity abides as your steadiness.

Ever yours in Truth,
Nome

≡
•

[A repsonse to a seeker whose questions can be inferred from the answers:]

March 6, 2009

ॐ Dear . . . ,

Om Namo Bhagavate Sri Ramanaya
Namaste. Thank you for your messages.

A pleasant sensation minus the happiness essence associated with it is meaningless for all. The happiness is what all desire. The Self is this happiness.

Pain represents no suffering for those who know the Self to be bodiless.

It is in the very nature of bodies to move toward what is pleasurable for them (e.g., food when hungry, rest when exhausted, absence of pain) and to move away from what is painful (e.g., alleviation of pain, treatment of wounds and sickness, etc.) Such, in itself, is not bondage. He who misidentifies with the body suffers in the bondage of the cycle of pleasures and pains, and births and deaths. He who knows himself as the Self abides liberated from all that and is ever happy and at peace. The same holds true for being in the company of another or not.

The reference to pranayama (affecting the animating life energy by regulation of the breath) by the Maharshi is an allusion to what Adi Sankara explains in his *Aparoksanubhuti* (*Direct Experience*). Therein, he describes the raja yoga (the royal yoga) in 16 steps, which is a more detailed and expanded form of astanga yoga (eight-limbed yoga). Pranayama is explained in Jnana (Knowledge) terms as exhalation of the misidentification with the body (deham naham, the body is not I), inhalation as ko'ham (Who am I?), and retention as So'ham (He am I; "He" refers to Siva). While it is fine to meditate in this manner with the breath, the original intention of the spiritual instruction by Sri Sankara and Sri Ramana is purely that of Jnana, referencing the breath in a symbolic way only.

The passage to which you refer is, perhaps, from the *Katha Upanishad*. The recitations in Sanskrit and English toward the conclusion of satsang are from several sources. Some are from various Upanishads, some are from *Bhagavad Gita, Ashtavakra Gita, Avadhuta Gita*, and similar traditional scriptures. Usually, chapters from the *Ribhu Gita*, in Tamil and English, are recited during retreats at the SAT Temple. You can easily determine which text is being recited, and sometimes even the section or chapter, by referring to the catalogue of recordings for the date of any particular satsang.

May your inquiry be deep so that the Self remains revealed in all of its perfection.

Ever yours in Truth,
Nome

[This is a response to a message from a person who was visiting Tiruvannamalai and had begun to read Sri Ramana's

teachings and attempt to practice Self-inquiry. She had listened to a few recordings of satsang at the home of friends there and expressed an intention to visit for satsang during an anticipated visit to California. Her questions can be inferred from Nome's response given below.]

March 16, 2009

ॐ Dear . . . ,

Om Namo Bhagavate Sri Ramanaya
Namaste. Thank you for your message.

You may find that reading and meditating upon the significance of the preamble and initial paragraph of Sri Bhagavan's *Who am I?* answers your question about bliss and the body perfectly. His instruction about Bliss that appears later in the same holy text would also be of immense benefit. In addition, but not as a substitute, appropriate passages from *Self-Knowledge* may be found helpful for you. [name omitted] and [[name omitted] may have that book with them.

Bliss is identical with Being. As Being is formless, eternal, not dependent on causes, bodiless, and of a self-existent nature, so is Bliss. Bliss is indivisible. There are not different kinds of bliss, just as there are no divisions or types of Being. The apparent false multiplicity is due only to delusive superimposition of limitations. If one misidentifies with the imagined limitations, bliss is correspondingly limited, as for example, in the case of misidentification with the body.

Even the most pleasant sensations are minute in contrast to the Bliss of the Self. They are transient, unsteady and can change character at any moment to pain, etc. The profound Bliss of Self-Realization is not like that.

Who is it that knows about the body, the right side, the shifting of mental attention, the surges, the obstacles, leaving and returning, etc.? What is her nature? It cannot possibly be a body. Inquire within to know yourself.

Self-inquiry is of the nature of Knowledge that is neither

perceptual nor conceptual. It is not a mere change in mental attention. True Knowledge transcends thought and the various modes and states of mind. The means of practice must be of the same nature as that which is to be realized. In Self-inquiry, the end manifests as the means. The Self is eternal. Self-Knowledge is eternal. It is evident that mental attention is not eternal. The Maharshi says that what is not eternal is not worth seeking. Inwardly seek to know yourself. Inquire into the nature of the inquirer.

Yes, if while you are visiting California, you find the opportunity to attend satsang at the SAT temple, you will be warmly welcome.

Absorbing yourself in Sri Bhagavan's teachings and ardently practicing them will certainly yield the highest result. May your inquiry be deep, so that, with the false assumption of individuality (ego) and misidentification with the body abandoned, you abide in the Self as the Self, undifferentiated Being-Consciousness-Bliss, the unborn and imperishable, and thus remain always happy and at peace.

Ever yours in Truth,
Nome

≡
•

[What follows is a series of responses to several lengthy messages from a spiritual seeker. The questions raised, difficulties encountered, and experiences had by the seeker can be inferred from the answers.]

March 22, 2009

ॐ Dear . . . ,

Om Namo Bhagavate Sri Ramanaya
Namaste. Thank you for your message.

As you discern, peace and stupor are not to be equated. The former is only a mode of tamas guna. Sattva guna is said to be the quality of the meditating mind. Self-inquiry reveals the Self to be gunatita (beyond the qualities).

The condition of the body is determined by many factors. They are unreliable and transient. The Self is bodiless and remains the same whether the body is still or moving, loose or rigid, strong or weak, well or sick, alive or dead.

Dullness in practice is due to lack of inquiry, especially manifesting as the conjuring of delusion and adherence to the same. The latter manifests as the illusion of continuity of ignorance. Here are two points that ensure spiritual practice is sparkling. Be sure to actually inquire, questioning your very sense of identity. Secondly, included in the inquiry, destroy vasanas, as the Maharshi has instructed. Vasanas are tendencies. They are the forms of the assumed ego. Examining your own mind and experiences, hunt for tendencies and destroy them by inquiry. Even the decision to do so will awaken one from the dream of ignorance, and actual practice even more so. You can see this demonstrated, or at least alluded to, in some of the dialogues recorded in *Self-Knowledge* and in some of the satsang transcripts that appear in *Reflections*. One must, oneself, practice in such a manner.

May you always abide in That which, though ever the same, is ever fresh and fascinating, and realize that to be your very Self.

Ever yours in Truth,
Nome

April 5, 2009

ॐ Dear . . . ,

Om Namo Bhagavate Sri Ramanaya
Namaste. Thank you for your messages.

Compassion initially derives from the perception that the ignorance that creates the suffering or the karma for and by someone else bears similarities, perhaps, to the ignorance and actions of one's own mind, speech, and body. Upon deeper inquiry, it is born of the recognition of the needlessness of suffering and the unreal nature of the ignorance that is its cause.

Are there two selves that one should gain or lose the other? To think the "I" will stay in or step out of the "I"-less Self still includes the false assumption that is to be abandoned. Inquiry, steady, continuous, deep, nonobjective, and complete, accomplishes this in the revelation of the one Self without a second.

Destruction of vasanas is wise. Perseverance fueled by the desire for Liberation is very beneficial.

In response to your question about vegetarian diet: Sri Ramana gave very few specific directions regarding actions, for his instruction is of Self-Knowledge. He did, though, advise "sattvic food in moderate quantities." The same is standard in numerous other teachings, texts, among the yogis, etc. Sattvic food is defined as traditional vegetarian diet (includes dairy foods), in which the lives of no creatures are taken. The reasons for this are multiple. First, since very ancient times, it has been known that the quality of the food affects the quality of the mind. Some present day health practitioners may be arriving at a similar conclusion. Second, the karma of taking lives is there, whether one recognizes such or denies it. Third, the reason for carnivorous diet among humans is often due merely to desire (habit, supposed convenience, etc.) and not actual need of that for nourishment. Fourth, considering the body to be a temple, consideration is given regarding what is offered in it. Fifth, there is the matter of integrity. Would you actually slay the cow or other animal yourself, or would you not but will pay someone else (the butcher in the slaughterhouse) to do the deed? These can be considered in relation to this topic.

The Self, though, is not a body, does not consume food, is beyond life and death, is untouched by a mind, is beyond all karma, is desireless, is all in all yet beyond all, is action-less, and is the Self that dwells in the hearts of all as their very Being.

Consume a steady diet of inquiry so that you are full of Knowledge.

Ever yours in Truth,
Nome

April 9, 2009

ॐ Dear . . . ,

Om Namo Bhagavate Sri Ramanaya

Namaste. Thank you for your messages.

As you know, the Self is described as Sat-Cit-Ananda (Being-Consciousness-Bliss). These are not three parts or aspects but three terms combined that refer to one, indivisible Reality. In an Upanishad, the same is described as Satyam-Jnanam-Anantam, which means the True, the Knowledge, the Infinite. In other texts, it is referred to as Satyam-Sivam-Sundaram, the True, the Good, and the Beautiful. Whatever there is that is true, good, and beautiful, in whatever manner, wherever and whenever, it is the Self that thus shines forth. It is that which is dear in all and which is dear for all. It is that which is loved. When realized conclusively, love exists as the indivisibility of Being and has no opposite.

It is wise to continue to persevere in the questioning as to the source of happiness until peaceful detachment, unmoved by craving and aversions, expectations and fears, is constant and steady. The true Self is always unattached, ever free, and bliss itself. Your vairagya (detachment, dispassion) and jnana (knowledge) manifesting as deep inquiry are simply the clarification regarding your actual identity. Free of misidentification, the Self is the perfect fullness. Inquire, inquire, inquire. Like a light, there will be no darkness for you.

Ever yours in Truth,
Nome

April 18, 2009

ॐ Dear . . . ,

Om Namo Bhagavate Sri Ramanaya

Namaste. Thank you for your messages. Focused, intense meditation to know the Self yields freedom from the illusory limitations. This is to be regarded as true concentrated meditation and not the mere riveting of mental attention or the combating with thoughts. One should neither remain with the thoughts nor fight with them, as if they were real entities or as if they had any validity apart from the belief posited in them, but one should inquire and know himself in thought-transcendent Knowledge.

All the happiness ever desired and all the love for which you have ever yearned exist within you. Finding such, you become delighted at heart and ever peaceful. This Truth is to be realized in all its perfect fullness, whether you are alone or in a relationship. You may wish to refer again to the earlier instruction about depth of love and egolessness. That advice reveals both what is within and also the way to relate.

Yes, though written as an autobiographical description at the request of the President of Sri Ramanasramam, *Timeless Presence* is actually, for the most part, much more a description of realizing that is "samanya," common to all or universal, a dissolution of the falsely assumed individual and an expression of what an Upanishad declares, in the description of how the ancient sages realized, to be like the tracks of the birds in the sky.

Ever yours in Truth,
Nome

171

April 26, 2009

ॐ Dear . . . ,

Om Namo Bhagavate Sri Ramanaya
Namaste. Thank you for your messages.

You certainly will be warmly welcome at satsangs and retreats. Some find retreats very beneficial because of the continuous focus during all the days of the retreat.

Yes, Meister Eckhart's sermons and letters glow with transcendent clarity. Indeed, at SAT, a woman named Shanti, who was with us for many years until her bodily death a few years ago, translated into English all of his writings from the original middle-high German. The translated material remains in manuscript form at present.

May you abide as that which is of the nature of Being-Consciousness-Bliss, realized by profound inquiry by those endowed with sincerity of purpose, equanimity, detachment toward all things in the passing dream of the world, devotion to Truth, humility, perseverance, and the desire for Liberation from all of the imagined bondage.

Ever yours in Truth,
Nome

May 8, 2009

ॐ Dear . . . ,

Om Namo Bhagavate Sri Ramanaya
Namaste. Thank you for your messages.

The Self, unborn and imperishable, is always the same. One who knows the Self is the Self that is known, for that is one without any other.

Therefore, inquiring to know the Self, remain as the Self, without misidentifications or attachments. The Bliss of Being is the perfect fullness, and this Self alone is real. Therefore, it is natural to abide unaffected by pleasure and pain, gain and loss, good reputation or defamation, acceptance or rejection, and all the other dualities imagined within the context of the false individual.

The Self is all in all, at all times, yet, in the Self, which is homogeneous Being, there is nothing to be conceived as all.

For your earnest aspiration to realize the Self, there is illimitable Grace. It is always present; one need only be aware of it.

Ever yours in Truth,
Nome

May 20, 2009

ॐ Dear . . . ,

Om Namo Bhgavate Sri Ramanaya

Namaste. The essential inquiry is summed up, in English, as "Who am I?" However they may be phrased, the various spiritual instructions, inclusive of that which is phrased as questions, have the purpose of coaxing the seeker to actually inquire so that the Self is realized conclusively as it truly is. They do not represent other practices.

The inquiry is of the essence of Knowledge. It transcends thought, mental attention, sensory perception, and action. If you understand and adhere to the instruction expressed in *Who am I?*, your efforts will bear fruit. In that scripture, the Maharshi's instructions succinctly, fully explain the nature of happiness, the nature of the Self, what the mind is and how to transcend thought, the nature of the world, detachment, Self-inquiry and much more.

Inquire and, in the Knowledge of the Self, repose in Bliss.

Ever yours in Truth,
Nome

173

May 28, 2009

ॐ Dear . . . ,

Om Namo Bhagavate Sri Ramanaya

Namaste. Grace is ever present. Whenever the ego subsides, and to the degree it subsides, Grace is experienced. If the nonexistence of the ego is realized, Grace is found to be the ever-existent Self.

Yes, prasad means Grace. It can also mean bright clarity. It is also a term to designate the blessed food that has been offered to God or to a spiritual teacher that is then consumed by the devotee. Even other blessed items, such as bhasma (sacred ash) and kunkum (vermillion powder) are sometimes spoken of as prasad.

You may find that contemplation upon "what is present" still includes the non-discernment concerning happiness, identity, and reality. The temporary respite such offers is due to the reduction of thoughts, including those constituting the emotions. That result is not permanent and lacks the immense scope of actual Self-inquiry. Some familiarity with scriptures shows a noticeable absence of mention of that mental mode as a means to Liberation. It is not harmful or obstructive; it is just not sufficiently deep. The Knowledge-essence is that which enables any practice to work as well as it does. This Knowledge-essence composes the inquiry and also causes devotion to shine.

The discrimination that regards as real only that which is eternal, without beginning or end and free of interruption, is wise. Being-Consciousness-Bliss is the very nature of the Self. This is timeless, free of the past, the present, and the future. This is nonobjective and absolutely undifferentiated. You may find it beneficial to read pages 291-293 in *Self-Knowledge*. The detailed commentary on verse 15 of Sri Ramana Maharshi's *Saddarsanam* as contained in *Saddarsanam and An Inquiry into the Revelation of Truth and Oneself* may also yield more clarity regarding this.

May you ever abide as That, realizing which one is happiness, itself, and which leaves nothing else to be desired. It is the perfect fullness.

Ever yours in Truth,
Nome

June 8, 2009

ॐ Dear . . . ,

Om Namo Bhagavate Sri Ramanaya
Namaste. Thank you for your recent messages.

It is wise to continue to distinguish the eternal from the non-eternal, disidentifying and remaining detached from the latter so that the former is revealed as the very nature of your Being.

Ardent inquiry to know the Self as transcendent of the mind, along with a keen cognizance of life and death, eliminates tamas. Awareness of the precious opportunity for Liberation and deep devotion also bring one out of inertia.

Knowledge of happiness being within frees one from rajas.

Knowledge of the Self beyond all states and modes even transcends sattva.

May you abide firmly in the Knowledge of the Self, full of bliss and peace.

Ever yours in Truth,
Nome

[This is a message from a person intending to write a book about surrender and who wished to ask his own questions, too. Nome's response follows.]

March 24, 2009

Hi Nome,

I am working on a book that focuses on surrender. It seems that most spiritual and mystical paths incorporate the act of surrendering. This act appears to play a key role in one's awakening and spiritual growth. I have tried to surrender hundreds of times over the past twenty years, only to be met with frustration, because I did not realize until recently that surrendering is not a conscious act of the mind, rather it is the act of the ego/mind letting go, giving up and surrendering. Under these circumstances, the ego lets go and enlightenment/awakening/healing occurs. I wonder if you would agree with that statement.

I had an inspiration to create a book of spiritual teachers from various faiths and spiritual paths and ask them the same five questions regarding surrendering. The book would be a compilation of teachings on surrender. The readers will experience surrender in a myriad of ways and, most importantly, find a path or practice that will bring them to surrender.

I am inspired to reach out to you to seek your participation. I would be honored if you would consider sharing in this book. Your life's work has inspired me in many ways and will inspire countless others through this book. In addition to your contribution on surrender, your section will include your bio, a listing of your books, DVDs, CD's, contact information so that readers who are moved can contact you or your organization.

Here are the five questions:

1. How would you define surrender? Who or what is one surrendering to, in your opinion? God, Universe, Self, Soul, What Is, present moment...?

2. Is there a practice/methodology to surrender that one can follow that does not cause suffering? I.e. some paths try to create madness so that the ego surrenders. Is there a joyful methodology?

3. What happens when you surrender?

4. What is the ego or mind? What's holding on?

5. Is there a practice/methodology you follow that would create surrender? If so, please share!

Thank you so much for considering my request and for your teachings.

With Love,

ॐ Dear . . . ,

Om Namo Bhagavate Sri Ramanaya
Namaste. Thank you for your message.

Sri Ramana Maharshi has given spiritual instruction (as found in *Origin of Spiritual Instruction* and elsewhere) that states the goal, or purpose, of the path of devotion and that of the path of knowledge are the same. Adi Sankara has elucidated the same in *Vivekachudamani* and other texts. As Self-inquiry constitutes the essential practice in Knowledge, so surrender does for devotion. In practice, there is no division between them. The result is Self-Knowledge, or Self-Realization as we often call it.

In answer to your questions:

Surrender is the dissolution of the ego, which is the false assumption of existing as an individual entity, and the delusive tendencies (vasanas) that appear as its forms. Surrender is only to God, which is the Self. That which is known as God in the context of the universe and which is known as the witnessing Consciousness in relation to the mind, is realized to be the nondual Self upon profound inquiry or complete surrender. That alone is real, and That alone exists. It is infinite and eternal, and Realization of it is of the same nature. Surrender should not be misinterpreted to mean some transient emotional change or temporary placement of mental attention on some objective thing such as the immediate sensory perceptions, a fleeting moment of time, etc.

The path to Self-Realization, whether practiced as inquiry or surrender, is completely joyful. It is sweet in the beginning, middle, and end. Ignorance alone is the cause of suffering. Surrender, or inquiry, destroys the ignorance by revealing it to be only ignorance. Both the delusion and its effects are found to be illusory. The Reality, which is of the nature of Being-Consciousness-Bliss, remains. That which is the end manifests as the means.

177

In surrender, attachments and misidentifications are abandoned, and happiness, the sense of reality, and identity return to their source, which is the one Self, or God. The false notions of "I" and "mine" compose ignorance, bondage, and suffering. Absence of "I" and "mine" is real Knowledge, Liberation, and limitless happiness. Self-inquiry eliminates the "I" and, with it, the "mine," while surrender eliminates the "mine," and, with it, the "I."

If one keenly discerns the nature of the ego or mind, there is found to be no such existent thing as an ego or a mind. Or it may be said that the individual "I" is Being misperceived and the mind is Consciousness misperceived. However, who is it that so misperceives? It cannot be the true absolute Self; nor are there two selves. If you inquire in such a manner, there is no misperception or one who possesses such.

One need not wait for or do something else previous to surrender. What has been indicated above can be practiced even now.

I hope that you find the above spiritually helpful, whether it finds a place in your book or not. If you decide to include it, it may benefit the reader to see the rest of this letter, as well. All the information about SAT, books, CDs, DVDs, downloads, etc. can be found at www.SATRamana.org. If you are going to include a list, you may find it beneficial to check this site close to your publication date, as there are new books about to be printed and new recordings being released frequently.

May you ever abide in That, as That, to which all surrender in one form or another, which is in truth that which all are, which is the innate, the unborn and imperishable, reaching which one does not return to samsara again, finding which one knows what is to be known, and merging with which one abides in happiness and peace that never end.

Ever yours in Truth,
Nome

[These are two messages from an aspirant in India who met Nome in Bangalore in the mid 1990's. Nome's response follows.]

April 25, 2009

Namaste Sri Nome,

Om Namo Bhagavathe Sri Ramanaya.

As I say every time, I continue to practice. But activity takes over me after this. I am not surrendering my work to the Lord. But I hear things will get favorable by Grace alone and this will help me to seek Liberation. You always advise me to not bemoan myself.

I do not know if I can tell you that I am in difficulty. Will this be for my entire current life (birth)?

I am taking liberty in asking this question since I thought I may try asking this to a Jnani. Will external worldly issues be dealt with by my own effort? I will be very happy if you can help me with this answer. If you can say, please give your wise counsel.

I was extremely reluctant to ask this question.

With Yours in Bhagavan,

April 26, 2009

Namaste.

Om Namo Bhagavathe Sri Ramanaya !

In the normal meditation that we practice, we remember the Lord and continue our practice. This is very beneficial because, as Sri A. R. Natarajan also reminds us, the remembrance of the Sadguru makes the Grace start functioning on our meditation.

The mind is nothing but the food we supply it with. The more we are turned toward the Lord the better we can meditate. The ability for the thoughts or the tamasic state like sleep or dullness is also not allowed to overtake one by the power of the Grace, by reminding ourselves of Grace or the Lord Himself, which becomes part of devotion.

179

I think one might have learned the first lessons when he recognizes that he can disassociate himself from the thoughts and the ability not to allow them to take over the mind. Then, the meditation flows.

In this way when the ego comes out, we ask the "Who am I?" and then again the mind subsides.

I felt like sharing this so that I may get even more suggestions or hints on practice of meditation, and I am just a beginner on the way.

Yours in Sri Bhagavan,

ॐ Dear . . . ,

Om Namo Bhagavate Sri Ramanaya

Namaste. By the Grace of the Sadguru, one is even able to commence meditation. By this same Grace, the meditation deepens. By this same Grace, the meditation reaches the zenith of perfection. Sri A. R. Natarajan knew fully the infinite extent and eternal nature of this Grace. In highest truth, Bhagavan, Grace, and the Self are identical.

Yes, remember Him, the Self, speak of Him, listen about Him and read of Him, think of Him, devote yourself to Him, contemplate Him, rely on Him, reflect on His spiritual instruction, deeply meditate upon that, Him, and, most importantly, inquiring "Who am I?" abide absorbed in Him, the Self, as the Self.

Self-inquiry not only causes the mind to subside temporarily, but also permanently in the realization of the nonexistence of the mind. Such is Self-Knowledge.

Ever yours in Sri Bhagavan,
Nome

[This message came from a Ramana devotee who is frequently at Sri Ramanasramam]

May 23, 2009

Dear Sir,

I attended the Maha Puja at Ramanasramam last Monday 18th.

I came across a person whom I helped when he came to CMC Hospital, but he did not recognize me and smiled at me. But I went and asked him. This hurts and I brood in my mind.

2. My colleague's daughter got more marks relatively. This, too, hurts my mind.

This does not affect me, and I do not even care. Why do these things affect my mind?

Why does Ramana fail to come to my rescue? Though the matter is nothing, these things brood in my mind.

With regards,

Yours in Sri Ramana,

ॐ Dear Sri . . . ,

Om Namo Bhagavate Sri Ramanaya

Namaste. Thank you for your message.

When you help someone, the joy in doing so derives from the indivisibility of the Self. That transcends the body and the mind and is free from the idea of a "person." It does not make any difference whether you receive appreciation or not, whether the person helped recognizes the fact or you or not. The joy is in the love that motivates you to help.

Similarly, it does not matter what is achieved or left unachieved. Inquire as the Maharshi instructs and abandon the false notion of being the performer of any action. As you define yourself, so do you conceive of others. Know yourself as the Self by relinquishing, through inquiry, the false definitions attributed to the Self. Thus, you will be at peace.

Similar is it with family relations. By Bhagavan's Grace, strive to realize your unborn nature. Then, you have no relations, though you are everyone. That is, attachment vanishes, and the blissful Existence of the Self remains.

Sri Ramana never fails. He has even brought you to the present point so that you can ask these questions. As

Ramana states in *Who am I?*, the disciple, for his part, must follow the path shown by the Guru. The brooding in the mind remains or returns only so long as you continue with that particular form of ignorance. When the ignorance is destroyed, peace shines. That which shines as peace then exists always. Therefore, there is no necessity to continue with such delusion. If you continue with the pursuit of what the Maharshi has taught, a time will come when you see that none of your ideas are true and the mind does not exist. Grace is ever present, just as the Self is ever-existent.

If you surrender all to Him, this will bring the same fruit.

You are fortunate to be at the Asramam. You are very fortunate to even know of Sri Ramana. You are blessed and fortunate beyond all measure to be able to practice according to His instruction, for in this are to be found liberation from all of the imagined bondage and the Realization of the Supreme Truth.

Ever yours in Sri Bhagavan,
Nome

[This message was from a devotee of Sri Ramana who is located in southern India.]

June 4, 2009

Dear Sir,

Last year, my daughter got through successfully in her higher secondary. She (and I, too) is interested in studying medicine. She was selected for graduate nursing course. In that batch, certain students entered with poor marks. She is now continuing with nursing course. As a rule, she is not supposed to appear again for medical entrance. Is it the will of God? At certain times, when these thoughts pass through my mind, I am depressed.

As per Gita, is it the will of God?

Yours in Sri Ramana,

ॐ Dear Sri . . . ,

Om Namo Bhagavate Sri Ramanaya

Namaste. Yes, all happens by the power of God and is ultimately for the highest good. Since all rests in God, we should, in our devotion, always acknowledge that fact and carry no attachment to anything of this illusory world. One who rests in God is absorbed in God and, having lost the falsely assumed separate individuality, remains undifferentiated from God. The happiness of that can never be disturbed.

Bhagavan cares for all. Rest in the knowledge that He knows what to do and when and how best to do it. Thus, the cause of suffering vanishes.

Ever yours in Sri Bhagavan,
Nome

[Another response to a seeker who had sent several messages expressing anxiety concerning health difficulties and relationships.]

June 25, 2009

ॐ Dear . . . ,

Om Namo Bhagavate Sri Ramanaya

Namaste. Thank you for your messages.

In the realization that the Self is not the body is found immense freedom and peace. The body is not the Self and, therefore, one should not misidentify with it. The body, though, is a temple, and should be treated accordingly. The body is a transient image in an unreal dream. The body is also to be regarded as an instrument to be used for divine service. The body is mere, inert matter. The body's lifetime is a precious opportunity not to be wasted. What pertains to a body is of no lasting significance. The body, itself, is a wondrous manifestation of the Supreme. One should not misidentify, and one should know the Self.

Better than oscillating between tamas and rajas, inertia and agitation, is steady inquiry in quest of the Self. If there are problems with the health of the body, better than dully pursuing previous habits and engaging in repetitive anxiety in the mind is to learn and discover how to care for your temple, your instrument, while liberating yourself from the tendency to misidentify with it.

Several times, you have described your worry about acceptance and the fear of rejection. They are two sides of the same idea. No one and nothing can give you what is innately yours, which is the happiness and love that you seek. When you finally look within and discover the treasure of Bliss-Consciousness, which is your very Being, you will see how needless was the worry and how false were the fears. Growing in wisdom within and thus attaining detachment from worldly illusions, you will joyfully comprehend the dissolution of bondage. Knowing your nature beyond the notion of existing as a person, you will find the perfect fullness, the infinite and the eternal. By profound inquiry to know yourself, you must discern the ignorant concepts for what they are, and, being concerned with the Reality rather than the miniscule imaginings surrounding an unreal ego, become absorbed in the real Self.

May you always abide in the Knowledge of the immutable Self and thus be ever happy at heart.

Ever yours in Truth,
Nome

[This message is in response to a seeker who asked about how to improve concentration in meditation and finished his question with: Every activity is predetermined by God. Are meditation and peace of mind also predetermined, or am I able to control them? Please clarify.]

July 8, 2009

ॐ Dear . . . ,

Om Namo Bhagavate Sri Ramanaya

Namaste. Concentration upon the inquiry is proportionate to the intensity of the desire for Liberation. Self-Knowledge is peace. It is not pre-determined, though it is perpetually existent, for the Self ever is, and the Self never is nonexistent. The inquiry, which is the deepest meditation, is always available. Dive within and realize.

Ever yours in Truth,
Nome

[The following message is from a seeker who lives at a distance from the temple. Nome's response follows.]

July 9, 2009

Namaste Nome,

Meditation is going well, but I am still working to build a more consistent strength of mind. What seems always critical is marshalling the alertness and presence to claim my identity as the mover of attention; otherwise, I slump into the lazy habit of an unquestioning follower of thoughts.

A dear friend is dying of cancer—only a few more days left. She brings a strength and a grace and lack of anxiety that seems to point to a deeper confidence, a confidence that I've not heard her talk about. I hold the Advaita bhava in my heart and remember that all this appears in Brahman alone.

I probably should be asking more questions. I am thoroughly hearing and contemplating the CD/DVD offerings of SAT and reading the *Gita*.

Many thanks and Aloha,

July 9, 2009

ॐ Dear . . . ,

Namaste. Thank you for your message.

Before birth, throughout life, and after death, Brahman is. That alone truly is. Appearances do not alter it in any degree. That is the formless, bodiless Self. That alone you are. That is the existence of all.

Observation of death can be a powerful reminder of immortal Being, the illusory character of worldly appearances and detachment from the same, the bodiless nature of the Self, and the importance of intense, focused spiritual practice of Self-inquiry to realize the Self.

You are ever the unmoving Knower of all modes and states of mind, inclusive of attention and diffusion. The Knower is Consciousness. It should not be misidentified with any thought, mode, or state.

Listening and meditating, as well as reading the *Gita*, are beneficial.

May your meditations continue to deepen, and may you abide as the deathless Being-Consciousness-Bliss, in perfect peace.

Ever yours in Truth,
Nome

[This is a response to a seeker who expressed feelings of joy experienced while listening to recordings of satsang at SAT as he drove to work.]

July 15, 2009

ॐ Dear . . . ,

Om Namo Bhagavate Sri Ramanaya
Namaste. Thank you for your message. Limitless happiness is innate. Being is, itself, Bliss. Self-Knowledge simply reveals the ever-existent Truth by its own Light. If you are able to visit SAT in California, you will be quite welcome.

Ever yours in Truth,
Nome

[As can be inferred from this response, a seeker raised questions about higher experience and samadhi, the loss of such experience, detachment from action, sorrow concerning personal problems, and a mental technique of the "redirection" of anger that he was attempting to use. This is Nome's reply.]

July 15, 2009

ॐ Dear . . . ,

Om Namo Bhagavate Sri Ramanaya
Namaste. Thank you for your several messages.
There are innumerable modes of mind. One self-luminous Consciousness knows all of them. Savikalpa means "with differentiation." Nirvikalpa means "without differentiation." Various yogis and rishis have employed these terms in various ways. For some, savikalpa signifies samadhi with some aspect of perception or thought, such as upon the indivisible nature of Existence, and such, while nirvikalpa is

187

that in which all perception and thoughts are absent. In the short text entitled *Drg-drsya-viveka (The Discrimination of the Seer and the Seen)*, Adi Sankara, the wondrous Acarya, defines savikalpa samadhi in terms of the means of entrance, such as meditation on the unreality of the world, and such, and further delineates interior and exterior kinds of these, while nirvikalpa samadhi entails entrance without differentiation, with the essence of the samadhi being the same in all. The same description is found in *Talks with Sri Ramana Maharshi* and is reiterated in the glossary of *Ribhu Gita* and the *Song of Ribhu*. Certainly, the distinctions and the questions regarding such do not arise in samadhi. Abide as the Self, and samadhi is found to be the natural, innate (sahaja) state.

Whenever the ego dissolves and in proportion to its dissolution, higher experience shines. If the ego emerges and in proportion to the misidentifications and attachments conjured up, the higher experience fades. First the ego is imagined, and the experience is considered objective rather than one's very Existence. Then, it becomes memory. Then, it fades, unless one practices. Therefore, Self-inquiry should be ardently practiced until the notion of individuality is impossible.

Along with detachment from action, detachment from the results of action, contemplation upon transience, and discrimination regarding happiness, the very idea of being a performer of action (kartrtva), which involves misidentification with the body, senses, and mind, should be questioned.

It is beneficial to wisely examine in order to destroy the root cause, along with the manifest thoughts, etc. of "problems." It is worthless to bemoan oneself, which involves the repetitive adherence to unexamined ideas, or to ascribe outer causes for one's own imagined ignorance, bondage, or unhappiness. So, continue to inwardly discern the inner Bliss of Being that is the actual source of happiness and love. Truly discern ignorance as ignorance, and it will be gone.

While sadness or despair may be a starting place for spiritual aspiration, such as expressed by Rama in the opening portion of *Yoga Vasishta*, it vanishes, along with the ideas constituting such, as soon as a deep inquiry commences, as expressed in the entirety of the remainder of that scripture and countless other texts.

Anger (krodha) is rooted in kama (desire) and avidya (ignorance). Destruction of the ignorant root is essential for freedom from it. Redirection of the anger, let alone, at the Maharshi, is not advisable. By doing such, the preposterous and presumptuous character of doing so may seem so starkly evident that it affords some relief from or temporary abeyance of the anger, but the causes will still be left intact to resume later, and, moreover, such redirection is fraught with far too many errors and delusions than can be elaborated upon here in this message. Destruction by true Knowledge is fruitful, and the fruit endures. If you must redirect, redirect the anger, or the intensity lent to the anger, at the anger, itself, intent upon no longer carrying on with such illusion.

The above answers a number of questions and points raised in your messages of the last three weeks or so. I hope that you find these answers and comments helpful.

May you abide absorbed in the Bliss of the Self, and, by the Grace of Sri Bhagavan, remain in the steady Knowledge of That, as That, itself.

Ever yours in Truth,
Nome

[After an absence of more than twenty years, a seeker visited satsang again and sent a message, the gist of which can be inferred from the response.]

July 21, 2009

ॐ Dear . . . ,

Namaste. Thank you for your message. If you examine finely, you will observe that some kind of ego-dissolution is the cause of every deeper or higher experience, every freedom from fear, every shining of joy and peace, etc. Egolessness is the real Knowledge-essence. The Knowledge-essence is what makes any spiritual practice fruitful and is the root of all that is true, good, and beautiful. You are always welcome to attend satsang.

Ever yours in Truth,
Nome

≡
•

[A seeker wrote: I have a question. Prior to consciousness, there is no appearance. The Self is prior to consciousness. When the appearance of being a body-mind organism goes back to the elements, the awareness is still the same. What is meant by the term "Parabrahman"? This is the reply.]

July 26, 2009

ॐ Dear . . . ,

Om Namo Bhagavate Sri Ramanaya
Namaste. Thank you for your message.
Parabrahma means, of course, Supreme Brahman. "Brahman" is without a direct translation into English, though we could say "the vast (literally, expansive) Absolute," in order to express some sense of its meaning.
As stated by you, the Self is prior to the awareness that conceives of objects, often referred to as the mind. Prior should be understood not only as in time but as the Self's

190

nonobjective nature, which is perpetual and entirely free of the awareness (mind, mental attention, etc.) and its imagined objects, be they gross (the world, senses, etc.) or subtle (thought, etc.). Indeed, it is only from the supposed position of a mind, or the misidentification as the individual "I," that one can speak of its appearance and such. If, as Sri Bhagavan instructs, one inquires as to who is this "I," the individuality or mind, being unreal, vanishes, and the Self alone remains. For this Self, which is unborn, there is no creation or appearance. The Self alone is real. This Self is Brahman and is also called Parabrahman. Thus the mahavakya-s (great aphorisms), Ayamatma Brahma (This Self is Brahman) and Aham Brahmasmi (I am Brahman). It is realized with the Supreme Knowledge innate to the Self that shines upon profound inquiry. That Knowledge is pure Consciousness. Thus: Prajnanam Brahma (Supreme Knowledge is Brahman). In this Knowledge, Being and Knowing are one and the same.

As with Dakshinamurti, regarding the Truth of the Supreme Brahman, the Maharshi's Silence is most eloquent.

I hope the above is of some help for you.

May you ever abide in Brahman as Brahman, without the least trace of misidentification or differentiation, and thus be always happy and at peace.

Ever yours in Truth,
Nome

[A response to another seeker:]

August 2, 2009

ॐ Dear . . . ,

Namaste. Thank you for your message. Working in a way to help others is noble. Such can go on simultaneously with inquiry to know the Self.

The humble recognition that one is in need of Self-Knowledge motivates the introspective practice of Self-inquiry. Earnest application of the spiritual instruction within yields the joyful fruit of peace and happiness. The freedom for which you yearn is within you.

May your meditations be deep as you find the fountainhead of joy within, your true Self.

Ever yours in Truth,
Nome

[This is a response to a seeker who had temporarily fallen under the influence of the rhetoric of someone who disparages some spiritual leaders, teachers, etc. He returned to calmness, yet said in his message, "I must go this road without any guru."]

August 4, 2009

ॐ Dear . . . ,

Om Namo Bhagavate Sri Ramanya

Namaste. Thank you for your message. It is good to see that your mind is calmer and expres sive of the peace and love that are natural for you.

May I offer a friendly suggestion? As with any suggestion, you are free to accept or reject it. If you find it useful, it is yours. If you find it otherwise, you can dismiss it as being only so much prattle. You need not respond to it, though you may if you so desire.

Upon examination, one finds that how he approaches—the orientation of his mind—very much determines his understanding and experience. Just as one does not realize nonduality from concepts of duality, or arrive at happiness by increasing the causes of suffering, so one would not wish to use worldly or delusive ways of thinking, or mentalities, in the pursuit of his spirituality.

It is quite evident to many that Bhagavan Sri Ramana Maharshi is a Sadguru, which is a true Guru who reveals the Truth. Of course, his view of himself is only the sole-existent Self. Yet, for those of us who are ever grateful for his Grace and revelation of true Knowledge, he remains the Sadguru, as well. That a few websites decry him, that some supposedly have written nasty and false things about him, and that Sri Ramanasramam has been forced to defend itself in litigation (Sri Ramana was even called upon to be a witness!) for many decades are of no consequence. Why? It is because such samsaric activities are carried out by a few individuals who are delusively bound in their own dreams, and such has nothing to do with the vast Truth and the purpose of spirituality (let alone the purpose of Advaita Vedanta). I would recommend that you deeply pursue Sri Ramana's teachings.

The approach to one's spirituality is very important. Therefore, at some point, you may find it beneficial to examine what approach aggravated your mind. It is not just a matter of what makes one a gullible victim of propaganda, though those who attempt to perpetrate such probably count on that mentality to wield influence and promote hysteria, so that even what is true, good, and beautiful is made to appear as if otherwise, and distorted false appearance is made to seem as if real. How does one formulate his opinions? Why does he formulate such opinions or use his mind in such a way? Is there any difference between that mentality and that of worldly-minded individuals who are not endowed with a spiritual practice? Is such helpful at all or even wholesome? Is judging others, let alone on what basis, helpful or antithetical to knowing oneself? Is not such actually utterly unrelated to spirituality? Is it necessary to mix such with one's practice? Is such contrary to the blissful wisdom one is attempting to realize? What is the cause of anger, frustration, fear, and hysteria? Is any good purpose served in ridiculing others or employing caustic expletives in one's speech? Would it be wiser to be thankful for whatever benefit comes from anywhere and dive within by inquiry? This list of questions could continue, but this much should suffice as an example of how it is possible to examine and question. Besides, as this body has Parkinson's Disease, it is nearing its limits for typing at this time.

So, the suggestion is twofold: Dive deep into the inquiry and Knowledge revealed by the Maharshi and question. Question much more than what you may be accustomed to, and be sure to direct your questioning to the workings of your own mind. In this way, that which is sublime unfolds.

Please accept apologies for the length of this message. At SAT, we always try to do our loving best for anyone who even once expresses interest in Sri Ramana and his teachings. If the above is not to your liking now, you may wish to consider printing it out and retaining it to read in the future.

May you abide in the joyful peace of the Knowledge of the Self.

Ever yours in Sri Bhagavan,
Nome

[From the same seeker came another message in which he said, "There are too many charlatans in the advaita field. I am concerned that the message be delivered as clearly and as truly as possible, the way Ramana delivered it." He also wished that Nome would do something to refute the defamatory falsehoods stated by that disparaging person mentioned above that had upset him. Here is the response from Nome.]

August 5, 2009

ॐ Dear . . . ,

194

Om Namo Bhagavate Sri Ramanya

Namaste. Thank you for your message. If someone knowingly says falsehood about someone else and is refuted, he will just create another falsehood for he retains the same motivation. If a person uses the mind in such a way as to be susceptible to believing in such falsehoods, the refutation will not necessarily clear his confusion or doubt. Therefore, pursuit of such preservation of one's good name is not truly worthwhile. In light of the eternal, what does it matter? Even in a mere ten thousand years, who will remember? Purnam (perfect fullness) and Ananda (Bliss) are within, so what does it matter? In the illimitable Brahman, what does it matter? Even in this mere vast universe, what does it matter?

Whether you think that there are charlatans or not is not significant. Is your purpose to gauge others or to inquire within yourself? Why waste time forming the mind into opinions about individuals who do not actually exist? Who will determine who is to be held in higher esteem and who not and upon what conceived basis? Ask yourself if such concerns do anything to eliminate the illusion of ego and bondage.

Anyone can put into practice that which Sri Bhagavan Ramana teaches and find the truth of it himself.

If anyone finds what SAT does helpful, he can avail himself of it as he pleases. If that is not so, one is free to look elsewhere. The same is so for any other place, event, teacher, etc.

May you abide in the unconditional happiness and peace of the Self.

Ever yours in Sri Ramana,
Nome

[From the same seeker: "I think what was happening to me was fear. The no-thing, awareness, is what is real. There is no claiming this fear, so what to worry. I apologize for such short

195

*sightedness. Peace and love always." The reference to "your sug-
gestion" in Nome's response refers to a suggestion regarding
health.]*

August 6, 2009

ॐ Dear . . . ,

Om Namo Bhagavate Ramanaya
Namaste. Thank you for your suggestion.
As you may recall, Sri Ramana was known to make
good use of everything. It is a lesson for all not only regarding physical matters, but spiritually as well. At your leisure,
you may find it useful to review the messages sent to you,
as well as what you wrote, to see how much more can be
learned from such. The Maharshi said that Self-Realization
is attained by destruction of vasanas (tendencies). So, hunt
for the vasanas commented upon or implied, or expressed
in what you wrote. Recognize them, discern the ideas composing them, and trace those ideas to their root definitions,
which are the misidentifications. Then, destroy them with
the inquiry (Who am I?).
For example, you mentioned fear. Fear is only in duality
and is always fear of something known. Apart from the
ideas constituting that known thing (state, condition, etc.),
there is no emotion of fear. The same holds true of anger,
etc. So, of what is the fear? Determine with precision that
idea or those ideas. Then, trace inward as just described. By
such Knowledge, which is of the nature of the essential
inquiry, you truly and permanently free yourself of the fear,
emotion, etc. The tendencies are not merely observed; they
are destroyed, as darkness is in the presence of light. They
become impossible. Likewise is it for moods, etc. The unreal is destructible. The vasanas are not real.
In addition to the discrimination regarding vasanas and
freedom from them, other aspects were expressed, implied,
or demonstrated by example in the replies sent to you. You
can search for and observe them and make them your own.

If there remain any further questions regarding how a person falls into delusion so that he misdirects the instruments of his body, speech, and mind and creates karma and such, you can refer to the *Bhagavad Gita* chapter 2, verses 62 and 63, which are best understood by reading Sri Sankara's commentary upon them. It may serve to explain the mentality of those whose activities agitated your mind.

May your inquiry be so profound that the very seed of illusion is found to be nonexistent, so that your peace abides forever.

Ever yours in Truth,
Nome

[Upon the publication of Saddarsanam and an Inquiry into the Revelation of Truth and Oneself and Advaita Devatam, copies were sent to Sri Ramanasramam, among others. A reply was received, and this was written in response to that reply.]

August 14, 2009

ॐ Dear Sri . . . ,

Om Namo Bhagavate Sri Ramanaya
Namaste. Thank you for your two messages.

It can readily be seen that, while the content of devotion to Sri Bhagavan and reveling in his sublime teachings is the same as that to which all devotees of Sri Ramana are accustomed, some of the manner of expression, most noticeably the format of the books, is, in some respects, a little different. This, it is hoped, will not detract or distract from the essential message. Whether or not either or both of them are suitable for Sri Ramanasramam's book depot is not known by me.

As for the price of the books: the cost is allowing us at SAT to joyfully give them to you for free, should you decide that these books may serve some purpose for devotees there. It would be unthinkable for us to receive funds from Sri Ramanasramam. The treasure of Grace and Knowledge bestowed by the Guru is immeasurably vast and precious beyond description. What little we are able to offer is symbolic of our heartfelt gratitude.

As for the appearance of the names of [names omitted] in the introduction, your point is, of course, true and very well stated: "Sri Bhagavan is the only One in Sri Ramanasramam always acting in action." Please permit me to offer some explanation, albeit a bit light-heartedly. In accordance with this understanding, it may also be said that it can be considered well-established that, when devotees fondly mention, with regard, other devotees, even thankful for their devotion and the selfless service that manifests such, it is actually the Existence of the Guru that is acknowledged and praised. The Guru is within them, indeed is their very Being, without there really being any "them" or "their," but only Him and His. So, it is Sri Bhagavan who is acknowledged in the introductions, even if this is also expressed in the names and forms of His devotees. Thus, to paraphrase the well-known passage of the Upanishad, the devotees are loved for the sake of the Self, [name omitted] of Sri Ramanasramam is loved for the sake of the Self. Having surrendered your bodies, minds, etc. to Sri Bhagavan, they and their activities belong to Him completely. They have become implements in His hands, and mention, with respect and love, of the implements held and wielded by those divine hands serves only to glorify that God who holds them and who is the one Power and One Existence in all. That One is and always will be Sri Ramana. Thus, any fault in expressing thankfulness in the introductions ought to be excused due to the sincerity of motive, and likewise should that accidentally happen again in the future.

In light of "Sri Bhagavan is the only One in Sri Ramanasramam always acting in action," the natural humility and purity of heart are revealed. Such are considered praiseworthy by the wise. Of course, this deep humility and purity of heart manifest as a refusal to accept expressions of gratitude and a redirecting even of the appearance of such to Sadguru Ramana, which is also lauded by the wise. So, as you can see, I now need to be excused again for this "problem" of loving appreciation for you who are dear.

Awaiting your further response, at your leisure, and remaining One with you in Him,

Ever yours in Sri Bhagavan,
Nome

[A response to a seeker:]

August 14, 2009

ॐ Dear . . . ,

Om Namo Bhagavate Sri Ramanya

Namaste. Clarity of knowledge regarding the Self is the cessation of ignorance, which is in the form of misidentifications and attachments, and its consequent suffering. Happiness is of your very Being. That is timeless. To conceive it as past, present, or future may still be regarded as partial, for the eternal Self is all-transcendent. Therefore, the Maharshi revealed Self-Knowledge and taught the nonobjective inquiry of "Who am I?" Whoever so steadily inquires knows the blissful Truth of the Self and is what she knows.

Ever yours in Truth,
Nome

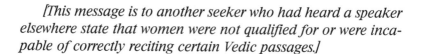

[This message is to another seeker who had heard a speaker elsewhere state that women were not qualified for or were incapable of correctly reciting certain Vedic passages.]

August 18, 2009

ॐ Dear . . . ,

Namaste. In light of our conversation on Sunday, here are a few additional points.

The purport of the Veda is supreme Knowledge. This is the Knowledge of Brahman, which is neither male nor female nor any other conception.

The Self is bodiless and is Brahman. It cannot be male, female, or any similar conception.

"The knower of Brahman becomes Brahman." That is, to know Brahman one ceases to misidentify with the body and such, including the attributes of such, and remains as Brahman; and only the bodiless Self can know itself.

Any interpretation of the scriptures that liberates one from imagined limitations (upadhi-s) is true. Any interpretation that maintains or extends the bondage is a misinterpretation, for the scriptures are for a divine purpose and not for binding one more to the delusions of samsara.

If the above is comprehended, the discrimination about what was said by the speaker to whom you were listening will be self-evident.

Now, for some speculative considerations:

Adi Sankaracarya may or may not have said what that speaker attributed to him. Supposing that such was said by him, the reason may be found in the passage cited if such can be located. For example, when Sankara says "just as" (yatha) and inserts an example before saying "just so" (tatha), it is the exemplified that is the truth and no emphasis is placed on the validity or otherwise of the example. So, if he were to say, with an example conforming to the custom at the time, just as a woman does not recite the Veda, just so the mind cannot know the Self, it would be the latter that is the truth, and the former serves only the purpose of an example and does not at all indicate any kind of injunction.

Practical considerations at a given time, such as the requirement of one kind or tone of voice should not be considered of any spiritual weight for those endowed with a practice of jnana. Similarly, rules that define the performance of rituals in the karma khanda do not relate to those who practice the jnana khanda. The goal, purpose, practice, and qualifications for jnana are distinct from that of karma, with the exception that the karma can be considered purifying for the mind to prepare some seekers for jnana who have not entered the jnana marga directly. What is said of jnana is also true of bhakti; thus the incident of Jnanadeva causing the buffalo to recite the Vedas when he was challenged by those whose narrow minds had missed the intention of the Vedas.

Symbolic expression, also, must be understood and not misunderstood. When men and women are on either side of a temple, the significance is not the separation of the men and the women. For example, the murti of Siva (and his entire shrine) is on the left and that of the Devi is on the right (His left). The men and women worshippers are divided, according to the tradition of the temple, so that they are aligned to the murtis in that manner or so they, themselves, are in that configuration. Similar is it with the rest of what is in the tradition. It should be deeply understood for one's benefit and not misunderstood for one's detriment.

To say that women cannot correctly recite is an absurdly useless statement. If mispronunciation is what is desired, there are plenty of men who can do a fine job of making a mess of a recitation! It is not an attribute that can be claimed for women alone. If what is meant by "recite" is "knowledge," only the unmanifested Brahman (Siva, symbolically male) in you can do so truly and correctly, and not the manifested or manifesting shakti, symbolically female.

The same holds true of Gayatri. That which is the vivify-er and illuminator of all the minds, the one to be worshipped, the Knowledge of which is secret from the ego and the worldly, which is to be known by those who identify as Brahman that courses through the three states and is the one Existence in all the triads, is obviously neither male nor female.

I hope that the above offers some further clarification for you.

Ever yours in Truth,
Nome

[Here is a letter written by a seeker who wrote a few times previously, obtaining answers to his questions. Nome's response follows.]

August 19, 2009

Namaste guruji. Many thanks for taking my questions. There is a song that goes, "torn between two lovers, feeling like a fool" that describes my current confusion. I understand when Sri Bhagawan says, "Go back to where you came from" as to follow the breath or "I thought" and see where they arise from. That is the Self-Brahman-Consciousness. So it is said in Mahavakya "aham brahmaasmi." According to Sri Nisargadatta Maharaj, "Follow the I-thought and remain in pure consciousness and beyond will take over." As he explains, I understood consciousness is temporary because it depends on the food-body. When it is no more, the consciousness merges into Absolute-Parabrahma. So, my confusion is this: Sri Bhagawan never mentions Parabrahma, but I am sure they both are talking about the same thing. All these different words—atma-self-consciousness-turiya-parabrahman-paramaatma-make it hard for me, who am looking for the way home. Once and for all, tell me what is my home and how do I know I am not in the wrong house?

My second question is why is so much emphasis placed on getting out of the cycle of birth and death, when, in each life, we don't remember who or what or where we were in a previous life! If all this maya is God lila, so He can experience it all, why the "Who am I?" to stop or deny that? If I had a wish, I would tell God to give me many human lives with no ego to go with it and remembrance of Self in each one.

Third question: Why are kanchan (gold) and kaamini (women) called the main roadblock to Self-realization? What is the logical connection? Women I can understand because it keeps one rooted in body-consciousness—or the physical level, but how about wealth?

These are the questions occupying my mind for a long time. I want to put them to rest before I come to the retreat, so that, when I am sitting with you, I am there completely without any monkey business from my mind to sidetrack me.

I hope this letter finds you in good health. My greetings to Saswati and the rest.

Namaste and thanks again.

August 19, 2009

ॐ Dear . . . ,

Om Namo Bhagavate Sri Ramanaya
Namaste. Thank you for your message.

There is only one Self, and that alone is the true abode. If you were required to select among several objects, a mistake could be possible, but the Self is nonobjective and, therefore, there is no multiplicity, choice, or division for it.

This Self is Brahman (ayamatma brahma, aham Brahmasmi, etc.). Inconceivable, but realized in Self-Knowledge, Saccidananda is a description of it. The very same Being is called Parabrahman to indicate its absolute nature, that that alone exists, and to indicate transcendence of any conception of saguna (with attributes) Brahman. In relation to the three states, it is called Turiya, and, describing it as beyond all states, it is called Turiyatita. It is the Self, Atman, but, if such is conceived by the seeker as jivatman (individual), he is instructed to know the Supreme Self (Paramatman), which alone is truly the Self. In relation to all the minds and thoughts, this same Consciousness is called the Witness, and in relation to the universe, it is known as God, the Supreme Lord, the All-pervading One, etc. To inquire into the nature of your very Existence and thus know it as it is, free from the least trace of misidentification, is essential. If that is accomplished, the significance of all these terms and instructions is self-evident.

Citta, vijnana, etc., which perhaps may be better translated as mind, awareness or intellect, etc., being unreal, are connected with the other sheaths and pass away, but the innate Consciousness (Cit), which is Being, is unborn and imperishable. I do not know if Bhagavan employed the term "Parabrahman" often or not, but certainly the *Ribhu Gita*, recited frequently in his presence and referred to by him often, uses the term hundreds of times.

In your wish, you say that you want to always know, or remember, the Self and to remain egoless. One who knows the Self is only the Self. Not having been born, he does not die. For that which neither is born nor dies, there is no rebirth. For this Self, there is no maya. Maya means that which is not. The Realization of such to be the case is its cessation. The assumption that one is an individual leads to the conception of embodiment and, from there, illusorily appears the entire samsara, like things imagined in a dream. The destruction, or abandonment, of that ego-notion is the end of the imagined cycle, which seemed so real in delusion, but which is found to be nonexistent in the light of Self-Knowledge.

If you accept that all at all times is the play (lila) of God, you should also consider that there is nothing with which God can play other than Himself. There is no second thing to limit God's infinity or to appear within God's indivisibility. So, God is the material and efficient cause of all ever, without actually becoming a cause at all. Uncaused and indivisible is God, so that God alone is, and it is only the mind's conception that there is a play and such. To surrender the ego means the dissolution of even that mind. This is to give yourself up to your original source. God alone remains, the beginning-less and endless.

By "women, gold, etc." in the scriptures is meant detachment. Attachment, born of confusion regarding the source of happiness, is the obstacle. Inert "gold" is not. A "woman" is not, unless the seeker of Liberation is a woman, in which case, she would want to disidentify from her body, just as a man would need to disidentify from his. With knowledge of the source of happiness (it is within, and within is the Self, thus Sat-Cit-Ananda), one becomes nonattached to all things in the world and is at peace.

It is good that you raised these questions. You need not worry if any "monkey business" of the mind arises during the retreat. With the Maharshi's teaching, all "monkeys" are cared for perfectly.

Ever yours in Truth,
Nome

[A message was received from a seeker that expressed his questions and doubts about care for the body, desires, and fears. Here is Nome's response.]

August 19, 2009

ॐ Dear . . . ,

Om Namo Bhagavate Sri Ramanaya
Namaste. Thank you for your message.

It is natural that every creature values its life. Transcendence of the bodily form and of the prana (animating life energy) and detachment, which are attained by Knowledge, are not antithetical to care of the body. However, whether or not the care is temporarily successful, and all bodies are transient, one is thereby (by the transcendent Knowledge) free of suffering.

To know that happiness is within and not dependent on anything else, such as things and circumstances, is the dawn of wisdom.

Yes, as the Upanishad proclaims, where there is duality, as it were, there is fear. Freedom from dualism is freedom from fear. Therefore, ardently inquire to know yourself.

If you are not already doing so, you may find it helpful to read, even a little, each day from teachings of Sri Ramana, Sri Sankara, or from books like *Self-Knowledge*.

May you abide in the deep Knowledge of the Self and thus be ever happy.

Ever yours in Truth,
Nome

[In response to several messages from a seeker, the following message was sent. The nature of the questions can be inferred from the answers.]

August 30, 2009

ॐ Dear . . . ,

Namaste. Thank you for your numerous messages during the last ten days. Between the retreat just completed, other matters that required attention, and this body's Parkinson's Disease, which limits the dexterity required to type, this is the first opportunity to respond in writing.

With a little examination, it should be easily observable by you that the confusion and suffering in the mind are due to an undue emphasis on, or preoccupation with, the supposed individual and his desires (materially fulfilled or not). When this occurs, the mind provides turmoil for itself accompanied by sadness. Sense of proportion is lost, and the delusive tendency that conceives that such a state (both internal and external) will continue forever may be generated. On the far tail end, the angst and suffering may even become so manifested in one's conduct that the behavior or communication lends itself to promoting the very thing feared or that one desires to avert. In addition, one sorrows over supposed lost opportunities while ignoring the present opportunity.

Turn inward and become peacefully nonattached in the understanding of the source of happiness. Thereby, the sense of proportion will return or be found anew. Reflect on what you have read, heard, and observed regarding happiness.

Consider how much "space" would be in your mind if you ceased to conjure up the clutter of the racing, yet circular, patterns of ideas that are illusorily fixated on the personality that is the outgrowth of the ego notion. Bemoaning one's plight and wallowing in misplaced self-pity over one's supposed incompleteness are not to be equated with the self-critical examination to destroy misconceptions that proceeds to the inquiry that reveals the innate perfection. Discriminate when you use your mind for either and choose the wiser path.

Each seeker may feel that his bondage is the worst, his darkness the densest, his capacity the most inadequate, his path the longest, his obstacles the most difficult, his problems unique, etc. In truth, such is not so. Whatever you encounter in your experience and practice has been met by those who have trod the path before you. Having found freedom from the entire illusion, they hold forth their hands, as it were, and beckon you to join in the bliss, showing what is true and how to find it, rousing you from delusion's dream, revealing the fulfillment of the purpose of life, unveiling the Truth within you.

The ego is unreal. So, there is little point in cogitating over what kind of ego one supposedly has. Deeply inquire into who you are, and Self-Knowledge will dawn.

May you abide in the perfect fullness, which is Brahman alone, and know that alone to be your Self.

Ever yours in Truth,
Nome

[This message was sent by a devotee who had returned to India for a visit. Nome's response follows.]

September 2, 2009

Dear Nome,

Namaste.

Yesterday was Vamana jayanti, the avatar taken by Vishnu to destroy the ego for the demon king Mahabali, who was supposed to have ruled Kerala during that time. It is celebrated as Onam festival. We read chapters in Srimad Bhagavatam that described the rule of Mahabali, birth of Vamana murti etc. I am sure that Sept. 1st event would have gone very well.

Reflecting and meditating upon the teachings of Sri Ramana heard during retreat and satsangs have been filling up this mind in vacation. It is indeed very peaceful.

Om Namo Bhagavate Sri Ramanaya
Om Namah Sivaya

ॐ Dear . . . ,

The pervasive One, the Supreme, who seems as if small due to subtlety, is realized as limitless, transcendently "striding" over the three worlds, as soon as the ego is humbled, even so much as by giving the opportunity to observe the extent of that true Self, leaving the apparent "I" to engage in conducting only what pertains at the lowest level, the manifested experience, and that, too, in devotion and only by the divine Grace of that Supreme One.

September 1st went very well here.

Om Namo Bhagavate Sri Ramanaya
Om Namah Sivaya

Ever yours in Truth,
Nome

[This is a response to a seeker whose mind was mired in anger at others and who asked questions that can be inferred from the response.]

September 14, 2009

ॐ Dear . . . ,

Om Namo Bhagavate Sri Ramanaya
Namaste. Thank you for your recent messages.

If you perceive the needlessness of the ignorance that is the cause of what you may find deplorable, you will be endowed with compassion rather than be swept up in anger, hatred, etc., which are rooted in delusion. Furthermore, by the realization of the divine Self within you, you will see the same Self in all and everywhere.

It is also quite useful to not employ the mind in sweeping generalizations of people, such as the formation of opinions about them. Are all people of a certain category conceived in the mind like that? Has one even met all of them, let alone been able to know them? Even simple questions can unravel the absurd tendencies of manifested ignorance.

The craving for acceptance and the fear of rejection are two sides of the same erroneous concept regarding the source of happiness.

However you practice, for final Realization, you must know yourself. How else is one to know the Self except by constant, profound inquiry? If you find various methods of meditation helpful to acquire concentration, then use the concentration thus gained to dive into Self-inquiry. The inquiry, though, is always available and does not depend on any preliminary method. Self-Knowledge alone is Liberation from all of the imagined bondage.

May your continuing earnest efforts bear the fruit of steady Knowledge of the Self, so that you abide in lasting peace and bliss.

Ever yours in Truth,
Nome

[Another response to the same seeker.]

September 17, 2009

ॐ Dear . . . ,

Om Namo Bhagavate Sri Ramanaya
Namaste. Thank you for your messages.

Concentration is a mode of mind that derives its intensity from the luminous Self, yet is placed within the context of thought or mental attention. The concentration may be external, that is upon some object or the breath, or internal, upon some mental conception or mental image, such being of a spiritual character. The value of such lies in the abeyance of other thoughts, though temporary, and the faith in the spiritual ideal contemplated. Dharana (concentration) is not an end in itself, and the yogis say that one should proceed to dhyana (meditation). Such should involve the dissolution of the mind or the transcendence of thought. This, also, is not the end, but one should then enter into samadhi, your questions about which were answered previously. The highest and nonobjective form of meditation is Atma-vicara (Self-inquiry), which reveals sahaja samadhi or sahaja sthiti, absorption or steady abidance in the Innate as the Innate, which is Self-Knowledge. Such inquiry and Knowledge are jnana. The inquiry, thus, is not a mere shift of attention or the repetition of a mental mode, but a profound questioning of your very identity to inwardly discern your Being as it truly is. Such inquiry is inherently mind-transcendent.

You may find it helpful to refer again to the previous comments in several messages about happiness, detachment, and viewing things in proportion. Otherwise, as you can observe with some reflection, an idea such as a desire seems to occupy your entire experience, just as, if one places the small tip of his smallest finger before his eye, it seems to occupy the entire scene and blocks out the view of all else, for example large mountains, the sky, the stars, etc. It is perfectly alright to read and reflect upon the same passages again and again until the inner comprehension dawns. Some books, such as *Self-Knowledge*, are intended for such use.

From another angle of vision, from what you have been relating in your messages, you can see how even one idea can continually rise and appear so important when you project even a drop of that which is of the Self upon it: happiness, identity, and reality. If, with wise discrimination, the same importance were placed upon Self-Realization, for the sake of the direct experience of that full happiness, true identity, and absolute Reality, how focused, intense and consuming would your spiritual practice become?

A tendency many times repeated may require sustained effort to be destroyed. Such effort should be perseverance in knowledge in the form of profound inquiry.

From still another perspective, if you are destined to be married or have a companion in the future, all the anxious thought and craving concerning it will amount to so much wasted time and purposeless suffering. If you are destined to live singly, all that anxious thought and craving will be a waste of precious time that could be spent more joyfully and wisely. Either way, the depth and purpose of life is to be found and fulfilled within.

Find within yourself that which is perfectly full regardless of whether you are alone or in the company of others.

If the inner understanding is clarified, and thus one is endowed with inquiry and detachment that blossom as Knowledge, the actions will become harmonious of themselves.

> Humility is essential.
> It is natural for anyone who
> Abides as the Self,
> Inquires to know the Self,
> Comprehends the vastness of Brahman,
> Knows the Truth,
> Perceives the magnitude and depth of the
> great sages,
> Considers the significance of immortality,
> Sees the approach of death,
> Notices the fragility and precariousness of life,
> Contemplates upon God,
> Observes the play of his own mind,
> Discerns the insignificance of his own thoughts,
> Considers the immensity of this mere, entire
> universe,
> Recognizes the smallness of his transient body,
> Feels the fullness of love,
> Experiences the magnificent perfection that
> is always,
> Or who has found Grace.

Ever yours in Truth,
Nome

[A brief response to a seeker:]

September 17, 2009

ॐ Dear . . . ,

Om Namo Bhagavate Sri Ramanaya

Namaste. Your note arrived today.

By inquiring deeply and steadily within, you will find the Self as it truly exists. In this Self, as this Self, there is no division or separation at all. Abide blissfully in this supreme Knowledge.

May you ever abide on the Knowledge of the eternal, infinite Being-Consciousness-Bliss, the sole-existent Self, your only true "I," and thus be ever happy and at peace.

Ever yours in Truth,
Nome

[These are two responses to a seeker who expressed worry over some mistakes that he had made and raised some questions about love.]

September 22, 2009

ॐ Dear . . . ,

Namaste. Thank you for your message.

If a man understands a mistake that he has made as a mistake, he is no longer mistaken. Further, if he discerns the causes of his mistake in his mind, and dissolves the causes by clear inquiry or by deep devotion, he is free from the rep-

213

etition of that mistake from then onward. He discovers the abode of Truth in his own heart and abides at the very source of happiness, which is the fountainhead of love.

If you dive within, you may find that you have far more control over the direction of the use of the instruments of body, speech, and mind than what you have been assuming. In that responsibility also lays freedom.

Steady, ardent spiritual practice can bring about transcendence of any tendency. If you so practice to become wise, you will find the plenitude of Grace.

Ever yours in Truth,
Nome

September 22, 2009

ॐ Dear . . . ,

Namaste. It is necessary that you find the source of happiness and love within you. Within means the Self. You must know yourself.

You are completely free to become involved with a woman or not. Either way, you must find the love within, the Bliss of Being.

Love is not a commodity. Being is neither an activity nor a thing. Inquire within to realize the true nature of your Existence.

Ever yours in Truth,
Nome

[This message is from a seeker who lives at a distance from the SAT temple. Nome's response follows.]

September 25, 2009

Om Namo Bhagawate Sri Ramanaya.

Dear Nome. Namaste.

I would like to share my recent experience of Sri Bhagawan's grace and guidance. One early morning, in my silent sitting, I was deeply touched by the understanding of my wrong and deep-rooted belief that all the objects of the material world that my senses sense are out there, and I have a sensory impression on the screen of my mind in here, in the head or my body. Now, I am awake to the truth, more and more, that such is not the case. Objects that look solid are just vibrations of / in Consciousness, including my own solid-looking body. So, where is in, and where is out? How can I get something or loose something? As I sink deeper in my understanding of this line of thinking, there is no limitation of my little body and mind, and I feel oneness as and with the whole Existence. I hope my rambling has made some sense to you, but, then again, you have understood all my rambling before, so this is not new. Right after this experience, during that morning, two books that I was reading - *Saddarshanam* and one by Sidharameswara Maharaj—they both point at the same idea or truth. That is all for now. I deeply appreciate your loving kindness. Convey my namaste to Saswati.

In and as Self,

ॐ Dear . . . ,

Om Namo Bhagavate Sri Ramanaya
Namaste. Thank you for your message.

Grace immeasurably vast manifests in innumerable ways.

Far from rambling, your words reflect the truth. Free of misidentification with the body, you, yourself, are beyond all considerations of inner and outer. This Self, of the nature of Being-Consciousness-Bliss, alone exists. If there is all, this Self is all, to such an extent that there is nothing else to be referred to as "all." If there is no such thing as all, the one, indivisible Self alone exists. For this Self, there is no gain or loss, birth or death, beginning or end, or creation or destruction. For one who truly, deeply inquires, there can be

215

no "wrong path," and, for one who knows, ignorance and illusions of duality are impossible.

May you abide in the everlasting Knowledge of the Self and thus remain in the happiness of the perfect fullness.

Ever yours in Truth,
Nome

[The questions raised can be inferred from this response.]

September 27, 2009

ॐ Dear . . . ,

Om Namo Bhagavate Sri Ramanaya
Thank you for your several messages.

You need not have any worry concerning whether or not it is appropriate to write what you have written to me. If such writing benefits your practice, perhaps as a means for gaining better perspective, use it. The explicit details represent no harm.

Some of what you have written is, indeed, pointing in the right direction. Yet, better than guessing, even intelligently, at the state of a jnani, how the jnani views such-and-such, what the Self may be, what Self-Realization may be, etc. is to experientially inquire and directly realize. For otherwise, whether cloudier or clearer, it remains an idea, and the Truth of Absolute Being, the self-luminous infinite Consciousness, and the perfect fullness of Bliss are undoubtedly transcendent of any idea.

In your messages, you expressed how you have been engaging in somewhat of a debate on certain websites. At some time, you may wish to consider the value of such. Whether your viewpoint or that of another prevails in such a debate, ask yourself what purpose it serves. Is this the best use of your time and effort? If you are inspired, is this the best way to share what you have found? Does such debate help your practice or deepen your experience at all?

From your fears regarding bodily discomfort, pain, etc., as described by you, you can discern the need for actual, deep, thorough inquiry to liberate yourself from suffering. An intellectual grasp of ideas thought to correspond to the real essential teaching does not have the capacity to reveal this freedom, unveil the innate Bliss, or bestow lasting peace. Therefore, more profoundly assimilate what has been said and written, in satsang, correspondence, and in sacred books, by persevering inquiry that uproots the misidentifications by which you falsely define yourself. Self-critical examination of your mind (not egotistical self-judgment that depresses) is helpful, just as the humility that is natural for anyone who is aware of the scope of That is superior to futile confidence rooted in the ego's assertion. Therefore, joyfully and ardently seek to know your Self, which is utterly free of the ego-notion (individuality) and far, far beyond the tiny concerns of the phantom-like personality and the illusory moods and modes of an unreal mind.

May you be ever happy at heart, discovering how imagined your pseudo-bondage is and finding the purpose of life fulfilled within you—the immortal Bliss of the illimitable Self.

Ever yours in Truth,
Nome

[In answer to a question regarding destiny and free will.]

September 28, 2009

ॐ Dear . . . ,

Namaste. Concepts of destiny and individual free will are entertained only so long as the individual to which either pertains is assumed to exist. In Self-Knowledge, both ideas are absent, for the ego does not exist. Self-inquiry reveals this Knowledge. The unreal ego has no part in it, for the nature of the inquiry is of the Knowledge-essence. If one asks about the "I" that seems as if implicit in the inquiry, the answer is found in the Maharshi's analogy of the stick used to turn the burning pyre. Therefore, inquire into the nature of the inquirer.

Ever yours in Truth,
Nome

[A response to a seeker whose mind was both inspired and plagued by tendencies.]

October 9, 2009

ॐ Dear . . . ,

Om Namo Bhagavate Sri Ramanaya
Namaste. Thank you for your numerous recent messages.

Your messages express both worthwhile spiritual reflection and repetitive patterns of thought. They do not have equal validity. One reflects that which is true and profound, while the other is mere repetition of imagination given undue emphasis. The latter is based on egoism and non-comprehension of the source of happiness and lends itself to worldly craving and fear. The former is of the nature of sattva and points in the right direction, which is the nirguna (quality-less) Truth. Examine the play of your mind, discern, and direct accordingly.

At the root of your ideas are the definitions that are misidentifications. The root of all misidentifications is the assumption of individuality, or ego. Inquire to become free of all of them.

The abandonment of misidentifications reveals the true Self. Such is inquiry.

The Self is actionless. It remains so regardless of the activity or inactivity of the body. Likewise is the Bliss of the Self.

That which is vast, eternal, deep, infinite, utterly beyond the personality and its concerns, bliss itself, illimitable Consciousness, formless, constant, imperishable, and non-dual, and so knowing which there is nothing else to experience, is ever cherished by the wise. Focused on that, devoted to that, inquiring to know that, finding the utter insignificance of all else in light of that, with that as their support, delighting in that, absorbed in that, the wise realize that to be the sole-existent Reality and remain completely content, at peace in the perfect fullness.

Ever yours in Truth,
Nome

≡
•

[To a seeker who sent several messages, the varied content of which can be surmised from the response presented here.]

October 13, 2009

ॐ Dear . . . ,

Om Namo Bhagavate Sri Ramanaya
Namaste. Thank you for your several messages.

Certainly, you may feel at ease in writing whatever you wish to express.

One's ideas about others tend to reflect his ideas of himself. From that perspective, "observations" are, perhaps, more interpretation than observation. You may find it helpful to consider this in relation to your views of the happiness, sadness, etc. of others.

It may also be helpful to examine, in the light of spiritual freedom or aspiration toward that, how you are using your mind. If repetitive patterns of thought, such as craving, fear, frustration, etc. plague your mind, from where is such force or vividness derived, and from where does this repetitive, undue emphasis come? Is it necessary to continue to conjure confusion?

Spiritual humility is more joyful than assertive arrogance and its corollary of depressed shame.

The ideas that objects, circumstances, etc. provide happiness and that the Self or Brahman may be a lonely, desolate state are not based on actual experience or wisdom. The great rishis, sages, saints, etc. have not been those who are unhappy or lonely, but, rather, they are truly full of bliss and are at peace.

Whether or not you should administer medications to your body to becalm your mind is a question that I cannot answer. I have no experience or familiarity with such.

There are many aids known since the most ancient times to create, enhance, and maintain a sattvic state of mind. Have you attempted such and continue with such?

It is incumbent upon the spiritual seeker to change from his limited conception to embrace the vast Knowledge of the Self. The attempt to reduce the Knowledge to fit within the existing conception will not liberate. Similarly, if one does not understand the meaning of a saying, scriptural passage, etc., he would do well to seek explanation, reflect and contemplate such, and deeply meditate so that the meaning becomes clear for him. It may not be necessary to change the words, and it may prove that the expressions of the wise, born from silence, contain profound meanings that may be lost by prematurely replacing the terms with ones that fit in with the existing conceptions mentioned earlier.

If your opinion is that some aspect of the teaching is pedantic, that is, obsessed with doctrine and a parading of book-knowledge, such could appear to be so because of a lack of experience that may make the absence of deviation from Reality seem like a fixed doctrine and, also, not yet understanding the depth of experience that can be had with spiritual literature and the reasons for references to such.

The stiffness or rigidity of this body noted by you is a symptom, one among many, of Parkinson's Disease. By the innate Knowledge of the Self and by the Grace of Sadguru Ramana, to whom one can never be too thankful, the body and its states, living or dead, present no bondage. The one Self, unborn and imperishable, alone exists. That is perfectly full. (Om purnamadah purnamidam, etc.)

I hope that you find what has been written here helpful.

May you ever abide in the happiness and peace of the Self, which is Brahman, God.

Ever yours in Truth,
Nome

≡
•

[This is a response to a seeker who frequently attends satsangs and who was struggling with unhappiness at that time.]

October 15, 2009

ॐ Dear . . . ,

Namaste. Thank you for both of your messages.

It makes little difference what words are used to phrase the question or if no words are employed at all. What is important is that you come to understand the nature of happiness and that you find it within you.

Deep meditation transcends thinking, even concentrated thinking, on a sentence. It is inner experience. The attainment of that is referred to as true Knowledge.

You say that you are miserable. No one likes to be miserable. Rather, everyone wishes to be happy. This is an intuition of your natural state, which is unmixed happiness. No object or external experience or circumstance can supply this to you. It is within you awaiting discovery. When the ego subsides, along with its erroneous ideas, the innate happiness shines forth in its fullness and without obstruction.

If you meditate on what is stated here and in the previous message to you, how to proceed will become clearer for you, and you will become happier.

Ever yours in Truth,
Nome

[Here is a message from a seeker who lives at a distance from the temple and attends retreats, along with Nome's response.]

October 16, 2009

Om namah Shivaya.

Namaste, dear Nome and Sasvati,

I received the warm welcoming letter from Sasvati. The experience took me to days and times when Sri Bhagawan used to remember and arrange for the transportation for any devotee coming to Tiruvannamalai. There was one incident about a devotee coming from Columbo, Sri Lanka by steamship and had written a letter to the ashram. Sri Bhagawan remembered the arrival date and all other details and then made sure that he came safely from Madras to Tiruvannamalai. Every time I read or think of that incident, I get teary-eyed at Bhagawan's compassion and also his grace in making all of us know and be exposed to him and his teaching and staying with us every step of the way.

When I read one statement by Sri Bhagawan in one issue of "Reflections," it hit me like lightning. He is telling a devotee, "There is nothing but the dreamer. Where does the question of dream people—real or unreal—arise? We are all unreal. Why do you doubt it?"

Even a few days before, I was experiencing more and more that "I" and "this" both rise and subside together. They are thoughts, perceptions and conceptions only, which means they are not real. Between "I" and "this" is included everything except the Self, which remains after "I" and "this" merge-subside-disappear. After reading Sri Bhagawan's statement, I felt like I was the devotee he was talking to.

There was this question about Bliss being the nature of Self and me not feeling it. Today, on my morning walk, I started thinking about it. It hit me that it is like that old saying, "I want to have my cake and eat it, too." I want to have bliss and, at the same time, be there to experience it, too. Either I go or bliss goes. So, it is back to self-inquiry to realize beyond doubt my true nature as the Self, Existence and Consciousness.

Please explain or make clearer to me the following statement by Sri Bhagawan, also from an issue of "Reflections" (May-June 2005), page 2. Bhagawan: ".......There is the creed of only one Self, which is also called the creed of only one jiva. It says that the jiva is only one who sees the whole world and the jivas therein."

With hope and prayers for your well-being,

ॐ Dear . . . ,

Om Namo Bhagavate Sri Ramanaya

Namaste. Thank you for your message. It is by Sri Bhagavan's Grace that any journey, outer or inner, reaches its destination.

Yes, the innate Bliss shines unobstructed, upon the abandonment of the merely assumed individual. The ego cannot experience Bliss anymore than the ego can realize Being. The ego is not. Being is Bliss.

The idea of multiple jivas is for, by, and contained within a jiva. Usually, the multiplicity is defined by the misidentification of the Self with a body, gross or subtle. As Sri Ramana explains, such a jiva is really the Self conceived as a seer who can see other jivas, the world, etc. So, if jivas

223

appear, they are only for the one jiva; other beings are for "I." The Self, though, transcends any "I," even defined as a mere perceiver. The real nature of the jiva, thus, is only the Self. So, also, the Self is said to be the Self of all jivas. Yet, there is neither a jiva nor many jivas in the one Self. It is forever undifferentiated.

May you ever abide in the Knowledge of the Self, the immutable, illimitable Being-Consciousness-Bliss.

Om Namah Sivaya
Ever yours in Truth,
Nome

[Here is a seeker's question about sattvic diet and Nome's response.]

October 21, 2009

Hello . . . ,

While reading some of Ramana's writings, I noticed he recommended a satvic diet. Can you please direct me to a resource where I can learn what are the components of such a diet?

Thanks,

ॐ Dear . . . ,

Om Namo Bhagavate Sri Ramanaya

Namaste. Mention of sattvic diet appears in numerous texts and in a few places in the printed records of Sri Ramana's teachings. Generally, a sattvic diet is said to be a traditional vegetarian diet; that is, a vegetarian diet that includes dairy products. In addition, a more sattvic diet may be further determined by the individual regarding the effects on the body, prana, and mind from different amounts of items that stimulate, induce torpor, etc.

From a more transcendent perspective, sattvic diet is that which is consumed free of the ideas of being the body, being the eater, being the enjoyer or experiencer, and such.

Finally, a sattva (of the nature of Truth, of Being) diet consists of fasting from all misidentifications and false concepts, never consuming the least bit of the ego assumption, and imbibing continuously the immortal nectar of the Knowledge of the Self to thus be utterly satiated with lasting Bliss.

I hope that the above is of some help for you. May you ever abide in the Knowledge of the Self and thus dwell always in peace.

Ever yours in Truth,
Nome

[This is a response to a seeker's messages, the content of which can be inferred from the reply.]

October 21, 2009

ॐ Dear . . . ,

Om Namo Bhagavate Sri Ramanaya
Namaste. Thank you for your messages.

The Maharshi's teachings reveal something far vaster and deeper than the resolution of personal problems. To apply them to such problems, of course, works, just as applying the whole ocean to extinguish an ignited match that is singeing your finger will certainly work, but we would not say that this is the entire purpose and scope of the ocean.

If you turn within, you will find the illimitable source of happiness, which is also the abode of love. Becoming absorbed in that, you will see how false, needless, and purposeless have been all the ideas of cravings, fears, hatred, anger, and the other tendencies with which your mind has plagued itself.

Understanding that a thought is transient may be a fine place to start. It is not the end and, by itself, does not destroy ignorance, which will produce the idea, the attachment, the suffering, and the problem again. For permanent freedom, inquiry to know oneself is the direct means.

It is also important to fully use your capacity to engage in spiritual practice.

May your inquiry be steady and deep so that you leave behind the imagined bondage of the mind and remain happy at heart and at peace.

Ever yours in Truth,
Nome

[A message was received from a seeker, who had never visited the SAT temple, regarding attending satsangs at SAT. Nome's response follows.]

October 21, 2009

Hi,

I was planning to attend the satsang at your place as suggested by Richard of Arunachala Grace blogspot. I was wondering if there is any cost involved? I attend a satsang group of Ramana Devotees that are linked to Arunachala Ashram run by [name omitted] and that tends to be a pot luck like thing.

I am keen on visiting Nome, hence want to know if we are expected to pay for the satsangs conducted by your organization.

Thanks,

ॐ Dear . . . ,

Om Namo Bhagavate Sri Ramanaya
Namaste. Thank you for your message. You are warmly

welcome to attend satsang at the SAT temple. There is no cost for satsangs. Similarly, there is no cost for the holy events that occur at the temple on other days, such as meditations, Ramana Darshanam, etc. If you wish, you can look at the website at www.SATRamana.org to see the schedule of events. If you wish, you may give a donation, but it is not mandatory. I, myself, have made it my consistent custom to offer a donation to every ashram, temple, center, etc. that I have ever visited, but no one is required to do so at SAT. Those who wish to give, do so; those who do not, do not.

May you ever abide in that priceless treasure of Self-Knowledge in which all worldly attachments do not exist and in which one is ever absorbed in the perfect fullness.

Ever yours in Truth,
Nome

[This piece of correspondence, from October 2009, is a response to two seekers who have long been devoted to Sri Ramana, living at a distance from the SAT temple and thus not able to attend frequently. One of them had become seriously ill.]

ॐ Dear . . and . . . ,

Om Namo Bhagavate Sri Ramanaya
Namaste. Thank you for your message.

It is evident that the body is subject to decay and is transient. It is a natural response to attempt to heal illness and to preserve life. The Self abides transcendent of all of that and is ever at peace. True Knowledge is found by the abandonment of the misidentification as a body or as an embodied individual and identification solely with the birthless and imperishable Being-Consciousness-Bliss that you truly are.

Ever yours in Truth,
Nome

≡
•

[A seeker who asked about sattvic diet wrote again. In his message, he expressed appreciation for the previous answer, mentioned his plans to visit along with questions about arrangements, listed the several books he was reading, many of which are authored by contemporary writers, but a few of which contain profound teachings of Sri Ramana, and spoke of his intention to stop reading every book, except Who am I? *because "reading is a waste of time." Here is the response sent to him.]*

October 22, 2009

ॐ Dear . . . ,

Om Namo Bhagavate Sri Ramanaya
Namaste. Thank you for your message.
If you travel also to California, please know that you will be warmly welcome to attend satsangs, meditations, Ramana Darshanam events, etc. at the SAT temple. You can look at the website www.SATRamana.org to view the schedule and descriptions of events. There is no cost involved, and, though donations to the temple are helpful and appreciated, they are not mandatory. Similarly, no service is required of those who attend, though some SAT members volunteer their efforts to help the temple operate.
Better than the reduction or elimination of the reading of spiritual literature is to find a wiser way to approach such literature. Such a wiser way includes keen discrimination, actually inquiring while reading, and absorption in the Truth indicated. It involves the traditional Vedanta approach of sravana (listening, though in this case reading), manana (reflection), and nididhyasana (profound, continuous meditation), either serially or simultaneously. Since

ancient times, certain sacred books were written and carefully preserved by those who knew their value for centuries and millennia to help seekers realize "that before which all words and thoughts turn back unable to grasp," as the Upanishads and *Gita* proclaim. The same is so even now.

Hopefully, the above is of some use or benefit for you. May you deeply inquire so that the innate Knowledge of the Self shines unobscured, in all of its peace and bliss.

Ever yours in Truth,
Nome

[This message is from a seeker who resides at a distance from the SAT temple. Nome's response follows and alludes to other messages sent by the same seeker.]

October 24, 2009

Dear Nome,
Om namah Shivaya.

Namaste. In my prayer room, I have a picture (one of many) of Sri Bhagawan. On the bottom, I have pasted a little handwritten strip of paper with one of his quotes, "You are Knowledge," but I have written the Tamil words for it "Arrive Nan." Every time I look at that picture, I imagine that Bhagawan is telling me himself in person.

The word "everything" means mind that holds the idea of I as individual, idea that I am the body, idea that there is "this," all duality of I and this, subject and object, and all triads of knower, knowing, and known. If all this is gone—forgotten—then what is left is pure knowledge itself. Where there is no one to know any thing and nothing to be known by anybody, and no knowing going on for anyone, just knowledge or Consciousness remains. That is what Sri Bhagawan is saying: "Arrive Nan". Also, that is same as Tat Tvam Asi. When "I" is removed from all its upadhis or so-called labels, like ego, body etc., there is no difference between I and That. Knowledge of I am is Brahman. As long as I stay with this understanding, there is

229

peace and joy. I know you will say, "Why do I come out of that understanding?" For that, I do not have any excuse.

Previously I said, "I imagine Sri Bhagawan is telling me in person." Behind that statement, there is a deep desire in my heart to hear his voice on some recording or such. Is it possible?

Hope everything is fine there. Must be getting a little cooler. Give my regards to Sasvati.

Namaste,

ॐ Dear . . . ,

Om Namo Bhagavate Sri Ramanaya

Namaste. Thank you for both of your messages.

Your analogy of light and a prism is quite apt. The original light or source is unmodified. Due only to the prism of imagination in the form of the ego, the very same light seems differentiated into all else, jagat-jiva-para.

The Knowledge of Consciousness is Consciousness. The one who knows is only this Consciousness. There is no other to know or to not know, and no one to be ignorant. Thus, Knowledge is said to be without attainment, for you are Knowledge.

Bhagavan is always speaking in resounding Silence to those who dive within, inquiring to know the Self.

Who comes out of the understanding?

Bhagavan refused the attempt to record his voice, saying that his voice is Silence.

Sasvati sends her love.

May you ever abide as the one Self, the real Knowledge, in Bliss.

Ever yours in Truth,
Nome

[This message is from a visitor at Satsang. Nome's response follows.]

October 26, 2009

Namaskar Master Nome,

Thank you for the great Satsang yesterday.

In Ramana's quote below, is "God" a conceptual, formalized God?

Otherwise, it doesn't make sense to me. For me, God is the Infinite. I would appreciate your response.

Verse 289. "The Infinite is like the screen on which the moving pictures appear; the soul, the world, and God are like the moving pictures; the Infinite alone is real." (From *Guru-Ramana-Vachana-Mala*, by "Who".)

Thank you,

ॐ Dear . . . ,

Namaste. Yes, this refers to God as conceived and not to God as Brahman. Jagat-jiva-para is the term commonly used to express this, which means the universe (or world), the individual (or individual soul or individual self, jivat-man) and the Supreme (or God). The three are three only so long as the one who knows them is unknown. Upon true Knowledge of the Self, there is no ego to be a jiva, to experience a world, or to conceive a God differentiated from the infinite Brahman, which alone is the Self.

Ever yours in Truth,
Nome

[This is a message from and a response to a seeker who was visiting Sri Ramanasramam.]

October 31, 2009

Om Namo Bhagavate Sri Ramanaya
Dear Nome and Sasvati,

Namaste.

Just a quick note to say that I arrived at Ramana Ashram and all is well. [Name omitted] sends his best wishes.

I'm having the best of meditations. Will be going up to Skandashram and Virupaksha Cave this afternoon. Ahhhhhhhh - the Bliss of Ramana and Arunachala.

Om Namo Bhagavate Sri Ramanaya
Namaste.

ॐ Dear . . . ,

Om Namo Bhagavate Sri Ramanaya
Namaste. We are glad to know that you arrived safely and that, according to [name omitted], you even obtained your luggage.

Please convey our love and respects to Sri [name omitted] and his wife, if you have not already done so.

Seeing with an eye of a different form or nature (Virupaksa), attacking (Skanda) with the vel (lance) of Jnana the illusion of differentiation, meditating on the nature of the meditator, realize the unmoving (acala) Being (A)-Consciousness (Ru)-Bliss (Na) to be the only Reality, One without a second.

Ever yours in Truth,
Nome and Sasvati

[Here is a response to a seeker who was troubling himself and others with his anger and related tendencies. The reference to knowing the thoughts of others is in response to the seeker's statement about the purported powers or claims of such of a famous spiritual teacher. The other questions raised by the seeker can be inferred from the response.]

ॐ Dear . . . ,

Om Namo Bhagavate Sri Ramanaya
Namaste. Thank you for your many messages.

So, you now see how mistaken your mind was, with the delusions and fears, projecting the same on to others and forming ignorant opinions accordingly. This is so not only regarding the people whom you see at the places you may frequent, but also others about whom you know little or nothing but of whom you have been vehemently proclaiming your hatred in your messages, such as humanity in general, and the entire world. Fortunately, they do not entertain the same aggressive thoughts about you. It would be wise to take full responsibility for the workings of your own mind, cease to hate anyone, abandon violent fantasies, and find fulfillment within yourself.

Though one can always imagine a better set of circumstances, bondage is one's own making; likewise is spiritual freedom.

Anger is created by delusion in one's mind. Only you apparently rob yourself of your innate happiness. Blaming others for such is absurd. Find the source of happiness within.

If you examine what you have written, you will perceive that, in the vehement portions, your ideas are equal to or worse than the qualities of which you accuse those other people.

As for Mahatma Gandhi, first accomplish within and outwardly what he accomplished, and then you can offer criticism if you wish.

In general, forming opinions about others in such a manner is spiritually worthless.

Regarding knowing the thoughts of others, especially when directed to oneself: In Jnana, the undifferentiated Consciousness is known to alone be real, and thoughts, their objects, and the thinker are unreal.

In Self-Realization, individuality is effaced, and only the one indivisible Being-Consciousness-Bliss remains.

Therefore, the attempt to count the number of realized beings is like asking for a dream calculation of the number of waking "Consciousnesses."

Please accept whatever seems critical here in the right spirit, for you truly are the Self, not an ego, and can abide in lasting peace and bliss. Therefore, with some lessons learned, become your own answer to the illusory problems, shine with what is true, good, and beautiful, love others as your Self, treat all as you would wish them to do to you, and find your true nature.

Ever yours in Truth,
Nome

[A message from a seeker visiting Sri Ramanasramam and Nome's response.]

November 5, 2009

Dear Nome,

Om Namo Bhagavate Sri Ramanaya

I have had time today to go through the suggested verses. All of the verses are wonderful, and your selections have left me in a puddle of blissful tears. Such undivided Love and absorption into the Heart are expressed in these Divine words. My Oh My..what an inspiring and all encompassing sweep of Truth. I want to include all of them! Oh, what a wonderfully difficult task to select from such Wisdom and Grace.

These days I feel that I'm being swept up in a torrent of endless Knowledge and Grace. I feel an ever-deepening certainty that my nature is the Absolute. For example, I woke up about 4AM today with the body feeling a bit out of sorts and the mind foggy. I opened *Saddarshanam* to meditate, and it was difficult to experience directly what the words were expressing. But I knew to focus on my existence until that became clear before reading further. In doing so, the state of the body and mind dropped into the background and the

Reality began to shine. Then, as I returned to verses, I became absorbed, and the marvelous clarity of Ramana's teaching spilled forth. More and more, I know the path inward, and it becomes shorter and shorter every "trip", so much so, that the "trip" is continuous at an evermore deepening level. The momentum moves in the direction of Truth.

Namaste.

ॐ Dear . . . ,

Om Namo Bhagavate Sri Ramanaya

I trust that, in Wisdom and Grace, your "wonderfully difficult task" is continuing.

In the inner path, the one that shows the way, the one that illumines the path, the space of the path itself, the goal of the path, and the one who knows these are the same One. For the bodiless and mind-transcendent Self, naturally egoless, there is no modification. It is ever existent and the only real Self. Any other, an unreal self, is ever nonexistent. For the Self, no ignorance exists, and the Self, itself, is Knowledge. An unreal individual, spoken of as the seed of all delusion, does not actually exist and so has neither knowledge nor ignorance. The self-luminous Self is. By Sri Bhagavan's Grace, may there be abidance in this Truth, as this Truth.

May your momentum continue to reach dissolution, like a river when it joins the ocean, and like space empties into space.

Ever yours in Sri Bhagavan,
Nome

•

[This message is from a seeker in India. The response from Nome follows.]

November 7, 2009

Dear Sir,

I have been working in CMC hospital, Vellore. Recently, after a little illness, I expected my colleague to carry out little routines. She does it only when I say. All these days I was doing it. I am the senior person doing all the works without any expectation, but, more recently, I am expecting the juniors to do it, even though I am capable of doing it. Is it my ego? Also, when she talks to others, I feel she talks about me. Kindly advise me how to overcome this problem.

Yours sincerely,

ॐ Dear . . . ,

Om Namo Bhagavate Sri Ramanaya

Namaste. Thank you for your message.

The worries and frustrations, indeed, have their source in the ego, which means that they have ignorance, or illusion, as their basis. The ego manifests as the misidentification with the body, as the performer of action, as a person in the world, etc. If one ascertains the source of happiness to be within, that basis of delusion dissolves, and he becomes nonattached. This yields steady peace regardless of circumstances. That which is within is the Self. Abidance as the Self is perfectly full joy without end.

A keen awareness of Sri Bhagavans's Grace, and complete reliance on it, yields steady peace, so that all feels as light as air.

For those blessed with such Grace and who dive inward with the inquiry to know the Self, it is natural to view all with an equal eye and to shine with love for all beings, even for those whose actions are not completely to your liking.

May you ever abide in the Knowledge of the Self and thus dwell in peace and happiness always.

Ever yours in Truth,
Nome

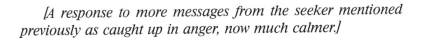

[A response to more messages from the seeker mentioned previously as caught up in anger, now much calmer.]

November 17, 2009

ॐ Dear . . . ,

Om Namo Bhagavate Sri Ramanaya

Namaste. Thank you for your several messages.

Here are a few suggestions that you may find helpful upon meditation upon them.

Self-critical examination can be quite useful for the seeker of Self-Realization who wishes to destroy vasanas (tendencies), but such must be in the context of an ardent desire for Liberation and the understanding that such examination and destruction are for the purpose of revealing the innate perfection of the Self.

In light of this, consider egocentric thinking, whether assertive or depressed, as delusive. Contemplation upon how much one uses his mind for such useless thinking, the imagined tales (or should we say tails, after which one chases) of an illusory character, should inspire him to completely alter the way he uses his mind, thereby revealing much freedom as it unveils great peace.

The deep spiritual aspirant knows that the illusions of his mind are entirely his own making and that he is free to set himself free of them, dissolving the misidentifications that are their root, so that, abandoning even the false assumption of an ego (an individual), he abides in the Self as the Self, full of bliss.

Life is fleeting, and one does not know how much time remains. Use it wisely in a worthwhile manner, so that you have no regrets later.

Free of the least bit of misidentification with the instruments of body, speech, and mind, the wise naturally use these instruments in a selfless manner, for such is a manifestation of that which is divine. It may be helpful to consider this, examine your activities with these instruments, and determine if and how you would wish to change based upon such spiritual principles.

May your meditations be deep and your life suffused with illumined happiness.

Ever yours in Truth,
Nome

[From India, a woman wrote on behalf of her father requesting instruction concerning how to overcome fear. This response was sent.]

ॐ Dear . . . ,

Om Namo Bhagavate Sri Ramanaya

Namaste. Thank you for your message.

As Sri Bhagavan has taught, there are two ways by which peace can be attained. One can inquire to know the true nature of the Self and, in this case, realize that it is ever peaceful and changeless, beyond the three states of waking, dreaming, and deep sleep. Identifying with the Self, the root of all fears and binding ideas (the ego or separate mind) is destroyed. The vast, peaceful Self alone remains. Alternatively, one can recognize that all is ever in the Supreme. Whether approached as God or Guru, that is the sole power. Thereafter, having given up all worries and attachments, with no scope left for the ego and its troubles, one rests dissolved in the Supreme Self, as the Supreme Self.

In either approach, it is wise to examine the fear, which is composed of thoughts that contain the belief in a loss of existence or loss of happiness or both. If one recognizes the specific thoughts that compose the fear, he can trace those ideas to their underlying false definitions or misidentifications. Those, in turn, can be traced inward to the "I"-notion or ego. Self-inquiry, as revealed by Sri Ramana and actually practiced, dissolves the fears, the ideas composing them, the underlying misidentifications, and the falsely assumed ego, leaving the Self as it is. "Where there is a second, as it were, there is fear." "A second" means the individual who seems as if separate from the Self and all dualism. Abidance in the nondual Self, which is Self-Knowledge, is freedom from fear, for it is abidance as the imperishable Existence, which is the unconditional Bliss.

Therefore, if one relies on the Grace of the Maharshi and earnestly seeks the Knowledge of the Self, all will be right.

I hope that the above is of some help to you and your father.

Ever yours in Sri Bhagavan,
Nome

[Here is a message from a seeker and the response.]

November 19, 2009

Prior to the I am arising, the absolute is eternal, the sat chit ananda, our true nature. Sri Nisargadatta states that when the consciousness dissolves, it returns to the elements, which return to the universal consciousness. In order to be consciousness, a body is needed. Prior to a body, mind and world arising, nothing is remembered. Also awareness is aware, but there is no self awareness. There is nothing that I can do except rest in awareness. Is there a difference in awareness and consciousness? Presently, I am rereading the final talks of Sri Nisargadatta.

ॐ Dear . . . ,

Om Namo Bhagavate Sri Ramanaya

Namaste. Perhaps, because, in part, of the manner of translation of some of the books expressing the teachings given by Sri Nisargadatta Maharaj, there may be some lack of clarity regarding the meaning of the terms "awareness" and "consciousness." A similar difficulty can arise with certain Sanskrit terms that may correlate with the Marathi terms. They are used in various ways by different sages and others and at different times. For example, Cit is Consciousness, citta is mind or memory, Jnana is Knowledge, but jnana can also be any kind of knowledge, caitanya is Consciousness (absolute) or awareness (relative) or sentience, and vijnana is Supreme Knowledge, intellectual knowledge, or awareness (relative) by the intellect. The words Sat, sata, and sattva similarly carry a host of meanings. One must understand the context and also must have the capacity to discern the intended meaning, which comes from one's own inquiry or Knowledge. To assist the spiritual seekers with this, in SAT publications, terms that refer to the Absolute Self are capitalized, and those employed with another meaning are placed in lower case letters, but such capitalization is actually not in the Sanskrit language. This approach is not necessarily followed by other publishers.

Addressing what you have written here, the Svarupa (True Nature) or Atman (the Self) is forever undifferentiated Being-Consciousness-Bliss (Saccidananda—Sat-Cit-Ananda). It is as it is eternally. It is only from the supposition that there is another that one speaks of prior, origin, arising, etc. With the supposed rise or appearance, only in imagination, of the notion of "I," all else appears or arises. Just as, in illusion, the real Being (Sat) appears as if individualized, so the reflected light of Consciousness (Cit) appears as a mind or awareness, of which one aspect is the senses, and within such appears the entire world or objective sphere of experience. Of course, all of this is conceived only in the mind, which also is not real, and is not the Truth.

Without the body, no world is perceived. This is also explained in Sri Ramana's *Saddarsanam*. The worldly

240

awareness requires the activity of all of the five sheaths. Apart from the mind, there are no senses, body, or world. The belief in an entity called "mind" is due only to lack of inquiry or Knowledge. Memory and forgetfulness are also merely modes of the mind. True Knowledge is beyond all of that and is nonobjective.

Consciousness is self-luminous; it knows itself timelessly. Such Knowledge is innate. The mind or awareness has no knowing capacity of its own, either to know Consciousness (the Self) or to know itself. There is only one Consciousness. If you feel that you are aware, trace the awareness or knowingness to its source, the original Light, which is the invariable pure Consciousness. In other words, seek the nature of the "I" that seems to be aware so that you realize the egoless true Self as your only identity. That is Sat-Cit-Ananda.

I hope that you find the above to be of some help. May you know yourself as you truly are and thus ever shine in Self-Knowledge, full of Bliss.

Ever yours in Truth,
Nome

[From a seeker who attends satsangs often. The response follows.]

November 25, 2009

Namaste, Master Nome!

I want to tell you how important and profound your advice to me to read *The Song of Ribhu* has been. Immediately after you recommended it during our lunch conversation at the August retreat, I was in the bookstore, and [name omitted], from India, came up and volunteered that he would recommend that I read *The Song of Ribhu* and be sure to read it aloud. (Divine reinforcement!) That's what I have been doing, and I eagerly look forward to the reading each day and am now on Chapter 35.

It speaks to me so directly and powerfully.

My friend [name omitted], who came with me one Sunday to SAT, was also reading it, but stopped. A few days ago I mentioned my continued reading to him, and he said, "That Ribhu really knows how to brain wash."

I said, "Yes, but it's a good brain washing, and I want my brain washed."

A "brain-washing" (cleansing, redirection, awakening, remembering) to develop the certitude of the "I am Brahman" presence is certainly desirable! I'm experiencing increased connections to Spirit through Self-inquiry and the "I am Brahman" presence.

One question I have concerns love. Most scriptures and sages affirm God as love, and of course the Bible does so quite directly. In *The Song of Ribhu*, love is never (up to Chapter 35 anyway) used to describe the Supreme Brahman or Consciousness. What is your understanding of that? Is love assumed to be an aspect of purity, Bliss and Consciousness? Does the Maharshi equate God or Brahman with love?

Thank you.
Sincerely,

ॐ Dear . . . ,

Namaste. Thank you for your message. I am glad to know that you are finding *Song of Ribhu* to be so beneficial.

Yes, there are passages of the recorded teachings of the Maharshi in which he equates love and the Self. In the *Ribhu Gita* and *Song of Ribhu*, love is there, too, though it is usually mentioned in the context of the love of the Lord by the devotee. Similar is it with other Vedanta scriptures and such in which God is said to lovingly bestow Grace and sages lovingly give their instruction.

In Truth, love is the indivisibility of Being. Being is Consciousness and Bliss. "Pure" means unmixed with anything else. In Being-Consciousness-Bliss, which is the nature of the Self, there is no differentiation whatsoever. To abide as That is the supreme love, or, as Sri Sankara refers to it, "parabhakti," supreme devotion. Perhaps, because of the tendency of the mind to think in terms of the lover and the beloved, and thus imagine division, the term "love" is not frequently employed in texts such as Ribhu, but there can be no doubt of the height of love that this knowledge reveals.

By profound inquiry to know the Self, by dissolution in the love of God, may you ever abide in That, as That, itself.

Ever yours in Truth,
Nome

[This message is in response to a letter from a seeker that described her experiences of love, inquiry, and her plans to re-visit India.]

November 25, 2009

ॐ Dear . . . ,

Namaste. Thank you for your letter of the 22nd, which arrived today.

Yes, the Heart, which is quintessential Being, is all. That words and thoughts do not arise certainly represents no problem.

Whether in the USA or in India, blissful is it to abide as the unmoving, the timeless, the location-less.

Abide as that in which Knowledge and love are one, in which Being, Consciousness, and Bliss are identical, and in which peace and happiness are always.

Ever yours in Truth,
Nome

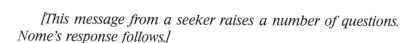

[This message from a seeker raises a number of questions. Nome's response follows.]

December 8, 2009

Namaste.

I've called a few times in the past 3 weeks, and you were kind enough to speak with me and answer my questions (thank you very much).

I ordered and received several books from your website, and am very much enjoying reading the Maharshi's writings.

Question: I find myself worrying about what I would consider to be certain "injustices" in this dream-world my ego thinks it's an inhabitant of. Sometimes I am frustrated with myself for not doing more to help correct some of these seeming injustices.

Would the Maharshi say that, rather than worry about things like that, inquire as to who is worrying about those things? (and you'll find that the worrier doesn't exist?). One of the Hindu saints said "Reform yourself first; then you will automatically (help) reform thousands".

I can appreciate that perhaps the best thing I can do to help anyone / everyone in this "dream" (not sure what else to call it) world is to attempt to remove the ignorance that is preventing me from seeing that this Self is already realized.

It's difficult to stand or sit by and do nothing when I see certain things going on around us that we believe in our heart are wrong. I hope I wouldn't stand by and watch a person standing next to me be beaten senseless; I hope I would come to that person's aid.

I understand that this world and everything physical in it is illusion / delusion / maya / ignorance / not-real. But does that mean that we do not reach out to help others, that we just turn within and inquire as to the nature of the worrier, the doubter, etc.?

Is that really the best thing we can do to help make this world a better place? Part of me says it must be, as I won't be able to help spread peace and knowledge in the world unless I am at peace, and that to me means a mind without thought, a silent mind, and subsequently, no mind, when the Self appears.

When I say "I", I understand that there is no small "I". I'm just not sure how to correspond in writing otherwise. I could write: "This self has a question for your self," but that seems a bit tedious. Can we just assume that when I refer to "me" as "I", that I understand this is just the "I" thought speaking from a place of ignorance, and that underneath this, I understand that all there is is Self, God, Guru (one and the same)?

Thank you. Appreciate your time and patience.
With best regards, (Namaste),

ॐ Dear . . . ,

Om Namo Bhagavate Sri Ramanaya

Namaste. Thank you for your message.

Simple, natural communication is fine, such as in the casual use of the word "I." The intended sense of it is understood. We do not wish to fashion some particular mode of speech, but rather abide in the transcendent Knowledge of the Self. When wise sages seem to employ a particular expression, it is for the purpose of revealing the Truth of the Self to the listener or reader, and it is not intended that one should mimic such expression. Rather the meaning should be inwardly realized.

Much of the answer to your question can be found in your question itself. That is, you have fairly well answered it yourself.

If the misidentification of being a performer of action is abandoned by deeper knowledge, the question of to do or not to do dissolves. The Maharshi has stated that, within the dream, one must do his best to help his fellow beings, but he should not misidentify or mistake the world to be real. In addition, as you have observed, you can give only of what you have, so that establishing yourself in steady peace is of the utmost importance. Moreover, Sri Bhagavan has set the best example. Can there be any doubt about his attainment being the supreme good? Just observe how much graced benefit is constantly emanating from that!

May your inquiry be profound so that the innate freedom and peace of the Self remain perpetually self-evident.

Ever yours in Truth,
Nome

[A message from a Sri Ramana devotee who resides in India. The practices that he describes were not suggested by Nome.]

December 11, 2009

Dear Sir,

I started Ramana mantra meditation and flow life meditation. I was able to face the stress, etc. I was okay. Now, I am seeking your assistance. Due to dream in my sleep, felt a vague pain and a catch in my calf muscle. The reason for it I could not make out. The same day, my student went without recognizing. Known people went without recognizing me. Some wished me with the left hand. These things bothered me, and I felt okay after sometime. How to ignore these things so they do not affect me? It should vanish immediately (not after long time.) How should I view good and bad equally?

Looking for your advice,
Yours in Ramana,

ॐ Dear . . . ,

Om Namo Bhagavate Sri Ramanaya

Namaste. Thank you for your message. Sri Bhagavan has bestowed the liberating teachings that reveal the blissful Truth and has shown the example for all.

Knowing that all happiness is in the Self, recognizing that external objects and events do not affect the Self and do not provide happiness, why should one suffer by thinking that what happens with others (events and circumstances) is a factor in this happiness? Just as the objects do not have the capacity to create happiness or to remove it (that is, create suffering), so the body and its sensations do not. Whether all goes according to your wishes or goes contrary to your wishes or is a combination thereof, remain at peace, with this nonattachment, relying entirely on Sri Ramana's Grace, and absorbed in Self-Knowledge. All will be seen equally, and your bliss will be undisturbed.

May you be unmoved in the certitude of the Self within, the Purnam (perfect fullness), and thus happy and at peace always.

Ever yours in Sri Bhagavan,
Nome

[This is a response to a seeker who wrote and received guidance earlier. He was afflicted by vacillating tendencies in his mind and wrote about such.]

December 11, 2009

ॐ Dear . . . ,

Om Namo Bhagavate Sri Ramanaya
Namaste. Thank you for your message.
Examining your mind, even as expressed in your messages, some observations should easily be recognized by you. First and foremost, there is an unrelenting spirit, manifesting as the desire to be happy, that shines in your aspiration and even remains coursing along when pursued in ignorant ways. Next, you should be able to discern that, while inner happiness and peace are alone satisfying in life, the tendencies of the mind still romp around in such a way as to cause confusion, bewilderment, and suffering for you. Next, you should recognize that, though the path to freedom is direct and not difficult, persevering effort is needed

to remove the self-generated tendencies. Some of these tendencies even cause the basic principles to be a challenge for you, as in the case with understanding ahimsa, which is counted as the first of the yamas, the yamas being the first stage of yoga. In this context, Jnana may be regarded as the final stage of yoga, or that to which yogis devote themselves at the culmination or zenith of their practice.

Still, you are inwardly drawn to the highest. You may notice that, although hearing and reading the Truth, your mind continues in repetitive modes of ignorance and its suffering, though light has begun to dawn so that the delusion is not quite as solid-seeming as previously. To eliminate the ignorance may, at first, seem a daunting task, because of its repetitive character, and because of its apparent multiple facets, but, with honest, earnest spiritual practice of Self-inquiry, it proves to be insubstantial, an illusion, and dissipates as you cease to conjure it up. Practice in such a way that the dips into delusion are not repeated. This means to utterly detach and disidentify. When ignorance is recognized to be only ignorance, it vanishes forever.

The inner yearning for Self-Realization will not die in you, but you need not suffer the oscillating patterns in your mind. Dive within, deeper and deeper, so that, the ego vanishing, you become certain of the nature of your Self. Thus you will wisely dwell in peace, awake from the dream of the repetitive samsara, with a profound happiness that does not fade.

Ever yours in Truth,
Nome

[This message is from a seeker who met Nome in Bangalore in 1995. Nome's response follows.]

December 26, 2009

Namasthe ,
Om Namo Bhagavathe Sri Ramanaya !

I am writing to you after a long time. How can a human, a mortal, understand Bhagavan's working? Whatever suffering I am going through is because of my mistakes and my own ignorance. If I remember Bhagavan or see or listen to anything on him, certainly, like most people, I know the importance of his grace. He has advocated Self-enquiry as the practice of prime importance.

I can only say that, wherever I go and whatever I worship, still I return to him, remembering him almost daily. This is just the fortune of having his vision or darshan when I came to him in 1994-95 I guess. This is not to boast in anyway.

A few months earlier, he appeared in a dream and asked me to repeat Om Namo Bhagavathe Sri Ramanaya. This happened a couple of months back.

Surrendering the fruits of work and practicing devotion, as well as the enquiry he taught, is perhaps our effort to be.

I just took an opportunity to write to you, and, like earlier times, I am just hoping you will excuse me if I have acted in anyway wrong with any of Ramana's devotees or family.

With Yours in Bhagavan Ramana,

ॐ Dear . . . ,

Om Namo Bhagavate Sri Ramanaya

Namaste. Thank you for your message. I am glad to hear that you are endeavoring to practice Sri Bhagavan's teachings. Surely, His Grace is omnipresent and always. If, being devoted, one keenly inquires as instructed, the Self is assuredly realized, full of lasting peace and bliss.

If you are still residing in Bangalore, you may find it helpful to attend RMCL and listen to Dr. Sarada. You can even obtain a few of the publications of SAT there (they are usually not available at Sri Ramanasramam), which you may also find beneficial. You can also find writings, satsang transcripts, etc. at the SAT website at www.SATRamana.org that may be helpful

249

May you ever abide in the Knowledge of the Self and thus ever shine in spiritual joy.

Ever yours in Sri Bhagavan,
Nome

[Sarasvati, a devotee who participated at the SAT temple for many years, lived at Tiruvannamalai for approximately the last year of her life. When she died there, a message was sent by two seekers who live at Tiruvannamalai. Nome's response follows.]

December 28, 2009

Sarasvati passed away about 10:45 AM this morning. She had been sick and was getting sicker. When [name omitted] went to take her to the doctor today, she was unconscious, and passed away while the ambulance was on its way.

She had said that the move to Tiruvannamalai was the last she was going to make. And today is a most special day for the Tamils. This is the day they say that the Devas open the gates to "heaven," so those who die this day are Realized automatically. So, to die in Tiruvannamalai on this day is about the best that a body can do.

She was happy here.

We cremated the body this evening. Some of her western friends were there, as were Rajan and the other rickshaw drivers that had befriended her.

The body dies. Was she the body?

Om Arunachala,

ॐ Dear . . . and . . . ,

Om Namo Bhagavate Sri Ramanaya

Namaste. Thank you for your message and the information about Sarasvati's passing. Yes, the body dies, but the

Self does not perish. Unborn, it is indestructible and is neither burnt, nor wetted, nor withered, nor buried in earth.

Yes, death is said to occur in a holy place. Yet, "What is death if scrutinized?" says Sri Bhagavan. Where is the Self not? It is comparable to speaking of where in a dream one passes away. The ever-existent Self alone remains, and that alone is real.

Thank you for your kind help to her during this last period of her life.

Om Namah Sivaya
Om Arunacalesvaraya Namah

Ever yours in Truth,
Nome

[A reply to a seeker who experienced a vision of Sri Ramana:]

December 29, 2009

ॐ Dear . . . ,

Om Namo Bhagavate Sri Ramanaya
Namaste. Thank you for your letter of the 22nd, which arrived today.

That the Maharshi appears in your experiences is auspicious. Proceed higher. Visions are according to the seer, even if the visions appear to be physical. Inquire to know the nature of the seer. For this inquiry, there is Sri Bhagavan's Grace.

I trust that [name omitted] is well, too. Of course, you are always welcome here when you find the opportunity to come.

May you ever abide in the Knowledge of the Self, the eternal all-illuminating Consciousness, and thus dwell joyfully in peace always.

Ever yours in Truth,
Nome

[In response to a message from Shanti's son, a Christian seeker who reveres the Maharshi:]

December 30, 2009

ॐ Dear . . . ,

Namaste. Thank you for your letter of the 26th. Thank you for the offerings to the temple that you enclosed. In addition, thank you for the CD of your music. You have selected an especially profound section of John's Gospel. Your letter is written very well and is expressive of an affinity for the very same spiritual depth to which Shanti devoted herself and in which she was absorbed.

Obstacles and challenges are of a phenomenal or bodily character. The Truth of the Self is transcendent. It is as natural to abide steadily in the Knowledge of the Self, in God, as it is to exist. As there is no obstacle to Being and no difference between the Self and oneself, so it is with Self-Knowledge. The manifestation of that which is true, good, and beautiful derives from this one, absolute source. Thus, for That, in That, there are no "ups and downs."

You are always warmly welcome to visit or to write. Yes, we are brothers in Spirit.

May you ever abide in, and as, the Eternal, which is declared in the Vedas as Brahman, which is praised and worshipped as God, the Lord of the universe, and which is realized as the Self by all who cease to imagine a separate individuality, and thus be ever happy and at peace.

Ever yours in Truth,
Nome

[This is a response to a seeker who had corresponded several times previously.]

January 5, 2010

ॐ Dear . . . ,

Om Namo Bhagavate Sri Ramanaya
Namaste. Thank you for your message. Two beneficial perspectives can be reflected upon. The first is the orientation of the entire life. If the central focus and what is valued the most is Self-Realization, the supreme good will result. Attachments will dissolve, and the mind will be consistently introspective, even while in the midst of various activities. The precious time of this life will be used wisely, which is joyful. The second is, since you, the Self, are not the body, you are never the performer of action, and, since you, the Self, are the Bliss, you do not depend on external activities to provide you with happiness. Thus, you can be fully happy and at peace regardless of the work, activity, health, energy level, etc. Therefore, the entire experience becomes profoundly transcendent continuously.

Listen (sravana), reflect (manana), profoundly meditate (nididhyasana), and remain absorbed in the Truth.

Ever yours in Truth,
Nome

[A family in India who had no previous contact in any way with SAT sent a message in which they described the sudden

onset of symptoms of disease of a family member who was diag-
nosed as having "stage four" lung cancer. They requested "spe-
cial prayers" on his behalf. Here is the response.]

January 11, 2010

ॐ Dear . . . ,

Om Namo Bhagavate Sri Ramanaya

Namaste. Severe illness, injury, impending death, or the occurrence of death, for a loved one or for oneself, call one to meditate upon and firmly abide in the Knowledge of the Self. It is the misidentification of the Self with the body that is the cause of the fear, anxiety, and sorrow. If this misidentification is relinquished, suffering ceases, and the supreme peace of the Self prevails. The Existence of the Self never ceases. It does not begin or end and does not perish when the body perishes. Therefore, neither for the living nor for the dead do the wise grieve.

To thus remain at peace yourself is a powerful form of prayer for your brother, one that has its basis in that which is immortal.

At some time or another, every form vanishes; all that are born inevitably eventually disappear. The Self is not born with the birth of the body and does not cease to be when the body ends. The Self of all is this Self. Rest in the certainty of this eternal Truth.

Illness of the body does not touch the true Self. Pain does not touch it. Water does not wet it, and fire does not burn it. Wind does not wither it, and the earth does not cover it. It remains, ever changeless and perfect.

Whatever be the outcome of the present situation, all is by Grace. Nothing is without a divine purpose. Both life and death, good health and ill health, are within the scope of this Grace.

Bhagavan Sri Ramana Maharshi reveals this divine Truth, with infinite Grace. Devotion to Him, surrendering all of one's worries, and the individual who worries, to Him,

254

yields sublime peace and transcendence over the transient dream of this world.

Self-inquiry and surrender are supremely potent "prayers."

Yes, prayers are always beneficial. Let your prayers for [name omitted] be such as to see all dwelling in and merging with the Supreme Lord, who is like an immovable mountain. If the health of his body is temporarily regained, such is by Grace, and, if the life of that body concludes, such is also by the same Grace.

The Knowledge and devotion indicated above do not preclude taking every active step that he, you, family and friends can take to attempt to preserve [name omitted]'s life. For this purpose, included below is a letter from my wife regarding treatments for cancer about which [name omitted]'s doctor may be ignorant. No treatment is guaranteed to be successful. Since you have access to a computer and the web (internet), you can read about what is possible for yourself by looking at the websites mentioned. If you cannot travel to these places, you can implement some of these treatments at your own place or find a clinic in India that treats patients in a similar manner. The patient owes no allegiance to the doctors who cannot help him cure himself. So, remain peacefully detached from the body, yet try your very best; try your very best, yet remain detached from the body.

Ever yours in Sri Bhagavan,
Nome

[This is a message from a very dear devotee of Sri Bhagavan at RMCL. Nome's response follows.]

January 15, 2010

Dear and respected Master Nome,

Your letter written on the date of Bhagavan's Advent in the human form comes as a great blessing to me, to my mother, and to the Centre. I am deeply touched by the donation that you have sent. As you have rightly said, everything is in Sri Ramana's hands always. Whenever His grace gives me this awareness of His infinite power and love, nothing is a problem. However, the clouding of the mind due to ignorance sometimes makes me identify with the illusory body and its appendages with all their ups and downs.

The books not only arrived promptly but were lapped up by the seekers of truth visiting our Centre. I was wondering whether we could carry extracts from the book in a serialized manner in the Ramana Way.

I am sending you two CDs, "Ramana Suprabhatam" and "Ramana Bharat" along with the letter.

Once again thank you for your great love that flows directly from the Self.

With deep regards to you and Sasvati ji,
Yours in Ramana,

ॐ Dear . . . ,

Om Namo Bhagavate Sri Ramanaya

Namaste. Thank you for your message and your letter of December 25th, which were received on the same day.

Of course, you are free to use any portion of any SAT publication in the *Ramana Way,* each issue of which is always a delight to read.

Thank you for sending the CDs. They are eagerly awaited.

Once, when traveling from the holy RMCL to Sri Ramanasramam escorted by your beloved Appa, we conversed, in the Light of Sri Bhagavan's Grace and Supreme Knowledge, about the nature of the mind, the practice that destroys the mind, what is meant by "freedom from thought" and such. Here is the gist of what was discussed.

In truth, there is no mind, of any kind or form, at all, in the Self, which is the sole-existent Reality.

256

If an existent mind is imagined to be, it is an illusion or a misperception of Consciousness, which is actually ever without modification.

The root of the mind, as Sri Ramana has explained, is the "I," or ego-assumption. Thus, the mind is only "I" in various guises. If there is not inquiry, if the path to know the mind's nature is not yet pursued, the mind appears as a bundle of thoughts, as explained by the Maharshi, apart from which there is no form of the mind. Ignorance is only misidentification, which manifests in various imagined forms within the mind. One of them, which is pivotal, is the misidentification with the body.

Freedom from thought or destruction of the mind is essential. Initially, such is the sufficient focus of an inward turned mind to pursue the spiritual quest, unobstructed by the ridiculous ramblings conjured up by an extroverted mind. From that, freedom from thought is the ability to discriminate as ignorance the thought forms and patterns that are based upon misidentification. This causes them to be abandoned. From that comes the discerning of Consciousness that is beyond thought as distinct from thought. With a steady poise in the "I" by inquiry, the ignorance and the thoughts that form such or sprout from such, vanish. When we ask, "For whom are the thoughts? Who am I?", the very supposition of an existent mind or existent thought disappears. This is absolute freedom from thought or complete "destruction" of the mind, for in the limitless, undifferentiated Self, such things have never been created.

This, in brief, is the gist of what that dear devotee of Bhagavan, Sri A. R. Natarajan, and I discussed during the journey. It is related here in the event it is of interest.

No matter the ups or downs, truly, just as the Self is utterly unchanging, so Sri Ramana's omnipresent Grace is ever there, all around and within you, to such an extent that we know that there is really nothing to us but Him. The bliss of such Grace erases without a trace whatever was imagined in the mind.

257

Sasvati sends her love. Please convey our love and best regards to Smt. Sulochana.

Ever yours in Sri Bhagavan,
Nome

[A seeker was directed to SAT by another seeker in India. Her questions can be inferred from this response.]

January 21, 2010

ॐ Dear . . . ,

Om Namo Bhagavate Sri Ramanaya
Namaste. Thank you for your message.

You say that you are unsure as to where to start. The best "place" to start is with that which is absolutely certain, about which you have no doubt at any time. That is your very existence. It is not possible to doubt your very existence, though it is possible to doubt that which is not actually your existence. Even if you would have a doubt regarding it, you would still assume that you exist to entertain or know the doubt. You may wish to refer to the beginning of Sri Sankara's *Svatmanirupanam (True Definition of One's Own Self)* for more on this point.

Focused on your very Existence, commence to discriminate between what is this Existence and what is not but illusorily associated with it in delusion in the form of misidentification. Cease to regard what is objective and transient and whatever appears and disappears, gross or subtle, as yourself. What is not the very Existence is not you and is not real. What is real is always so. What is true regarding the Self is always so. You may wish to refer to the Maharshi's *Who am I?* and to *Self-Knowledge* for more on this.

Whatever is not continuously present regardless of the three states (waking, dream, and deep dreamless sleep) cannot be your very Being. This applies to the various experiences of the senses by which the world is conjured, the body, various modes of mind (fear, "presence," etc.), thoughts, the mind itself, and even the assumed individuality or ego, which is the supposed experiencer of the aforesaid. Only that which always is, and is without increase or decrease, without appearance or disappearance, is true and truly you.

For whom is life and death? For whom is the appearance of the body? For whom is unity and multiplicity? For whom is perception and conception? For Self-Realization, which is Liberation from all of the imagined bondage, you must find, within, the answer to the question, "Who am I?" Inquire.

What do you mean by "life"? Is it the tiny, fleeting experiences perceived through the senses? Is it the minute thoughts of the mind? First, find out who you are, and then you can say what is life.

Freedom from attachment, which is confusion regarding the source of happiness, will yield clarity regarding your question of "trust."

The Upanishad declares, "Where there is a second, as it were, there is fear." A "second" is dualism. The primary dualism, upon which all illusion is based, is the notion "I." Conversely, where there is no such false notion of "I," there you abide as the infinite and the eternal. That alone is your true state, or real identity. That is Brahman; that is the Self. That you are (tat tvam asi).

I hope that you find what is briefly stated here beneficial. You may also find it useful to read some of the teachings of Sri Ramana Maharshi and some of the works of traditional Advaita Vedanta, such as *Ribhu Gita*, for inspiration, instruction, and to understand the context of what has been mentioned here.

May your Self-inquiry be profound, so that, serenely unattached to the unreal, you know yourself as the Self and thereby abide in the perfect fullness of Bliss always.

Ever yours in Truth,
Nome

[This is a response to a seeker who had corresponded several times previously. His questions can be inferred from the answers.]

January 21, 2010

ॐ Dear . . . ,

Om Namo Bhagavate Sri Ramanaya

Namaste. The *Bhagavad Gita* says: For that which has birth, death is certain; for that which has death, birth is certain. If there is the individual, incarnation will follow. Is there the individual? Ask yourself: Who am I? For the Self, unborn and immutable, there is no incarnation, no death, and no rebirth. If you consider the nature of Self-Realization, that is, its nondual nature in which the Knowledge is only Being, itself, why the scriptures declare the absence of rebirth for a jnani is clear.

As for the supposed blackness, blankness, or nothingness, there must be one who knows such. Who is he?

We should abide as That in which there is no ego and which is reached by those who embrace what is true, good, and beautiful. We should not waste our breath or even a thought on the peculiar karma-producing activities of deluded egos. To say this bluntly in, perhaps, an overly simplified manner: there are plenty of good people to speak of, why bother about those who insist on wrong-doing?

260

Abidance in the Knowledge that perceives the true Self of all is best.

Know that within you which is the perfectly full, immortal Bliss. In That, all fears are gone, all desires are dissolved, and that which is real is self-evident.

Ever yours in Truth,
Nome

[This is a response to another seeker. The questions raised by her can be surmised from the response.]

January 21, 2010

ॐ Dear . . . ,

Om Namo Bhagavate Sri Ramanaya.

Namaste. The purpose of the manifested life may be said to be Self-Realization. Thus, the Paramartha (Supreme Truth) is the final artha (purpose, truth) of the purusa-artha-s (human purposes or goals) and is called Moksa (Liberation), as described in the Vedas. This Self-Realization is attained by a profound Self-inquiry. For whom is the perception of "life"? The same one Self is regarded as God, the solitary power of this universe, or as the unmoved Witness of the entire mind, or as uncreated, undifferentiated Being-Consciousness-Bliss, according to the depth of understanding of the experiencer, the meditator, or the Knowledge of the Self, itself.

Yes, ignorance creates an illusory mess. Suffering is only imagined bondage. Bondage is only ignorance. Ignorance is composed of misidentification. Liberation from misidentification is the self-illumined revelation of the ever-indestructible Purnam (Perfect Fullness) of the Self. Know yourself. Inquire.

The concept of being the performer of action depends on misidentification with the instruments of body, speech, and mind. Inquire to discern your true nature, which is not to be defined by such objective things.

The Silence and Grace of the Maharshi are ineffably sublime.

I hope that, upon meditation upon it, the above is helpful for you.

Ever yours in Truth,
Nome

[This is a response sent by Nome to a seeker who commented favorably on some of the translation work published by SAT.]

January 25, 2010

ॐ Dear . . . ,

Om Namo Bhagavate Sri Ramanaya
Namaste. Thank you for your messages.

It is enough if one realizes That before which all words and thoughts turn back, unable to grasp. That is of the nature of Absolute Silence. Having realized That, whatever may be the expressions that pour forth, they are correct for they shine with divine Truth.

Ever yours in Truth,
Nome

[This is a message from a seeker who resides at a distance from the temple. Nome's response follows.]

January 26, 2010

Namaste Nome,

I've noticed recently in meditation and otherwise that there is a feeling of unsettledness, diffused focus, etc. Rather than resist this unwanted mental activity, I try to remember that the gunas come and go for someone and to keep inquiring. Also, I try to remember to unburden my ego load to Ramana-Shiva.

It's pretty silly to try to use thought to become unbound from thought.

Thank you for Advaita Devatam. I'm using it as an aid to meditation. Any other suggestions for its use?

I'm also wondering about the linkage between the two words, "jagat" and "jagrat." I understand jagat to stand for the world and jagrat to stand for the waking state. The world appears and disappears along with the waking state's rise and fall. Is this the reason for the similarity in the words?

Om Namo Bagavate Sri Ramanaya
Aloha

ॐ Dear . . . ,

Om Namo Bhagavate Sri Ramanaya
Namaste. Thank you for your message.

Regardless of the guna of the mind, your nature is ever the entirely peaceful, unmoved, clear Consciousness. Know this with certainty by profound inquiry. In addition, investigate to determine if there is some unexamined vasana that is the cause of the mental mode.

Inquiry, being transcendent of the mind, is not limited in its capacity to liberate you from the illusory bondage of thought.

The book *Advaita Devatam* is for devotional and meditation purposes, as well to further the nondual understanding of the symbols described. The CD entitled *From Advaita Devatam* is for meditation purposes, though it is not intended as a substitute for actual inquiry.

Jagat means moving, movable, that which is alive, the world, the universe, and even humankind. It is said to derive from the root gam, which means to go, move, to pass, or to undergo a condition or state. Jagrat could be transliterated as jaagrat, considered a participle, the root of which is said to be jaagri, which means waking. So, while a connection of the two words is not readily apparent, what you have said regarding the world being only an appearance in the waking state, rising and falling with it, is quite true.

Repose in the happiness that Ramana-Siva is the support of all, the Light, and your very Self.

Ever yours in Truth,
Nome

[A response to a letter received from another seeker who resides at a distance from the temple. Each paragraph is in answer to a question or a comment upon a statement that can be inferred from the response.]

January 28, 2010

ॐ Dear . . . ,

Om Namo Bhagavate Sri Ramanaya
Namaste. Thank you for your letter of January 25th, which was received today.

When happiness surges forth from within, it is the Bliss of your own true nature, the Self, that thus shines. When serenity floods your experience, it is the peace of your own true nature, the Self, that thus shines.

When the illusion of depressed modes of mind and similar suffering cast a veil, such is due to misidentification and its concomitant falsely placed emphasis on thoughts

264

that are not true, not you, and not real. As revealed by Sri Bhagavan, inquiry destroys such misidentifications along with their effects, the mental modes.

Suffering is self-imagined; profound happiness is the Self's nature. Neither is caused by an external cause.

You always have the ability to discern the true and to abandon the false.

For that which has birth, death is certain. The Unborn is immortal, and, in that, there is imperishable peace.

Ever yours in Truth,
Nome

[A response to a message from another seeker:]

February 2, 2010

ॐ Dear . . . ,

Om Namo Bhagavate Sri Ramanaya
Namaste. Thank you for your message.

Though you say that you lack confidence in that which is real, you are completely certain of the fact of your existence. Focused upon that, inquire to abandon the misidentifications, so that the Knowledge of the Self, the sole Reality, becomes certain.

The Self is only one, and the individual is not real. Death of the body does not necessarily equate with destruction of misidentification. The *Gita* says that for that which has birth death is certain, and for that which has death birth is certain. Therefore, it is wise to realize your nature, bodiless and egoless, to be unborn and thus imperishable. Removal of an object in one's experience will be replaced by another, even if the other is an absence or a blank, which will also be replaced in time. Inquiry into the subject, apart from which the object has no existence what-soever, yields permanent Liberation from all dualism, bondage, and birth-and-death.

Happiness is of the very nature of Being. Thus, one does not wish to cease to exist. Realize your innately immortal Existence as the bodiless, egoless Self, and thereby abide in happiness and peace without end.

"Fear is where there is duality, as it were," says an Upanishad. Nonduality is fearlessness. Know the Self that is One without a second.

Ever yours in Truth,
Nome

[Here is a message from a seeker, along with the response from Nome.]

February 11, 2010

Om Namo Sivaya

Dear Nome,

Namaste from [name omitted]. All is well here. Hope for same there. I have this question that is coming up for a while now. In meditation/contemplation, I find it easy to just sink into the Self when my eyes are open because, when I look at the surroundings, all objects have this neon sign on them that says "go home" right away. I am aware of the "I" who is seeing them, and, right at that instant, I know and feel my real existance separate from that "I." There is no thought or word; there is the feeling of "ahhh, finally home." But if I try to capture the same (capture is not the right word, but you know what I mean) with my eyes closed, I feel that I am still hanging or floating around in mental world. There is a lack of that big push/punch from visual objects.

I tried asking "Who does not see any object?" But that does not seem to work, so please help me. My day starts with reading of *Sat Darshanam* and ends with listening to satsang cds. For longer and

266

longer periods, there is awareness of absence of "I" thought, the hook on which any and every thing can possibly hang. There are certain passages in *Sat Darshanam* that serve as stepping stones to the inward plunge.

Thanks again for your loving, kind guidance.
Namaste.

ॐ Dear . . . ,

Om Namo Bhagavate Sri Ramanaya
Namaste. Thank you for your message.

Inquire for whom the mental realm, whether with thought forms or blank, appears, so that, with your focus entirely nonobjective, the ever-present Consciousness stands revealed. That is the same with or without objects, and that alone is the Self. There is not an individual self, a second, to leave the true "home" of yourself. The Existence of this only Self is equally real at all times. All point to that; all are only that. Any apparent difference is an illusion born of misidentification. The opening and closing of the eyes do not make the difference. By inquiry, repose in the Self, as the Self, in peace and bliss.

Sri Bhagavan's *Saddarshanam* is of utmost profundity.

Om Namah Sivaya

Ever yours in Truth,
Nome

[A message from a seeker and Nome's response]

February 16, 2010

Dear Nome,

Om Namo Bhagavate Sri Ramanaya.

Namaste. Thank You for ever-present Existence which is Being, Identity, and Peace. My heart is full and happy in the Self as the Self. I humbly ask for Your help. I think I might have been out of line when we had the private conversation, for thereafter I could not/would not maintain the level or depth of inquiry that I was proclaiming during the private conversation. I became misidentified with old vasanas in the form of love and happiness being external/connected with forms/relationships and clinging to / believing in these ideas. I realize more clearly now that, if I am suffering, I made a mistake. I now can proceed to recognize these as mere ideas and not the Reality. The Self is too precious to cover over, causing one to "move about listlessly" as Sri Bhagavan so clearly describes.

Thank You once again for Being,
Ever Yours in Truth,

ॐ Dear . . . ,

Om Namo Bhagavate Sri Ramanaya

Namaste. Thank you for your message. The later appearance of residual delusive tendencies does not invalidate an earlier, clearer state of inquiry, but it does show the need for continued, even deeper inquiry.

He who knows that his mistake is, indeed, a mistake no longer repeats it and can no longer be regarded as mistaken.

Where love is identical with Being is your true abode. Realize this by devotion, by inquiry, and by the Grace of Sri Bhagavan.

Ever yours in Truth,
Nome

[This is a message from a gentleman from Scotland who had never written previously. Nome's response follows.]

February 17, 2010

My dear people,

I have just returned from Arunachala where I met with some wonderful people from SAT. Though I did not abide with them very long I was introduced to the *Ribhu Gita* as translated by Nome and Dr .H. Ramaoorthy. It is to these that I offer my heart-felt gratitude. This translation reaches to the very highest that language and words can attain before they disappear into the Silence that gave birth to them. Nowhere except in the words of Bhagavan Ramana have I felt such intimacy of Truth and Grace.

Nome has given the world a most fragrant and sacred gift. It is right that we should all give deep thanks for such a work, for here I feel are the very sounds of Siva uttered just prior to the arising of the identified mind. I know also that a gentle and beautiful being dropped her body in complete surrender to That, in the Grace of our dear Maharshi whilst I was there. Her name was Sarasvati and, although I spoke with her only a few times, her spirit reached out to me in my suffering, silently and completely. When I learnt of her passing, my heart cried, though I hardly knew her, but I knew also of a great wordless significance that I cannot explain.

For all of this and my time within Arunachala, I send you all at SAT my deepest love and fondness for a woman that I never knew.

I thank you, Nome, with the wordless love I have for Bhagavan and his dear disciple Sri Muruganar. I cannot say anymore.

ॐ Dear . . . ,

Om Namo Bhagavate Sri Ramanaya

Namaste. Thank you for your message. It is always a joy to hear from those who deeply love Sri Ramana.

We are glad to know that you are finding the *Ribhu Gita* to be beneficial and to know of your attunement to this sacred text that reveals the Truth of the Self, the Reality. When you have the opportunity, you may wish to look at the *Song of Ribhu*, too, which is an English translation from the Tamil version of the scripture. The *Ribhu Gita* is the translation into English from the Sanskrit original. Some find them to be good "companion" volumes. If you

269

look at the SAT website, you can see more about these and other similar literature and recordings.

For that which has birth, death is certain. For the Unborn, immortality is innate, as Existence, which is the Self, can never become otherwise. That is the true abode, the imperishable, the bodiless, and the undying fount of love. That is the very nature of Grace and is the perfect fullness. That, of the nature of beginningless and endless Being −Consciousness-Bliss is alone what you are.

If you are ever in California, please know that you would be very warmly welcome to visit the SAT temple.

May you ever abide as the Self, in the inconceivable Knowledge of itself, in the Silence in which neither the assumption of "I" nor any other misidentification is possible, and thus dwell in peace and happiness always.

Om Namah Sivaya

Ever yours in Truth,
Nome

[Here is a message from a devotee of Sri Ramana at Tiruvannamalai, who had written a few times previously. Nome's response follows.]

February 27, 2010

My dear sir,

Two days back, I developed a catch in the hip. I assumed it is because of depression. Whenever there is any problem, I think it is a depressive disorder.

I showed to the doctor, and he examined me and said that that is due to age related factor.

I developed 20 years back a problem. I worked beyond my limit. Later, I suffered and it made my mind very confusing and something came to me.

I myself met the doctor. I was labeled as bipolar.

Later, when any problem comes, I think of that depressive disorder. But ultimately, it is not so. If I could have met the doctor, they would have suitably advised.

Now I am better .

Kindly advise me how to trace properly, in what way I can approach Bhagawan.

Yours,

ॐ Dear Sri . . . ,

Om Namo Bhagavate Sri Ramanaya

Namaste. Thank you for your message.

Approach Bhagavan with a heart full of devotion and with complete trust in Him. Approach Bhagavan with humility and faith. Approach Bhagavan with conviction in His teachings and ardently, consistently, eagerly practice them.

By whatever name called, the shifting of mental moods is only the play of delusion. Trace them to the misidentifications that form their root. That will destroy the mood. Inquire to know the Self as it is, and the innate continuous happiness will shine as the revelation of your true Self. Moods are changeful illusions dependent on the content of thought. The one who knows them is unchanging and is the un-conceived knower of all thought. Who is that one? Ask yourself, "Who am I?"

Regardless of bodily ailments and their symptoms, it is wise to know the Self as free from the body, for in this is found true peace and immortal Bliss.

May your inquiry be profound so that you abide in the perfect Self, as the perfect Self.

Ever yours in Sri Bhagavan,
Nome

271

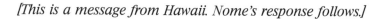

[This is a message from Hawaii. Nome's response follows.]

March 26, 2010

Namaste Nome,

I came across this quote on page 114 in *Day by Day*, and I'm not entirely clear that I understand it:
Though I have become you and you alone exist
Undestroyed the 'I' persists
As I within that knows
And I that turns to what is known,
The many things knowing and unknowing

Thayumanavar

What is he getting at here?
I probably ought to be asking more questions than I do.
I'm getting a lot from the DVDs and CDs—being connected in the company of the wise—even from a physical distance.
I'm finding the inquiry valuable upon waking in the morning and it's still dark and quiet—just lying there in bed, old vasanas, concerns, fears—fear of death—can bubble up. This 'Who am I?' interrupts the following of these worthless thought trains. Just now, on reflecting though, I see that I'm stopping short of really trying to trace the source of the individual who just appeared upon awaking.

Om Namo Bhagavate Sri Ramanaya
Much aloha,

ॐ Dear . . . ,

Om Namo Bhagavate Sri Ramanaya
Namaste and Aloha! Thank you for your message.
Tayumanavar's words are interpreted differently according to the depth of the readers. Since Sri Bhagavan selected the verse in question and, in effect, combined it with the

verse mentioned on the previous day along with the verse by Nammalvar, we must understand such from the view of pure Advaita, which is the zenith of both knowledge and devotion. The highest unity of Siddhanta and Vedanta is also stated in Sri Ramana's *Upadesa Manjari (Origin of Spiritual Instruction)*. Thus, the first line determines the rest of the meaning, that is, that "You alone exist." "You" signifies Siva, who is the Supreme Self. "I have become You" signifies the complete destruction of the falsely assumed individuality, so that That alone is known to solely exist. Then, the "undestroyed I" can refer only to Consciousness, the real Existence. Elsewhere, the Maharshi states that where "I" vanishes, another "I"- "I" shines forth. That alone constitutes the knower and the known. One Consciousness illuminates all knowing, and it illuminates even a state of unknowing, as well.

I hope that this clarifies the meaning for you.

If you pursue the inquiry to the essence of "I," the fears and concerns will be destroyed by Knowledge, and deathless peace will remain. Seek not so much for the temporary calming of thoughts as, rather, the utter uprooting of them in True Knowledge of what the Self, your only Self, is. To support and lead you in such inquiry, there is limitless Grace.

Ever yours in Truth,
Nome

[This is a response to a seeker who had communicated several times previously.]

March 30, 2010

ॐ Dear . . . ,

Om Namo Bhagavate Sri Ramanaya

Namaste. Thank you for your messages.

Ardent spiritual practice is beneficial. By doing your utmost to practice the inquiry to know the Self, the significance of the spiritual instruction already given will be understood more and more deeply. Become free of the self-imposed, imagined limitations, the unreal ego and all its illusory, delusive manifestations, and realize your true Being as the infinite and the eternal. This is true Knowledge.

May you ever abide in the innate happiness and peace of the Self.

Ever yours in Truth,
Nome

[This is from a couple, written by the husband, who were regularly attending the SAT Temple but who had recently moved out of the country. Nome's response follows.]

April 7, 2010

Namasthe Nome,

Finaly, after two weeks, we are settled in home. I don't know how I am going to find a job here. I hope I will get a job.

Nome, I have a question. For the last 2.5 years, I was staying home without any work. Is this my mistake by having taken a wrong decision or was it per my fate? Our relatives advised me that I have taken a wrong decision to come to U.S., but I have got the good opportunity to practice Sri Ramana Maharshi's teachings.

Thoughts are rising from the mind even without thinking about that particular person or situation. Are these thoughts already decided or am I able to prevent these particular thoughts? Some thoughts rise about what happened several years before, even though it is after eliminating those thoughts by enquiry.

Do our thoughts rise based on our karma or do they rise based on environment?

Namasthe,

274

ॐ Dear . . . and . . . ,

Om Namo Bhagavate Sri Ramanaya
Namaste. Thank you for your message.

It is good to know that you and [name omitted] are better settled there now. All occurs by one supreme power, so there is never a real reason to be anxious or to suffer.

That which encourages introversion and prompts inquiry is a wise way. That which furthers bondage in samsara is an ignorant mistake. That which causes devotion to spring up is wise. That which causes the mind to stagnate in worldliness is ignorance. That which takes one beyond thoughts, revealing that your Self can never be an object of thought, is wise. That which brings about misidentification and entanglement in thought is a mistake.

The environment is itself a thought. So, how can it be said to be the cause of thought? Action (karma) and its result are inert, declares the Maharshi, and are also forms of thought. So, how can they be the cause of thought? It is better to discriminate and trace the sense of identity to its origin and, thereby, liberate oneself from thought and its assumed cause.

Grace it is that brings one to Sri Bhagavan. This Grace dissolves both the ideas of free will and fate. This Grace reveals itself as the very nature of the Self.

Ever yours in Truth,
Nome

[This is a message from a seeker who read Essence of Enquiry. Nome's response follows.]

April 23, 2010

Hello...a note to Nome if he is available;

I have read several books about Ramana over the years and find that I resonate to them most strongly compared to others I have read, e.g. [six names omitted], to name a few. I recently started reading *Essence of Inquiry* and found it to be the most powerful yet with respect to the degree of clarity, depth, resonance....on and on....words are too inadequate to express the feelings that arise as I imbibe the spirit carried by these words.

As I set the book aside, I find an insistent question arising: is there a next step? Is it time to be in the Presence of someone like Nome? The readings seem to indicate that the Self that shines through Nome and others is the same that shines within this BMO. Inquiry is all that is necessary. In other places in the readings, it is said that there is no substitute for being in the Presence of Self-realized Beings. Can you offer some light into this confusion?

I have had the experience of touching that which remains when inquiry is made and the illusion of the "me" dissolves leaving only awareness, several times, in fact, unless I am deluding myself, (a distinct possibility). It is possible to make the inquiry at any time that awareness arises and return once again to that stillness. Yet, the self, thought, arises yet again and the veil descends. Again, can you cast a guiding light?

All is well,

ॐ Dear . . . ,

Om Namo Bhagavate Sri Ramanaya

Namaste. Thank you for your message. I am glad to know that you resonate with the teachings of Sri Bhagavan and that you are finding *Essence of Inquiry* beneficial.

With regard to your first question, it would be wise to first ascertain what is meant by "presence." Can it mean "in the proximity of some body"? If not, how is the location to be determined and, indeed, what actually is the presence? If it is the bodiless Self, which is the real identity of the realized and oneself, near and far, now and then, and in and out lose their significance. If one conceives of a personal view of the realized presence, such is confusing the real and the unreal. It is best to inquire, which reveals that the Real

276

ever is and the unreal never is. That undivided Reality is the Self and the only Existence. Of course, scriptures and wise sages recommend seeking the company of the wise as being very helpful. You may also find such to be so by your own experience.

As for the second question: for whom is the "arising"? Who returns and who knows such? To what do you return? There cannot be two of you. Who are you?

If you visit the SAT temple, you will be warmly welcome.

May you ever abide in the Knowledge of the Self, which is "the Self that dwells in the hearts of all," of the nature of unborn, uncreated Being-Consciousness-Bliss, and thus always remain happy and at peace.

Ever yours in Truth,
Nome

[This is a response to a seeker who wrote on April 30, 2010, describing her depression in relation to the pressures at work and requesting guidance.]

ॐ Dear . . . ,

Om Namo Bhagavate Sri Ramanaya
Namaste. Thank you for your message.

The work demands the use of your body and that aspect of the mind required for such activity. It does not demand that you suffer or worry. Suffering and worry are due to confusion, which consists of overlooking the ever-present source of happiness within and mistaking yourself to be the body and such. Repose in the deeper Knowledge that you are actually the Self, free of the difficulties that pertain to the body.

Never forget that Bhagavan indwells your heart. Devoted reliance on Him yields peace.

Though the manifested events can be said to be related to previous karma, suffering is not so. Turn within, inquiring to know the Self, and you find yourself to be free.

Keep the present troubles in perspective. They are only external and transient. You, who are the Eternal, need not be adversely affected by them. Consider also the abundant Grace shining in your life, and you will see this life as precious, and your heart will fill with gratitude. Moreover, in contrast to what some others undergo, such as those with dire illness, starvation, pain, etc., your difficulties are not so great. In these ways and others, retain a sense of proportion.

Whenever you have any opportunity, read some of Sri Ramana's teachings or any of the SAT publications. The attempt to do so daily may be beneficial, even if it is just a little. Likewise, with listening or viewing satsang recordings on occasion.

Write (email) whenever you wish. I am always with you and in you.

May your inquiry, dissolving all apparent obstacles, reveal the Self, so that you abide in imperturbable bliss and imperishable peace.

Ever yours in Truth,
Nome

[This is from a seeker who wrote previously. Nome's response follows.]

April 30, 2010

Namasthe Nome,

I have a question. Normally, our minds focus on the outside, looking at all things as an object, but, when I am doing enquiry, it is very difficult to focus on the nonobjective Self. Per Ramana's teaching, being the Self is our real nature. How is it possible to merge with the Self? Please advise me.

If I pray to Ramana for a job, is it right? Per Ramana's teaching, the world is unreal. So, I am asking for something from the unreal.

Namasthe Nome.
Thanks and Regards,

ॐ Dear . . . ,

Om Namo Bhagavate Sri Ramanaya
Namaste. Thank you for your message.

It is fine to direct all your prayers to Sri Bhagavan. In this manner, you devote yourself to the all-powerful Source. Yet, deeper, yearn for no material or physical thing, but to know His Presence within you. In this way, your devotion becomes joyfully transcendent, and you remain unattached to the world. Deeper still, inquire to know Him as the one Self and to know all else as merely illusory. In light of this, true Knowledge dawns, and He, the one Self, alone exists, free from the least trace of an ego, with all desires resolved and all imagination destroyed.

By negation of misidentification, you are said to merge with the Self. Truly, the Self is ever nondual and undivided, and the ego, or separate individual, is ever unreal. This is abidance in Self-Knowledge.

Ever yours in Truth,
Nome

[This is from the same seeker. The response follows.]

May 7, 2010

Nameste Nome,

Om Namo Bagavathe Sri Ramanaya

I got a part-time job in a retail field in which I had work experience in India. It is very near to our apartment, so it is very convenient to pickup [name omitted] after school. Last week, I was walking in the park. I felt the peace in my mind, even though I was not doing any pranayama or yoga. How can the mind be silent without doing anything? I am able to watch the mind and enquire, "Who am I?" Can the mind subside without doing anything?

When listening to your satsang cd, I hear you say that there is no form of the mind, it is just a collection of thoughts, and the real Self within us, also, has no form. Is there a chance that I can misunderstand the mind as the real Self? Please clarify.

Namasthe,

ॐ Dear . . . ,

Om Namo Bhagavate Sri Ramanaya

Namaste. The peace that may be experienced with pranayama and yoga is actually innate. Peace is of the very nature of the Self.

When the form of the mind vanishes because of Self-inquiry, Consciousness, which is the mind's essence, remains. This is formless. This Consciousness, formless and egoless, for which there is no individual perceiver and which is eternal, is the Self.

Work has now been found by you. So, you can see how any anxiety over the matter was needless. In Grace, all is ever alright.

Ever yours in Truth,
Nome

[These next two messages are from a seeker who resides in another state, and Nome's response follows each one. The term "dharmasankatha" can be interpreted as a perplexing situation

or a dilemma, but in the reply it is also interpretted as a holy conversation or a discussion about Truth.]

May 14, 2010

Om Namo Bhagawate Sri Ramanaya
Dear Nome,
Namaste from [name omitted].

With Bhagawan's grace and your guidance, things are changing. There is longer abidance in and as consciousness and less and less identification with individual identity. Today, in my reading of *Sat-Darshanam* verse 24, it is said that the body does not know and the Self is not born. Between the Self and the body, a third imagined concept of "I" seems to exist. So, here is the confusion—if there is only Consciousness-Self existing, how can the ghost of the ego be said to be between Self and body, which is also nonexistent? Am I right to understand that this explanation is only at the body and mind level, only for the waking state, which is no different than the dream state? If I wake up, there is no body, no ego, no knot, no "I" and all those no's.

My warmest greetings to everybody there.

Om Namo Sivaya.
Thanks for everything.

ॐ Dear . . . ,

Om Namo Bhagavate Sri Ramanaya
Namaste. Thank you for your message.

Less or no misidentification with the individual is indicative of clear spiritual progress. The utter absence of the individual is of the very nature of the Self.

Spiritual instruction about the ego, illusion, etc. is only for the purpose of revealing their unreality, which is referred to as their destruction. So, if the ego is assumed or a connection between the Self and the body is supposed, Sri Bhagavan has graciously bestowed this spiritual instruction of utmost clarity that liberates one from this assumption or

281

supposition. Thus, the Reality of the Self stands revealed, transcendent of all differentiated individuality, illusion, etc., and even negation does not describe it. In this Truth lies your supreme Bliss.

May your inquiry be steady and deep so that you ever abide in blissful Self-Knowledge.

Om Namah Sivaya

Ever yours in Truth,
Nome

May 16, 2010

Om Namo Bhagawate Sri Ramanaya.
Namaste Nome.

Thanks for the email. All day yesterday, I was thinking thusly, "Is it all right and possible to keep just a tiny, tiny ego at the end, so I can hear and see all that is about Sri Bhagawan and your satsang dvd and all that describes the truth." Then, in my morning reading of Sat Darshan today, what do I read?

"There is no happiness in ego." So, please pull me out of this "Dharmasankata" catch 22.

Thank you and namaste.

ॐ Dear . . . ,

Om Namo Bhagavate Sri Ramanaya

Namaste. The ego sees nothing, as it is not endowed with Consciousness or any actual existence. Indeed, you see and hear the Truth, about Bhagavan, etc. without the ego illusion, and blissfully so. Taking the liberty to re-interpret the term, the true Dharmasankatha (dharma-samkathaa, pious coversation) is that of perpetual, luminous Silence, full of Grace and Truth, and all of our speaking and corresponding occurs within it. So, there is no catch or binding, but only the vast freedom of the true Self.

Om Namah Sivaya

Ever yours in Truth,
Nome

[A seeker who had attended satsang about 25 years earlier returned for a single satsang in 2009. Several months later, he wrote, describing some perplexity in his practice of inquiry, wishing to know if the "person" should fade away, and asking if this was the case in the story of Nome's spiritual practice and Self-Realization. Here is the response.]

May 16, 2010

ॐ Dear . . . ,

Om Namo Bhagavate Sri Ramanaya
Namaste. Thank you for your message.

Yes, passing mental modes, even clearer and happier ones, are not the finality, though the clarity and happiness do, indeed, have their deep source in the Self.

Seek not so much to stop seeking, but to know the seeker, for, in this way, you find, and you, yourself are that which is found, thus fulfilling the reason for the search.

Dissolution of the "person" by the cessation of misidentification is beneficial and is in keeping with realizing the nonexistence of an ego.

Be certain that the inquiry is not merely mental, for, if it is, you will experience the understanding of "there being no one there," as described by you but still conceive of yourself as an individual entity, one who is endowed with difference, a mind, a body, objects, etc. In profound inquiry, no such dualism prevails. Inquiring to know the inquirer, the Self knows itself as it is, and not even a trace of the ego and its personal story is found to exist. All of that was the adventure of someone who was never even born.

You may find it helpful to read *Essence of Inquiry, Saddarshanam and an Inquiry into the Revelation of Truth and Oneself,* and that which is on the SAT website www.SATRamana.org (downloads, Reflections, etc.)

You are always welcome at satsang. I hope that you find what is presented above helpful.

Ever yours in Truth,
Nome

[A seeker attended satsangs for several years until about 1986. He corresponded a few times in recent years and then became quiet. In May 2010, he wrote again, with this message. Nome's response follows.]

May 18, 2010

Hi, and good day to you.

Dear Guru Nome, I bother you only to write quickly and tell You what I found from You.

Just these last two days, I realize that my bigger problem has been not knowing that anyone who comes inside to SAT should observe reverence I apologize, but I have been following a hippie view that all people, whoever, can do whatever they do, but I have always remembered ahimsa, that no one should ever do violence.

The whole time that I spent at SAT, we always were taught and were trying to practice the highest level and this has regard for reverence. Now that I have found this, as like a precept, I see that I have missed the boat, all the way, until now. I think that if I see that reverence is mandatory here, then so much more I will be on the right track. I feel so darn strong in what I share with You, which is from You, (thanks), that I really do believe this is cool. I want to direct towards Your way the biggest, loudest shout I can muster for the observing of reverence for what goes on at SAT.

I really am so thankful that You taught that to me.

God Bless You, and Your Good Guru Ramana Maharshi.

Lots of love,

ॐ Dear . . . ,

Om Namo Bhagavate Sri Ramanaya
Namaste. Thank you for your message.

The reverence of which you speak is the natural manifestation of spiritual love and the dawning of wisdom that dissolves the ego-notion. However, you need not worry about the past, as your heart's love was always evident. With what you now know, you can appreciate and experience the Knowledge revealed by the Maharshi, Self-Knowledge, more profoundly. That which you revere also dwells within you.

Grace is ever present. May you abide in the Truth of the Self and thus dwell always in happiness and peace.

Ever yours in Truth,
Nome

[This is a message from a seeker who writes on occasion, with Nome's response.]

May 24, 2010

This is a question to master Nome. The eight negations of Nagarjuna, the Self or the Absolute, is this deconstructed also? Or is it said to exist or not to exist. No one to know or not to know. Om Namo Bhagavte Sri Ramanaya. Peace. Please comment.

ॐ Dear . . . ,

Om Namo Bhagavate Sri Ramanaya
Namaste. Thank you for your message.

Numerous ways of expressing the Truth have been brought forth by sages and saints and even by the intellects of scholars. The Truth, itself, remains ineffable and inconceivable, yet these expressions fulfill the worthy purpose of pointing one inward and act as an aid to discrimination, as well as being inspirational.

Negation is a prime means of such discrimination to reveal the Self (neti neti). The Reality, itself, can neither be affirmed nor negated for it is nondual, free of the notion of an individual to know or not know, and is ever-existent. Even if one thinks that there is nothing, still there is the "is" of that, which is to say, the Being-Consciousness of the one who knows the multiple negations can never be negated.

Though Self-Knowledge may be said to be reasonable, it transcends logic and all other forms of thought. It is wise to remain poised in a nonobjective, non-conceptual inquiry to thus realize the Self conclusively.

May you ever abide in the supreme happiness and peace within you.

Ever yours in Truth,
Nome

[This message is from a seeker who, along with her husband, had been to the SAT temple several years previously. Following a telephone call from them a few days earlier, she sent this message. The allusion to "Zero" is a reference to Lane Langston. Nome's response follows.]

May 26, 2010

Dear Nome,

Thank you for the very special telephone conversation. We were relieved to hear you sounding so well. We hope that your body will be well also!

There are some words I remember from many years ago that were from Zero. They were about what happens to the one who lays her life at the feet of her Guru, follows his instruction with one pointed intensity and turns life completely into service to the Guru. She also mentions disassembling of her ego. These words deeply touch my heart, yet I fall short. Would you please offer some instruction along these lines?

In deep love and gratitude,

ॐ Dear . . . ,

Om Namo Bhagavate Sri Ramanaya
Namaste. Thank you for your message.
Illness is only for the body. The Self, unborn and imperishable, remains blissfully as it is. Even upon the dissolution of the instruments of the body, speech, and mind, the Self, of the nature of Being-Consciousness-Bliss, abides unchanged, at peace and existing forever.
The Maharshi declares that God, Guru, and the Self are identical. The nature of the Guru, therefore, is not an object or an individual, but rather that Being-Consciousness-Bliss. Sri Ramana further instructs that what the Guru, who sees no difference between himself or others, does by means of spiritual instruction is to cause the disciple to abandon the illusory differentiation, which is in the form of misidentifications, so that she abides in the Truth of the Self and thus dwells fully in the innate bliss.
The phrase "feet of the Guru" found in devotional texts, verses, etc. signifies the manifested Guru, meaning that the "major portion" is unmanifested, just as the Upanishads state that the entire universe is but "one quarter" or "one portion" of Brahman. By means of association with the manifested, which includes receiving and practicing the spiritual instruction, the unmanifested, formless Silence of Being, which is the real Being of the Guru and the Self, is found. Surrender means subsidence of the ego, inclusive of its concomitant misidentifications, attachments, etc. When one knows the source of happiness within, attachments in the mind vanish, and she becomes naturally concentrated upon the quest of Self-Knowledge. Such quest and abid-

ance in Self-Knowledge are also the highest devotion, as mentioned by Sri Bhagavan, Sankara, Ribhu, and others. Firm abidance in the Self is the most profound service, and in those who are devoted to That is found all that is true, good, and beautiful.

To destroy the ego, seek it, inquiring to know yourself. If you so inquire, the ego will be realized to be nonexistent, and its effects, being unreal, will vanish. There are not two selves: an ego-self and a true Self. The Self is only one and is indivisible. The real ever is; the unreal never is.

I hope that you find the above helpful. Please covey my best regards to [name omitted].

May you ever abide in the profound depths of the Knowledge of the Self, which is the very source of wisdom and love, and thus be always happy and at peace.

Ever yours in Truth,
Nome

[This is a message from a devotee of Sri Ramana in Bangalore who has written several times since 1994. Nome's response follows.]

May 26, 2010

Dear Sri Nome,
Om Namo Bhagavathe Sri Ramanaya.

Namaste.
Please accept my namaskars. I hope that your health is fine and you are keeping well.

I went through some of the recently posted videos on the SAT website, and they are wonderful, especially the short snippet, the talk on "Who am I?". Yes, I am very much convinced and through my own experience that it is the everlasting bliss which has to be sought after, that it ever is. However we are caught in time, the process of birth and death.

What I understand is that Bhagavan's relation to each devotee or individual is eternal. However we need to strive for the same. The very process becomes the experience.

I feel intuitively, or it may be my own conviction which makes me feel, the athmic power which is always there with this. With continued practice and by Bhagavan's grace, we may proceed to grow and experience the same.

I just wanted to write to you from couple of days and I happened to visit the SAT website. I am not sure how much time is left for me to correspond with your physical presence.

I have not visited Sri Ramanasramam for long and just continue to practise in the morning hours and engage myself in work after that. I feel I need to put more effort for sadhana.

As always, I will look forward to your reply with the hope that I will strive well for seeking the true meaning of life.

Yours in Bhagavan,

ॐ Dear . . . ,

Om Namo Bhagavate Sri Ramanaya
Namaste. Thank you your message.

Though the health of this body is not well, the Truth of the bodiless, unborn, and imperishable Self, as revealed by Sri Bhagavan, is self-evident and ever is.

To be free from samsara, the illusory cycle of birth and death, destroy the ego assumption. To destroy that false assumption, inquire. Thus, there is blissful Self-Knowledge.

Grace and Knowledge are of the same nature. The very Existence of them is really the Self.

Whether at the Asramam or anywhere else, the Self exists. It is not more in one place or less in another. Within is the "place" of meditation, bodiless and world-less, and one who realizes the Self abides in That, as That, alone. That Self, of the nature of Being-Consciousness-Bliss, is infinite and eternal.

Persist in your earnest inquiry and devotion to the Maharshi. Not a drop of spiritual effort is in vain.

289

May you ever abide in the deep Knowledge of the Self, which is ever undivided and is that which you truly are, full of happiness and peace.

Ever yours in Sri Bhagavan,
Nome

[This is another message from the seeker who wrote on May 26th. Nome's response follows.]

May 28, 2010

Dear　,

Thank you for your compassionate reply. I understand more clearly what devotion and service are pointing to. Because I do not know the condition of your health, I feel an urgency to reach out to you for answers.

These are my questions: What should my day-to-day life look like in terms of maintaining true practice?

What is all this love that I feel permeating my heart and how do I use the strength of that in a positive way in my practice?

What is the feeling in my forehead that I feel when I do inquiry? Am I focused on the wrong thing?

I still wonder about how to disassemble my ego?

Knowing me as you do, what is the most important instruction that you could give me to keep me moving in the right direction and deeply immersed in practice? What instruction would help me stay dedicated moment to moment?

I understand life's purpose and do not want to waste this life.

I have been so very blessed in this life to know you and be with you. I am so grateful to you , Nome, so very grateful always.

All love,

ॐ Dear . . . ,

Om Namo Bhagavate Sri Ramanaya

Namaste. Thank you for your message. Due to the retreat held at the temple this weekend, this is the first opportunity to respond to you.

In answer to your questions in the order in which they were asked:

If you feel that you have a daily life, it is wise to engage in constant, profound inquiry to discern for whom it appears. If, as a result of such inquiry, you abide in the certainty of Knowledge regarding the bodiless, sense-transcendent, and mind-transcendent nature of your Self, the concept of a daily life vanishes, and the self-luminous real Existence remains. That Existence is truly your only existence. In light of this, it is like asking what does Brahman do with its "daily life"" or what should God do with His "daily life." More discussion on this appears in *Saddarsanam and an Inquiry into the Revelation of Truth and Oneself.*

Love may be said to be the bliss of the indivisibility of Being. It is wise to know that the love is for the sake of the Self, which dwells in the heart or as the essential Being of all.

Regardless of whether or not sensations, gross or subtle, are experienced, seek to know the knower of them. Inquiry pertains to Self-Knowledge, which is Realization of that which is infinite, eternal, nonobjective, and free of the duality of "I" and "this." Sensations of any kind are obviously transient, limited, objective, and are the "this" aspect of illusory duality. Your very Being is not a mere sensation and does not depend on such to know itself. Making your vision nonobjective, inquire to know who you are. This and other points regarding Self-inquiry and Self-Knowledge are found in *Self-Knowledge.*

Inquiry to know your true nature will assuredly destroy the ego, as light is said to destroy darkness, for the individual, or ego, is unreal and depends on non-inquiry even to be assumed. Trace your knowledge of existing to its core, and no ego will be found.

291

If you know the source of happiness, you remain serenely unattached, absorbed in the Bliss of the Self. If you inquire within, you abide free from thought as the self-luminous, illimitable, infinite Consciousness. If you know yourself, you abide in the Self, as the Self, of the nature of undifferentiated, eternal Being. By the clarity of Knowledge, happiness, reality, and identity return to their origin or true "place." If only one knows herself, she will find that to be indivisible, absolute Being-Consciousness-Bliss, without beginning and without end. If you imagine that you do not know the Self, earnestly inquire as to the nature of the one who does not know. As far as instruction regarding the Truth is concerned, silence is most eloquent. When even Sri Bhagavan and, in ancient times, Dakshinamurti were silent, who else could convey such by speech?

The Self is not an object apart from you, and you are not an individual apart from the Self. If you sincerely, intensely yearn for Self-realization, which is liberation from all of the imagined bondage, the way will be clear within you.

May you, devoted to the highest, repose in the Self as the Self, and thus abide in unwavering bliss and changeless peace.

Ever yours in Truth,
Nome

[This is a response to a seeker who wrote with questions about inquiry in a thoughtless state.]

June 4, 2010

ॐ Dear . . . ,

Om Namo Bhagavate Sri Ramanaya

Namaste. Thank you for your message.

With or without thoughts, you exist. This Existence, which is truly the nondual Self, is the foundation and goal of Self-inquiry and the teachings regarding Self-Knowledge.

True Knowledge is thought-transcendent. Thoughts possess no knowing power. They neither know each other nor know themselves. Consciousness, which is the Self, alone knows. This Consciousness knowing itself nonobjectively, not through sensory perception, mental conception, etc., is inquiry.

The inquiry is constituted of nonobjective knowledge. If thoughts appear, inquire for whom they appear. If a state that contains no thought appears, inquire for whom such appears. Whatever be the case, it is essential to know yourself. Inquire, "Who am I?"

Pursuit of this Self-inquiry as revealed by Sri Bhagavan is certain to yield blissful results.

Ever yours in Truth,
Nome

[Another message from the same seeker with the response to it.]

June 5, 2010

Dear Nome,
Om Namo Bhagavate Sri Ramanaya

Namaste.

Thank you so very much for your response to my questions. I deeply feel your support and appreciate how much you give to me. I was fortunate to also receive the CDs and DVDs I had ordered as well as the gift CD. I thank you with all my heart for your Grace!

I know I must inquire always. My thoughts, especially my worry thoughts, seem to overwhelm my intention to stay with my practice. I will continue to inquire and never give up.

I am curious about "the Supreme does all" and "free will". When I look back on this life, I see good and bad, things I regret, things I feel good about. Are my mistakes done by my free will or was all done by the Supreme? When I do something I feel good about, it seems it is being done, but not by me. Please clarify my confusion.

In deep love and gratitude,

ॐ Dear . . . ,

Om Namo Bhagavate Sri Ramanaya
Namaste. Thank you for your message.

If one knows where happiness is to be found, she will be steadily focused within. Worry involves confusion concerning happiness and existence. Happiness and Existence are truly the nature of the Self. If you deeply realize that happiness is in the Self and that the Self is ever-existent, you will be free of worry.

The questions concerning free will and divine destiny arise only so long as the ego's existence is assumed. In the undifferentiated Self, which has not the least trace of individuality, neither pertains and all doubts are resolved. If the Supreme Self, which is the Supreme Lord, alone exists, and, if there is "all," that alone is the existence of all and the power of all. If there is no "all," the Self alone exists, and doubt or differentiation cannot be imagined.

The concept of being the performer of action should be questioned. Its falseness can be discerned by understanding what is stated above and by the cessation of misidentification with the body.

The Self may be said to be the source of all that is true, good, and beautiful, and, whenever the ego subsides and to the extent that it subsides, this Self shines.

Additional instruction concerning fate and free will is contained in verse 19 of Sri Bhagavan's *Saddarsanam* and the commentary on such.

May your inquiry be deep so that you steadily abide as the Self that you really are and thus dwell in happiness and peace always.

294

Ever yours in Truth,
Nome

[This message is from the same seeker who asked about thoughtless meditation. Nome's response follows.]

June 8, 2010

Namaste Nome,

Thanks for your reply.

How do I find my way to self-inquiry? I can understand what you are saying about the Self, but, when I am doing inquiry, I have a doubt about where can I focus: on thoughts or who is watching all thoughts or the origin of thoughts that are rising.

Please help me to clarify my doubts.

Thanks and Regards,

ॐ Dear . . . ,

Om Namo Bhagavate Sri Ramanaya

Namaste. In answer to your question concerning which of the three possibilities mentioned by you should be your focus in Self-inquiry: "on thoughts" is objective, and so that cannot be the focus of inquiry. Moreover, you already focus on thoughts even without inquiry, so such would be redundant. If you inquire into the knower, the seer of all thoughts, or into the origin of thoughts deeply, the same realization of Consciousness as the nature of the Self will result. Consciousness, which knows, cannot be objective and is innately free of thoughts. In relation to thoughts, it may be said to be the witness, the substrate, the origin, etc. In itself, the Self transcends all such views. Inquire to know this Self.

Ever yours in Truth,
Nome

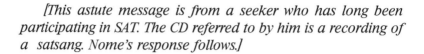

[This astute message is from a seeker who has long been participating in SAT. The CD referred to by him is a recording of a satsang. Nome's response follows.]

June 13, 2010

Dear Nome,
    Namaste!
    This morning while listening to the 9 May 2010 CD "Only One Self", the statement: "The scriptures declare that it is impossible to define Maya, illusion, for how could that which has no existence be defined?" stimulated a reflection on the nature of illusion. Please correct me if I'm wrong. I recall that the traditional concept of Maya refers to the power that produces what is not absolutely real nor absolutely unreal and is itself neither absolutely real nor unreal. It seems like a non-definition on the face of it, but it is a way of "defining" an experience that is dependent. Once there is an experience, it can't be said to 'not exist' because it's being seen, or talked about. I suppose all experience except for the experience of "being" could be called illusion. I'm not sure illusion is the best word because, in general parlance, an illusion is generally something that can't be used in a practical way. It is like the difference between drinking actual water and trying to drink illusory water. However, I don't believe there is an English word for Maya other than illusion. I recall the Sanskrit term mithya to define Maya and its product as what is not absolutely real and not absolutely unreal. Absolutely unreal refers to the nonexistent, like the horns on your head. It's not even in the realm of common illusion. Your horns simple don't exit and never could exist.
    I'm only reflecting on the thoughts that come up when I heard the above statement. As it is very clear when you speak, Ramana, and Ribhu speak, everything phenomenal can be regarded as nonexistent in the face of the sole existence. Even the scriptures that declare it's impossible to define Maya are themselves nonexistent to my true nature. But, I'm thinking the infinite beingness can include infinite imagination. It wouldn't seem reasonable to restrict the infinite by saying there couldn't be imagination in it. Imagination

is not a movement of consciousness because consciousness doesn't move. So what is it then? It simply can't be explained as anything other than imagination, and I don't see any other explanation. It's something that appears in consciousness, but has no actual reality. It doesn't obscure consciousness because its essence is nothing but consciousness. However, imagination should be seen for what it is, in order to see my reality as I actually am.

OK, enough of that. I should also say, I guess, that all the above, as well as this here and below, is only imagination. So, in this dream, there is an appreciation for the imaginary teacher who stands fast in the vision of the non-imaginary reality. If you are not my self, then who is? And if I'm not my self, then who is? And if the self is not all there is, then what is?

Ever grateful to you, Ramana and Ribhu for reflecting the truth as it is,

ॐ Dear . . . ,

Om Namo Bhagavate Sri Ramanaya

Namaste. Thank you for your message. What you have stated is clear, so please regard what is said here in response as additional comments and not as corrections.

In Monier-Williams Sanskrit dictionary, maya is defined as illusion, unreality, deception, an unreal and illusory image. A few other definitions are listed but they are not so directly connected to the use of the term in Advaita Vedanta. Sri Bhagavan says maya is "That which is not" (ma = not that ya = which). Mithya means false. The dictionary lists the meanings as inverted, incorrect, wrongly, falsely, untruly, to no purpose, etc.

There is only Existence. "Nonexistence" may be said to not exist or be only Existence; it amounts to the same.

When attempting to understand or interpret the spiritual instructions bestowed by wise, Self-realized sages, such as that which is preserved in the scriptures, it is important that they be approached from precisely the meaning, or state, from which they are uttered and not from dualistic or qualified nondualistic perspectives that are born of superimposed limitations, or misidentifications. Otherwise, the true significance is overlooked or misapprehended. So, the sayings of the wise are to reveal the Reality as it is free of all suppositions. The suppositions, such as the individual and the world (the objective sphere of experience), "I" and "this," are already known, or imagined, by one in delusion or bondage, and so an interpretation of the scriptures and such that is in accord with such suppositions would merely be redundant ignorance. True understanding transcends that context and is realized by Self-Knowledge.

Is that which "produces what is not absolutely real or absolutely unreal" itself real or unreal? If real, it is not maya or "illusion or unreal." If unreal, it does not exist. If the concept of it is a combination of real and unreal, is that combination real or unreal? If real, Liberation, which is the purpose of spiritual instruction and such, becomes impossible, and this runs contrary to all that has been declared by the wise sages, Advaita Vedanta, and to the very nature of the nondual, undivided Brahman. If unreal, it does not exist. If again both real and unreal, such represents an unending regression composed of only thought due to non-ascertainment of the Reality of the Self, pure Being-Consciousness, by thought-transcendent Self-inquiry.

Things seen, spoken of, etc. in a dream are just as illusory as the things not seen to occur in that dream. Practicality of dream things within the dream does not endow them with any additional reality. The senses cannot possibly be regarded as capable of discernment of Knowledge of Reality; likewise the mind. If one inquires for whom experience, sensation, thought, etc. appear, so that it is clear that there is no "it" at all apart from "I," and further inquires, "Who am I?" he realizes Absolute Brahman, the one Self free of even the least trace of illusion, difference, appearance, etc.

What pertains to "illusion and unreality" also applies to what is "false." To think that the false is true or partially true is the very definition of ignorance, which "inverts."

That the infinite Consciousness alone exists, without anything else whatsoever, represents no restriction. A snake-less rope is no bondage. The absence of the unreal or the imaginary is no loss. The apparent endlessness, solidity, vividness, etc. of the merely imagined may be said to be entirely reflected or borrowed from the real Self in order to direct one to realize that real Self. In Truth, though, the Real ever is and the unreal never is, as declared by *Bhagavad Gita.* The Self is the Reality. For whom would the unreal be?

Who imagines what? The one Self exists. How can we speak of it imagining? Another "I" is not. Even if referred to as "imagined," there is no other to do so, and it cannot imagine itself. All explanations of maya are only to show that it is not, for the Self-revelation of Reality.

The Truth is clearly revealed by Sri Ramana, Ribhu, Adi Sankara, and others. We can never be too grateful to them. That which they reveal, that which they are, that which I am, is that which you are. That is as it is, and That alone is. In this Light, blissful, perfect fullness exists always.

May you ever abide happy in the Self as the Self.

Ever yours in Truth.
Nome

[Here is the response to Nome's response.]

June 14, 2010

Ready, aim, fire!!! Dead and gone!
Illusion/imagination shot down by the execution squad of non-compromising total adherence to the non-dual truth.
Thank you for your comprehensive dissection and dismissal of illusion, and total revelation of reality as it is.

Ever grateful,

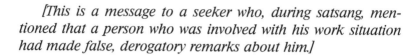

[This is a message to a seeker who, during satsang, mentioned that a person who was involved with his work situation had made false, derogatory remarks about him.]

June 20, 2010

ॐ Dear . . . ,

Namaste. Regarding the topic of which you spoke during satsang:

One's own thoughts are not true definitions of the Self. How much less are those of others! Remain transcendent.

In delusion, a person may project his/her view of himself upon others. This encompasses the obvious misidentifications with the body, as an ego, etc. as well as the projection of tendencies, traits (e.g. "laziness") upon others. Perceive the utter foolishness of the formation of opinions regarding others, and remain wise yourself.

Underlying the projection, generally, is the fear that that trait, etc. is one's own. See the Self that one truly is, even if that person is oblivious to such.

The tendency to ruin another's reputation is a perverse one born of misery that just makes more misery for himself/herself. Abide happily at the very source of joy.

Some friends or acquaintances may be so fearful of becoming the target of rejection (defamation, name-calling, etc.) themselves that they appear to distance themselves from the targeted person or pretend that they are unaware of the facts actually experienced by them. Inwardly they pay the price of conscience. Do not depend on them but have compassion for them.

The Truth is the Truth, no matter what anyone says. Likewise, the facts are the facts no matter what anyone says. God sees all and is not fooled by false statements. Repose peacefully in God.

What may seem momentous now, will be as if nothing later. Abide in the eternal as the eternal.

Ever yours in Truth,
Nome

[A seeker wrote concerning the death of his mother. The response to him follows.]

June 22, 2010

Dear Nome,
My mother passed this morning. No tragedy, she was more than ready to go.

Om Arunachaleswaraya namah,

ॐ Dear . . . ,

Om Namo Bhagavate Sri Ramanaya
Namaste. There is no grief over the inevitable when one knows the imperishable nature of the bodiless Self.

On Namah Sivaya
Om Arunacalesvaraya Namah

Ever yours in Truth,
Nome

[Another seeker wrote that she was ill. She also wrote about freedom from thought. This is the response to her.]

June 28, 2010

ॐ Dear . . . ,

Om Namo Bhagavate Sri Ramanaya

Namaste. Thank you for your letter of the 25th, which just arrived.

I am glad to know that your bodily health is recovering. Though you have not supplied the details concerning your health, from what you have written, it seems that this illness is not one from which you are able to quickly recuperate. The bodiless Self, though, remains unaffected and serene.

To see the importance of freedom from thought is correct. Moreover, it should be realized that the Self is ever beyond thought. It is inconceivable, undefined, and unconfined by any thought. In Self-Knowledge, that thought is purely illusory, being the imagined superimposition of the objective upon Consciousness, and does not actually exist, is certain. Free from thought, abide in the bliss and peace of the Self.

Ever yours in Truth,
Nome

[These are two messages from a seeker, with responses to each.]

July 5, 2010

Hi, my companion and I would like to visit with Nome and would like to know if Nome attends the Friday night sessions. We live 500 miles away and have the funds only for a one night stay in Santa Cruz, and we would not want to miss seeing Nome. My friend needs his grace and guidance. Thanking you in advance,

Arunachala Shiva!

ॐ Dear . . . ,

Om Namo Bhagavate Sri Ramanaya

Namaste. Thank you for your message. I am present at all the events at the SAT temple. You will be warmly welcome at any of them. The calendar of events can be found on the SAT website at www.SATRamana.org.

May you abide in the Knowledge of the Self, absorbed in That which is of the very nature of Grace, and thus be always happy and at peace.

Om Namah Sivaya
Om Arunacalesvaraya Namah

Ever yours in Truth,
Nome

August 3, 2010

Beloved Nome, I cannot express in words my joy and thanks at being able to see you again after so many years. How I wish I could meditate with you and "catch the Samadhi habit" that you so generously offered those many years ago. I feel my time in the body is quickly running out, and I have a fear of dying in ignorance yet again. Perhaps Providence will come to my rescue and allow for it to happen.

My friend [name omitted] was with me and remembers all that you said and feels that you were speaking to her directly. She was duly impressed and hopes for your continued guidance.

Arunachala Siva,

ॐ Dear . . . ,

Om Namo Bhagavate Sri Ramanaya
Namaste. Thank you for your message.
The body is, indeed, transient, but you truly are the Self, which is unborn and imperishable. Ignorance is considered

303

the obstacle to Self-Realization, but for one who ardently inquires within, the ignorance dissolves and the obstructions prove to be imaginary.

Just as the Self is ever-existent, so Grace is ever present. Guidance shines from within, and, if you and [name omitted] feel it to be beneficial, is available in a manifested manner, too. What is truly important is to put the instruction into practice to the best of your ability and find the blissful Truth of your very Being.

May you ever abide in the Knowledge of the Self and thereby be ever happy and at peace in the perfect fullness of the Self.

Om Namah Sivaya
Om Arunacalesvaraya Namah

Ever yours in Truth,
Nome

[A message from another seeker, followed by Nome's response.]

July 21, 2010

Hello Master Nome:
Being no difference in samsara and nirvana, one has a glimpse of consciousness. What is it to steadily abide as the Self?

Namaste.

ॐ Dear . . . ,

Om Namo Bhagavate Sri Ramanaya
Namaste. Thank you for your message.
Consciousness alone is the Reality. Misidentified as an ego, the imaginary assumption of an "I," it, itself, appears as

samsara. From the perspective of being in samsara, Consciousness appears as if a state, called "nirvana" because of the extinguishment of the "I" and its supposed samsara. Turning inward and inquiring into the very nature of "I" to know the real Self, one then may speak of glimpses. Yet, who sees what? Who sees otherwise? Thus inquiring, the notion of two selves vanishes, and only indivisible Being exists. The notion of two knowers disappears, and only one Consciousness exists. That alone abides as itself. That is the Self. That is who you are. The innate immutability of the Self is the steadiness of Atma-nishtha (Self-abidance, being in the Self). In sadhana (practice), abandonment of attachments and misidentifications by depth of inquiry yields steadiness.

Ever yours in Truth,
Nome

[Another message from the same seeker. The response by Nome follows.]

July 22, 2010

Good morning Master Nome:

As I reflect on what I thought was a glimpse of peace, joy and quiet, I observe that I was working as a hospice volunteer on Tuesday, and, in so doing, all that was coming out of my mouth were words of inspiration from Bagavan Sri Ramana Maharshi, Buddha, St. Francis of Assisi, and I seemed to be gone. There was peace, joy, energy. Yesterday, after some time at the office, I returned, in the form of thinking, and feelings arose and questions as to the feellng of the doer, which has been so present in this life. I realize that all of the "doing" this I thinks it has done is just that, a thought, nonexistent. May the turning to the subjective be deeper by the grace of Bagavan Sri Ramana Maharshi for this mind seems not to be sharp enough.

305

Om Namo Bhgavate Sri Ramanaya
In Devotion,

ॐ Dear . . . ,

Om Namo Bhagavate Sri Ramanaya
Namaste. Thank you for your message.
When the ego subsides, the words of wise sages are
one's own.
    If one ceases to misidentify with the instruments of
body, speech, and mind, all concepts of being the performer of action are gone.
    Bhagavan's Grace is always. Turning inward, the ever-
existent is realized.

Ever yours in Truth,
Nome

[This is a message from a seeker, with Nome's response.]

July 21, 2010

Dear Nome,

Om Namo Bhagavate Sri Ramanaya
    Namaste. I am feeling that you, my precious guru, are pushing
from the outside and pulling from the inside. I am happy to feel you
and I want you to always be with me. I have been thinking that the
strong attachment, the needy part of me, seems better. Still I want to
be one with my guru more than anything.

Please be well.
All my love,

ॐ Dear . . . ,

Om Namo Bhagavate Sri Ramanaya

Namaste. Thank you for your message.

At some point, you may find it interesting, and perhaps beneficial, to examine what you refer to as "the needy part." Though attachment represents a confusion regarding the source of happiness, what actually is that for which you wish? Deeply considered, the desire to be happy is an intuition of your natural state. Of course, such happiness is to be found within, and within means the Self. That is also the nature, or very existence, of the Guru. Thus, Sri Ramana says that God, Guru, and the Self are one and the same.

So, instead of attempting to modulate the sense of need, it is wise to determine what, truly, you need and how much you need it. Then, you will naturally make every effort, in joy, to realize it. All the wise have declared that truly only one is needed. Some call that one God. Some call that one Guru. Some call that one Self. Those who realize that one within know that to be ineffable.

Ever yours in Truth,
Nome

≡
•

[This message is from a seeker who corresponded previously. Nome's response follows.]

July 27, 2010

Namasthe Nome,

Om Namo Bagavathe Sri Ramanaya,

When doing Self-inquiry, one thought arose. I inquired, who created this thought, to whom, but suddenly another thought arose. So, I couldn't find the source of thought rising. Will I know by more practice of Self-inquiry, or I am doing wrong?

Please clarify. Now, I am reading *Yoga Vasista* book. It is really useful to understanding about oneself.

Thanks,

ॐ Dear . . . ,

Om Namo Bhagavate Sri Ramanaya
Namaste. Thank you for your message. Reading *Yoga Vasishtha* is excellent.

It does not matter how many thoughts appear. You know all of them. You remain as the ever-existent. They do not. Inquire to know who this unchanging "you" that is not the thoughts truly is. Keenly discern how no thought defines Consciousness, which is your true nature.

Continue to inquire in a nonobjective manner, and, with Grace, the Supreme Self will be realized.

Ever yours in Truth,
Nome

[This message is from a seeker who wrote previously. Nome's response follows.]

July 29, 2010

Om Namo Bhagavate Sri Ramanaya

Master Nome:

Please elucidate what the transitional "I" is and what notices it.
How does the awareness of the transitional "I" become awareness of it?

In Devotion,

ॐ Dear . . . ,

Om Namo Bhagavate Sri Ramanaya
Namaste. The phrase "transitional I" may be a result of translation and would be best considered in the context in

which it is used. It may be a way of describing the appearing and disappearing character of the notion of "I," the illusory connection between Consciousness and the body, the superimposition of individuality upon the Self, or the continuity of Consciousness that is the unbroken Existence amidst the transitory states of mind.

There is only one Consciousness, and that alone is the Self, the only true "I." Discern this real knower free from the known, such as the mind and the notion "I."

Sri Bhagavan said that devotion is the "mother" of knowledge.

Ever yours in Truth,
Nome

———
•

[Here is a message from someone who attended the earliest public satsangs in 1978, had been present during the previous, mostly silent years of satsangs 1974 to 1978, and was present during Nome's sadhana 1971 to 1974. He attended the celebration of Sri Ramana Maharshi's Self-Realization at the SAT temple on July 17, 2010. His message also discussed suggestions and information relating to Nome's bodily health and contained discussion regarding a commentary on Upadesa Saram by a respected Swami, and these have been deleted here. Similar editing has been performed on Nome's response, which follows.]

July 29, 2010

Dear Master Nome,

I was delighted to affirm our oneness without the illusion of a spatial separation. 32 years later, your realization is as palpable and timeless as the very first Satsang together!

Om Tat Sat,

Love,

P.S. If I can ever be of service to you in any capacity, I would be honored to do so and hope that you would call upon me. If you do wish to travel to the island of Hawaii, there will always be space in our home and our hearts, and there is a depth of unity that brooks no separation.

ॐ Dear . . . ,

Om Namo Bhagavate Sri Ramanaya
Namaste. Thank you for your message. Please convey my thankfulness to [name omitted] for so kindly sending the information, which arrived in yesterday's mail. The care she, you, and others have expressed is, itself, a sweet remedy.

Knowledge, the nature of which is Consciousness, is the very nature of our Being. Its freedom is boundless. It is possessed by none, but, in the nonexistence of the individual who would gain or lose it, it is realized, and what is realized we are.

I hope that the move to Hawaii is successful. Whenever you visit the mainland, be sure to visit us at the SAT temple.

We ever remain One.
Om Tat Sat

Ever yours in Truth,
Nome

[In early August 2010, a seeker wrote about her spiritual practice, her wondering whether or not she was experiencing enlightenment, and about some ridicule from a loved one, which she quoted extensively, towards her spirituality. This is Nome's response.]

ॐ Dear . . . ,

Namaste. Thank you for your letter of the 4th and this email message.

Rather than think, "Is this enlightenment or not?" in the attempt to evaluate your experience, it is wiser to continue to inquire. What comes and goes, increases or decreases, is not the finality. The Self is ever existent, and the realized Knowledge of it is invariable. It may be helpful to refer to the comments in *Saddarshanam and an Inquiry into the Revelation of Truth and Oneself* concerning this.

Peace and bliss cannot be wrong. Just continue to trace their source, so that you fully identify yourself as that.

It is absurd for the unhappy to ridicule the happy and for the disturbed to condemn the peaceful. Insistence upon others conforming to one's own opinion is narrow-minded and characteristic of the dense delusion that forms samsara. The quotations of [name omitted] given by you are, perhaps, not in a completely described context. Standing alone, they seem very contradictory, expressive of bigotry, may be hypocritical, and seem to be of an ignorance rooted in egotism and worldly attachment, as explicitly stated in the quotations. While it may be possible that such is the state of mind expressed, you are in a far better position to understand the context and to perceive if that is a mollifying factor or not. Whatever be the case, it is best for you to abide as the undivided Self and remain happy at heart.

Where the ego does not appear is true silence. The highest prayer is that in which the individuality of the worshipper vanishes. The presence of God precludes the existence of an ego. The joyful state devoid of attachment is according to God's will.

Ever yours in Truth,
Nome

August 13, 2010

Namaste Nome,

Om Namo Bagavathe Sri Ramanaya
I am working a part-time job. In this worldly life, any kind of action that happens for me that is positive or negative is affecting my peace of mind. I always remember that this action can't decide my happiness. So, I am inquiring about who is affected by this worry, but, mostly, within a moment, worries go deep into my mind even without time to think about inquiry. After some time, I realize that I am thinking like this. Then, I start inquiry about my thoughts and action of mind. In that situation, I am sitting in front of a Sri Ramana Maharshi photo praying for help. How can I be without any attachment in work and my personal life? My mind always sticks to something and creates worries or imagines some worldly happiness.

Thanks,

ॐ Dear . . . ,

Om Namo Bhagavate Sri Ramanaya
Namaste. Thank you for your message.
If the mind is not rooted in the Truth, but rather pursues its own delusive ideas, peace will be obscured. Sri Ramana advises those who desire Self-Realization not to pursue the delusive ideas. The result of such pursuit is unhappiness. Instead, inquire and abide happily as the Self.
Know with certainty that happiness is within. External objects and events do not provide or affect it.
If you know that happiness is within and seek to know the Self, you will remain at peace and will not suffer.
Thus, when the body engages in work, you will be unattached, and happiness and peace will still shine. For one who inquires to know the Self, activity and inactivity are the same.

Ever yours in Truth,
Nome

[A seeker started regular attendance at satsang. After three months, he wrote a lengthy message that was full of expressions of devotion, while also describing how he had been confused in his mind and questioning the signifcance of silence and if the spiritual pursuit is selfish. Here is Nome's response.]

August 15, 2010

ॐ Dear . . . ,

Om Namo Bhagavate Sri Ramanaya
Namaste. Thank you for your message.

The fullness of deep devotion is true Knowledge. The effort of spiritual practice and Grace are of the same nature. Bliss is of the very nature of Being. Who can say whether such is the beginning or the end of devotion, the dawn or finality of Knowledge?

Silence is the self-evident nature of the Self, for which there is no alternative and no other.

If the mind moves, determine who knows it. By such inquiry, the true nature of the mind becomes clearly known. If the misidentifications, which are the root of the perplexing thoughts, are destroyed, illimitable peace remains.

The Maharshi has set the supreme example: Egoless Self-abidance is the greatest good for all.

If you know yourself, you will always be happy, at peace, and free as immortal Being-Consciousness-Bliss.

Om Daksinamurtaye Namah

Ever yours in Truth,
Nome

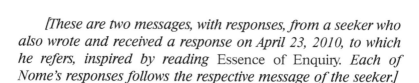

[These are two messages, with responses, from a seeker who also wrote and received a response on April 23, 2010, to which he refers, inspired by reading Essence of Enquiry. *Each of Nome's responses follows the respective message of the seeker.]*

August 18, 2010

Namaste.

Since sending these questions, I have almost finished your book, *Essence of Enquiry*, and your points are taken.

It seems to me that one of your purposes in writing the book is to compel readers to engage in a practice of inquiry. I have committed to do so, and it now seems to me that there is no other activity that comes close in value.

I must believe that enquiry is a practice, or was a practice, of yours and my question is: from your experience of your practice, can you make any recommendations as to the most effective and efficient practices beyond those described by Ramana in the book? Can you note any pitfalls to avoid?

The process, as I understand it, starts with the efforts of the illusory "me" doing the practice and ends with the disappearance of the "me", and the arising of the always-present Self. As I have been practicing, I notice a reduction of arising of thought and an increase in quiet mind and peace. I assume that the practice is continued until there is no more arising of thought and, in its place, is a continuous, effortless, presence of Self experienced as Sat, Chit, Ananda.

Any recommendations or corrections will be appreciated.

ॐ Dear . . . ,

Om Namo Bhagavate Sri Ramanaya

Namaste. Thank you for your message.

Sri Bhagavan's teachings are complete in themselves. When deeply understood, the teachings revealed by Ribhu, Adi Sankara, the sages of the Upanishads, and others only reiterate the same Truth and the same inquiry.

314

An illusory "me" does not actually practice, for how can that which is unreal have any part in the self-revelation of the Reality? The power, illumination, etc. of the practice of inquiry is rooted in the ever-existent Self. The inquiry, itself, is composed of mind-transcendent Knowledge; the end is the means.

If the nonobjective inquiry remains deep and constant, you will experience no obstacles or pitfalls. Always, the inquiry is into the very nature of the inquirer.

Peace and happiness are natural for one who inquires, for his very nature is Ananda, just as he is Sat-Cit. Regardless of whether thoughts appear to be few or many, inquire to destroy the misidentifications. When the nonexistence of an "I" is conclusively realized, there is the certitude of knowledge that there are never any such things as a mind, thoughts, etc.

If you are finding *Essence of Inquiry* helpful, you may also find benefit in *Saddarsanam and an Inquiry into the Revelation of Truth and Oneself* and *Self-Knowledge*. Both have Self-Knowledge and Self-inquiry as their sole focus.

Depth of inquiry is essential. As discrimination sharpens by discriminating, inquiry becomes deep, strong, steady, and clear by actually engaging in the practice of it.

May you, deeply inquiring to know your own true Self, abide in the Self, as the Self, free of the least trace of imaginary delusion and ever full of peace and bliss.

Ever yours in Truth,
Nome

August 19, 2010

Dear Nome,

Namaste. Thank you for the quick, comprehensive, and deep reply.

Again, I suspect several re-readings will be of benefit. I assume the readings you recommended are books, and I will search them out. Thanks for that, too.

You mentioned "deep" inquiry several times, and it caused an alert in me. Can you say anything more about deep inquiry vs. shallow, I suppose. Is there any way to gauge the depth of one's inquiry?

Again you say "depth of inquiry is essential." Since it is so important, I want to be sure to understand as much as possible about this essential aspect. How should I go about deepening my understanding of what you mean and, more importantly, applying it?

Thank you so much for the pointers and encouragement. Ever seeking truth,

ॐ Dear. . . ,

Om Namo Bhagavate Sri Ramanaya

Namaste. Depth of that which is nonobjective cannot be measured in objective terms. If, though, you keep your focus on the clarity of the knowledge of your identity, so that you abide free of misidentifications, your inquiry will be deep, and Being will remain self-revealed.

Inquiry is deep if it is experiential, though such is not sensory or a mental mode, just as you exist and you know that you exist. At that depth the inquiry should be.

If you inquire in such a way, vasanas (tendencies) of ignorance will vanish, and Self-Knowledge will shine.

Ever yours in Truth,
Nome

[Here are two messages from a seeker and responses to them.]

August 30, 2010

Dear Master Nome:

Om Namo Bhagavate Sri Ramanaya

The closing spiritual instruction in which you stated the message that Sri Ramana Maharshi indicated as part of the five verses

316

went deep; in which you stated that there is no consciousness in the body and that it would be as if the screen were in the moving film, was recognized as truth by truth itself.

Master, could you please elucidate what is called chit-jada-granthi? Is it understood correctly as being the knot of the ego which is partly consciousness?

In devotion,
Om Shanti shanti shanti

ॐ Dear . . . ,

Om Namo Bhagavate Sri Ramanaya

Namaste. The more the inquiry is continued, the deeper the Knowledge experienced. Yes, Truth alone knows itself.

The Cit-jada-granthi is the supposed connection between pure Consciousness and the inert. It is the ego. It is not conscious at all. It is entirely illusory and appears as if borrowing the knowing power of Consciousness and combining it with the body. When sought, it vanishes. Egoless, bodiless Consciousness is the only knower. That is the Self. That is who you are.

May you ever blissfully abide in the Self, as the Self.

Ever yours in Truth,
Nome

Om Namo Bhagavate Sri Ramanaya!!!

Master Nome:

As the reading of *Saddarsanam* continues to take place, the heart is increasingly joyous in truth. On page 206: "You know that you relate to another person only from the perspective of being a body. If not, there is blissful love and identity in truth, but there is no relating. The wise will understand this." Does this point to the truth that there is nothing objective, no relating, only Existence-Consciousness-Bliss.?

Yours in Devotion,
Om Namo Bhagavate Sri Ramanaya

ॐ Dear . . . ,

Om Namo Bhagavate Sri Ramanaya
Namaste. It is as you have stated. One undifferentiated Self alone exists. There is no "other" or anything objective at any time. This is "blissful love and identity in truth."
The height of devotion shines with true Knowledge.

Ever yours in Truth,
Nome

[This message is from a seeker. Nome's response follows.]

September 6, 2010

Dear Master Nome,

As always, I wait a little time to gain the true distillation of what was absorbed from the retreat. It is this: I can recollect not just with mind, but more importantly with feeling, the Silence of Dakshinamurti, or, in other words, the Essence of Reality, that Vibrant Stillness which is at the Source of all. Now, I feel more empowered to stay in that Stillness when disturbing things happen, and not just for that, but as a general practice throughout the day.

We will not be going to India this year. Instead we hope to come to SAT for the retreat. This was all [name omitted]'s idea!

Always with Love and Gratitude,

ॐ Dear . . . ,

Om Namo Bhagavate Sri Ramanaya
Namaste. Thank you for your message.

You will be very welcome at the retreat if you are able to attend. The Silence of Dakshinamurti is absolute. It is the Being of the Self. Abidance in that is to be that. It is also the perfect, transcendent sanctuary from all illusion.

Ever yours in Truth,
Nome

[A seeker attended satsang and wrote to Nome with questions about experiences of the chakras that the seeker was having, silence of the mind, and other topics. This is Nome's response.]

September 7, 2010

ॐ Dear . . . ,

Om Namo Bhagavate Sri Ramanaya
Namaste. Thank you for your message.
If your goal is Self-Realization, such is eternal. What appears disappears; what comes goes. The eternal is unchanging and nonobjective. It is your true Being. Therefore, meditation should be upon the very nature of the Self, and not merely upon that which is perceived and conceived.

Regardless of whatever experiences, gross or subtle, come and go, you are aware of them. Inquiring to know the nature of that "you" is the direct means to Realization.

Silence is the undifferentiated, absolute Existence in which the illusion of a separate "I" does not appear.

May you deeply inquire and thereby abide in the Self, as the Self, formless and unchanging, space-like and infinite, so that you are always happy and at peace.

Ever yours in Truth,
Nome

—
—
•

[A message was received on September 12, 2010 from a seeker who asked for advice regarding mental attention, sleep during meditation, and the meaning of the following anecdote that he found on a website.]

"A certain lady who had a lot of devotion performed a traditional ritual for worshipping sages whenever she came into Bhagavan's presence to have darshan. She would prostrate to Bhagavan, touch his feet and then put the hands that had touched Bhagavan's feet on her eyes. After noticing that she did this daily, Bhagavan told her one day, 'Only the Supreme Self, which is ever shining in your heart as the reality, is the Sadguru. The pure awareness, which is shining as the inward illumination "I", is his gracious feet. The contact with these [inner holy feet] alone can give you true redemption. Joining the eye of reflected consciousness [chidabhasa], which is your sense of individuality [jiva bodha], to those holy feet, which are the real consciousness, is the union of the feet and the head that is the real significance of the word "asi" ["are", as in the mahavakya "You are That"]. As these inner holy feet can be held naturally and unceasingly, hereafter, with an inward-turned mind, cling to that inner awareness that is your own real nature. This alone is the proper way for the removal of bondage and the attainment of the supreme truth.'"

September 13, 2010

ॐ Dear . . . ,

Om Namo Bhagavate Sri Ramanaya
Namaste. Thank you for your message.
Though directing mental attention toward spiritual matters and inward may be regarded as beneficial, such cannot be equated with absolute Consciousness, which is the Self, or with true Knowledge (Self-Knowledge), which is eternal and nondual. Nondual means that it is without divisions,

such as subject and object and, also, that it is of the very same nature as that (the Self) which is known, which is the knower himself. Attention is a transient mental mode that is apparent only if there are thoughts. It is not eternal. For Self-Realization, the means must be of the identical nature as the end, for that (the Self) alone is real, and the unreal cannot result in the real. Self-inquiry, which reveals Self-Knowledge, therefore, is of the nature of Knowledge and should not be misconstrued as the mere mode of the mind referred to as mental attention.

Now, in light of the above explanation, consider the profound teaching given by Sri Bhagavan, as quoted by you. He simultaneously reveals the true significance of the expression of devotion and lifts one's view from action, which is performed with the instruments of body, speech, and mind and which cannot yield Self-Realization, which is Liberation from all of the imagined bondage, to Self-Knowledge, which is the very nature of Self-Realization.

First, he reveals the identity of the Self, Consciousness ("shining"), the Reality, and the Sadguru. Implicit in this is the elimination of conceptions based upon the body, a person, or the individual. He then reveals this to be the only true identity, one's real Being, which alone is the true significance of "I." "Inward" is nonobjective. Contact is such as to merge or lose the false sense of a separate individuality. Such loss of the unreal, the ego, "alone can give you true redemption," that is, alone yields Liberation from the imagined bondage, for it consists of the egoless, true Knowledge.

Joining is the union with That or the clear Knowledge, in which Being is the Knowledge, of one's identity as That, the Self. It is the revelation of what is ever true and not the conjoining of two different things. Abhasa means reflected or a distortion or a false appearance. Cit (Cid) is Consciousness, which is real. There is only one Consciousness, and there are not different kinds of the Self. If, by inquiry, you trace the light, now seemingly reflected as a second knower or second awareness or mind, to its

321

source, such is the union referred to. This is by Knowledge (inquiry) alone, for thought cannot reach beyond itself and has no knowing power of its own. Jiva means the individual or individual life. Bodha signifies knowledge. Trace the knowledge of existence, of "I" or the sense of identity, to its source. In the union referred to, which is the utter dissolution of even the least dualism, the egoless nature of the only true "I," which is the Self without any trace of individuality, alone remains and is self-evident. That is the real Consciousness, which is one without a second.

"Asi" means "are." The meaning of the mahavakya can only be that of being That. That is Brahman, the real Self. Thoroughly elucidated by Adi Sankaracarya, the meaning is solely true Knowledge in which Being is Knowing. It is an instructional statement of absolute identity.

It is not possible for thought, attention, or any mental mode to be unceasing, but actual inquiry, of the nature of Knowledge, can be so. Natural refers to the innate. An inward-turned mind is one that abandons its own imaginings, such as the world, etc., and refers to nonobjective vision. Clinging to the inner (nonobjective) Consciousness (Awareness), can only be by knowing that alone to be real and oneself, without an alternative.

Thus, the unreal bondage, inclusive of the assumption of one to be bound, is destroyed, and there is the Self-revelation, or attainment, of the eternal Supreme Truth.

In light of what is actually declared by the Maharshi, it is not necessary to interpret it by reducing it to the play of mental attention. Indeed, with that interpretation, much of what is taught would remain an enigma. From another perspective, first-hand experience by practice will show the value and limitations of mental modes and the invaluable, illimitable nature of pure Knowledge. Moreover, the attention is something known, just as that upon which it is placed is known. Who knows?

There may be many factors affecting sleepiness. If you engage in Self-inquiry, which reveals Consciousness that is transcendent of the three states, sleep will not be a problem.

I hope that you find the above helpful.

Ever yours in Truth,
Nome

[This is a response to a message from a seeker.]

September 16, 2010

ॐ Dear . . . ,

Om Namo Bhagavate Sri Ramanaya

Namaste. Thank you for your message.

Everything is only in and of the Self. The perfect fullness of Absolute Being ever remains un-fractured, undiminished, and unblemished.

The ego is unreal. All sorrow is only in, by, and for it.

Therefore, as Sri Bhagavan said, quoting Vasishtha:

"That in which this entire universe is established, to which it pertains, out of which it arises, for which it exists, by which it comes into being, and which it really is, that is the Self-existent Reality, the Truth. Let us worship That in the heart."

Ever yours in Truth,
Nome

[In response to a seeker who wrote that he was caught in frustration and worry due to worldly concerns and lack of practice of Self-inquiry.]

323

September 16, 2010

ॐ Dear . . . ,

Om Namo Bhagavate Sri Ramanaya
Namaste. Thank you for your message.

Suffering, in the form of frustration, worry, and such, in relation to worldly things and circumstances, is experienced by all who do not truly know that the source of happiness is within. If this is truly known, one remains at peace, filled with serene detachment.

The mind wanders toward what is conceived as determining one's happiness and toward what is conceived as defining oneself. If you know that happiness is within, naturally the focus will be upon knowing what is within, that is, upon Self-inquiry. Self-inquiry reveals the true definition of one's own Self (svatmanirupanam), and such is Self-Knowledge, which is the highest bliss.

Deeply reflect and meditate upon the significance of what is indicated above, so that the precious time of this life is used wisely.

Ever yours in Truth,
Nome

═══
●

[A Ramana devotee from Russia sent a copy of his Russian translation of the book Maha Yoga. *This message was sent in response.]*

ॐ Dear Sri . . . ,

Om Namo Bhagavate Sri Ramanaya

Namaste. It is a joy to hear from you. Thank you for so kindly sending us a copy of your Russian translation of *Maha Yoga.*

To make the spiritual teachings of Sri Bhagavan available in various languages is a wonderful, holy service that is of immense benefit for the seekers of the supreme Truth who read those languages. Though, as with Dakshinamurti, Sri Ramana's perpetual Silence is the absolute teaching, His words are fully permeated by that Silence and explain in an unsurpassable, sublime manner the Knowledge of the Self and the inquiry that reveals it. Thus, the service you are performing, by His Grace, and the books you are writing are truly blessings for Russian-speaking people.

Should you ever travel to California, please accept our warm invitation to visit us at the SAT temple.

May you ever abide in the undivided Self, as the undivided Self, and thus be always happy and at peace.

Ever yours in Sri Bhagavan,
Nome

[A seeker sent two messages, one pertaining to a study of language and the mind and the other reproduced here. Nome's response follows.]

September 20, 2010

Hi Nome,

Om Namo Bhagavate Sri Ramanaya.
Namaste.

It was another great satsang as usual, yesterday. I was back this morning for another meditation and watching a satsang DVD. Listening to our past dialogs is especially helpful. To listen, reflect, and meditate on the dialogs again helps me to understand even more deeply.

It's quite wondrous how just a bit more effort at practice returns so much. Bookending the day with meditation, it's becoming easier and easier to recognize misidentifications and stop them before they gain any momentum. It's changing daily life into the "continuous meditative cruise."

Namaste.

ॐ Dear . . . ,

Om Namo Bhagavate Sri Ramanaya

Namaste. Thanks for your messages and the link to the article about language. Of course, interesting and observant as it is, the article presents just a bit concerning speech and the mind, not touching upon other aspects such as how the quality or state of mind affects language certainly as much or more than language affects the mind, the physical sound and subtle vibration and their effects on the mind as discerned by those yogis who are knowledgeable about mantras, etc., the levels or stages of "speech" usually classified into four ranging from the spoken word to Para (absolute, beyond) as described by some yogis and bhaktas, and the "language of Vedanta" that communicates that which is neither worldly nor bodily, which is neither tangible nor abstract, which is timeless and without location, and which is without an ego or an object. That aside, the article presents interesting points and perspectives in a readily comprehensible and sometimes humorous manner. It is a pleasant surprise to see such erudition in a newspaper article. Perhaps that is due to it being an adaptation derived from a book.

Yes, meditation at the beginning and at the end causes the middle to be free from deviation, too. Continue to inquire so that you destroy misidentifications earlier and earlier, indeed, so that they are destroyed before they begin.

As with the books, so with the recordings: each time you read or listen, in light of deeper practice, you hear what was not heard before, and you see what was not seen before. Thereby, you know that which, though apparently unknown, is truly best known and realize the ever-real.

Ever yours in Truth,
Nome

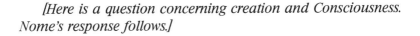

[Here is a question concerning creation and Consciousness. Nome's response follows.]

September 23, 2010

Please shed light on where the solar orb (the sun) plays in Advaita Vedanta. From the light comes the creation, eventually the consciousness arises, so how is this sun that will last another 4.5 billion years negated? At the pralaya, the consciousness is still as it is?

ॐ Dear . . . ,

Om Namo Bhagavate Sri Ramanaya
Namaste. Thank you for your message.

Consider your dream state. In a dream, a sun, world, senses, bodies, etc. appear. In dream time, the dream sun is billions of years in duration, and your dream body is of a much briefer duration. The dream time is as illusory as the rest of what appears in the dream. The same is so with the illusory, individualized, sense-connected, "awareness" of the dream character. The only thing that is real in the dream is Consciousness, which illumines (knows) and is its only substance, but that never appears as any of the forms, gross or subtle, in the dream. Upon awakening, Consciousness alone remains. Similar is the case with the waking state, the great dissolution (mahapralaya), etc. Consciousness is the Self and alone truly exists. It ever is as it is. If the misidentification with the body and as the ego is abandoned, the timeless Being of the Self will be clearly self-evident.

May you ever abide in the Self, as the Self, from which this universe is, by which it is, for which it is, in which it is, which it actually is, and in the Light of the Truth of which there is no universe at all.

Ever yours in Truth,
Nome

[This is a message from a seeker. Nome's response follows.]

September 24, 2010

Pranams,

I would like to take this opportunity to request your advice on the following spiritual question:

About a year ago, with Bhagavan Ramana Maharishi's grace, I had the glimpse of the Truth that I am not the body and mind. Everything disappeared before me, and I came to know the real "I" - the inner stillness, inner being, Self. After that, I saw my own thoughts as a mirage before me. Then, I saw that the same consciousness (formless being) present in my body is present in all the forms that I see. A month later, I had a similar experience. This really has broken the shackles of the mind. I experienced such an inner peace and bliss.

The inner peace lasted for several months. Now, I experience the inner peace, but there is some intermittent loss of peace. I completely understand, there is nothing to gain in this material world and live in the present most of the time and do the necessary activities as they are presented to me. But unable to abide in the Self at all times. I have the following question:

How could I sustain this inner peace for a longer period of time to make it as a permanent experience?

Please guide me. Appreciate your seva.
Namaskarams,

ॐ Dear . . . ,

Om Namo Bhagavate Sri Ramanaya

Namaste. Thank you for your message. We are glad to know of your experience of Sri Bhagavan's Grace.

If there is inquiry into the nature of the assumed "I" that conceives of the two states or experiences of peaceful abidance and absence of the same, the eternally-existent, indi-

328

visible Self will be found to be the sole-existent Reality. Who is it that does not abide? The Self is only one and cannot be otherwise or different from itself. The Self is never a known or unknown object.

An experience appears and disappears; what is born perishes. The Innate is unborn, indestructible, immutable, and inseparable from oneself. Your Being does not come or go. Inquiring into the nature of the experiencer in the quest to know yourself, realize with nonobjective Knowledge who you truly are.

By discerning misidentification to be only such and not the Self, even the supposition of being an individual, who can then be defined as an experiencer, a non-abider, etc., is abandoned. That which remains is absolute peace, and That which is realized you are.

I hope that you find the above helpful. Being within the Maharshi's Grace and following His spiritual instruction, you are certainly blessed. May you ever abide in the Self, as the Self, full of Bliss, the One without a second.

Ever yours in Sri Bhagavan,
Nome

[A seeker asked about fasting and pranayama. Here is Nome's response.]

September 24, 2010

ॐ Dear . . . ,

Om Namo Bhagavate Sri Ramanaya

Namaste. Regarding these practices: they may have some health benefit, they may be useful for inducing some yogic experiences, they may be of some use in temporarily effecting certain modes of mind and for some control of

329

the mind, and they are unrelated to Self-Realization, which is of the nature of Self-Knowledge.

Engagement in these practices requires care, an understanding of what one is doing, a suitable environment, self-discipline, observance of certain precautions, patience, etc. Though I do not offer instruction about these two particular practices, if you wish, sometime after a satsang, we can speak a bit about them.

Fasting from attachments and misidentifications, and the pranayama of exhalation of ignorance and the misidentification with the body, inhalation of the inquiry "Who am I?", and retention of identity as the Self, can be practiced by all, everywhere and always.

Ever yours in Truth,
Nome

[In reply to a message that described mental turmoil and doubts, this response was sent.]

September 25, 2010

ॐ Dear . . . ,

Om Namo Bhagavate Sri Ramanaya
Namaste. Thank you for your message.

The vasanas (tendencies) of the mind appear only to be destroyed. Be certain to inquire sufficiently deeply so that the misidentifications that are the root of those binding patterns of thought are dissolved. Without a cause, there is no effect.

In your heart, you know something that can never be imitated or afflicted by the mind. That is your true Being. Holding That as the dearest of the dear, inquire to know your true Being unveiled by the misidentifications. The delusive vasanas will vanish. The peace of the blissful Self will alone remain.

Bhagavan's Grace is always there.

Ever yours in Truth,
Nome

[This is a message from a seeker who had not contacted SAT previously. Nome's response follows.]

October 9, 2010

hello
I know you don't know me in person, but I wanted to ask you some questions that are really important to me in this time and place.
I am really curious to know how spiritual practice and a romantic relationship can exist with and aid each other. If one person is very serious about practice and wants to put the focus nowhere else, it seems impossible to have a marriage because of all the attachment.
How is this for you, if I may ask?

love

ॐ Dear . . . ,

Om Namo Bhagavate Sri Ramanaya
Namaste. Thank you for your message.
Love is identity in Being, the undivided true nature of the Self. It is delusive to equate that with attachment, which is based on confusion regarding the source of happiness.
The essential spiritual practice that yields Self-Knowledge is the inquiry to know oneself. Action pertains to the body, and the Self is not the body. Married or other-

wise, for Realization of the undifferentiated Self, which is perfectly full Bliss, you must know yourself.

I hope that you find the above helpful. May you ever abide in the Knowledge of the Self, of the nature of Being-Consciousness-Bliss, the One without a second, so that you are always happy and at peace.

Ever yours in Truth,
Nome

[Here are two messages from a seeker who resides in Bangalore, India. Nome's responses follow each message.]

October 13, 2010

Dear Nome,

My humble respects, from [name omitted], Bangalore, India.

I have a peculiar mix of demoniac thoughts and a powerful pull and push towards the Self (Divine).

I had a vision of Shiva while I was 6 years old along with one girl called Andaal. Can you please tell me the detailed background of that event? Why did I have the vision?

I also suffer from a thick, dark, formation of a man who gives constant demoniac and kama desires to me.

I have found my Guru [name omitted], but Mother right now ignores me.

Hence, I humbly pray to you to get rid of that formation, to get physical darshan of Mother [name omittedd]. and the past life history for the sudden Vision of Shiva from you.

Humbly,

ॐ Dear . . . ,

Om Namo Bhagavate Sri Ramanaya

Namaste. Thank you for your message.

If one has found his Guru, he has all that he needs. Absence of seeming outward attention does not mean absence of Grace, which is impossible.

Whether visions appear or not, if one inquires into the nature of the seer who knows the seen and the unseen, true Knowledge of the Self shines. That is Siva, eternal and real.

The inquiry to know the Self, of the nature of Being-Consciousness-Bliss and the very source of all that is true, good, and beautiful, as revealed by Bhagavan Sri Ramana Maharshi unfailingly destroys the darkness of ignorance and the delusive forms such takes.

May you ever abide in the Knowledge of the Self and thus be always happy and at peace.

Ever yours in Truth,
Nome

October 13, 2010

Dear Nome,

Humble respects for your reply, kindly considering me, this ego-mind.

Even though the highest level of explanation has been given by you, I suppose you are that Divine (Self) itself in the form of Sri Nome externally. Sri Nome's illusary 'I' thought was long back extinguished in the fire of Divine (Self). Hence, can I humbly request you to meditate upon this ego-mind [name omitted] and find out my past life details—the background behind the Shiva vision and the demoniac thoughts? Am I asking beyond my limits and the same thing again?

I very humbly request you to kindly consider the above and also immerse me in Nirvikalpa Samadhi the moment you read this mail. I know I can only do it for myself, but also it is equally true that a jnani can influence a mind beyond time and space.

Even though all these are momentary and relative knowledge, nevertheless I have this notion that I can better go only from the unknown to less known and finally to fully known.

Humbly,

333

October 14, 2010

ॐ Dear . . . ,

Om Namo Bhagavate Sri Ramanaya

Namaste. Yes, as you surmised, the present question is the same as the previous one.

It would appear that the memories of the present life are already burdensome to your mind, so why ask for those of other lives that will only add to the burden? One cannot ask one who sees the truth of non-ego, that the Self alone is, to think of an ego, mind, etc. Find the source of the thoughts, and you will be free of bondage. If you deeply determine that the source of happiness is within, the tendencies and attachments that now plague your mind will dissolve.

If you inquire to know the truth of the Self, you will find the Reality of Siva, which transcends time and space. Thereby, one is absorbed (samadhi) in that which is without differentiation (nirvikalpa) and without imagination (nirvikalpa). That in which one remains absorbed, without the least trace of ego ("me") is innate (sahaja). That is the true nature of the Self.

Grace is fully present. Apply your best efforts. No spiritual effort is ever in vain. Practice according to the instruction of the Guru.

May you steadily abide in the Knowledge of the Self, as revealed by Sri Bhagavan, and thus remain absorbed in profound peace.

Ever yours in Truth,
Nome

[A seeker wrote describing how he felt shaken at the possibility of death not being far off after obtaining "a Vedic reading" (perhaps astrological). This is Nome's response.]

October 14, 2010

ॐ Dear . . . ,

Om Namo Bhagavate Sri Ramanaya
Namaste. Thank you for your message.

Whether the body lasts for a long time or a short time, true Being is forever. Compared with the stars and galaxies, even a long life of the body is for a miniscule duration. Yet even this universe is momentary, while the Self, Brahman, endures eternally.

The true, profound purpose of the Vedas is the revelation of the Knowledge of the eternal Self.

One who knows the Self abides as the Self, and he is at peace, without fear, at ease in his own bliss always.

Ever yours in truth,
Nome

[This message was sent in response to a seeker who expressed his growing detachment from worldly life and his confusion regarding engagement in business activities and perplexity regarding the lack of approval from others regarding the spiritual direction of this life.]

October 26, 2010

ॐ Dear . . . ,

Om Namo Bhagavate Sri Ramanaya
Namaste. Thank you for your message.

Whatever are the activities in which the body engages, detachment is necessary. Detachment is rooted in the knowledge of the source of happiness and the purpose of life.

Whether active or inactive, Self-inquiry should continue, as it is not determined by the conditions of the body, senses, etc.

To pursue the quest for Self-Knowledge is the greatest good for all. It is also the most loving; indeed, it is to abide as love, itself. To unreservedly give yourself to this quest is to fulfill the purpose of life and to find the supreme bliss. The *Gita* teaches that one ought to dedicate his activities and the fruits of those activities to the Supreme. One should know himself and be free of the ideas of being a performer of action, an enjoyer (experiencer) of their fruits, and such.

Attachment born of ignorance gives rise to fear. Nonattachment and inquiry yield fearless serenity.

Ever yours in Truth,
Nome

[Here is a message from another seeker, followed by the response from Nome.]

October 26, 2010

Namaste,

Although this separation that is being perceived never existed, that is still not fully known to me, or I have not had full experience of it. When did this forgetting or un-knowing of truth occur? When I was first born, did I have this knowledge and eventually forget and create illusion? Is the purpose of this physical, illusory life to realize its own true nature?

ॐ Dear . . . ,

Om Namo Bhagavate Sri Ramanaya
Namaste. Thank you for your message.

When you say that the truth of non-separation is still not fully known by you, who is it that does not know?

The idea that illusion has a start is as illusory as the illusion, itself. The one Self alone exists eternally. The idea of another, of an "I," is entirely a false assumption. If one inquires for whom this assumption could be, imagination, being unreal, ceases.

Self-Realization is undoubtedly the supreme purpose of life. Therefore, one should earnestly and with utmost intensity strive for this Realization. In that, one finds that the individual was never born; this is spoken of as its "destruction."

It is hoped that you find the above to be of some help for you. May your inquiry be deep so that you abide steadily in the Knowledge of the Self and thus dwell always in lasting peace and happiness.

Ever yours in Truth,
Nome

[This response was sent to a seeker who expressed feeling insecure and anxious over the ill health of a loved one.]

October 27, 2010

ॐ Dear . . . ,

Om Namo Bhagavate Sri Ramanaya
Namaste. Thank you for your message.

Security cannot truly be found in the things of the world, body, etc. Lasting peace and perfection lie in the Self. Self-inquiry, resulting in the Knowledge of the Self, reveals your identity as That, and thus you abide in lasting peace, as lasting peace.

Bodies are inherently transient. The Self alone is eternal. If you cease to misidentify with the body, you will grieve for neither the living nor the dead, and, being free from anxious thought, you will know this eternal Self to be the one Self of all.

Ever yours in Truth,
Nome

[This message is from the same seeker who wrote twice previously concerning visions and past lives. Nome's response follows.]

October 27, 2010

Dear Nome,

I was persistent in asking a few questions about this ego [name omitted], but you showed great affection and love in replying to them.

I am writing this mail with frustration..

Is it very tough for you to read my past life and give a glimpse of my past history, please?

One side, the kama desire is just winning over me every night, and the whole day's efforts go to waste.

On other end, my Guru [name omitted], the Guru I have chosen, is leading a reclusive life, and I am not lucky enough to get a reply from her. Even as I write this letter to you, I strongly feel it is not proper to address my problems to you when I have already chosen [name omitted] as Guru.

In this circumstance, cannot you kindly consider to look into this individual ego [name omitted] past life? Or else can I humbly beg you for a taste of what it would look like when the mind subsides? Do you need any focus at your form from my part to achieve any of this?

I feel if you will look into my history you can, or rather, if it is in my script to learn my past life from you, I will.

Thanking you,

ॐ Dear . . . ,

Om Namo Bhagavate Sri Ramanaya

Namaste. Thank you for your message.

By the Guru's grace, all the illusory problems are overcome, but the disciple, for his part, must follow completely the instructions of the Guru.

For whom is the past life? For whom is the present life? For whom is the future? Self-inquiry to know the true nature of the Self is the means to realize the perfect fullness of Brahman. That alone constitutes full peace and happiness.

To desire to know the details of a past life is like craving to know the adventures of a man who was never born. What is truly desirable is freedom from the ego, and not more thoughts about the illusory adventures of the ego. Freedom from the ego includes the abandonment of erroneous ways of attempting to find the happiness that is, in truth, innate.

If one earnestly practices in the manner prescribed by Sri Ramana Maharshi, he finds within himself freedom from the ego, desires, and fears. It is wise not to waste one's time with that which is frivolous. Search for true wisdom within yourself, for it is in the Knowledge of the Self that one realizes immortal Bliss.

Ever yours in Sri Bhagavan,
Nome

[This is a reply to a seeker.]

October 30, 2010

ॐ Dear . . . ,

Om Namo Bhagavate Sri Ramanaya

Namaste. Thank you for your message.

Observing the outward tendencies of the mind, determine their root. Having determined the root, examine those misidentifications. Like darkness exposed to the light, such ignorance vanishes in inquiry. The ego proves to be unreal, and the Self alone remains. This Self is the very source of happiness; indeed, it is happiness itself.

Grace is ever present. One need only be keenly aware of it.

Ever yours in Truth,
Nome

[A message from a seeker, with Nome's response:]

November 1, 2010

Recently, I have been reading about Brahman, Paramatma, and Bhagavan as the three stages of realization. What is Bhagavan realization? (ie. relationship to Krishna)? What is the relation of that to what is taught by Ramana Maharshi?

ॐ Dear . . . ,

Om Namo Bhagavate Sri Ramanaya

Namaste. As Sri Ramana Maharshi revealed, the Self is undifferentiated, indivisible, and free of the least trace of duality. The nature of Self-Realization must necessarily be identical with the Self. The original meaning of the terms mentioned by you should be inwardly realized. The differences, stages, etc. are conceived within the mind, yet the Self and its Realization are transcendent of the mind, thought, and all conception. Inquire within to directly know that which is to be realized, yet is beyond the perceivable and the conceivable.

May you ever abide in that Absolute Self, as that Absolute Self, which is the indivisible Brahman and the very nature of Bhagavan.

Ever yours in Truth,
Nome

[A seeker wrote that he was confused upon reading and listening to the various spiritual views and practices of others. He concluded his message by stating that his "mind was running a million miles an hour." This is Nome's response.]

November 1, 2010

ॐ Dear . . . ,

Om Namo Bhagavate Sri Ramanaya
Namaste. Thank you for your message.
There may be many ideas about the Truth, that is, the Self, yet the Self, itself, is quite beyond all of them. If you discern and understand that the aim, Self-Realization, is eternal and of the nature of infinite Being-Consciousness-Bliss, transcendent of all thought, the path to that Realization will become clear for you.
Your mind may run, yet the one knows it is unmoving. Inquire within yourself to know who he is.

Ever yours in Truth,
Nome

[In response to a message from a seeker, this reply was sent.]

November 8, 2010

ॐ Dear . . . ,

Om Namo Bhagavate Sri Ramanaya

Namaste. Thank you for your message. Examination in the light of Truth is always beneficial. Trace the moods or modes of mind to the thoughts composing them. Trace the particular thoughts to the false definitions, or misidentifications, that are their basis. Dissolving the misidentifications, inquire into their very root, which is the ego assumption. Inquiring into the ego, it will be found to be nonexistent, and the Self alone will remain. This Self is the Heart, and devoted abidance in that is, indeed, bliss.

Ever yours in Truth,
Nome

[Here is a message from a seeker, followed by Nome's response.]

November 9, 2010

Om Namo Bhagavate Sri Ramanya
Dear Master Nome:

Always pointing to the truth of direct inquiry reveals that there is no question unless there is a mind and if such is the case, Who am I? is the first, middle, last and only true question.

In deep devotion,
Om Namo Bhagavate Sri Ramanaya

ॐ Dear . . . ,

Om Namo Bhagavate Sri Ramanaya

Namaste. Thank you for your message. Yes, "Who am I?" is the essential question, and one's own Being is alone the silent answer.

Ever yours in Truth,
Nome

[A seeker wrote about the sickness of another seeker. This message was written in response.]

November 9, 2010

ॐ Dear . . . ,

Om Namo Bhagavate Sri Ramanaya

Namaste. Thank you for your message. Please convey my best regards to [name omitted].

It is quite evident that the body is subject to decay, disease, and death. Yet, the Self is truly not the body. It remains as perpetual, formless Being, and birthless and undying Consciousness, the perfection of which is immutable Bliss. One who knows the Self as such is herself that Self and remains at peace with or without the body.

Thus, Sri Bhagavan has revealed the spiritual remedy for any kind of suffering associated with the body and its conditions. By abidance in this Truth, you will be at peace, and that peace, in which you abide, you, yourself, are. Inquire within to verify how this is so.

Ever yours in Truth,
Nome

[This is a message from a seeker. Nome's response follows.]

November 21, 2010

I have begun practicing japa, which has been helping me to turn inwards and meditate. I have heard that it is very beneficial to

343

receive mantras from a self realized guru. Would you happen to have any to prescribe? Also I remember reading somewhere, but I may be mistaken, that Ramana said japa will lead one to the same place as bhakti and meditating with the intent of turning inward and knowing "who am I?". Is this true?

ॐ Dear . . . ,

Om Namo Bhagavate Sri Ramanaya
Namaste. Thank you for your message.

No spiritual effort ever goes in vain. With the inward strength that you gain from your practice of japa, turn even more deeply inward to find the source of all mantras, which is Brahman, the true Self. Such turning entirely inward, so that the ego disappears and the divine, real Self remains self-revealed, is bhakti and jnana.

Ever yours in Truth,
Nome

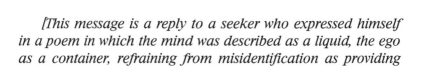

[This message is a reply to a seeker who expressed himself in a poem in which the mind was described as a liquid, the ego as a container, refraining from misidentification as providing glimpses of freedom, and ended with:

Then with the absence of the imaginary wall
the liquid (river) will enjoy the freedom
continue its journey in its course
until it merges with the sea.
At that point, the liquid (river) no longer exists.

Namaskarams..]

November 25, 2010

ॐ Dear . . . ,

Om Namo Bhagavate Sri Ramanaya

Namaste. Thank you for your message with the verse.

As you have observed, the real Being of the Self is entirely formless, just as a liquid intrinsically has no shape of its own but only seemingly appears in the shape of its container. By the inquiry revealed by the Maharshi, no container is found to exist, and the Reality of the Self shines as absolute, One without a second.

Just as there are no individual drops in the ocean, and just as there are no corners in boundless space, so there is no individual in Reality. As you have said, the ego is an imaginary wall. Such is also the case for all of its concomitant bondage For whom is this imagination? By such Self-inquiry, as graciously taught by Sri Bhagavan, the imagination, both as the assumed cause and the supposed effect, vanishes, being unreal, and the blissful Self alone remains. It is, as he has said, "like a river when it joins the ocean."

May you ever abide in the Knowledge of the Self, fully absorbed in That, as That, and thus dwell in lasting peace and happiness.

Ever yours in Truth,
Nome

[Here is a message from a seeker accompanied by Nome's response.]

November 29, 2010

Om Namo Bhagavate Sri Ramanaya
Dear Master Nome:

You are ever with me. In Love, there is no you and no me, simply the truth of Love. As events unfold, the teaching of Bhagavan which you make so clear, which you are, is ever present. There is no way to offer thanks. It is Grace. There are no words, just Love, Love, Love.

In devotion,
Om Namo Bhagavate Sri Ramanaya

ॐ Dear . . . ,

Om Namo Bhagavate Sri Ramanaya
Namaste. Thank you for your message.
The truth of love is ineffable. It is the indivisibility of
Being. Blissful it is to know this by abiding absorbed in it.
May you ever happily abide in That, as That, the secret of
love, the Knowledge of Truth. In this manner, the teachings
of Sri Bhagavan shine in you.

Ever yours in Truth,
Nome

*[This is a response to a seeker who asked to be put in con-
tact with someone who could give him shaktipat and thereby
provide awakening through arousal of kundalini.]*

December 4, 2010

ॐ Dear . . . ,

Om Namo Bhagavate Sri Ramanaya
Namaste. Thank you for your message.
You may find it worthwhile to inquire as to whether or
not the Self is an object to be given or received. For it to be
eternal, the nature of Self-Realization must be of a nature
that is identical with the Self. Therefore, it must be free of
duality, nonobjective, and timelessly existent.
It is ignorance alone that causes one to believe that
oneself is different from the Self. Self-Knowledge alone
destroys ignorance, as light causes darkness to vanish.
Transient action cannot do so, for it is within the context of
that very ignorance.

Shaktipata literally means the handing down, falling, bestowing, or flying of power. Alternatively, it may mean the "prostration of strength." One has to inquire to determine what is the true power and what is its source. True power lies in eternal peace. It is that which brings one from the unreal to the real, from darkness to light, and from death to immortality. How could such power be associated with a body or a subtle body? It is none other than the power of Consciousness, itself, which is eternal, formless, unborn, and imperishable. Know yourself.

Ever yours in Truth,
Nome

[A seeker wrote about being flooded by fond memories of her satsang experiences, the value of her past friendship with a now-deceased seeker, seeing the importance of intense inquiry and deep surrender, and questioned how she will become free of distractions. Here is Nome's response.]

December 20, 2010

ॐ Dear . . . ,

Namaste. Thank you for your message.

Appearing in the context of sweet memories, there is an indestructible essence of true Knowledge, which is the actual loving experience, that is inextinguishable.

The body of Saraswati may have perished, but that which she loved in the innermost recesses of her heart is unending.

It is evident that you have become aware of the preciousness of that which is spiritual: the Truth, Self-Knowledge, the Guru, the spiritual instruction, deep spiritual friendship, joyful devotion, holy books, etc. There is noth-

347

ing in this world that can compare to the depth of happiness that is found or expressed in these.

Certainly, whenever you wish to visit here, you are warmly welcome. Obviously, the same is so for [name omitted].

The Self is not defined by the body or by location. It is within you, and it is truly you. The idea that you are distinct from the Self should dissolve. Such dissolution is accomplished by the profound inquiry to know the Self. Deep surrender is the same. For one who practices, illimitable happiness is found to be the natural state of the Self. Distractions, worries, and other forms of delusion are only ignorance. The more that you determine ignorance is just ignorance and not the truth, the more you will find yourself to be free of it. Ignorance always involves a mistaken notion about the source of happiness, what is real, or who you are. The profound Knowledge of the blissful, real Self, found by deep inquiry and thorough devotion, eliminates such ignorance, just as light is said to destroy darkness.

Please convey my best wishes to [name omitted]. May your meditations be filled with the joy that is the innate.

Ever yours in Truth,
Nome

[This is a message from a seeker, along with the response from Nome.]

December 21, 2010

Om Namo Bhagavate Sri Ramanaya
Namaste Master Nome:

While reading the *Advaita Bodha Deepika*, I have come across the following: "... Maya has no antecedent cause because it is not the product of anything preceding it, but remains in Brahman, self evident and without beginning. Before creation, there could be no cause for its manifestation, yet it manifests and it must be by itself."

Can you please explain the meaning of this? Is Maya equivalent to Shakti in the Shiva Shakti dance? Is it all Brahman, pure Being, inexpressible as is Maya or Shakti? If Maya is not real and yet not unreal because it is experienced, are we then seeing Brahman everywhere until we disappear into Being Brahman with no manifestation?

Om Namo Bhagavate Sri Ramanaya
In devotion,

ॐ Dear . . . ,

Om Namo Bhagavate Sri Ramanaya
Namaste. Thank you for your message.

Maya can have no antecedent cause because the causality, itself, would be a figment of maya. Similarly, it cannot be a product of a nonexistent preceding thing. Though it may be said that maya remains in Brahman, for there is nothing external to Brahman, Brahman remains homogeneous, undivided, and without any quality such as maya. Self-evident refers to Brahman. Maya, illusion, cannot be said to be self-evident. By whom is it known and by what means is it known? It cannot know itself, yet the idea that there is another existent one, someone other than Brahman, to know it is also only in illusion, or maya. Brahman is without beginning or end, for it is ever existent. Maya is also said to be without beginning for two reasons. Within maya, illusion seems to have been going on forever. In the knowledge of Brahman, maya is seen to never have started, for that which is unreal cannot have a real beginning. Therefore, illusion is only for illusion. For the Reality, there is only Reality.

In the teachings that pertain to Siva and Shakti, the emphasis is on the undivided reality, which is Siva, and the Shakti, or power, is only of the very nature of Siva, and not

349

anything apart. As Brahman is inexpressible, so Siva is ineffable.

The statement that, "Maya is yet not unreal because it is experienced," is merely an expedient teaching and should not be taken as a statement of the final truth. Who experiences what? By what means is it experienced? If taken at face value, without further deeper inquiry, such a concept can lead to the idea of a duality of states, such as one with maya still appearing and one without, but the Reality is only one, without conditions, and free of the least trace of multiplicity.

Maya is that which is not. Yet, in truth, there can be no such thing as an existent nonexistence. Brahman, which is the one Existence that alone is, is alone the nature of all. The experiencer, the experience, and the object of experience are only Brahman, yet there is not the least trace of that triad in Brahman. All is Brahman. This means that Brahman alone is, and there is no such distinct thing as all.

It is hoped that you find the above helpful and clarifying. May the Light of Nondual Knowledge ever shine within you so that you, free of the least illusion, abide in bliss.

Ever yours in Truth,
Nome

[The Ramana Maharshi Centre for Learning and SAT have maintained loving relations rooted in deep devotion to Sri Ramana for many years. After the dropping of the body of Sri A. R. Natarajan, who was the founder and leader of the RMCL, the leadership of the Centre came into the able hands of his daughter, Dr. Sarada Natarajan. Here is a message that she sent in December, with Nome's response followed by his article.]

December 23, 2010

Dear and Respected Ramana brother, Master Nome,

Namo Ramana!

It gives me great joy to convey that by the ever full, all-knowing grace of Bhagavan, this year we complete thirty years of publication of "Ramana Way", the monthly journal of Ramana Maharshi Centre of Learning, Bangalore.

In this connection, as a celebration of three decades of learning and sharing Bhagavan's life and teachings, we plan to bring out a special series of the journal in the year 2011-12. The first of this will be the March edition of "Ramana Way" as the journal commenced in March 1981.

In this first special March edition, we are inviting senior devotees from different Ramana Centres, in India and the world, to share their experience of Bhagavan's blessings, His life, works and teachings.

I would feel deeply blessed, if you could contribute an article for this inaugural special edition of "Ramana Way." You may write on any aspect of Bhagavan's life and teachings, say within a thousand words.

As the issue would need to go to the press by mid-February, it would be best if we can receive the article by January end, or latest by end of first week of February.

My warm regards to Shashvatima and all others of the Ramana Family at SAT.

Yours in Bhagavan,
Sarada Natarajan

ॐ Dear Sri Ramana Sister, Dr. Sarada,

Om Namo Bhagavate Sri Ramanaya

Namaste. Thank you for your kind message, which I received yesterday, the day for Sri Bhagavan's Jayanti celebrations here at SAT. Actually, we will celebrate again on the 30th. One can never engage in too much devotion...

The "Ramana Way" is a spiritual delight for all the devotees who are fortunate to read it. Your idea of a celebration of three decades of publishing it is splendid.

351

In response to your request, yesterday the attached article was written. I hope that it falls within the guidelines suggested by you in your message. It contains 751 words.

Sasvati sends her deepest love.

Please convey my best wishes to Sulochana.

Ever yours in Sri Bhagavan,
Nome

Inconceivable, Yet Self-evident

Om Namo Bhagavate Sri Ramanaya

His Silence, His Being, is ineffable, indeed, inconceivable. He is known only by Himself. To Himself, He is self-evident. Where differentiation is impossible, that in which there is nothing "else" whatsoever, He is. If inconceivable, how is one to know Him? In the disappearance of the illusion of existing as a separate individual, we can be said to know Him, That, the sole-existent Reality. The Reality is self-evident to itself. Who is to conceive otherwise? Only to an illusion could the Reality of the Self appear as if unknown, but an illusion is not real at all. So, how could its ignorance exist? He, the inconceivable One, is the self-evident One.

Inconceivable, yet self-evident, is His teaching. Just as "there are not two selves, one to know, or realize, the other," as He has instructed, so there are not two selves, one to be ignorant of the other. The means to realize the Truth, which He reveals and is, is summed up in the question "Who am I?", yet the true significance of the inquiry is the inconceivable Knowledge regarding the self-evident Truth of the Self. Every particle of His teaching shines fully with the light of this Knowledge. The self-evident Truth is the ever-existent Self, which, being of the nature of the innermost, nonobjective Consciousness, is ever inconceivable. Transcendent of ideas learned and forgotten, His spiritual instruction shines with the same full power of His absolute Silence. His sparkling, eloquent, spoken and written instruction, always brimming with exquisite, nondual clarity that leaves no darkness, reveals the formless yet exceedingly precise path to realize the formless. His teaching is the shining of Reality, itself, and reveals the self-existent, which is the self-evident. Who can say what His teaching is? It is nonobjective and inconceivable, yet entirely real and self-evident, the very revelation of Reality in which Being is Knowledge. It is never a known or unknown concept, and it stands as the eternal revelation of the eternal, the Self's revelation of itself.

His life shines with a sublime holiness that is the pinnacle of spiritual perfection. However much we laud it, our praise can hardly describe it. All, and more, that is needed to wisely approach everything in life is fully explained by His life. He may be said to be the very manifestation of the unmanifested Brahman, the Self, yet His identity as That renders even such a description futile, for it imagines differences where there are none. Even still, He shows that life in That, as That, is natural and innate, for such is "the egoless state, the only real state that there is," as He has declared. Yet, His life is the Existence of the Self, which neither is born nor perishes. Unborn and immortal, His Existence is inconceivable, yet it is self-evident, for He is the Self of all forever.

His grace is immense, vaster than the vastest, with innumerable manifestations, while its nature remains utterly transcendent. Did he not declare that "grace is of the Self"? How can one conceive of such grace? All the thoughts of it and different experiences of it are still only an infinitesimal particle of it. As the Self is ever existent, so His grace is ever existent. Just as one cannot actually be separate from the Self, so it is impossible to be outside of grace. Knowledge of it in any manner whatsoever is also His grace. For those who are devoted to Him, relying on His liberating spiritual teachings for their freedom from all illusion, their hearts full of love for Him, depending on Him for their peace amidst all experiences, seeking refuge in Him, and finding bliss in Him, His grace shines as self-evident.

Inconceivable, yet self-evident is He. Bhagavan Sri Ramana Maharshi: the inconceivable, self-evident One. Who can conceive of Him, yet who can be apart from Him or not know Him? The Being of real existence, the Consciousness of true knowledge, and the Bliss of all happiness is He.

He, our only true Self, in us abides, and we in Him, the infinite, dwell. He, the eternal, is always with us, and we, who are nothing else, are ever in Him.

What little has been said here is only of Him. That He is utterly inconceivable is quite self-evident. May we ever remain blissfully absorbed in Him, the One without a second.

Om Sri Ramanarpanamastu

Written on this sacred Jayanti of Bhagavan Sri Ramana Maharshi, December 23, 2010, by Nome.

[A message from a seeker who attends satsang and Nome's response.]

January 5, 2011

Dear Nome,

Om Namo Bhagavate Sri Ramanaya

With the goal of making my practice/understanding more effective, I seek your wisdom in response to a few questions I have regarding the following saying by Bhagavan:

"You need not eliminate any false "I". How can "I" eliminate itself? All that you need do is to find out its origin and stay there. Your effort can extend only so far. Then the Beyond will take care of itself. You are helpless there. No effort can reach it."

My questions:
1. Isn't it "I" (ego or non-Self) that "apparently" does the self-inquiry since the non-dual Self cannot be the doer?
2. I conceptually understand that eventually the inquirer ("I") vanishes upon inquiry, but the Inquiry, i.e. Self-Knowledge, alone remains as the Self. Is this "apparent" elimination of the "I" not brought about as a result of apparent deep and intense self-effort, i.e. thought transcendent inquiry/meditation by the yet-to-be-eliminated "I"?

3. Or is it that "I's" self-effort, no matter how deep and intense, does not eventually result in the apparent elimination of "I"? I.e. does the apparent Self-Realization eventually happen when it happens and is independent of the self-effort? And if so, what is the role of self-effort?

Pranam,

ॐ Dear . . . ,

Om Namo Bhagavate Sri Ramanaya

Namaste. Thank you for your message. As always, Sri Bhagavan's instruction is of the utmost profundity.

"You need not eliminate any false I": There are not two existent selves, that one should eliminate the other. The Self is always only one, and that alone is real.

"How can I eliminate itself?": The so-called, false or unreal "I" does not exist. If it is assumed to be real, how will the ego eliminate itself? If the ego is truly unreal, which means that it does not exist, how could something that does not exist eliminate or do anything else to itself or to anything else? The ego, being unreal, is insubstantial and utterly powerless. The Knowledge that completely destroys ignorance cannot possibly be for or by the ego. True Knowledge is of the very nature of Being, which is the Self.

"All that you need to is to find out its origin and stay there.": One should trace his very existence, or identity, to its origin, that is, to its true nature. Such finding or tracing consists of Knowledge in the form of Self-inquiry. To "stay there" signifies steady abidance in the Self, as the Self, without the least false assumption of individuality. It is to remain free of misidentification.

"Your effort can extend only so far.": We can speak of effort only in the context of spiritual practice. The effort to be applied intensely is that of profound inquiry to know the Self as it is. Since the Self is nonobjective, and, therefore, neither lost nor attained, the effort is primarily directed toward negation of the misidentifications that constitute ignorance.

355

"Then, the Beyond will take care of itself.": "Then" may be understood to be upon Self-Realization or the word may be understood to mean therefore. The Self is always the Self and knows itself by its own innate Knowledge. That is eternal, which means that it is without beginning and without an end. The Self knows itself, and there is no individual "I" involved.

"You are helpless there. No effort can reach it.": The ego, being unreal, is powerless. The Self, being ever-attained, is not to be attained anew. Effort is applied only to the elimination of ignorance. That being accomplished, the innate Self-Knowledge remains. The Self is truly the only existent Reality. Who is different from it? Who is to reach it? Whose is the effort?

In answer to your first question, Self-inquiry destroys the imaginary ego and is not done by an ego. In truth, the Self alone exists and therefore has no inquiry. If we speak of inquiry, it signifies the end manifesting as the means. That Knowledge which the Self is manifests itself as the inquiry. Knowledge belongs only to the Self. There is only one knower. The unreal or imaginary has no capacity to know. Self-inquiry is Knowledge and is not to be regarded as an activity. Knowledge alone yields Liberation; action cannot do so. Actions are performed with the body, speech, and mind. Self-inquiry transcends all of those. A performer of inquiry cannot be spoken of when the inquiry eliminates the very ideas of a performer and of action.

Not a drop of deep, intense, spiritual effort ever goes in vain. The inquiry should be of utmost intensity and should be continuous. Your practice should be as intense and as continuous as you wish for the state of Self-Realization to be. If you want partial happiness and peace, practice partially. If you want full happiness and peace, practice fully.

Self-realization is not an event and does not "happen." The Realization is of the very nature of the Self that is realized. The Self is not an event. What happens ceases. What comes goes. What should occur for whom? The Self is only Being. Know yourself.

May you, by the Grace of Sri Bhagavan, deeply inquire and thus know the Self that you really are and, thereby, abide always in lasting peace and happiness.

Ever yours in Truth,
Nome

[On January 8, 2011, a seeker who lives at a distance from the Temple wrote a message that contains several questions relating to his spiritual experience and the perception of the illusion of the world through the senses. He also expressed his deep devotion and faith in Sri Bhagavan's grace. In response, Nome sent this message. The questions raised by the seeker can be inferred from the response.]

ॐ Dear . . . ,

Om Namo Bhagavate Sri Ramanaya
Namaste. Thank you for your message.

Inquire within yourself: who is it that becomes ensnared by the senses? The Self, which is pure Consciousness, cannot be bound, and, for it, there is no differentiation such as the senses, the objects, etc. If there seems to be another "I," inquire into the nature of that "I." Such inquiry will reveal that there is only one Self, and that alone exists.

From another perspective, recognize that, although the senses appear and disappear, the Consciousness that illumines them, apart from which they cannot even appear, is ever the same and neither comes nor goes. You are the Consciousness, so how can the senses affect you? In addition, contemplation along the lines mentioned by you will certainly be beneficial, especially if you absorb yourself in the actual, essential Knowledge in which the bodiless Self shines clearly beyond illusion's dreams. If you cease to misidentify, to regard the unreal as real, and to imagine that happiness lies in anything other than the Self, what will it matter if the senses appear or disappear?

For whom is this universe? If the seer is inquired into, the objective outlook is abandoned, and the true Existence is realized. When you see the snake, you do not actually see a snake but only a rope imagined to be a snake, for only the rope is there. Similar is it with the world and the Self. The Self alone exists, eternally, both when it is imagined to be differentiated into an experiencer and a world and when it is known just as it is.

The world, the senses, the body, and the mind do not declare their own reality. You say that they are. If that "you" is known in its true nature, all such imagined differentiation, being unreal, vanishes. Your own Self has been imagined as all these things. Self-inquiry reveals the nonexistence of the very root of such imagination, and the Self alone remains.

Of course, you are always welcome at the SAT Temple; Ramanasramam is also a very holy place to visit. Whether there, here, or at your own home, that which is essential is the profound Knowledge of the Self, for in this alone are perfect peace and bliss.

Ever yours in Truth,
Nome

[On January 9, 2011, the same seeker wrote the following:]

Om Namo Bhagavate Sri Ramanaya

Dear Nome,

Namaste. One point that is still not convincingly clear like a amala fruit in my hand is the everlasting, unborn nature of Being-Consciousness. Either because of lifelong proximity or not deep enough vichara, I cannot imagine beingness without the body. It is said that in deep sleep there is no body, but there is beingness. But are not breathing and heartbeat going on even in deep sleep? Please help me get over this hurdle once and for all. Thank you for your time and help. Namaste.

[Here is Nome's response.]

ॐ Dear . . . ,

Om Namo Bhagavate Sri Ramanaya
Namaste. Thank you for your message.

The idea about breathing and heartbeat continuing during the deep sleep state is conceived in the present waking state. In deep sleep, itself, there are no such ideas. Yet, without perception of a body and without conception of ideas, you still exist. That existence is the same now, too. Know yourself to be the invariable Existence, which remains immutable regardless of the apparent changes of the three states.

Even to think of a body, you must exist. This "you" cannot be the body. That which knows the body and which knows the mind that thinks about it is free of both. Even to entertain the idea that you cannot exist without a body, you, the bodiless one, must exist.

Unborn, attributeless, and imperishable is your real Self. Being is bodiless and nonobjective. Consciousness is free of thought. Bliss is innate.

If, by the Grace of Sri Bhagavan, you deeply inquire, what is indicated here will be found to be self-evident. Thus, you will remain absorbed in the blissful Truth.

Ever yours in Truth,
Nome

[A message from a seeker followed by Nome's response.]

January 12, 2011

Om Namo Bhagavate Sri Ramanaya

Namaste Master Nome:

Chit, pure consciousness, and chidabhasa, reflected consciousness, are not personal as I understand it. The "I" that understands is not personal. It seems there is nothing personal. Reincarnation is not personal either, nothing personal, no individual.

Please comment.

In devotion,
Om Namo Bhagavate Sri Ramanaya

ॐ Dear . . . ,

Om Namo Bhagavate Sri Ramanaya
Namaste. Thank you for your message.

Chit or pure Consciousness is absolute and invariable. If that is known as it is, no idea of another can arise.

Chidabhasa or reflected consciousness is spoken of to explain how any appearance, such as the mind, is known or experienced. The reflected consciousness is not personal in the sense of being contained within a personality, yet it can be conceived of as such only in reference to some kind of appearance, which, in turn, must be for an "I."

The idea of a person is for the "I," so, in that sense, the "I" is not personal. Yet, that "I" should be inquired into so that the egoless, true nature of the Self is realized.

Reincarnation is for one who is presently incarnate. It involves the ego notion, the collection of subtle tendencies (samskaras) that can manifest as the illusory person, and association with a body or bodies. In that sense, such may be regarded as personal.

In truth, you are the impersonal, absolute Consciousness. You are not any kind of person. You have no birth, and you will not be reborn. Know yourself as you truly are. In this lies liberation from the imagined bondage of the cycle of birth and death, from reflections and appearances of any kind, and from the false assumption of an ego entity. This is the way to unalloyed happiness.

Ever yours in Truth,
Nome

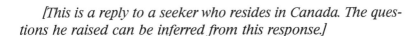

[This is a reply to a seeker who resides in Canada. The questions he raised can be inferred from this response.]

January 12, 2012

ॐ Dear . . . ,

Om Namo Bhagavate Sri Ramanaya
Namaste. Thank you for your message.

If you surrender to Sri Bhagavan, problems will no longer be felt to be problems. In the nonattachment that results, peace and happiness remain full regardless of the circumstances.

The way to get beyond worldly life is an inward one. As you have seen, a change in outer circumstances does not necessarily mean increased happiness. One's mind still goes with him, and, if there is ignorance in it, suffering continues. Nevertheless, happiness exists as the very nature of the Self. Turn inward, and you will find it shining in its fullness. Attachment is confusion regarding the source of happiness. If one truly knows that happiness is within, he is detached and cannot suffer. Indeed, he is his own bliss.

Of course, when you are able to visit the SAT temple, you will be warmly welcome. In the meantime, you can very easily read the SAT publications, other books about Sri Ramana's teachings, and avail yourself of all that is on the SAT website, such as listening to and watching satsangs, etc.

According to the Maharshi, the truth about karma yoga is discerned by inquiry as to whose is the karma. Yoga means union and should be understood to mean union with the Self. Karma yoga, therefore, implies abidance as the egoless Self and free of misidentification with the body, even as it engages in various activities, which should be dedicated to the Supreme.

He who, in his heart, is fully devoted to the Realization of the Self, by the Grace of the Sadguru, finds happiness to which nothing in the world can compare and which nothing in the world can diminish.

Ever yours in Truth,
Nome

[This response is in reply to a message dated January 17, 2011 from a seeker who resides at a distance from the SAT temple. The questions asked can be inferred from the answers.]

ॐ Dear . . . ,

Om Namo Bhagavate Sri Ramanaya
Namaste. Thank you for your message.

It is essential to know yourself as you truly are. The Self is not an ego, or individual, and similarly is not to be defined by personal attributes. Being the source of all that is true, good, and beautiful, the Self is yet transcendent of all qualities, attributes, and activities. So, you are not a deficient individual; you are not even a confident individual. Being is truly free of individuality and, in this, lies its limitless bliss.

You have noted that whenever you engage in an act of kindness or service that you feel a greater sense of love, goodness, etc. Your own experience thus shows you how to proceed. In the midst of such action, the ego recedes or subsides. Therefore, the natural happiness of the Self shines. One's entire life can be permeated by such egoless joy. Your description contains the explanation of your experience: "it makes a huge difference in how I view myself and others." Actually, it is the view of yourself that gives rise to the selfless approach, the joy, and the view of others. One who has this inner knowledge, or is in quest of it, has no need for anxious thoughts regarding esteem, etc.

362

May you abide in the profound Knowledge of the Self, the one source of all happiness and love, and thereby be full of peace.

Ever yours in Truth,
Nome

[In response to a message sent by a Sri Ramana devotee who resides in India concerning how his mind becomes disturbed in reaction to circumstances with others, Nome wrote the following:]

January 19, 2011

ॐ Dear . . . ,

Om Namo Bhagavate Sri Ramanaya

Namaste. Thank you for your message.

When one overlooks the innate bliss of the Self and imagines that his happiness is determined by outer circumstances, his mind becomes unclear and agitated. Then, he thinks that his unhappiness is externally caused. Abandonment of such ignorance, by knowing that it is only ignorance, removes all the suffering and enables one to rest in the innate happiness of the Self. If you deeply examine your own experience, you will find that what is stated here is true, and you will know the way to be free.

In addition, for the Self, what does it matter what anyone else says or does? For one who is immersed in Sri Bhagavan's Grace, what does it matter, whatever happens and by whomever? Understand in this way and be at ease.

Ever yours in Truth,
Nome

[In answer to a seeker's question, Nome responded:]

January 19, 2011

ॐ Dear . . . ,

Om Namo Bhagavate Sri Ramanaya
Namaste. Thank you for your message.

In whatever form and by whatever name the "I" seems to appear, it is wise to inquire for whom it is, that is, "Who am I?" Then, it is realized with absolute certainty that the one Self alone exists, eternally, and that there is neither an individual nor the objective sphere of experience.

May you abide unwaveringly in the Knowledge of the Self, which is forever unmodified, and thus be delighted at heart.

Ever yours in Truth,
Nome

[In another message, the same seeker wrote:]

January 20, 2011

The self is neither a nothingness or a void. Does it still know itself without an expression? I feel the underlying fear is nonexistence in any way, an idea of just being complete emptiness.

[Nome replied:]

ॐ Dear . . . ,

364

Om Namo Bhagavate Sri Ramanaya

Namaste. Yes, the Self is neither a thing nor a void. It is pure Existence, for which there is no alternative. Even in the case of a "nothing," there is still Existence. The nothing exists. The nothing is not real, but the Existence is. Truly, that which is conceived as being nothing does not actually exist, but Existence always exists. Therefore, there is truly no such thing as nonexistence.

Existence is Consciousness. In your inquiry, you may find it easier to discern the truth just stated by observing that the nothing is something about which you know. Even in a supposed state of "nonexistence," you still exist to know that. That "you," which is formless and without beginning or end, is the pure Existence. So, it is not possible for you to cease to exist or for you to even imagine your own nonexistence, without you existing to know that.

With or without any expression, the Self ever is. By inquiring to know who you are, and thus liberating yourself from all misidentification as an ego and as a body, you will know the non-dual Truth and thereby become fearless. In such inquiry, Sri Bhagavan's Grace is evident.

Ever yours in Truth,
Nome

[A seeker who attended satsangs in the 1970's and who visited for a celebration in the SAT temple in 2010 wrote a message that contained quoted passages from the teachings of Ch'an Buddhist Master Lin Chi along with the expressions of his own understanding here. Nome's response follows.]

January 22, 2011

Dearest Master Nome,

Om Namo Bhagavate Sri Ramanaya

I have just finished reading, *Ch'an and Zen Teaching Vol. 2* by Lu K'uan Yu (Charles Luk), which I thoroughly enjoyed and want to share some passages for your enjoyment.

I have always been annoyed and taken exception with the current propounding and insistence of Zen teaching that thought has to be silenced. Here the teaching is quite clear that the problem is not thoughts but the division into self and other that reflects one's ignorance and confusion which leads to isolation and suffering. Herein is the understanding of, "one without a second."

I want to acknowledge that in your presence you have always radiated your insistence that all of us are even now as we wish to be and that understanding alone is the key to the Kingdom - Self-abidance.

Lin Chi passed away in May of 863, yet his words are as true and accessible today as then.

From the notes regarding this passage: In China, the heart is believed to be the seat of thought, or intelligence, and its Western equivalent is mind. A true man of no fixed position is the mind which, according to Huang Po, "has neither location or direction" because it is as immense as space.

I thought you might appreciate this statement for the similarity with Sri Ramana Maharshi's view. My understanding, given what has been stated here about the nature of mind, is that the reference to the heart is as Ramana expressed.

During our time together, many moons ago, you shared a fondness for the Ch'an tradition of instantaneous enlightenment. Since our true nature is timeless and not different than our Self, I do find enjoyment when that same understanding is expressed in different ways and offer this letter in recognition of your essence and for your amusement.

Om Tat Sat,

ॐ Dear . . . ,

Om Namo Bhagavate Sri Ramanaya

Namaste. Thank you for your message replete with the Ch'an Buddhist quotes. It is good to hear from you again.

The idea that thought has to be quieted presupposes that thought is actually existent and, most importantly, takes for granted the assumption of an individual conceiver or perceiver of it. Upon this assumption is based the idea that one is separate from the Self, the thoughts supposedly creating the barrier or chasm that divides oneself from the one Self. It is certainly silly, yet nothing to be annoyed at, for neither such erroneous notions nor the individuals who entertain them are real.

The passages that you have selected certainly express the essential non-dual Truth. Such is our very Being, which is without gain or loss, free of differences of all kinds, and without an alternative. Forms of expression or the words employed do not matter, whether referred to as Brahman or Tao or God or Self or Mind or by any other term. What is important is the realization of the Truth, which is of the nature of the nonobjective Knowledge that is identical with Being.

That which is here is also truly the nature of you, for such is the Self that dwells in the hearts of all. May you ever abide in That, as That, of the nature of Being-Consciousness-Bliss, for such is your true abode, the Self itself, the home of paradisiacal peace. This is timelessly so.

Again, thanks for sending these passages.

Om Tat Sat

Ever yours in Truth,
Nome

[January 23, 2011, a SAT seeker sent a message in which he explained at length his spiritual experiences, practice, and the obstructions to his practice. His message ended with: "It just seems that no matter what, there is always an objective experience that pertains to this mental awareness I call "i" or feel as "i" in my enquiry. When you referred to the three states and

these being mere modes before the Self, that easily shows that this mental awareness I call "i" is an obstacle, because he comes and goes....What to do?" Here is Nome's response.]

ॐ Dear . . . ,

Om Namo Bhagavate Ramanaya
Namaste. Thank you for your message.

The best way to be liberated from the individual (ego) is to find out whether or not you are an individual to begin with. Focused on your true Being, inquire as to who you really are. Every form of the apparent "I" is objective and cannot possibly be a true definition for the Self. Eliminating such objective definition by clear inquiry, discern what the "I" is in its own nature. In truth, there is only one Self, and it is never individualized. Inquiry reveals this and thus sets you free of the illusory bondage.

May you ever abide in the Knowledge of the Self and thus repose in blissful peace always.

Ever yours in Truth,
Nome

[This message is from a seeker. Nome's response follows.]

January 24, 2011

Om Namo Bhagavate Sri Ramanaya

Dear Master Nome:

Namaste

I have a question regarding a verse in which Bhagavan stated, "Having investigated the various states of being, and seizing firmly by the mind that state of supreme reality, play your part, O hero, ever in the world. You have known the truth which is at the heart of all kinds of appearances. Without ever turning away from that reality, play in the world, O hero, as if in love with it."

What does "...seizing firmly by the mind that state of supreme reality..." mean?

In devotion,
Om Namo Bhagavate Sri Ramanaya

ॐ Dear . . . ,

Om Namo Bhagavate Sri Ramanaya

Namaste. The quotation of Sri Bhagavan may derive from *Yoga Vasishta.* The emphasis of the passage is that one should abide firmly in Self-Knowledge, even while one's body is engaged in the activities of the world. To indicate that such is an inner state and not a bodily state, the text says that the state of the supreme Reality should be seized firmly by the mind. If the mind does so, its limitations are destroyed and even the form of the mind vanishes, leaving pure Consciousness as the residuum.

Ever yours in Truth,
Nome

[This is Nome's reply to a seeker whose questions can be inferred from the response.]

January 27, 2011

ॐ Dear . . . ,

Om Namo Bhagavate Sri Ramanaya
Namaste. Thank you for your message.
Sri Bhagavan has, indeed, said that the destruction of vasanas is necessary for Self-Realization. The vasanas are

merely tendencies of ignorance, which true knowledge alone can destroy. Knowledge is not an action, so there is no question of being a performer of action in the destruction of the vasanas. It is ignorance alone that causes the false assumption of individuality and its concomitant false sense of deficiency. So, it is a bit silly to think that you are deficient in the ability to destroy the ignorance. When ignorance is recognized to be ignorance, it ceases to exist. What remains is the ever-existent, perfect fullness that is innate to the Self.

If you examine the definitions that falsely lend a sense of solidity to the ego, you will find them to be not true and thereby abandon them. If you inquire, "Who am I?", the assumption of existing as an ego entity will vanish, for it is unreal.

The Maharshi has taught that the idea that there is an obstacle or a difficulty should be the first to go. He has also indicated that, if one makes the effort, the practice will not be found to be difficult at all. How could Self-Knowledge be difficult? For whom would the difficulty be?

That [name omitted] has found a spiritual teacher whose instruction is fully satisfying for him is good. May he ever abide in the blissful Truth of the Self. Of course, he is always welcome here at the SAT Temple.

Grace is ever present. It exists as the Self of all and shines as the love within your heart. This Self has no tendencies, and abidance as this Self is freedom from all illusion.

Ever yours in Truth,
Nome

[This is from another seeker who lives at a distance from the temple, followed by Nome's reply.]

January 29, 2011

Namaste Nome,

I very much appreciated talking with you several weeks back.

The two major things I took from the conversation were to go about finding in myself the source of happiness via turning within (in inquiry) and then, to stay focused and go deeper in meditation, its good to clearly intend my purpose in the beginning,"Know thyself" with a short reading from the Maharshi, scripture etc. and making the Self-quest an offering to the divine.

I've been applying this and finding that I'm more avidly turning inward during a meditation than previously.

This morning, my mind had lots of reasons (thoughts) about why I shouldn't continue:."intellect isn't keen enough", "body feels off", "I'm really not focused", "it's just not working", etc. I found that I could inquire into each excuse, go past and deeper as a result.

Thanks for the instruction and your unflinching abidance in Truth.

ॐ Dear . . . ,

Om Namo Bhagavate Sri Ramanaya

Namaste. The perseverance in inquiry as you experienced in the meditation described by you is just what is needed. There are no valid excuses for bondage; there are endless reasons to be free. The divine Knowledge of the Self reveals the truth that you, of the nature of Being-Consciousness, are the happiness you always desire. The question is not whether to continue with meditation, but why should you continue in the imagination of non-meditation?

May you ever abide as the Self, the One without a second, and thus be at peace always.

Ever yours in Truth,
Nome

371

[This message from a seeker is followed by Nome's reply.]

February 1, 2011

Aum Namo Bhagavate Sri Ramanaya
Namaste Master

Thank you for the reply you gave me. It helped a lot. In Timeless Presence, you talked about your asthma and the chance of you not living for much longer, since there was no cure, and that you decided to practice right down to the end in hopes for liberation. In the end, you conquered death and the disease disappeared. Is this possible for someone like me? Can destiny really be overcome?

In deep devotion and gratitude,

ॐ Dear . . . ,

Om Namo Bhagavate Sri Ramanaya
Namaste. The Realization of the deathless Self is undoubtedly possible for all who, full of devotion, earnestly inquire to know who they are. Where is destiny for one who abides as the timeless Self? Therefore, have deep conviction in the path of Self-Knowledge and, in the dissolution of the ego, find Liberation to be the eternal, innate state.

Grace is always.

Ever yours in Truth,
Nome

[A message, dated February 8, 2011, from a seeker was received that described his feeling that he was caught in ignorance, quoted passages from Yoga Vasishta Sara *about bondage to sense objects, and requested instruction to help him overcome the tendencies of his mind. Here is the response from Nome.]*

372

ॐ Dear . . . ,

Om Namo Bhagavate Sri Ramanaya
Namaste. Thank you for your message.

Reading and meditating upon spiritual texts is certainly beneficial. Discrimination must be developed so that you discern their true meaning and inwardly verify that truth within yourself.

You need not continue to suffer. Suffering is born only of ignorance. Ignorance is certainly not effortless. It involves thinking in limited, repetitive patterns. Such ignorance is a mistaken attempt to know oneself, to know reality, and to find happiness.

Both verses cited by you refer to the mental tendency, the mistaken concept, that happiness is to be found externally, such as in objects. Certainty in the knowledge of the true source of happiness is a wonderfully strong basis for spiritual practice that results in Self-Realization. It is for this reason, that the Maharshi presented such knowledge in the preamble to the booklet *Who am I?* and taught more about this later in the same text. Knowledge of the true source of happiness is essential for deep nonattachment and for the intense desire for Self-Realization.

You may also find it helpful to read the passages in the second section of *Self-Knowledge* that deal with the nature of happiness and immortality.

May you, discovering happiness within, become serenely detached from all worldly things and, keenly inquiring to know your own true nature, abide in the Self, as the Self.

Om Namah Sivaya

Ever yours in Truth,
Nome

February 9, 2011

Om Namo Bhagavate Sri Ramanaya

Master Nome: Namaste

Hearing your words during Satsang on Sundays gives rise to the joy of truth. Bowing in gratitude and devotion, more of it is sought.

What exactly is the meaning of "Abide in the Self"? While Bhagavan Sri Ramana Maharshi answered seekers' questions, the questions arose from the perspective of relative or personal illusion, and the answers provided were suitable for the questioner yet arose from Self Realization.

Abiding as the non-dual Consciousness of the Self, can one then play in duality, which is illusion? Are there approximations to Self-Realization, or is it all or none?

I am the body is illusion. I am is truth. Reflecting on the truth, one realizes oneself, yet, while one lived under the spell of being the body, there were ignorant acts which were undertaken by the delusion of the doer thought. As acts committed in ignorance carry momentum, how are they to be cut at the root and not cause suffering to others who are dependent on the financial resources such acts engendered?

Yours in Devotion,

ॐ Dear . . . ,

Om Namo Bhagavate Sri Ramanaya
Namaste. Thank you for your message.

Abidance in the Self is truly abidance as the Self. It is Being left free of even the least trace of misidentification. In Sri Bhagavan's spiritual instructions, one finds the Absolute Truth, the destruction of the misidentifications that seem to veil the Truth, the means to realize, and more.

If there is abidance as the non-dual Consciousness, which is the Self, there is no individual entity to engage in duality or illusion. The illusion cannot be for the real Self. For whom is it?

The notion of being closer to or further away from Self-Realization is like the idea of being closer to or further away from the Self. For whom would it be all, none, or partial? Who is it that is supposedly apart from the Self? Can there be two selves? The real Being is indivisible.

Acts committed bring their results. If you transcend the misidentification with the body, the idea of being the performer of action and the one who reaps its result, and even the idea of being an experiencer, you stand completely free of karma.

You do not have the power to make another happy or sorrowful. Happiness is within and exists as the Self of all. If it is unknown, then, due to misidentifications and attachments, one suffers. The suffering is merely the veiling of the innate happiness by ignorance. Any amount of worldly treasure will not make one happy.

Your own abidance in the Self, as the Self, replete with the perfect fullness of supreme happiness, is the greatest good that can be achieved and given to all. Abidance as indivisible Being is the deepest love.

Ever yours in Truth,
Nome

[Two more messages from the same seeker were received at that time, one of which is printed here with Nome's response.]

February 11, 2011

Om Namo Bhagavate Sri Ramanaya

Dear Master Nome:

Namaste

Yesterday there was a feeling of defeat. The realization that the I can do nothing for seeing the Self yet persist in questioning Who am I? On the morning walk, I usually repeat "I am Brahman I am," but the feeling of sadness was such that repetition of the mantra was thought to be useless.

This morning appeared a revelation that "I am Brahman I am" does not arise from I, the mind. The "I am Brahman I am" arises from the heart, and this may be the reference to "thoughtless thought"?

This morning reading a statement from the heart itself, Bhagavan Sri Ramana Maharshi, in *Guru Vachaka Kovai*, "Bhagavan: Questioning "Who am I?" within one's mind, when one reaches the Heart, the individual "I" sinks crestfallen, and at once reality manifests itself as "I-I". Though it reveals itself thus, it is not the ego "I" but the perfect being, the Self Absolute."

Bhagavan is ever guiding. The heart melts with gratitude for the teachings, for SAT, for Nome!

Yours in Devotion,
Om Namo Bhagavate Sri Ramanaya

ॐ Dear . . . ,

Om Namo Bhagavate Sri Ramanaya
Namaste. Thank you for both of your messages.

Perhaps referring to a different translation for verse 204 of the *Garland of Guru's Sayings* may lend some clarity for you. Professor K. Swaminathan has translated the same verse as: Know well that perfect Selfhood, peace serene, all thought in stillness lost, identity with Being-Awareness, this alone is pure Siva-puja.

It is thus evident that identifying oneself by Self-Knowledge as the one Self is the zenith of devotion.

When you say that there is nothing that you can do to see the Self, do you conceive of yourself as one thing and the Self as another? How could the Self be powerless to know itself?

Repetition of a mantra is not useless, though it cannot substitute for the actual inquiry that reveals the true significance of "I am Brahman."

The other verse mentioned by you in this later e-mail message very much resembles verse 20 of *Upadesa Saram* and verse 30 of *Saddarshanam*.

Because His guidance and grace are ever there, and because one's true nature is indeed the Self, the very idea of defeat is absurd. The same is so with any other idea that produces sadness. If the ego subsides, bliss shines resplendently.

Ever yours in Truth,
Nome

[From the same seeker followed by the response to him.]

February 14, 2011

Om Namo Bhagavate Sri Ramanaya

Dear Master Nome:

Namaste
When effort is exerted who exerts it? Who is the doer? When does the Grace of the exertion reveal the doer? Does exertion go to waste if the doer is not revealed? When is exertion done?

There has been exertion for many years and an understanding that it is all sacred while karma takes its course. If the body idea had been fully removed, karma would have gone as well. The body and mind idea must live still, so it is clear that not enough exertion has been undertaken, yet there is an awareness that no matter how much exertion the idea of a body is still there, though there is a conviction of not being the body or the mind. The exertion requires deeper inquiry, how does that happen?

Many questions today.
The joy felt at satsang and the grace of the teachings are magnetic!

In gratitude and Devotion,

ॐ Dear . . . ,

Om Namo Bhagavate Sri Ramanaya
Namaste. Thank you for your message.

If by effort and exertion you refer to the power of motion manifested in all bodies throughout the universe, the source of such can only be one. That alone accomplishes all.

If by effort and exertion you refer to the spiritual quest to realize the Self, that destroys the doership notion along with the other misidentifications. Such is of the nature of knowledge alone and cannot be any action performed with the instruments of body, speech, and mind. Such power can have only one source. It may be called Grace and should be realized as the Self.

No spiritual striving ever goes in vain, though the results are determined by the proportion of the knowledge-essence in the practice. When the possibility of the false assumption of an ego has become impossible, the striving is complete, and that which remains is the reality of Being-Consciousness-Bliss.

Inquiry becomes deeper by engaging in it.

Ever yours in Truth,
Nome

[From another seeker, followed by Nome's reply.]

February 20, 2011

Om Namo Bhagavate Sri Ramanaya
Namaste.

What is the best way to serve one's Guru and give back for all the Grace that has been bestowed upon the disciple? What is the proper way to make use of that Grace that is overflowing so compassionately from the Guru?

ॐ Dear . . . ,

Om Namo Bhagavate Sri Ramanaya

Namaste. Thank you for your message.

The best way to give for the Grace bestowed is to steadily abide in the Knowledge of the Self. The best way to serve is to blissfully dissolve the falsely assumed ego. The proper use is, knowing with certainty the incomparable value of the truth, the steady inquiry to know the Self. With a heart full of devotion, to deeply meditate upon the indweller of that heart so that your identity is revealed as That, is to abide in Grace.

If this is comprehended, whatever expressions of love, devotion, gratitude, and such that may manifest will be natural.

Ever yours in Truth,
Nome

[This message was sent to a seeker who wrote several times during recent years and engages in reading SAT publications. It was written in response to questions posed by him, which can be inferred from the answers.]

February 23, 2011

ॐ Dear . . . ,

Om Namo Bhagavate Sri Ramanaya
Namaste. Thank you for your message.

Abidance in the Self is truly abidance as the Self. In truth, because there are not two selves, there is no forgetfulness or remembrance and no going in or out of the Self. If one truly realizes the Self as it is, who is to stay where? The innate Self is completely free of any such differentiation and is One without a second.

The Self is the very Being of all. If you cease to misidentify as some kind of individual, others are perceived likewise.

The difficulty or challenge does not lie in mere interaction, but rather it lies in the vasanas or tendencies that stem from misidentifications. Such ignorance is composed of the stuff of imagination, yet seems as if solid when it is lent the sense of reality and identity that truly belong to the Self. Thus, for one who inquires, there are no actual obstacles.

Trace your experience to the thoughts forming it, and trace the thoughts to the misidentifications from which they spring. Inquire, "Who am I?"

When, through inquiry, the misidentifications and their corresponding tendencies vanish, true love remains, which is the indivisibility of Being.

The actual discernment of the Self involves the disappearance of the ego notion. If the individual or ego vanishes, because it is unreal, in true Knowledge of the Self, the indivisible, undifferentiated, non-dual Self alone remains. That is the ever-existent Reality, and there is no one else to claim that he sees it or does not see it, is in it or out of it.

Though, in truth, we cannot speak of effort for the Self and its Realization, in practice, every effort should be made to realize, for in that alone are bliss and immortality to be found.

Grace is illimitable and ever present. This is evident for those who earnestly strive to know the Self.

Inquire so that your sense of identity remains as the Self alone. What you seek to realize, you are.

May you ever abide as the Self that you really are, of the nature of Being-Consciousness-Bliss, and thus be at peace.

Ever yours in Truth,
Nome

[In response to a seeker who expressed his fear of dissolution of the mind by turning within, Nome wrote:]

February 23, 2011

ॐ Dear . . . ,

Om Namo Bhagavate Sri Ramanaya
Namaste. Thank you for your message.

To state it quite simply, you have nothing to fear by diving within. Within is the source of bliss.

In actual experience, though there may be fear for an aspirant prior to diving within, such fear utterly dissolves once he actually dives within.

Fear is born of duality and is concomitant with the ego. Ego clinging may be fearful, but ego loss is always of the nature of happiness.

The idea that the mind will not like the spiritual truth is based upon two false premises: the idea that the mind is a separate knowing entity apart from Consciousness and the idea that overlooks the fact that the mind, even if still regarded as such an entity, is always in quest of happiness. That happiness is intrinsic to the Consciousness which is truly the Self.

The wise who have turned inward and completely abandoned the falsely assumed ego are not at all fearful. They abide happily in this supreme Reality, as That itself.

There is no need to engage in a battle with your mind. Rather, deeply inquire to know your true identity, which is of the nature of Being-Consciousness-Bliss.

Ever yours in Truth,
Nome

[A message was received from a seeker whose plans to return on a vacation visit to his native India were meeting with difficulties about which he was constantly worrying. This is Nome's response.]

381

June 8, 2011

ॐ Dear . . . ,

Om Namo Bhagavate Sri Ramanaya
Namaste. Thank you for your message.

Wherever your body may be, for unbroken, undiminished happiness, you must know yourself. The guarantee of Grace is not that all of one's wishes or desires will be met in a physical manner, but rather the certainty of transcendent peace that exists within, regardless of circumstances. Relying on Grace, dive within by inquiry and realize the Self, which is the perfectly full happiness.

Ever yours in Truth,
Nome

[A message from a seeker followed by Nome's response.]

June 28, 2011

Om Namo Bhagavate Sri Ramanaya
Dear Master Nome:

Namaste

Bhagavan wrote, "My son, you should experience advaita within your Heart at all times, but never, even for a moment, should you express it in your outward actions. Advaita is appropriate in (all) the three worlds, but it is never appropriate in relation to the Guru."

Could you please clarify: it is never appropriate in relation to the Guru?

Yours in Bhagavan,
Om Namo Bhagavate Sri Ramanaya

ॐ Dear . . . ,

Om Namo Bhagavate Sri Ramanaya

Namaste. Thank you for your message.

The same instruction appears in the works of Adi Sankara, in the teachings by Ribhu, and elsewhere. Advaita is of the nature of Being, of Knowledge of Being, and not an action or set of actions. To think that there is a nondual way to act is to attempt to define the Self as the performer of action, which is delusive. It is to attempt to define the bodiless in terms of a body, and that in which there is no world in terms of the world, which is illusory.

You may already know the answer to your question by the power of devotion, which includes humility and gratitude. After all, you began your message with Om Namo Bhagavate Sri Ramanaya, and not saying salutation to your name, and you concluded with Yours in Bhagavan, and not yours in your own name.

Ever yours in Sri Bhagavan, ever yours in Truth,
Nome

[This question from a seeker relates to the meaning of a nondual verse. Nome's answer follows.]

July 4, 2011

Dear Master Nome,

I've been reading Gaudapada's *Karika* on the *Mandukya Upanishad* and am troubled about the translation in one passage. I'm hoping that, if you have time, you could help me find the Sanskrit word I'm curious about.

There are two translations I'm reading. The familiar translation by S. Gambhirananda and the other by S. Nikhilananda. The passage is in Chapter III. 36— "Brahman is birthless, sleepless, dreamless, nameless, and formless. It is ever effulgent and omniscient. No duty, in any sense, can ever be associated with It." (S.N.'s translation)

Gambhirananda's translation adds, "Brahman is birthless, sleepless, dreamless, nameless, formless, ever effulgent, everything, and a knower."

Honestly, I have difficulty with the idea of Brahman as a "witness," and so I'm really curious what Sanskrit words are being used here. I have the feeling S.N. shared my feelings and that's why he didn't include knower in his translation.

Thanks so much for your time.

ॐ Dear . . . ,

Om Namo Bhagavate Sri Ramanaya

Namaste. Thank you for your message. I am glad to know that you are delving deeply into Gaudapada's illustrious, profound teachings.

Regarding verse 36 of the third prakarana (chapter), the following can easily be observed. It is assumed that you are not in possession of the itrans Sanskrit and transliteration fonts, so I will type the Sanskrit words in a sort of hodge-podge English, using double vowels in place of long vowels, etc. A few of the terms have a variety of meanings.

First, the word Brahman does not appear in the verse. It is implied by its appearance in verse 35.

The first line is ajam (unborn, birthless), anidram (sleepless), asvapnam (dreamless), anaamakam (nameless), aruupakam (formless);

The second line is sakrid (forever, simultaneously, instantly) vibhaatam (luminous, shining, effulgent) sarvajnam (all-knowing, omniscient one) nopacaarah kathancana (no practice, no proceeding toward, no ceremony, no offering, no conduct in any way whatsoever).

For sakrid, forever fits the context more than the other possibilities.

The term about which you asked, sarvajnam, compounds two words. As one term, it means omniscient. Split into its parts, it can be interpreted as all (entire, everything) and knowing (knower, one who is wise, etc.).

384

So, both translators are correct. Of course, the intended meaning is revealed in radiant clarity by Adi Sankaracarya in his commentary.

The idea of a witness (sakshi) is not actually presented in the verse, for, in light of the first line of the verse, there can be nothing objective to be witnessed, and, in light of the second luminous line, the indivisible, absolute nature of Consciousness is clearly self-revealed.

I hope that the above is of some help for you. May you ever abide as the one Self, Brahman, in the certain, nonobjective Knowledge of the Self, and thus be happy and perfectly at peace as That which is innate and without beginning and without an end.

Om Namah Sivaya

Ever yours in Truth,
Nome

———
•

[A seeker who is a writer sent messages requesting information about an anecdote. She wanted to know from which book the passage was derived, on what page it could be found, etc. Nome's response follows.]

July 6, 2011

Dear SAT,

Thank you for your prompt reply! I made a mistake; the passage I want to quote is actually this one:

"Even a grain of rice or a mustard seed lying on the ground would be picked up, dusted carefully, taken to the kitchen and put in its proper tin. I asked him why he gave himself so much trouble for a grain of rice. He said: "Yes, this is my way. Everything is in my care, and I let nothing go to waste. In these matters, I am quite strict. Were I married, no woman could get on with me. She would run away."

Can you help? I would also need the publication date of the relevant edition, if possible!

Thanks so much,
greetings in Bhagavan,

ॐ Dear . . . ,

Namaste. The passage that you cited is located on page 219 of the fourth edition 2010 of *Ramana Smrti*.

May you, not letting even the least "grain" of the innate ability to realize the Self go to waste, ever abide in That which is perfectly full, as That which is perfectly full, and thus, by His Grace, always dwell in happiness and peace.

Om Namo Bhagavate Sri Ramanaya

Ever yours in Sri Bhagavan,
Nome

[Here is a message from a seeker who says that he read teachings of Sri Nisargadatta Maharaj. Nome's response follows.]

August 1, 2011

Hello Nome,

Several months ago, I read the book *I am That* of Nisargadatta Maharaj. While reading this book, I had some experiences. During the night, while in sleep, I ran into a state in which nothing exists. Just an indescribable feeling of joy and peace. In that state, nothing was perceived, and the feeling was that I am one with everything. No thoughts. During these states, I was crying. When I woke up from those dreams, I had a state of bliss that slowly faded during the day.

Now, all those experiences disappeared, and I am dealing with a long period of depression because of that. I have the feeling that I

386

lost something, and I cannot make those experiences come back. Due to this depression, I am drawn more and more into the chaos of my life. I understand how to do Self-inquiry, but no matter what I do I cannot make it last. It is like a weight that my body alone cannot lift. My question is: do I need to find a living master that by his/her grace I will be able to lift the weight or I should continue my day by day existence in what sometimes appears to me like a living hell?

Thank you,

ॐ Dear . . . ,

Om Namo Bhagavate Sri Ramanaya

Namaste. Thank you for your message.

That which appears inevitably disappears. The true Self neither comes nor goes. It is wise to inquire to discern what is truly your Self.

The Self is, itself, the joy and peace. Misidentification is the ignorance that yields suffering. It is wise to inquire to know the nature of the sufferer and thus remain released from that.

What is it that you refer to as your "life"? It is wise to discriminate between delusive assumptions and what is truly your Existence.

As for the need of a Guru, your experience, as well as the sastras (scriptures), should suffice to answer your question regarding such.

I hope that you find the above to be of some help to you.

May you ever abide in the Knowledge of the Self, realized by mind-transcendent inquiry, which is of the nature of beginningless and endless Being-Consciousness-Bliss, which is free from the waking, dream, and deep sleep states, and which alone is the Reality, and thus always dwell in happiness and peace.

Ever yours in Truth,
Nome

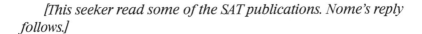

[This seeker read some of the SAT publications. Nome's reply follows.]

August 3, 2011

Namaste:

I have been increasingly practicing inquiry and am amazed at how often the "me" and its story arise in awareness. There have been occasions when that which arises is of an angry nature and often quite negative. It seems to color all forms that arise. It is shocking because it is not how I usually experience myself. It is quite painful, and I must make efforts to not let it bleed over into my interactions with others and sometimes must leave situations in order to not dump this on others. Am I doing something wrong? Is this a reaction of the egoic processes in response to continually questioning its existence? If I need to correct something, please let me know. If this is a common reaction, that understanding would help, too. The arisings are so strong and sustained that it is almost impossible to break through them to inquire.

Thanks for any comments you may have.

ॐ Dear . . . ,

Om Namo Bhagavate Sri Ramanaya
Namaste. Thank you for your message.

As is mentioned in the *Bhagavad Gita,* from avidya (ignorance) comes kama (desire), and from kama comes krodha (anger). To be free of such is essential, for anger is unhappiness, and that runs contrary to your true nature.

Ask yourself the fundamental question: what is the source of happiness? The answer to that question dissolves all desires and removes all anger. If one truly knows that happiness is within, not only will he not become frustrated due to delusive ideas that only give rise to suffering, he will also be endowed with a one-pointed motivation to inquire to realize the Self in order to abide in lasting bliss.

388

To actually continuously question the very existence of the ego leaves no scope for ignorance and its later developments, such as anger. Ignorance has no strength or enduring power of its own, for it is made of imagination. This imagination does not conjure itself. It is you who imagine and make such imagination seem as if solid. In a sense, such can be regarded as a testimony to the power of the source, which is the reality. Only, your natural state is to remain quite free of ignorance and all kinds of suffering. You can destroy this unreal imagination by the power of your own inquiry. What remains, in the Knowledge of the Self, is pure Being-Consciousness-Bliss.

In addition, considering the magnitude of the Grace that is shining for you, as well as your opportunity to realize the supreme truth, about what should you be angry? It would be wise to meditate on this.

Ever yours in Truth,
Nome

═══
•

[This message is a reply to a seeker who wrote about his confusion regarding the need for a guru.]

August 4, 2011

ॐ Dear . . . ,

Om Namo Bhagavate Sri Ramanaya
Namaste. If one truly knows the source of happiness is within, he no longer suffers at all.

The concepts of an interior and exterior in relation to the Guru endure only so long as one's misidentification with the body goes unquestioned.

"God, Guru, and the Self are one and the same," says Sri Bhagavan. The question is not whether or not a Guru is

389

necessary, but, rather, if the ego of the disciple/spiritual seeker is necessary. Bliss is characterized by the absence of the ego, or the false assumption of individuality.

You may find it beneficial to more thoroughly, deeply meditate on the content of the previous response, as well.

Ever yours in Truth,
Nome

[A response to a seeker, dated August 8, 2011.]

ॐ Dear . . . ,

Om Namo Bhagavate Sri Ramanaya
Namaste. Thank you for your recent messages.

Grace is always present. It manifests in myriad ways, though its essence remains formless. Whenever, and to the extent that, the ego subsides, Grace is experienced, and bliss and peace shine. Turning within, you will find its existence within you, indeed, as the very nature of the Self.

Ever yours in Truth,
Nome

[A response to a seeker who was dealing with suffering and fear in relation to some problems with his health.]

August 8, 2011

ॐ Dear . . . ,

Om Namo Bhagavate Sri Ramanaya

390

Namaste. As you attempt to treat the body and remedy its illness, also deeply inquire and know the Self as free of the limitations of the body, and thereby remain inwardly at peace and without the suffering of anxiety. Grace is present; turn inward and realize the undecaying and the indestructible.

Ever yours in Truth,
Nome

[A devotee of Sri Ramana who lives at Tiruvannamalai wrote describing his attempts to deal with his anger. This is Nome's reply.]

August 8, 2011

ॐ Dear . . . ,

Om Namo Bhagavate Sri Ramanaya

Namaste. Thank you for both of your messages.

That your conscience weighed upon you because your mind became irritable and angry and expressed the same to this woman is, in a sense, a form of grace, for it is an intuitive discrimination that the mental mode of anger is not natural for you, whose true nature is Bliss. So, you should not desire that to disappear, but, rather, it would be wise to realize the unaffected Bliss within, of the nature of Being-Consciousness, so that anger is not created in the first place. Anger follows from desire, which has its root in ignorance. By such ignorance, one overlooks the perfect, innate happiness of the Self and imagines that it may be elsewhere or thinks that someone or something else has stolen it. Be free of such ignorance by finding the Self to be the very source of happiness, by practicing the teachings of

391

Sri Bhagavan. Indeed, the Self is Bliss. Therefore, due to what should you become upset? Abide in peace in the light of such Knowledge.

Ever yours in Truth,
Nome

[This message is from the same seeker who wrote on August 3, 2011, accompanied by the response from Nome.]

August 10, 2011

Dear Nome,

Namaste. Thank you for your prompt and thorough reply.

Based on your reply, I will stop entertaining concerns about doing the inquiry practice incorrectly and apply the suggestions you recommend. The outbursts of anger passed and will no doubt return in some way, at some time.

Correct me please if I am wrong about the following. It seems that there are situations in life where the operation of the "me" is necessary. Moving through a world based on thought and ego identities, it seems necessary to engage this "world" in kind. Communication with others is the most difficult time regarding remaining in an inquiry frame of awareness. Who am I? Who are you? What are we doing? If upon inquiry the "me" dissolves, who is going to carry on the communication? As yet, I have been unable to not fall back onto the usual modes of ego communication.

As I read your books and listen to your audios it, sounds like you are responding from a sense of self and other, as do we all it seems. Do you move into and out of Inquiry and conceptual reality? When I'm by myself, it is much easier to spend more time in inquiry and less in thought. I just can't seem to communicate without thought entering in. The world is thought constructed, if I understand Ramana. How do I relate to and with those who see only their world? It seems I must respond in kind or it won't work. To ask them to inquire or to respond from that understanding seems inappropriate and unacceptable to most people.

I'm rambling, but perhaps you can tease out the gist of my concerns.

ॐ Dear . . . ,

Om Namo Bhagavate Sri Ramanaya

Namaste. You may find it useful to reflect some more on the previous advice in order to be certain that you are free from the ignorance that gives rise to the illusory anger. One need not wait for delusion to grossly manifest in order to cut the root of it. The opportunity to liberate oneself from all of the imagined bondage is always.

Regarding your other questions, here are some suggestions:

"the operation of the "me" is necessary"—How could something that does not actually exist be necessary? It would be wise to first inquire as to what is signified by "me."

"that there are situations in life"—Such is conceived only after the individual, or ego "I", is assumed.

"Moving through a world"—It may be better to say that the world appears in you than you move in the world. You are not the body. As Sri Bhagavan has declared, has anyone ever experienced a world without a body? An unreal world does not demand you to misidentify. You alone project your own reality, identity, and happiness upon it, though it does not actually exist at all. If you recognize that the world is only the thought of such, that the world and the mind arise and set together, and that true Existence, which alone is real, ever is as it is changelessly, and that what appears and disappears is not actually real at all but is merely a supposition based upon the false assumption of "I," the idea that the world can create your confusion will seem silly, and you will no longer retain it.

"communication with others is the most difficult time regarding remaining in an inquiry frame of awareness."—Is it the communication that presents difficulty, or is it how the so-called others and yourself are conceived that gives difficulty? Actually, the Existence of the Self is always the

393

same. You are the Self, transcendent of the body, the mind, and all else. The Self is not individualized and has neither "I" nor others. The supposed difficulty is only apparent and not real. Profound inquiry is composed of Knowledge, is continuous, and transcends all mental modes. From another perspective, considering the true nature of everyone, who is communicating with whom and how could there be a difficulty with that?

"who is going to carry on the communication?"—This is like asking, upon awakening, "Who is going to continue the dream actions?" The very notions of their continuance or cessation do not apply. The "me" dissolves upon inquiry because it is unreal. If it were real even to the least degree, it could never disappear. Again, from another perspective, the love, which in essence is the oneness of Being, that constitutes the very core of one's relations with the so-called others is the actual substance of "communication," and the ego never has any part in that. So, the ego is neither real nor useful.

"you are responding from a sense of self and other"—What is the definition of this "you"? Is it not according to the definition attributed to the "I" for whom it seems? Abandoning the misidentification with the body, how can there be a "you," an "I," and such? There is no movement in and out of the Self; nor is there any individual to do so. If the significance of "the Self alone is real, the Self alone exists," is realized, inherent in which is the knowledge that the world and individual are not real, how this motionless immutability is so will be self-evident.

It is not necessary for the others to inquire in order for you to firmly abide in the knowledge of who you truly are. The tendency to misidentify with the instruments of body, speech, and mind can be questioned, so that you are free from misidentification as a performer of action with any of them.

Your existence is absolutely one. If this existence is the absolute Self, for whom are these apparent obstacles, confusions, etc.? If you examine finely, you will be able to discern when you assume an identity other than the Self and associate what is not the Self with the Self. Then, inquiring to know the nature of the one who so discerns, you will find yourself to be only the one Self, in which the realizer and the realized are identical.

I hope that you find the above to be of some help. May you, setting yourself free of the objectifying outlook, deeply inquire to know the Self that you ever are and thus abide in undiminished, immortal Bliss.

Ever yours in Truth,
Nome

[A message came from another Ramana devotee in India, expressing her suffering over comments uttered to her by others, failure to obtain a diploma, and similar difficulties. This is Nome's reply.]

August 20, 2011

ॐ Dear . . . ,

Om Namo Bhagavate Sri Ramanaya
Namaste. Thank you for your message. Your true value lies in the very nature of the Self. Your Being is innately divine. No worldly success can add to it. No worldly failure can detract from it. Praise does not make it better, and criticism does not diminish it. If you inwardly inquire to know this Self as it truly is, yours will be perfectly full happiness and imperishable peace.

Sri Bhagavan did not obtain any diploma. Was He upset about that? Of course not, for He realized that which is the supreme treasure, which is eternal. If you remain devoted to the realization of that, you will be happy at heart.

Ever yours in Truth,
Nome

[This message came from a seeker who has never been to the SAT temple. Nome's response follows.]

September 4, 2011

Dear SAT (or Nome),

I am having a little trouble trying to cut off the enjoyment during eating. I want to remove all external enjoyment, as I find that this enables me to experience the inner clarity of self-consciousness with greater ease. Enjoyment during eating seems to be a problem for me. For regular foods, I try to eat them cold, or mix them with bitter ingredients to kill the taste, but when it comes to fruits, I cannot really "kill the taste" of fruits. Also, I find that fruits greatly increase sattva-guna, so they are helpful to eat. But, how to remove all sensual enjoyment while still satisfying the body's requirements? Should I try to read a book of Bhagavan's teachings while eating? Or, is it better to practice self-attention as intensely as possible while eating, so that I am not conscious of eating, and the mind cannot go out through the taste-sense?

I appreciate your help. If the tongue is conquered, the body-identification is much easier to shed.

Sincerely,

ॐ Dear . . . ,

Om Namo Bhagavate Sri Ramanaya
Namaste. Thank you for your message.
As Sri Bhagavan and Adi Sanakaracarya have made completely clear in their spiritual instruction, Liberation is of the nature of Self-Knowledge and not a product of action. Therefore, transcendence comes with detachment and not by a rearrangement of sensations or the objects of

396

the senses. Rather than contend with the tastes of various foods, it would be far wiser to inwardly determine the real source of happiness. Such discernment regarding the real nature of happiness is the true root of detachment. A simple lack of culinary skill is not to be equated with wisdom and does not automatically grant peace.

You may also find it to be beneficial to reflect deeply upon the actual spiritual instruction bestowed by the Maharshi, for you may find that it is much more joyfully freeing than interpretations based on misidentification with the body and the senses. Attempts to "kill the taste of food" cannot possibly yield blissful immortality, but Self-Realization does. The nature of Realization is Self-Knowledge, which is found by Self-inquiry.

Om Namah Sivaya
Ever yours in Truth,
Nome

[This is a reply to a message from a seeker addressed to Sasvati and Nome that expressed appreciation for the temple atmosphere and the holy company in it.]

September 5, 2011

ॐ Dear . . . ,

Om Namo Bhagavate Sri Ramanaya
Namaste. Thank you for your message. The experience of being in holy company at the temple and imbibing spiritual instruction is sure to continue shining within you, especially if you continue to practice deeply.

Please convey our best wishes to [name omitted] for his speedy recovery. The body is transient and subject to ills, but the Self is eternal and is transcendent of all. One who knows this remains at peace, undisturbed by what may befall the body. The perfect fullness of the Self ever exists. This perfect fullness is also known as Grace.

May you, by the power of deep devotion and the revelation of knowledge, ever abide as the Self, of the nature of immortal Being-Consciousness-Bliss.

Ever yours in Truth,
Nome

[This is a response to a seeker who wrote a message about his experiences of ajna cakra (third eye) during meditation.]

September 6, 2011

ॐ Dear . . . ,

Om Namo Bhagavate Sri Ramanaya
Namaste. Such experience as you have described regarding this cakra is not uncommon. It may be associated with previous practices or may occur spontaneously. Whether it occurs or not, inquire to know yourself, for subtle experiences are not the finality, but Self-Knowledge is.

Om Namah Sivaya

Ever yours in Truth,
Nome

[This is the response to a prayerful message that expressed the desire to be immersed in love and devotion.]

September 6, 2011

ॐ Dear . . . ,

Om Namo Bhagavate Sri Ramanaya

Namaste. Just as effort in meditation is never in vain, sincere prayers for increased devotion never go unanswered. That for which you strive, upon which you meditate, to which you devote yourself, in which you truly abide, and which you truly are is the ever-existent Self, the sole-existent Reality. Practicing, inquiring, in light of this, you will realize freedom and unceasing bliss.

Ever yours in Truth,
Nome

[This is a response to a message from a seeker who wrote about surrender and some problems between her neighbor's dog, or at least the dog owner, and her own.]

September 6, 2011

ॐ Dear . . . ,

Om Namo Bhagavate Sri Ramanaya

Namaste. Thank you for both of your messages.

Yes, surrender yields peace. Be sure that the surrender is the dissolution of the false ego-notion in devotion to that which is the Absolute. This brings deep discrimination between the real and the unreal and detachment toward the illusion. Mere resignation to transient circumstances is temporary, lacks depth, and is no substitute for actual Self-inquiry or devotion.

Such devotion does not preclude taking action to better a situation, but it does yield freedom from the misidentification as a performer of action and nonattachment to the results of action.

I hope that all comes out right for all of the dogs, and their handlers, involved.

Ever yours in Truth,
Nome

[A Ramana devotee in India wrote about her father's illness, which she described as not serious but causing fear and asked how to overcome the fear. This is Nome's reply.]

September 15, 2011

ॐ Dear . . . ,

Om Namo Bhagavate Sri Ramanaya

Namaste. Thank you for your message.

As long as there is misidentification of the Self with the body, there is likely to be fear associated with its decay, becoming infirm, growing old, and eventual death. Sri Bhagavan has clearly revealed that the Self is not a body. Realizing that this is so by deep Self-inquiry, one destroys the imagination, or ignorance, that is the very basis of the fear.

Even if the symptoms are such as to naturally make the mind more attentive to them or given to more consideration as to how to heal the illness, one can still remain without fear or other suffering by absorption in this Knowledge of the bodiless nature of the Self.

Thus, if one is transcendent of the body so as to be able to meet serious illness or even death with peace, less serious sickness will certainly present no problem.

Please convey my best wishes to your father. May you ever abide in the Knowledge of the Self, of the nature of eternal Being-Consciousness-Bliss, and thus dwell in happiness and peace always.

Ever yours in Truth,
Nome

[A seeker wrote a message in which he described his spiritual practice, that he is a college student, his concerns over his parents' response to his reduction of activity and attending only the minimum classes, and his attempt to maintain solitude in his apartment. This is Nome's response.]

September 18, 2011

ॐ Dear . . . ,

Om Namo Bhagavate Sri Ramanaya
Namaste. Thank you for your message.
It is good that you have taken an interest in Self-inquiry, for it is in Self-Knowledge that lasting peace and happiness are found. Knowledge is not to be equated with a particular action, inclusive of the action of inactivity. Action of any kind, whether considered moving or unmoving, is only of the body. Freedom from the misidentification with the body, which includes freedom from the idea of being the performer of action, is essential for Self-Knowledge. The Self is the same whether the body is inactive or active and does not depend on any action or inactivity in order to be itself. One who knows this remains identified with the Self and no longer imagines that he is bound by activity even though his body may be engaged in action. You may find it helpful to reflect upon this.

What others may opine regarding your spirituality is not particularly significant, just as your opinions about the spirituality of others would not be of any significance. What is important is that you find the interior wisdom that yields freedom from imagined limitation and the revelation of the Self, which is Brahman, within.

Your determination to remain completely honest and to intensely pursue Self-Realization by profound inner inquiry will certainly bear fruit.

May you, deeply inquiring to know that which you truly are, which is of the nature of Being-Consciousness-Bliss, ever abide in the Knowledge of the Self and, thereby, dwell in happiness and peace always.

Ever yours in Truth,
Nome

[A seeker wrote on September 19, 2011 regarding her experience of her husband's ill-health and impending surgery. This is the reply.]

ॐ Dear . . . ,

Om Namo Bhagavate Sri Ramanaya

Namaste. Yes, fears, etc. arise for the spiritual aspirant for the purpose of her finding the deep resolution for such. The Self that you truly are is the Self of all. It is never separated from itself. Unborn, it is imperishable. This eternal Self transcends the limited body and its conditions. By Grace and by dissolution of the false ego with its idea of being body-bound, know this Self to be your only self, and, with joy, see the disappearance of the fear as your experience becomes absorption in peace.

Ever yours in Truth,
Nome

[A seeker wrote a lengthy message with several questions that can be inferred from the answers contained in Nome's reply presented here.]

September 25, 2011

ॐ Dear . . . ,

Om Namo Bhagavate Sri Ramanaya
Namaste.

In as much as your subtle experiences may have prompted you to recognize that the Self is not the body, they may be regarded as having been helpful. With or without such experiences, the innately bodiless Self exists. It would be wise to inquire deeply as to the nature of the one who knows the appearance and disappearance of such experiences and thus realize this Self.

Samsara should be renounced, but what is the samsara? It is only the delusion in one's own mind, and Liberation from that ignorance is found only in the inner Knowledge of the Self and not by outer actions.

One's pursuit of spiritual Truth is beneficial for all.

Steadiness and strength of practice arise within those who earnestly strive with perseverance and who ascertain the actual source of happiness. Continuity of Knowledge shines for those who inquire in a thought-transcendent manner.

What could be more direct than the nonobjective inquiry, "Who am I?" for Self-Realization? In whatever manner you may meditate and search, in the end, you must come to this.

Om Namah Sivaya

Ever yours in Truth,
Nome

[In reply to another message from the same seeker, Nome wrote:]

If meditation is upon the nature of the meditator, that is, Self-inquiry, abidance in Self-Knowledge is certain,

403

which is immortal bliss. May your meditations be deep so that you abide as the self-luminous Being-Consciousness-Bliss that you really are.

Ever yours in Truth,
Nome

[A seeker wrote on September 27, 2011:]

I'm stuck. The answer to "Who am I" seems to be "the brain," since it is the only non-replaceable organ. One can have a heart transplant and live, etc. But if someone has Alzheimer's, if he has a serious stroke, he disintegrates and dies because his brain has been damaged.

Please help me; I want to get past being stuck here. Thank you.

ॐ Dear . . . ,

Om Namo Bhagavate Sri Ramanaya
Namaste. Thank you for your message.

Though you may regard the brain tissue to be irreplaceable for the body in order that the body may continue to live, there is no need to misidentify with the body or that organ. Real Being is unborn and eternal. It does not begin when the body is born, and it does not end when the body is destroyed. It is bodiless and does not change when the neurons, etc. decay.

If you commence a deep inquiry to truly know the Self, that which is expressed above will become comprehensible for you.

Ever yours in Truth,
Nome

[In reply to a message from a seeker who was attending sat-sangs, Nome wrote:]

ॐ Dear . . . ,

Om Namo Bhagavate Sri Ramanaya

Namaste. Yes, if you can discern the source and nature of happiness, with this conviction, you will be able to free yourself of any binding attachment to anything of the world, and you will, indeed, find yourself endowed with a joyful, intense desire for Self-Realization and a heart full of devotion.

Om Namah Sivaya

Ever yours in Truth,
Nome

≡
•

[A seeker wrote concerning his attempts to practice Self-inquiry and about problems with his marriage. This is Nome's response.]

October 18, 2011

ॐ Dear . . . ,

Om Namo Bhagavate Sri Ramanaya

Namaste. Thank you for your message.

That you are attempting to practice inquiry is splendid. The inquiry should not be reserved to a particular time, for the Self is ever-existent, and, therefore, Knowledge of the Self ought to be continuous. So, inquiry should become continuous.

When both members of a couple, as one, keep their vision upon the Reality of the Self, maintain their aspiration

405

to the Realization of the Self, hold the Realization of that Truth as supremely dear, draw their love from the depths of the Self and, indeed, love this true Self, dissolve their minds and personal attributes in the course of the inner quest to know the Self, and, in Truth, abide as One as the One Self, the illusory troubles of which you speak do not arise and those that arose previously are gone, never to reappear.

You stated that you are doing all the household work. It seems that she is doing the work that is a livelihood to financially support the family. Whatever be the activity, it can be accomplished while one remains free of the notion that he or she is a performer of action.

May you ever abide in the Knowledge of the egoless Self, as this Self, the very source of love and of the nature of unlimited Bliss, so that you are always at peace.

Ever yours in Truth,
Nome

[A devotee had to leave a holy event early due to a burglar alarm at his home. The next day, this message was sent to him.]

ॐ Dear . . . ,

Om Namo Bhagavate Sri Ramanaya

Namaste. We were sorry to see you leave early last evening. Hopefully, it was just a false alarm at your house and not a burglar.

Prostrations to the One who steals the ego, who wears no disguise, and who establishes Himself in our true home and does not leave. Seeing Him, we do not raise an alarm, but welcome Him in with open arms and folded hands.

Om Namah Sivaya

Ever yours in Truth,
Nome

*[A seeker wrote expressing her anxiety over her husband's
impending surgery to Sasvati. Here is Sasvati's response.]*

October 24, 2011

Namo Ramana

Dear . . . ,

Namaste!

Sri Ramana says, "If a man considers he is born, he cannot avoid the fear of death. Let him find out if he has been
born or if the Self has any birth. He will discover that the
Self always exists, that the body which is born resolves itself
into thought and that the emergence of thought is the root
of all mischief. Find wherefrom thoughts emerge. Then you
will abide in the ever-present inmost Self and be free from
the idea of birth or the fear of death."

Sri Ramana tells us that thought is the root of all mischief. We think that we will die and are fearful, when, in
fact, it is only the body that dies. We think we will go out of
existence and are fearful, when, in fact, we are the
Existence. We cling to thoughts, in the form of memories,
hoping they will give us happiness, when, in fact, our nature
is happiness. We have thoughts that make us feel lonely or
fear loneliness, when, in fact, the whole universe in contained within us.

Ramana says, "...Why fear death? Death cannot mean
non-being. Why do you love sleep, but not death? Do you
not think now? Are you not existing now? Did you not exist
in your sleep?"

Sri Ramana tell us that Existence, our true nature, never dies.

He says, "...The ego in each one must die. Let him reflect on it. Is there this ego or is there not?" By repeated reflection, one becomes more and more fit."

The so-called ego exists only due to non-investigation into the non-reality of thoughts.

Be kind and loving with one another. Grace and love are ever-existent and ever-present. Take Ramana books with you to the hospital. Read them yourself and read them to [name omitted]. Meditate on the non-reality of thoughts.

Our love and prayers are with you both.

With love,
in Sri Ramana,
Sasvati

[This is Nome's reply to the same seeker to another message of hers.]

October 27, 2011

ॐ Dear . . . ,

Om Namo Bhagavate Sri Ramanaya

Namaste. We are very glad to know that [name omitted] is doing well. We hope that his recovery is swift and not too uncomfortable.

Peace is present in faith and reaches its perfect fullness in the deep Knowledge of the Self.

As Sri Bhagavan is ever-existent, so is His Grace. Thus supported by the indestructible, inquire deeply to realize the Truth He reveals so that your happiness and profound peace are full and never-ending. In this Truth, love shines as the indivisibility of Being, and separation is seen as impossible.

Please convey our love to [name omitted].

Ever yours in Truth,
Nome

[From a seeker who is frequently at the temple, followed by Nome's response.]

November 2, 2011

Namaste Nome,

Om Namo Bhagavate Sri Ramanaya
This body must attend a hospital inservice for our new Electronic Medical Record System this evening so I am unable to be at the SAT Temple. I will meditate as Consciousness, the screen upon which the universe is projected! Also, [name omitted] is kindly warming [name omitted]'s prasadam I brought over.

ॐ Dear . . . ,

Om Namo Bhagavate Sri Ramanaya,
Namaste. Thank you for your message. Yes, you are the unmoving screen of Consciousness that is ever changeless, unaffected by any projected image, neither being born when an image appears nor ceasing when an image disappears. In this Knowledge, remain blissful and at peace.

Ever yours in Truth,
Nome

[Another message from the same seeker, followed by Nome's reply.]

November 7, 2011

Gratitude and Meditations

Namaste Nome,

Om Namo Bhagavate Sri Ramanaya

This Heart is spilling over in love and gratitude for the Holy Being which the Maharshi/Nome graciously reveals so lovingly and freely. Revealing Existence to Existence is Truth and Bliss. This one continues to read, reflect, meditate, and take refuge in Shankaracharya's *Vivekachudanami*, it being so very potent and pithy. I move slowly then at times quickly, enlivened by the freedom from conceptual thinking, which is bliss. I encountered an area that requires deeper and more profound meditation in order to liberate myself from bondage. There was worrisome thought concerning the approach of two and three hour lectures on nursing theory materials, about preparing for it, how it in the past was demanding, etc. The misidentification with the anxious mind then swung into the depressive state which I am much too familiar with and consequently remained disidentified for a longer time than customary! The Maharshi's Grace lifts the veil of illusion to reveal Reality as Existence-Consciousness, which is my own innate happiness. Om. Love and gratitude surges.

ॐ Dear . . . ,

Om Namo Bhagavate Sri Ramanaya
Namaste. Thank you for your message.
Realizing that you are not the performer of action, inclusive of being a speaker, your mind will be free of worry regarding the lectures and such. Grace is always present, and it carries all. Where your love and gratitude surge, there is the knowledge of the Reality as Existence-Consciousness-Bliss. That which the Maharshi reveals, which is that which Sankaracharya reveals, which is that which ever so many sages reveal, is within you. May your meditations be profound so that your very sense of identity remains absorbed in the Self.

410

Ever yours in Truth,
Nome

[This is a response to a seeker who expressed how much she benefited by her recent stay at the temple and raised some questions about how to retain the experience she loves, thinking and not thinking, and how to deal with "issues."]

ॐ Dear . . . ,

Om Namo Bhagavate Sri Ramanaya

Namaste. As there is such beneficial effect for you in attending satsangs at the Temple, perhaps you could consider if it is possible for you to visit more often. Nevertheless, as your own experience reveals, the Consciousness, which is the Self, is ever existent everywhere and always perfectly full.

The spiritual instruction is not that "one should not try to hang onto an experience," for the desire to do so actually stems from the deep source of happiness within you. It is far wiser, then, to discern how that which is the essence of higher spiritual experience is actually not an objective experience but is your own true nature. It is only recurring misidentification that makes it appear as if that ends. The Self is beginningless and endless, is nonobjective, and is peace itself. The very nature of the Self is freedom, and the bondage is merely imagined due to misidentification.

Abidance as the Self is true. Thinking of yourself as otherwise is not true. That which is true is the best. Rather than concern yourself with whether or not there is thought, minimal thought, or no thought, it is wisest to abide in the Knowledge of the Self. For that, the appearance of thought or of no thought is inconsequential. In truth, thought itself is not existent. To have a little or a lot or none of what does not exist amounts to the same thing. Abide in the

Knowledge of the Self, which transcends thought and thinker.

If there is an "issue," as mentioned by you, there is no need to concern oneself with measurements as to how many thoughts about it one is thinking. It is far better to free oneself from the misidentification and attachment that make an "issue" to begin with. Practice discrimination in this way, and you will remain free, and your bliss will remain full.

Ever yours in Truth,
Nome

[A message from a seeker, with Nome's response.]

November 6, 2011

Hi,

I am sending this email after having been guided in my meditation to get in touch with Nome. I have been following the Vedantic philosophy and feel greatly guided by Bhagavan in my meditations. I am currently looking for different employment opportunities and one of the astrologers who did a reading for me said that they see me moving to California. Seeing Nome's videos put my mind so much at ease. I am wondering if there is any guidance that you can give me in this challenging time of looking for employment and trusting that a higher power is leading and guiding it.

Looking forward to your reply.
In sincere gratitude,

ॐ Dear . . . ,

Om Namo Bhagavate Sri Ramanaya
Namaste. Thank you for your message.
It is with joy that we come to know that you are follow-

ing the Vedanta and are being guided by Sri Bhagavan in your meditations. Certainly, if you visit or move to California, you will be very welcome at the SAT Temple.

Always, all are fully within the higher power of the Supreme Lord, who is, in Truth, the Self. In the light of this, remaining free from misidentification of being a performer of action is quite natural.

Knowledge that the source of happiness is within yields complete detachment from all things, activities, and events in the world.

In the Knowledge that one is not the body, the very ideas of being an actor or being in the world cease, leaving one's peace and happiness always undisturbed. This is true even while the body is in the midst of its activities.

May you ever abide in the Knowledge of the Self, which is of the nature of immovable Being-Consciousness-Bliss, and thus always dwell in peace and happiness.

Ever yours in Truth,
Nome

≡
•

[To a seeker who asked about the "knots of the heart."]

November 14, 2011

ॐ Dear . . . ,

Om Namo Bhagavate Sri Ramanaya
Namaste. Thank you for your message.

The "knot of the heart" refers to the ego notion, and the plural form of "knots" signifies the various misidentifications based upon that ego assumption. Indeed, all suffering is due to such. With Self-Knowledge, the ego and these misidentifications are destroyed, for they are found to be unreal, and so the knots are said to be cut. The innate Bliss thus shines without obstruction or veil.

Yes, the Light that is ever shining, which is only One and which knows the mind, is Consciousness, your very Being.

Sri Bhagavan's Realization is limitless Grace for all.

In love, as in Truth, there is no distance.

Ever yours in Truth,
Nome

[A seeker wrote with several questions that can be inferred from Nome's answers.]

November 20, 2011

ॐ Dear . . . ,

Om Namo Bhagavate Sri Ramanaya

Namaste. Thank you for your message.

We are glad to know that you have taken a deep interest in the teachings of Sri Ramana Maharshi. If pursued in earnest, the practice of Self-inquiry surely yields the Knowledge of the Self, which is perfect happiness and peace.

If you cease to misidentify with the body and, therefore, abandon the tendency to conceive of yourself as a performer of action, you will find that your concerns about working and such dissolve.

The differentiation of the universe, the individual, and the Supreme (jagat-jiva-para) delusively appears only so long as the ego notion is assumed. If that notion vanishes, differences, being unreal, also vanish. The ever-existent Reality of the Self alone remains.

The bodiless, location-less, world-transcendent Self, of the nature of Being-Consciousness-Bliss, is your true abode.

May you ever abide in the Self, as the Self, and thus be ever happy and at peace.

Ever yours in Truth,
Nome

[In response to a message from a seeker that raised questions about suffering.]

November 20, 2011

ॐ Dear . . . ,

Om Namo Bhagavate Sri Ramanaya
Namaste. Thank you for your message.

Happiness is one's very nature. Suffering is due to being ignorant of it. Though pains and the mortality of the body are unavoidable, suffering on account of such experiences is not necessary.

If there is suffering, it, like everything else, is for the ultimate purpose of the Realization of the Self. However, in the Self, there is neither suffering nor its cause, but only the vast, infinite expanse of Being-Consciousness-Bliss, which is the eternal Reality.

One who sees that the Self has neither birth nor death sees truly. This yields peace that is transcendent of all. Abide as That.

Ever yours in Truth,
Nome

[In reply to a seeker's questions:]

December 24, 2011

ॐ Dear . . . ,

Om Namo Bhagavate Sri Ramanaya

Namaste. Thank you for your message. We are glad to know that [name omitted] is continuing to recover and is feeling much better. Please convey our best regards from everyone here to him.

That which is "to be done" is the attainment of Knowledge of the Self. This is not an action such as would be carried out by one's limbs or senses. It is not even a mental activity. Rather, it is the profound ascertainment by interior Knowledge of what actually is your Self. It is a matter of what you regard as your identity.

When misidentifications dissolve, the natural freedom and peace of the Self shine forth. When misidentifications occur or resume, though the Self is ever existent, it appears as if veiled, and the freedom and peace seem obscured. If you examine your experience finely, you will be able to determine what these misidentifications are and then, by inquiry, dispel them. Your experience shows you that peace, freedom, and happiness are natural. If they seem absent, you naturally long for them, because they are of your very nature. Yearning should become intensity and continuity of spiritual practice. Thereby, the Self is realized.

If love reaches its origin, in devotion to the Supreme, the result is sublime beyond description.

Ever yours in Truth,
Nome

[Another reply to another message from the same seeker.]

December 30, 2011

ॐ Dear . . . ,

Om Namo Bhagavate Sri Ramanaya

Namaste. Thank you for your message.

As to the question regarding the "I" into which one inquires, the Self is only one, and there is, in truth, no other "I."

Sri Bhagavan referred to the ego as a spurious "I" because it is entirely false and has not actually been born. It is an illusion that seems to connect the Self, which is pure Consciousness, with the body. It is an illusory combination of the Self with the non-Self, the Real and the unreal, absolute Being with the nonexistent. This illusion is merely delusion, composed of imagination, and has no actual existence. Thus, the spurious "I" is the false assumption of existing as an individual, which, being unreal, "vanishes" upon inquiry into its nature. The inquiry to know the Self eliminates this false assumption and reveals that the only existent "I" is the one Self. Thereby, the delusive notion of being bound is destroyed so that not a trace remains.

There are not two of you, so that one could inquire into another. Who are you? Thus, the Truth is realized.

I hope that you find the above helpful. Tonight, the Jayanti of the Maharshi is being celebrated in the SAT Temple.

Ever yours in Truth,
Nome

[This is a response to two messages from a seeker who stated that his experience was confined to that which is sensory and wished to know if his meditation or inquiry were correct.]

January 10, 2012

ॐ Dear . . . ,

Om Namo Bhagavate Sri Ramanaya

Namaste. Thank you for your messages.

That which is sensed through the five senses cannot possibly be your true existence. For all that is objective, there is a knower, the nature of whom is nonobjective Consciousness. Self-inquiry is not an activity, but rather it consists of Knowledge. Whether you think your meditation is correct or incorrect, still you exist. Inquire deeply to discern the nature of this Existence, this Self, that transcends the mind and senses. Discriminate finely to determine what you merely conceive of as being yourself and what truly is the Self.

It is also wise to discern and to destroy tendencies that emanate from the misidentifications. This establishes one beyond desires and fears.

Ever yours in Truth,
Nome

[In the course of her message on January 11, 2012, a seeker wrote, "I am focusing more on listening to your Satsang CDs and Ribhu Gita CDs. I have a question. In Satsang CDs, I hear that happiness is our real nature, but in Ribhu Gita it is also mentioned, "You are neither happiness nor sorrow." May I request a clarification?" This is Nome's reply. The third paragraph is in reference to her request for blessings for her child with whom she was pregnant and expecting to give birth in several months.]

ॐ Dear . . . ,

Om Namo Bhagavate Sri Ramanaya
Namaste. Thank you for your message.

It is good that you are listening to satsang CDs and *Ribhu Gita* CDs to help you focus more clearly on Self-inquiry. That which is revealed as the Supreme Brahman in

Ribhu Gita and in the spiritual teachings expounded in satsang is truly your very Self. By profound realization of this, you will abide in imperishable Bliss.

Blessings, of course, are always there. Even now, you can prepare for the child by turning your mind inward so that your experience is filled with peace and love.

Your question revolves around the meaning of "happiness." If you conceive of happiness as merely an emotion, a state of mental elation, Ribhu negates that along with its opposite, which is sorrow. The Self is free of duality and is quite beyond all mental modes, states, and conditions, as well as the pleasures and pains of the body. If, though, you understand happiness to be the innate bliss of Being, the Maharshi declares that such happiness is actually our real nature. This happiness, or Bliss of the Self, is uncaused and eternal.

May you ever abide in this deep happiness of the Self, beyond the changeful modes of the mind and the transient experiences of the body, by the Knowledge of who you truly are.

Ever yours in Truth,
Nome

[This is a response to two messages from a seeker who resides at a distance from the temple.]

January 10, 2012

ॐ Dear . . . ,

Om Namo Bhagavate Sri Ramanaya
Namaste. Thank you for both of your messages.

The clarity and detachment indicated in the *Treatise in Deprecation of Acquisition That is the Non-Self* yield peace that is undisturbed regardless of the seeming surroundings.

Experiences of increasing clarity and spiritual strength are good indications of proceeding on the right path. Clarity is of the nature of true Knowledge, and spiritual strength derives from the solidity of real Being. That which is otherwise is not the reality. Understand that it is only delusion that is momentary and that which is of the depth is actually permanent. That is, cease to misidentify as the changeful mind, and know yourself to be the unchanging, infinite, eternal Self, of the nature of Being-Consciousness-Bliss.

Yes, the retreats at the Temple are scheduled in full for this year. Of course, whenever you are able to visit, you are very welcome.

Because you mentioned it, it may be said that the disease affecting this body seems to be progressing. It seems to be characteristic of this illness that the symptoms intensify sometimes and recede at others. Care continues to be given in an ongoing attempt to reverse or retard the disease. Sri Ramana's teaching and Grace are the perfect remedy for the illusion of birth and death.

That in you which recognized even before you understood has its source in the Self that you truly are.

By deep devotion and profound inquiry, may you realize the Immortal and thus dwell in peace without end.

Ever yours in Truth,
Nome

[From a seeker in India. Nome's response follows.]

January 11, 2012

Dear Nome,
Namaste!
Since we listen to your voice every day, we feel very close to you, even though we are separated by half of an imaginary world.

We are doing very well. I hope your body is not giving you too much trouble these days.

There is a sadhu who sits half way up the path to Skandashram. He calls himself the Wandering Swami of Tiruvannamalai. (Even though every time we see him, for four years now, he has not moved from the same rock on the path!) He apparently met you on one of your trips here, and he knows us as your devotees. The last time I spoke to him, he asked after your health, and I told him of your battle with Parkinson's. He wanted to make sure I told you that he sends his regards and blessings.

My practice continues to deepen, thanks to you and Bhagavan. I can say now, as I said to you a couple years ago, that I'm finally getting ready to begin inquiring!

Please give my love to Sasvati.
Love,

ॐ Dear . . . ,

Om Namo Bhagavate Sri Ramanaya

Namaste. Thank you for your message.

Yes, an imaginary world, with illusions of time and space, cannot divide the Self, of the nature of undifferentiated Being.

When you next have the opportunity to speak with the Wandering Swami who does not wander, please convey my fond regards and best wishes to him.

Though we may casually say that one battles with a disease, really, the Self, unborn and imperishable, is entirely bodiless. Just as, after you awake from a dream, neither the body nor experiences of the dream are found to exist, and you do not remain as an experiencer of any of the dream, so, if you inquire and thus abide in Self-Knowledge, you will realize that the Self, eternal and infinite, ever is just as it is. In this lies perfect peace.

Bhagavan's Grace is fully present always. Inquire.

Om Namah Sivaya

Ever yours in Truth,
Nome

[From another seeker in India, followed by Nome's response.]

January 17, 2012

Pranam Master,

Om Namo Bhagavate Sri Ramanaya
Though I could not be part of SAT physically, I am happy and feel blessed to be an instrument in supporting SAT in any little way I am involved.

I am not sure what to write to you. Just need Your Blessings and feel Your Grace at every moment. I miss the Satsangs.

Please accept my namaskaram.
Om Namo Bhagavate Sri Ramanaya.

ॐ Dear . . . ,

Om Namo Bhagavate Sri Ramanaya
Namaste. Grace is always present, just as the Self is ever existent. Diving within, you find interior satsang. Transcendent of the bodies, this Sat, or true Being of the Self, is free of differences and division. In this, the distance does not matter. May you ever abide in the Knowledge of the Self and thus remain always happy and at peace.

Ever yours in Truth,
Nome

[A message to a seeker who had just given a donation to SAT.]

422

ॐ Dear . . . ,

Om Namo Bhagavate Sri Ramanaya

Namaste. Thank you for your generous donation. The devotion that motivates your giving is also that which opens the gate to divine Knowledge and steady, blissful abidance as the Self.

May you ever abide as the imperishable Self, free of even the least trace of the illusory ego and its anxious thoughts, and thus be ever at peace.

Ever yours in Truth,
Nome

———
●

[This is a message addressed to "SAT." Nome responded.]

February 8, 2012

Dear SAT,

When a person has realized his/her true nature as Being itself, is there a sense of unlimitedness or of any other qualities? Thanks for any light.

ॐ Dear . . . ,

Om Namo Bhagavate Sri Ramanaya

Namaste. Thank you for your message.

One who has realized the Self is the Self alone, and no individuality or person remains. This Self is Brahman, and only Brahman knows Brahman.

The Self is said to be unlimited and nirguna (quality-less). If Being had a quality, it would be defined, and thus limited, by such. Being is undefined and thus unconfined. It is limitless and free of any quality.

423

As there is no other that exists, being the sole-existent Reality, it is called "unlimited." Similarly, as it is location-less, timeless, undifferentiated, and the only power, it is unlimited.

Inquiry as to "Who am I?" reveals that what has just been indicated is self-evident.

It is hoped that what is said here is found to be helpful.

Ever yours in Truth,
Nome

[From another seeker:]

February 8, 2012

Dear Nome,

Please help me. For the past few months I am so tense. Couple of months back, here in Dubai, a young lady committed suicide jumping from 15th floor when she realised that her kid slipped from the same window a few minutes back. This news devastated me totally. No other suicide news shattered me like this one in my whole life. Since then, I have developed a fear that it might happen to my family members and that some one may do that in my house. This fear is making me mad. When I meditate, I feel better, and again, after some time, this fear grips me. A pain in the chest starts with the fear. Though I know this is just a fear, this mere knowing is not help-ing me come out of the fear. I have started realizing knowing is just not enough. How do I start feeling it in my heart?

Please help me come out of this. Will more and more medita-tion help me? What is the missing link in my self-enquiry? Should I try any other methods for self enquiry so that I can come out of such fear? How do I come out of the fear of death? I am never afraid of my death but always worried about others.

Please help me, Nome. Almost every day, when I am traveling to office, I listen to one of your videos ("listen to something which he himself said") that I grabbled from you tube. This has given a confi-dence that you can help me.

Waiting for your reply.

Thank you.
Love and regards

ॐ Dear . . . ,

Om Namo Bhagavate Sri Ramanaya
Namaste. Thank you for your message.

It is obviously not sufficient merely to have an idea that the fear is just a fear. Fear is constituted of particular thoughts. The thoughts pertain to and are generated by certain misidentifications, which are ignorance. By inquiry, trace the "feeling" of fear to the concepts that compose it. Trace the concepts to the false definitions or misidentifications, and then inquire to determine who you truly are. When the false is truly known to be false, it ceases to exist. By "trace" is meant that the entire sense of reality, identity, and happiness should return to their true place or source.

Such ignorance as the misidentification with the body and the belief that the world holds one's happiness should be thoroughly questioned and examined. Destruction of the body by suicide is a deluded attempt to stop suffering (become happy) and to gain freedom from the limitation of the body, but it does not result in such at all.

The value and supreme efficacy of Self-inquiry as taught by Sri Bhagavan have already been indicated in previous correspondence with you, so such need not be reiterated here. You may find it helpful to reread the previous messages and what is available in the SAT website downloads, etc.

Meditation is always beneficial. Sincere devotion to the Guru also yields peace.

May you ever abide in the Knowledge of the immortal Self, the one conqueror of death that grants fearlessness, and thus dwell in peace.

Ever yours in Truth,
Nome

[Nome's reply to a seeker's message.]

February 20, 2012

ॐ Dear . . . ,

Om Namo Bhagavate Sri Ramanaya

Namaste. Thank you for your message. The Oneness that exists as the Existence of the Self, the Oneness that shines in the heart's complete devotion, the very essence of Mahasivaratri, is ever present yet most clearly experienced by those who, endowed with a deep conviction in the Truth, practice to the best of their ability. In this way, eternal peace and happiness are, indeed, found in their fullness.

We are glad to hear that [name omitted] is doing well. He has our best wishes for a complete recovery and for success with the hip surgery. Of course, he is completely welcome at satsang if, and when, he wishes to participate.

May you ever abide in the timeless bliss of the Self, which always is and can never cease.

Om Namah Sivaya

Ever yours in Truth,
Nome

[The father, "an ardent devotee of Bhagavan Ramana Maharshi," of a seeker was suffering with anxiety. The seeker wrote for assistance, raising questions that can be inferred from Nome's answers.]

February 21, 2012

ॐ Dear . . . ,

Om Namo Bhagavate Sri Ramanaya
Namaste. Thank you for your message.

If he is an ardent devotee of Bhagavan, there is nothing about which he need be anxious. If he meditates in love for Bhagavan upon the immensity and depth of His Grace, everything will be all right.

Yes, doubts, fears, etc. are composed of thought. Such thoughts are rooted in misidentification. The Self transcends all of that. If one inquires, misidentifications are destroyed, and, along with them, the ideas constituting the doubts, fears, etc. are also destroyed. Thereby, the innate peace of the Self shines without obstruction.

Certainly, this illusion can be overcome. Being a father of two children represents no obstruction to Liberation. Self-Knowledge is that which is important. Depth, thoroughness, and continuity of Self-inquiry determine the abidance in such Knowledge.

For happiness and equanimity, for freedom and steadfastness in peace, the sublime way shown by the Maharshi is supreme. It is also available for all.

Injuring the body or the committing of suicide is not the way at all but only perpetuates suffering for such actions are born of delusion. If one truly wishes to be free of delusion and suffering, he must joyfully turn within and know himself.

It is hoped that your father finds the above message beneficial.

Om Namah Sivaya

Ever yours in Sri Bhagavan,
Nome

—
•

[A seeker telephoned the temple office and requested some spiritual advice. He was told that he could raise his questions by email. Here is his message along with Nome's response.]

February 22, 2012

Dear Mr. Nome,

I have been asked by Ms. Sasvati to ask you a spiritual question or two I have.

I just finished the book by Maharshi, *Who am I?* The questions are from that book.

In this book, in answer to question 'what is happiness,' Maharshi ji says that the world is full of misery. The exact quotation is that when mind goes out it experiences misery.

My question is how is it that? Surely, at times, we see a natural beauty, and the mind is exhilarated. What to make of this? At that sight the mind is not miserable.

At another point, the book says that (my interpretation only) that this world is a creation of the mind only. I can see that my world (the subjective world) is the creation of my mind, but the objective world is not just a creation of my mind. But it exists as waves exist in ocean. True, the waves die out in the absence of the wind.

I hope you will find time to answer my inquiry.

Thank you sir.
Sincerely,

ॐ Dear . . . ,

Om Namo Bhagavate Sri Ramanaya
Namaste. Thank you for your message.

In the passage about which you raise your question, the Maharshi says, "Happiness is the very nature of the Self; happiness and the Self are not different. There is no happiness in any object of the world. We imagine through our

428

ignorance that we derive happiness from objects. When the mind goes out, it experiences misery. In truth, when its desires are fulfilled, it returns to its own place and enjoys the happiness that is the Self. Similarly, in the states of sleep, samadhi and fainting, and when the object desired is obtained or the object disliked is removed, the mind becomes inward turned and enjoys pure Self-Happiness."

Thus, he has already graciously answered your question. Happiness is the very nature of the Self. Just as the Self is not an object apart from oneself, so happiness is not an object and is not produced by the experience of an object. In the example cited by you, that happiness is purely of your own nature. The apparent limitations to the happiness are determined by the superimposition of limitations on your identity. So, if you misidentify with the body, the senses, as a sensing entity, etc., the experience of happiness, which is actually innate, will appear to be determined by the presence and absence of objects and limited to the condition and duration of such. If, though, you cease to misidentify, the happiness of the Self will be realized to be infinite and eternal. It is ever perfectly full.

An outward-turned mind may be understood to be one that believes in its own conceptions. An inward-turned mind is one that ceases such imagination and thus loses its own form. What remains is only Being-Consciousness-Bliss, which is the nature of the Self. This Self is the Reality. To ignore Reality and pursue imagination in the mind is ignorance and leads to all kinds of false bondage, which is the cause of suffering. The destruction of suffering results from liberation from the imagined bondage, which is realized by the dissolution of ignorance by Self-inquiry.

The idea that there is an existent, objective world is only in the mind. The idea of the creation of the world is also only in the mind. The idea of externality, an "out there," appears only in the mind. Explanations, such as waves, are only in the mind. The idea that there is a mind may also be said to be only in the mind. If the root or nature of the mind be sought by profound inquiry, neither a mind nor its content, the form of the world, is found to actually exist.

That which is real is ever existent. That which is unreal is ever nonexistent.

The objective realm of experience, or world, does not declare its own existence; you say that it exists. Who is this you? If you are not the body, where, then, is the world?

The transient images of a world of objects and activities that appear in a dream state seem as if real as long as one dreams. Upon awakening, one finds that none of that was the case. The only thing really existing there is one's own Being-Consciousness, though that is invisible to the dream sensations and thoughts. Similar is the case with the waking state.

It is hoped that you find the above helpful so that you can dive ever more deeply into the teachings of Sri Bhagavan. You may also find it useful to read the explanations given in such works as *Self-Knowledge, The Quintessence of True Being, Saddarsanam and an Inquiry into the Revelation of Truth and Oneself, Ribhu Gita, Song of Ribhu,* etc.

May you be endowed with the profound inquiry to know your true Self, which is mind-transcendent and world-transcendent, which is uncreated and imperishable, which is forever unmodified and always changeless, and which is the perfect fullness of bliss, and thus be ever happy and at peace.

Ever yours in Truth,
Nome

[This reply is to a seeker who has long attended satsang and who had mentioned his ill health in a message.]

March 5, 2012

ॐ Dear . . . ,

Om Namo Bhagavate Sri Ramanaya

Namaste. I hope that your health recovers quickly. Sri Bhagavan's instruction regarding the bodiless nature of the Self is the supreme remedy for the ills of illusion.

Ever yours in Truth,
Nome

[This is a response to a SAT seeker, whose questions in her message can be inferred from the answers in the reply.]

March 16, 2012

ॐ Dear . . . ,

Om Namo Bhagavate Sri Ramanaya

Namaste. Thank you for your message.

It is important to deeply, conclusively realize that the Self is not the body. This yields transcendence of bodily attributes, such as condition, location, etc. That which remains is the egoless nature of Being-Consciousness-Bliss. Is it not this Self that you love in all that are loved? It is without boundary and devoid of separation. Repose in the peace of this true Self, the One who dwells in your heart.

Ever yours in Truth,
Nome

[This message is from a devotee of Sri Ramana. Nome's response follows.]

March 20, 2012

Master Nome,

I wanted to thank you for the generous grace with which you showered me at the retreat. To say I am grateful would be an understatement of such tremendous magnitude that I would rather close my eyes and pranam to you from the depths of my heart.

Having arrived back in New Jersey yesterday, I felt an utter longing for your presence, for the divine. This is only due to your grace. Thank you.

It is superflous to ask, I know, but yet I must. Please be with me, each moment. Please nurture the longing in me. Please lead me to myself. Please do not allow me to fall by the wayside and wake up one day years from now, thinking that I have wasted my life.

I know that when Bhagavan was asked the same, he replied "You are standing neck deep in water and you ask for water." I know that grace is ever present. I know that grace was present prior to meeting you. Yet, today I feel a hope and confidence that I did not feel previously. So, to me, it is as if the grace is anew.

I pray that it may continue to flow. Thank you.

Pranam to your feet,

ॐ Dear . . . ,

Om Namo Bhagavate Sri Ramanaya

Namaste. Thank you for your message.

Yes, Grace is ever present. All that is required is for one to be keenly aware of it. Relinquishing misidentifications, one finds himself absorbed in it.

With your sincerity of purpose and earnestness, you are never forsaken. Not a single drop of devotion or effort in Self-inquiry ever goes in vain.

Not only did Sri Bhagavan say that one's situation is like asking for water when he is neck deep in water, but he also said that it is like water itself asking for water.

May you ever abide in the Knowledge of the Self, of the nature of Being-Consciousness-Bliss, and thus always dwell in happiness and peace.

432

Ever yours in Truth,
Nome

[This message is from the same Ramana devotee. Nome's reply follows.]

March 21, 2012

Hello Master Nome,

I was just sitting at my desk, deeply immersed in solving a computer problem that I had been working on for the last hour. Suddenly I felt a sensation on my head and my chest.

My eyes closed, and your smiling face flashed before my mind's eye. Suddenly, I went into a deep, spontaneous meditation. I felt myself lose awareness of my body. It was not a complete loss, but I could no longer clearly feel my arms or hands. I felt that I was expanding beyond the frame of my body. I felt a deep, vibrant silence.

As I sat, I tried to think, "to whom is this experience happening?"

This started a chain of mental activity. I put an end to it and just tried to stay with the feeling of expansion, still in the deep silence. I must have sat like this, motionless, for a few minutes.

Then, gradually I opened my eyes. I felt surprised to see my small body sitting in the chair, having felt so expansive a few minutes earlier. The thought crossed my mind, that if my awareness had expanded beyond the body, then the body must be in it, not the other way around.

If I were near you, I would come and pranam at your feet and relate this experience and sit content at your feet. Since this is not possible, I relate it through email, yet the pranams continue in my heart.

ॐ Dear . . . ,

Om Namo Bhagavate Sri Ramanaya

Namaste. The experience shows you that your nature is expansive and beyond the limits of the body. Transcendent of the body, silence shines.

433

The particular form of the experience, such as sensations or loss of sensations, is of a transient character. The Knowledge-essence is of a permanent nature. It pertains to your very Existence, which is continuous and eternal. It is this Existence that is free from the body and bodily limitations. Place emphasis on this Knowledge-essence.

In your thought, "to whom is this experience happening?", the chain of mental activity manifested due to the undue emphasis on the delusive "person." If, as the Maharshi instructs, one truly inquires, "For whom is this?" the egoless nature of the real Being-Consciousness, as the only reality, becomes self-evident.

May you ever abide in That, as That, which is the Self, the infinite and the eternal, and thus remain at peace.

Ever yours in Truth,
Nome

[This message is from a seeker. Nome's reply follows.]

March 20, 2012

Dear Master Nome,

Namaste!
Thank you so much for a superb retreat! Much of the discourse relating to simply being the Self was especially valuable for me, and just what I had been "requesting" to deepen my practice. Already I can tell a major difference during meditation. Also, your reading of *The Song of Ribhu* (which I still read daily, as you suggested) and the puja were special "take-aways."

Something you said near the very end of the discourse Sunday morning reminded me of related questions I have been pondering. How can God be the doer of the actions of jivas since jivas are imaginary? Similarly, what is meant by the Maharshi's teachings that all activities are actually God's and proceed as God's will? (God willing the actions of unreal beings?)

I am confused about the idea of God being the doer and actor of a dream world. I relate to the concept of the Supreme Brahman/Siva/Self/pure Consciousness being Absolute Reality, Existence, Consciousness, Bliss. However, the idea of God being responsible for all the actions of individuals and of God's will being responsible for all that happens in the world seems to suggest the traditional Christian concept of a bearded man in the sky pulling all the strings, which seems contrary to Advaita Vedanta. Perhaps some of the ideas and imagery about the doer are part of the expedient teaching to which you refer as being necessary at certain stages of learning.

Your clarification would be most appreciated.
In great appreciation and sincerity,

ॐ Dear . . . ,

Om Namo Bhagavate Sri Ramanaya

Namaste. Thank you for your message. I am glad to know the retreat was and continues to be spiritually beneficial for you.

In Reality, the Self, or Brahman, alone exists. In that, there can be no question of individuals, the world, or a God. Without these, there can be no concept of destiny or free will. This is egoless Knowledge.

If this is not deeply, conclusively realized, a question about manifestation will arise. For those who are perplexed by such, it is pointed out that the entire manifestation is but the imagining within the mind, and the Self is the unaffected, eternal Consciousness that is the witness of the mind and its content. Thereby, the idea of being a perceiver is abandoned. This is ego-dissolving Knowledge.

For those who do not comprehend this and who assume the reality of an external world, the question regarding the power that accomplishes all things arises. For them, it is pointed out that there is only one supreme power, which is of God, the supreme Lord of the universe. Thereby, the idea of the ego's importance is nullified. This is ego-attenuating Knowledge.

One cannot truly know that the jiva is unreal yet still hold that the world, in which actions appear, is real. If the nature of the jiva is discerned by deep inquiry, ideas of both destiny and free will vanish. One Existence alone appears as jagat-jiva-para. One Existence alone appears as God, the witness, and Brahman. This Existence is the Self.

It is hoped that you find the above clarifying. May you ever abide in the Knowledge of the Self, in which there is not the least trace of duality or difference, so that you remain always happy and at peace.

Ever yours in Truth,
Nome

[This message is from another Ramana devotee. Nome's reply follows.]

April 1, 2012

Dear Master Nome:

Namaskara. After my return from SAT with the great benefit of having met you and received the instructions, by His Grace, my mind is getting more focused on self inquiry. I pray never to veer from the path.

Though I understand that self inquiry must be ongoing all the time, I believe that to always inhere at His feet, at my stage, I should stabilize my practice in the morning and evening, and carry the momentum the rest of the day. I have been successful in spending an hour or so in the evening, and spend more time on weekends. However, I have not been very successful lately to wake up early and practice, and sporadically remember to practice during the day. Your words of wisdom will help.

Bhagawan's image and reading keep me inspired. I am reading *Essence of Inquiry*, and this work is making my understanding clear and motivating me. Thank you so much.

Also, I have started reading *Ribhu Gita*, and the mention therein that there was a Kannada publication even before Tamil has caught my attention. Since I was educated in Kannada, I may find that version easy flowing along side the English book that I have. Do you know where I can get the Kannada version? That will be of great help to me, I assume.

I appreciate a response at your convenience.

With deep respects,
In Bhagawan,

ॐ Dear . . . ,

Om Namo Bhagavate Sri Ramanaya
Namaste. Thank you for your message.

Bhagavan's Grace is ever present, even manifesting as the ability to inquire. If one's earnest prayer is to be endowed with inquiry, certainly all illusion will dissolve for him, and the Self will be self-revealed.

Inquiry reveals Knowledge and consists of Knowledge. Depth, thoroughness and continuity are important. The time of day for meditation is not important. Though it is common to wisely meditate at the commencement of the waking state or shortly thereafter and at the end of the waking state or shortly before, Self-inquiry that yields the timeless Realization of the Self transcendent of all states of mind does not depend on those times.

With the intense desire for Liberation, you will find yourself eagerly seizing every opportunity to dive within. Thereby, as the Maharshi has taught, the Self is readily realized.

I do not know where the Kannada version of *Ribhu Gita* can be found. The SAT temple does not have a copy.

May you ever abide in the Knowledge of the Self, so clearly, graciously revealed by Sri Bhagavan, Ribhu, and other wondrous sages, in That, as That, and thus dwell always in peace and happiness.

Ever yours in Sri Bhagavan,
Nome

[Here are two messages from a devotee of Sri Ramana. Nome's response follows.]

April 4, 2012

Om Namo Bhagawate Sri Ramanaya.

Dearest Master Nome,

Your words are greatly helping me. You simply make me happy.

Thank you!
Ever grateful in Bhagawan,

April 15, 2012

Dearest Master Nome,
Thank you for being the ever inspiring presence of Sri Ramana.
The Grace has been supplying efforts for my sadhana. However, I am not pleased with myself yet.
While reading *Ribhu Gita* Ch 2, verse 40, the line... "There are no gods such as Siva to worship..." shook me a bit.
Intellectually, I understand that the remover of all obstacles, Ganesha, is no different from the most beautiful ever Divine Mother, who is no different from the ever gracious Lord Siva, who is no different from my own Self. However, I love Lord Siva, who I believe manifests as great teachers to remove all ignorance and suffering. Moreover, sage Ribhu himself obtained the teachings from Lord Siva.
Please explain at your convenience.

438

With deep respects,
In Bhagawan,

ॐ Dear . . . ,

Om Namo Bhagavate Sri Ramanaya
Namaste. Thank you for your message.

Grace is infinite and ever present. We need only remain keenly aware of it.

It is natural to feel less than complete satisfaction until the Self is conclusively realized. It is an intuition of the natural state of the perfect fullness of Bliss. It serves as a goad that prompts one to deeper and deeper inquiry and devotion.

The thorough negations expounded by Ribhu must be comprehended in their proper context and by inner experience. Not only is any idea of "Siva" negated, but everything else including the world, all that is objectively perceived, all that is conceived, and even the individuality of the one who negates. That which can never be negated, remaining resplendent, is truly Siva.

The same scripture that expounds such negation also lauds devotion to the Supreme Siva. Ribhu declares that the source of this highest spiritual instruction that the Self alone exists is none other than Siva. So, Siva and the Self must be the same.

If some idea causes bondage, it is wise to relinquish it and destroy it. If some action is motivated by ignorance, it is wise to renounce it. Who, though, has ever been bound by devotion and its expression? Therefore, the spiritual instruction found in *Ribhu Gita* is intended for those who, filled with devotion and clear inquiry, are intent upon the Realization of the Supreme Truth. Even if duality would be imagined during the start of sadhana, the dualism ought to be abandoned and not the sadhana. With the abandonment of dualism, supreme bhakti flourishes, and such becomes abidance in Knowledge.

439

Om Namah Sivaya

Ever yours in Truth,
Nome

[A message from a Ramana devotee followed by Nome's response.]

April 15, 2012

Dear Master Nome,

Om Namo Bhagvate Sri Ramanaya.
Namaste and Pranams.
Through the mystery of grace, my practice of inquiry has been happening on a daily basis since my return from the ashram. How wonderful! I know that this is a function of grace alone, since when I tried to maintain a regular practice in the past, I have found it very difficult. Thank you.
When I sit to meditate, a thought comes up. I inquire, "For whom is this thought ?" and, finding no response, the thought and the thinker of the thought both disappear. I am left in a silent, peaceful state that feels wonderful. I sit like this for 20 minutes or so and the above process repeats numerous times.
Here is my question:
When I inquire, the thought and the thinker of the thought vanish, I am left in silence. However, I have read that whatever one perceives is not what one is. I perceive my body, so I am not my body. I perceive my thoughts, so I am not my thoughts, etc. However when I inquire and perceive peace and silence, then by the same logic, this is not I either. So, then, who am I? Is the peace and silence resulting from inquiry also just phenomena that must be discarded? Master, would you please clarify? I am confused.

Thank you,
Pranam,

440

ॐ Dear . . . ,

Om Namo Bhagavate Sri Ramanaya

Namaste. Thank you for your message.

When, through deep inquiry, the thinker and thought both vanish and silence alone remains, complete the inquiry by discerning the nature of the one who knows the silence. True Silence knows itself; the Self alone knows the Self.

There is no need to attempt to discard the peace and the silence. Rather, seek to realize the very nature of peace and silence, which is the Self. Sri Bhagavan declared that Silence is that in which no "I" appears. He also says that peace is of the Self. We should know that peace is rooted in the changeless. Therefore, if one inquires into the egoless, changeless Existence that he truly is, all confusion vanishes, and the nonobjective Truth shines for itself.

It is not necessary to continue with a conception that peace or silence is a transient experience or a state of mind. The peace and the silence exist forever as the very nature of the Self. If such a conception does arise, simply inquire for whom such is and, then, inquiring "Who am I?" realize your very Self to be the ever peaceful, eternally silent Reality.

One who understands that bliss lies within cannot do otherwise than practice continuously.

Ever yours in Truth,
Nome

[A seeker from Gujarat, India wrote a few messages that contain questions about renunciation, bhakti, jnana, Vedanta, study of the scriptures and such. Here are Nome's replies.]

April 27, 2012

ॐ Dear . . . ,

Om Namo Bhagavate Sri Ramanaya

Namaste. Thank you for your message. I am glad to know that you find *Ribhu Gita* and the *Song of Ribhu* to be beneficial.

The true renunciation is the abandonment of the ego and of the concept of an objectively existing world.

Complete detachment, born of the knowledge of the source of happiness, is necessary for Self-Realization. Renunciation may thus also be understood as the expression of such detachment in the form of cessation of those actions that are based upon, or motivated by, ignorance regarding the nature of happiness.

Vows of renunciation, wearing the symbols of sannyasa and engaging in a particular mode of life, etc. or not doing such are according to the temperament of the seeker. The appearance, actions, and condition of the body do not affect the Self. Knowledge of one's true Being, the Self, yields Realization. Actions performed by the instruments of the body, speech, and mind cannot accomplish this. Perplexity over activity and inactivity arises only so long as there is misidentification with the body. Upon inquiry to know one's own nature, this delusion vanishes.

Destiny is an idea of and for the illusory individual, or ego. Grace is the dissolution of that very illusion.

To choose wisely that which promotes the inner realization of supreme Bliss cannot be regarded as a fault.

The effects of polio or any other disease are only for the body and never touch the perfection of the Self, which is unborn and imperishable.

I hope that you find what is written here helpful.

May you ever abide as That, the bodiless and egoless, which is the goal of all renunciation, initiation, and such, which is the ever-existent Self, of the nature of Being-Consciousness-Bliss, and which is Brahman, and thus dwell in happiness and peace always.

Om Namah Sivaya

Ever yours in Truth,
Nome

April 27, 2012

ॐ Dear . . . ,

Om Namo Bhagavate Sri Ramanaya
Namaste. Scriptures and meditation upon what they declare are for the purpose of the revelation within us of that which is imperceptible to the senses and transcendent of the mind. That is Brahman. That alone is the Self.
Bhakti and Jnana are inseparable and not different.

Om Namah Sivaya

Ever yours in Truth,
Nome

May 1, 2012

ॐ Dear . . . ,

Om Namo Bhagavate Sri Ramanaya
Namaste. Thank you for both of your messages.
All differentiation is merely imagined and based upon the false assumption of, or misidentification as, an individual or ego. If that vanishes due to clear inquiry, differences are found to be unreal.
If one inwardly inquires as the nondual scriptures, such as those mentioned by you, are read, the experience will be

profound. Indeed, the depth is of one's own Self, of the nature of illimitable Being-Consciousness-Bliss.

By deep devotion and clear inquiry, abandoning entirely the objectifying tendency (vasana), abide in the Knowledge of the Brahman-Self. That alone is real. That alone exists. That alone is what you are.

Grace is ever there and always perfectly full.

Om Namah Sivaya

Ever yours in Truth,
Nome

[These are two responses to a Ramana devotee who wrote expressing his perplexity concerning making a decision regarding the direction of his occupation.]

June 1, 2012

ॐ Dear . . . ,

Om Namo Bhagavate Sri Ramanaya
Namaste. Thank you for your message.

Nonattachment born of the knowledge that the source of happiness is within is most important. With that, regardless of which occupation is chosen and regardless of the result of such choice, you will be free from worry and will be happy and at peace.

As Sri Bhagavan graciously teaches, you are not the body and, therefore, cannot be the performer of action. You are the immoveable Self. In light of this Truth, what is "to be done" and what is "not to be done," for you who are Brahman itself?

Whatever is done without attachment, free of the false notion of being the body and doer, and dedicated in devotion to Sadguru Ramana, the Supreme Lord, is the right way to proceed.

444

May you, by the Knowledge of the Self, ever repose in the peace that is imperishable.

Ever yours in Truth,
Nome

June 1, 2012

ॐ Dear . . . ,

Om Namo Bhagavate Sri Ramanaya

Namaste. In the initial paragraph of the book, *Who am I?*, Sri Bhagavan declares that happiness is the cause of love and that the Self is this happiness.

Upon meditation on what was mentioned in the previous email, the decision will feel as light as air.

As Brahman, the Self, one should remain free of all concepts. Inquiring, abandon the thoughts and the thinker as not-Self and as unreal notions about unreal things.

If you think that the mind decides, inquire and know for certain that you are not the mind and that its content, in the past, present, and future, does not pertain to you.

If you feel that all is universally ordained, inclusive of the decisions made by the mind and acted upon by the body, remain at ease in the state of non-identification with and detachment from all of that. He carries all and is, indeed, all.

If you think of yourself as making the decision, sincerely reflect on which course of action would best express and support your devotion to Sri Ramana and, detached from the fruits of the action, make your decision as an offering to Him. Thus, as proclaimed in the *Gita*, Brahman is the offering and that which is offered, and the one who offers, and Brahman indeed is reached by him in the samadhi of Brahman-action.

In brief, without the ego's intrusion, there will be found no cause for worry. All is alright always. Dive within and realize the ever-existent perfect fullness. It is the Self.

445

Grace is ever with you and within you.

Ever yours in Truth,
Nome

[A seeker in India wrote asking about the details of the life of Ribhu so that he could better "walk on the path of Krishna." This is Nome's reply.]

June 6, 2012

ॐ Dear . . . ,

Om Namo Bhagavate Sri Ramanaya
Namaste. Thank you for your message.

The little that has been described of the manifested life of Ribhu is found in the introductions to the English translations of *Ribhu Gita* (from the Sanskrit original) and the *Song of Ribhu* (from the Tamil version), both of which are published by SAT. It is very difficult to ascertain an historical date for him. The *Ribhu Gita* appears in the *Sivarahasya*, which is a very ancient scripture, so he must predate that time. Ribhu-Nidagha dialogue also appears in four Upanishads, so he may have flourished in Vedic times. The scriptures state that he is a mind-born son of Brahma and that his Guru is Siva Himself.

Perhaps, we should regard Ribhu's teachings about the Self, Brahman, as the true description of himself.

Sri Krishna declared, "The real ever is; the unreal never comes to be," and, "I am the Self that dwells in the hearts of all." Sri Ribhu's teachings could be regarded as a vast, profound instruction that reveals the ultimate significance of these declarations.

The very same Truth is revealed in the teachings graciously bestowed by Sri Ramana Maharshi.

You are encouraged to read the two books mentioned above and deeply meditate on their meaning by inquiring to know the Self as it truly is.

I hope that you find what is mentioned here to be helpful. May you, with a heart full of devotion, inwardly inquire and thus realize the Self, of the nature of Being-Consciousness-Bliss, and thus ever abide in happiness and peace.

Ever yours in Truth,
Nome

＝
•

[A seeker asked about the meaning of the declaration that the world is unreal and is a dream. Here is the reply.]

October 8, 2012

ॐ Dear . . . ,

Om Namo Bhagavate Sri Ramanaya

Namaste. Thank you for your message. Yes, Sri Bhagavan declares that the world is unreal. So do Adi Sankaracarya, Ribhu and other sages. That all that objectively appears is transient, not self-existent, appears only in a waking state of mind, seems to exist only from the perspective of misidentification with the body and the senses, and is a mere supposition that is utterly dependent on the "I" notion is indicative of its unreality. If the only real "I" is the Self, which is infinite, eternal, changeless, and undifferentiated, how could there be any scope for "this"?

You may find it helpful to read *Self-Knowledge*, mandala 8 and the chapter entitled "Self Revealed." The other chapters in part two of the same book also pertain to your question. In addition, the short book, *The Quintessence of True Being*, provides a thorough, albeit tersely expressed, explanation of the spiritual instruction that Brahman is real and the world is unreal.

I hope that you find the above helpful. If you inquire within deeply, the profound Knowledge of nondual Existence, egoless and worldless, will shine for you, as you.

Om Namah Sivaya

Ever yours in Truth,
Nome

[On October 28, 2012, a seeker from Canada, after referring to the Song of Ribhu 44:41-42, asked: "Is it absolutely necessary to wear triple stripes of ashes on the forehead and holy ashes all over the limbs as it is said? Is it only for sadhana or else? In the chapter 38, verses 24-27, it is said to renounce all kinds of devotions or habits, etc. It looks to me contradictory to the chapter 44 verses 41-42." Here is Nome's response.]

ॐ Dear . . . ,

Om Namo Bhagavate Sri Ramanaya
Namaste. Thank you for your message.

The spiritual instruction stated in *Song of Ribhu* pertains to Self-Knowledge. So, that which is described in chapter 38, verses 24 through 27, as also elsewhere in the text, should be comprehended in knowledge and not conceived as a particular action. That is, the "casting aside" is accomplished by Knowledge of one's Self and not by some bodily deed. Implicit in the "study of this treatise" mentioned in those same verses is the nonobjective inquiry into oneself, without which such "study" would not yield the Self-Realization sought.

The value of wearing vibhuti (sacred ash) is known by those who do so. Of course, if the significance of the ash as the residuum of Absolute Being, which shines as self-revealed upon the death of the ego and the destruction of the illusory triads, is realized, the rest will be understood, too.

One should "wear"" the undivided Knowledge always, with not a "limb" of the mind or experience left uncovered by it.

One thing is absolutely necessary: Self-Realization. How else to realize the Self except by the deep, constant inquiry to know the Self? It is wise to engage in whatever you determine to be helpful and supportive of this inquiry.

May you ever abide in the Knowledge of the Self and thus be always happy and at peace.

Om Namah Sivaya
Ever yours in Truth,
Nome

[On November 9, 2012, in a message, a seeker asked, "What is the best way to approach Self inquiry? When I am suffering, I ask myself: who is this sufferer and to whom does this pain arise? What can I do to maintain a steady practice?" This is the reply from Nome.]

ॐ Dear . . . ,

Om Namo Bhagavate Sri Ramanaya
Namaste. Thank you for your message.

Your very Being is entirely natural. Inquire by questioning inwardly so to discern this true Self free from whatever you may be accustomed to regard as yourself, such as the body, the mind, or the ego.

Suffering is due to not knowing the source and nature of happiness. Knowing the source of happiness tends to yield steady spiritual practice. Self-inquiry transcendent of thought is completely steady.

Earnestness and an intense desire for Self-Realization are the best approach. More details regarding the approach can be found in *Self-Knowledge* and in the "Requisites" booklet.

May your inquiry to know the Self, of the nature of Being-Consciousness-Bliss, be deep so that your happiness is full and your peace is always.

Ever yours in Truth,
Nome

[In the course of a message, a seeker asked, "Thank you very much for the suggestions when I will be at Ramanasramam. You tell me to focus entirely on Sri Ramana Maharshi with his supreme Wisdom and limitless Grace to guide me. Nome, what do you really mean objectively concerning Ramana Maharshi's Wisdom and Grace to guide me?" Here is Nome's reply.]

November 14, 2012

ॐ Dear . . . ,

Om Namo Bhagavate Sri Ramanaya

Namaste. Due to Truth Revealed retreat held at the SAT Temple, this is the first opportunity to respond to your message.

Grace is nonobjective, so no objective definition of it would be adequate. Grace is of the very nature of the purnam (the perfect fullness) of Brahman. Sri Bhagavan is always Brahman. The manifestation or not of a body, which is conceived only in the unreal mind of another who does not actually exist as such, for Brahman alone is the only Self, is of no consequence.

If the approach is one of ego-dissolution, what is meant by guidance with Supreme Knowledge and Grace will become clear. Such egoless clarity is natural for those who actually inquire to know the Self.

May your inquiry be deep, thorough, and profound so that you abide in the Self, as the Self, which has not the least trace of individuality or an objectified world, and thus dwell always in happiness and peace

Om Namah Sivaya

Ever yours in Truth,
Nome

[In a message dated November 25, 2012, a seeker asked, "I want to be free, but my worries of the future perpetuate my suffering. How can I transcend mental tendencies when they keep arising? Can Self inquiry/Self Knowledge transcend karma of the mind and body?" This is Nome's reply.]

ॐ Dear . . . ,

Om Namo Bhagavate Sri Ramanaya
Namaste. Thank you for your message.

The Self is perfect Bliss. If this happiness of your very Being seems to be veiled, such is due to ignorance, which is in the form of misidentification. If you examine the mental tendencies that cause you to suffer, you will discern that the root of the tendencies is the misidentification. The tendencies do not arise by themselves; you conjure them based on the misidentification. By inquiry that clarifies the knowledge of your identity, the very root of the tendencies is destroyed.

If you deeply determine the source and nature of happiness, you will be nonattached, and your worry will cease.

By Self-Knowledge one finds Liberation from all kinds of karma.

Steadiness is found by depth and thoroughness of inquiry to know the Self. Perseverance and devotion are great aids to such. You may wish to refer to the sadhana catushtya (four-fold practice) described in the "Requisites" booklet and in Adi Sankaracarya's *Vivekacudamani.*

Om Namah Sivaya

Ever yours in Truth,
Nome

*[The same seeker wrote again, finishing her message with, "
I always have faith in Bhagavan. I wish I could go see Him in
Arunachala and get His Darshan. Please help lead me out of
ignorance. Om Namo Bhagavate Sri Ramanaya. Om Namah
Shivaya." Here is the response.]*

December 11, 2012

ॐ Dear . . . ,

Om Namo Bhagavate Sri Ramanaya
Namaste. Thank you for your message.
When, through inquiry to know the Self, the misidentifications are abandoned, the anxious thoughts that constitute the emotions will subside.
Sri Bhagavan says that a, ru, and na signify Sat (Being), Cit (Consciousness), and Ananda (Bliss) respectively, and achala means unmoving. If you dive within to realize the Self which is of that nature, by His Grace, darshan will be granted in this quintessential true Being. Such darshan is forever.
Faith is the seed of profound, direct experience.

Om Namah Sivaya

Ever yours in Truth,
Nome

[A seeker who dwells near Arunachala regularly meditates on the holy mountain and wished to know how he could deepen his experience while moving about in that sacred place. He already recognized the importance of inquiry to negate misidentifications and expressed a yearning to identify with the motionless. Here is Nome's response.]

December 15, 2012

ॐ Dear . . . ,

Om Namo Bhagavate Sri Ramanaya

Namaste. Thank you for your message.

Existence, which is the Self, is ever unmoving and is always changeless.

From what vantage point do you perceive the movements and changes of the body? That which knows must be bodiless.

What is it that knows the changes of the senses and prana? That must be transcendent of them and unaffected by their changes and motions.

What is it that, unknown by the mind, knows the mind and its motions? That is innately mind-transcendent.

Consciousness, which alone knows, is the Existence, which alone is.

As the Self ever is, you are able to experience your true identity continuously and forever. The inquiry is the self-revelation of the very nature of your Being, which perpetually is as it is. This is the One without a second.

Inquire. Inquire deeply. Inquire thoroughly. Inquire consistently.

Just as, while walking on Arunachala, above and below there is Arunachala, and all of the motion is only on Arunachala and you do not depart from Arunachala, so it is with the motions of all and the Self.

Om Namah Sivaya

Ever yours in Truth,
Nome

[To a seeker who asked, "Can you please explain how bhak-ti yoga is similar to jnana yoga?", the reply was:]

December 16, 2012

ॐ Dear . . . ,

Om Namo Bhagavate Sri Ramanaya
Namaste. The similarity of jnana and bhakti is in the dissolution of ahankara (ego).

Ever yours in Truth,
Nome

[A seeker wrote asking if he could come to the SAT Temple to catch the Samadhi habit. Here is Nome's response.]

December 23, 2012

ॐ Dear . . . ,

Om Namo Bhagavate Sri Ramanaya
Namaste. Thank you for your message.
Sri Bhagavan says that samadhi is natural for sages, and those that associate with them catch the "samadhi habit." Understand samadhi to mean absorption in and abidance as the Self. Natural refers to that which is innate. A jnani, or

454

sage, retains no falsely assumed individuality, or ego, and thus, with Self-Knowledge, exists as the Self alone. The Self is bodiless, undifferentiated, and only one. This is the true Self of the seeker, too. "Association" is determined by depth of inquiry.

Of course, if you feel that attending satsangs and other spiritual events would be beneficial for you, you will be very welcome at the SAT Temple.

On Namah Sivaya

Ever yours in Truth,
Nome

[A devotee of Sri Ramana in India wrote: "When we are suffering from the prarabdhakarma, for a devotee of Sri Ramana, will Sri Ramana Maharshi come to our rescue or ease the karma? If a devotee is involved in service to humanity, will He ease it?" Here is the reply.]

January 16, 2013

ॐ Dear . . . ,

Om Namo Bhagavate Sri Ramanaya

Namaste. By Sri Bhagavan's gracious instruction, we know that it is only so long as there is misidentification as an ego and with the body that prarabdha karma appears to determine one's experience. Inquiring as He instructs, with a heart full of devotion and faith, you realize the Self, which is free of all kinds of karma.

Sri Ramana's "rescue" is always there. Knowledge of this yields deep peace.

Ever yours in Sri Bhagavan,
Nome

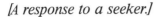

[A response to a seeker.]

January 22, 2013

ॐ Dear . . . ,

Om Namo Bhagavate Sri Ramanaya

Namaste. Thank you for your message. Though your caring concern about the disabilities of this body is appreciated, as long as it is possible to do so, I will continue to respond, albeit perhaps more briefly and concisely than in the past, so that you and others endowed with sincere interest can find the truth of the Self revealed within.

The ego that wanders in illusion is not real. The individual who conceives of the illusion in which to wander is not real. The Self, of the nature of Being-Consciousness-Bliss, is real. The Self is the source of the grace and the very nature of the one who finds herself absorbed in it.

May you abide always in the Knowledge of the immortal Self and thus be ever at peace.

Ever yours in Truth,
Nome

[A response to another seeker. The questions can be inferred from the replies.]

January 23, 2013

ॐ Dear . . . ,

Om Namo Bhagavate Sri Ramanaya

Namaste. Thank you for your message. In answer to your questions:

To inquire by tracing your Being inwardly beyond the senses and thought is fine. If you visualize it as a source of light, inquire as to who knows that. The knower can never be objectified. If you visualize the holy feet of Sri Bhagavan, continue to surrender, in deep devotion, so that the ego notion vanishes and, along with it, every objectified notion. They are not opposing ways of approach, so there is no difficulty. Continue to devotedly inquire until all ideas of "this" and "I" are gone, and only absolute Being, Sri Bhagavan's Grace, remains.

The Truth of no-creation is realized by Self-Knowledge alone. It is neither a particular kind of sensation nor an absence of sensations. One should never expect the senses to determine reality. The Self is not a body or a sensing entity. In Self-Knowledge, the "I" supposition and the delusive notion of a "world" are found to be nonexistent. The "sign post" about which you ask is the certainty regarding who you truly are, what is real. The peace and happiness of such are self-evident.

The goal of life as stated by you is clear. To give your full effort and attention to sadhana and to share Sri Bhagavan's teachings with your wife so that both of you can revel in His illuminative Grace are not contradictory. Both can very well be accomplished quite naturally.

May your inquiry be profound so that you ever abide in the nonobjective Self, as that Self, the One without a second.

Ever yours in Truth,
Nome

457

February 1, 2013

Om Namo Bhagavate Sri Ramanaya

Dear Nome

By the grace of Sri Ramana I have found SAT through Richard Clarke's blog. I wish to express my deepest gratitude for the Satsang videos. Self-inquiry is clearer now than ever. Thank you.

Some months before finding the teachings of Ramana Maharshi, I ate a very powerful, medicinal root from an African tree called Iboga. It is used for traditional spiritual and ritual purposes in the Congo by the Bwiti religion and also for treating drug addiction of all kinds in the west. Driven by an inner urge, I began to inquire during the experience, "Where do I come from, and what are my spiritual origins"? It was revealed to me, through an act of grace, that the self in me is the self in all and I and the light which words cannot express are one. There have been doubts arising since the rising of individuality subtly reappearing and due to not being in the bliss of that world-dissolving shining constantly. So, clearly there is work to be done. Is it good if the mind is kept constantly on the name Arunachala while remaining focused on the one repeating the name and inquiring into him?

It is understood that one must inquire to become established more fully in the Knowledge of the Self. After coming to Sri Bhagavan one year ago, I had a very powerful dream where He was not in human form, and I take it that He was pouring grace upon me. He is the Supreme Teacher and Sat-Guru for me. I am very blessed by this. On another occasion, Arunachala was a most beautiful orange color in an equally powerful and unusual dream. I ask only that even the subtlest sense of individuality may be completely absorbed in Arunachala, the real Self, and for guidance and confidence in inquiry.

With thanks,

[Here is Nome's response.]

ॐ Dear . . . ,

Om Namo Bhagavate Sri Ramanaya

Namaste. Thank you for your message. I am glad to know that you find the recordings of satsang beneficial.

The rise of the false assumption of individuality is the root of regarding the forever-nonobjective Self as if it were objective and fleeting. Inquiry dissolves that assumption and its concomitant dualism or differentiation.

Sri Bhagavan says that a, ru, and na signify Sat-Cit-Ananda (Being- Consciousness-Bliss), and achala (unmoving) signifies perfection. If one inquires into the nature of the worshiper, the meditator, or the one who knows the name, this Arunachala Siva reveals itself to itself, as one's own Self.

Graced with the Maharshi as your Sadguru, you can be quite certain about his instruction.

May your inquiry be deep and continuous so that you ever abide in Self-Knowledge, full of bliss, as the self-luminous Self, and thus remain absorbed in immortal peace.

Om Namah Sivaya

Ever yours in Truth,
Nome

[In a message a seeker wrote:]

February 7, 2013

Namaste Nome,

I have a question about an incident that happened today.

One of my friends Dad died suddenly in India due to heart attack. I called her for something else, and she mentioned this to me. Hearing this, I went to her house to console her. For a couple of minutes, she seemed very strong, and then, suddenly, she fell apart and started crying. Even yesterday, she talked about her dad and was saying that she is really concerned about her dad because he is getting sick more often. I kept telling her he would be fine.

When my friend started crying, I felt so bad for her, and I also started to fall apart. This body was not helping her anyway. I was thinking about my loved ones and what will this body do without them. Theoretically, I know even when they die, they will be with us all the time, and it is just the body that is no longer there.

Please advise me on how to focus. Situations like this can happen to me also. I don't have the courage to ask questions at Satsangs, and that is why I am emailing you.

Please help,
With Love,

[Nome's response:]

ॐ Dear . . . ,

Om Namo Bhagavate Sri Ramanaya
Namaste. Thank you for your message.

For that which has birth death is certain. This is the fact for your body and the bodies of others, including the bodies of loved ones. This loss brings sorrow to all except for those spiritual beings who turn within to find that which is immortal. That is God, or the Self.

For those who would be wise, death brings certain lessons. It can put everything into perspective so that one recognizes deeply what life is truly for, and it can reveal the existence of the Self, which is unborn and imperishable.

When you consider that, in less time than the space between two heart beats, death can snatch away all the objects to which one has grown attached and render utterly meaningless one's worldly activities and mental opinions and ideas, how are you going to use the remaining precious time of this life?

Your ability to comfort others who are being touched by death of their bodies or the bodies of their loved ones depends very much on your own spiritual depth. If you wish for this ability, you need to live and practice accordingly. Otherwise, as you have mentioned, what you will have to offer is mere theory or wallowing in the same grief. If, in your heart, you sincerely desire the eternal peace in which death presents no change or difficulty, consistently, deeply devote yourself to the Supreme Lord and intensely inquire to know the Self. For those who approach in this manner wholeheartedly and with full earnestness, persevering to destroy all of the mind's tendencies, Sri Bhagavan says the "I" (ego) is the first to die as they seek refuge in the Conqueror of death.

Om Namah Sivaya
Ever yours in Truth,
Nome

[In the course of a message, a seeker wrote: "Bhagavan says ultimately it is God that will help you realize, grace alone can will it, nothing else. What makes one receptive to grace? That is my goal right now in my sadhana; just to be receptive to this grace and wherever it wants to take me. I try to let go of the desire to become liberated since I have heard and read that desire of this can be an obstruction." This is Nome's reply.]

February 7, 2013

ॐ Dear . . . ,

Om Namo Bhagavate Sri Ramanaya
Namaste. Thank you for your message.
Grace is ever fully present. Sincerity of purpose, earnest and ardent practice of the teaching, faith, intense desire for Self-Realization, and such make one keenly aware of it.
Generally, if one attempts to be rid of the desire for Liberation, she desires something else, due to the persistence of the motivation to be happy. It is wiser to, endowed with the desire for Liberation, deeply inquire to know the

Self and thus destroy the ego-supposition and its false bondage by finding their unreality.

You will be very welcome at the SAT Temple.

Om Namah Sivaya

Ever yours in Truth,
Nome

[This is from a Sri Ramana devotee in India. Nome's response follows.]

February 22, 2013

Dear sir,

I have been repeating Bhagawan's name and I feel happy and the same day afternoon I could not do it, since my mind dominating and prevent from doing it.

Kindly give some suggestion. Why mind once again dominates? Thanks,

ॐ Dear . . . ,

Om Namo Bhagavate Sri Ramanaya

Namaste. If, repeating His name, you do so with a heart full of joyful devotion and faith, the waywardness of the mind will subside and it will no longer veil the Truth that Sri Bhagavan reveals.

Ignorance, in the form of misidentification, is the root of the illusions of the mind. Self-Knowledge destroys such ignorance. For this Knowledge, inquire "Who am I?"

For the earnest devotee of Sri Bhagavan, the tendencies of the mind appear only for the purpose of being destroyed.

As the Maharshi's Grace is always present, and as the nature of the ever-existent Self is Bliss, you have no real reason to ever be unhappy.

Om Namah Sivaya

Ever yours in Sri Bhagavan,
Nome

[In reply to a message from another devotee of Sri Bhagavan:]

March 7, 2013

ॐ Dear . . . ,

Om Namo Bhagavate Sri Ramanaya
Namaste. Thank you for your message.
Peace and freedom are experienced proportionately to the disappearance of ignorance. Inquiry reveals that they are of the very nature of the Self. Inquire so as to discern the false definitions of the "I" that seems to be distinct from the Self and, conceiving of a state other than the Self, thinks that he cannot be in the Self continuously.
Bhagavan's Grace is ever present. Rely on it completely and thus be always happy.
Whenever you are able to visit the SAT Temple, such as for a retreat, you are warmly welcome.
Om Namah Sivaya

Ever yours in Truth,
Nome

[A reply to a message from a seeker whose questions can be inferred:]

March 26, 2013

ॐ Dear . . . ,

Om Namo Bhagavate Sri Ramanaya

Namaste. Thank you for your message. I am glad to know that you have an interest in the teachings of Sri Bhagavan.

The source of the assumption of individualized existence, the ego or "I" notion ("I" thought), cannot be another thought, for other thoughts are subsequent to this supposition of "I," that is, they are further definitions of this "I." Rummaging through the piecemeal, sporadic, unreliable thoughts conceived as constituting memory will not do much to reveal the true nature of the Self, which is thought-transcendent, timeless, unborn, and imperishable. You, the knower of all thought, cannot possibly be a thought. Therefore, it would be wiser to seek to know yourself and realize what your Existence truly is. The nonobjective, introspective inquiry indicated by the question, "Who am I?" is for this purpose of Self-Realization.

Inquire inwardly, tracing your very sense of existence to its source. The source is not the body and is not the thoughts. Inquire so that you cease to misidentify with such forms.

"Heart" indicates your quintessential Being. Other uses of the term when applied to references pertaining to particular visualized, symbolic meditations mentioned in the Vedas and other Sastras, as well as in reference to yogic lore, must be understood in context. Some exercise of discrimination (viveka) will suffice to bring clarity about this for you. First, inquire and know the Self. Then, you can decide what the heart is, if you so desire.

I hope that you find the above helpful. If ever you find the time or interest to visit the SAT Temple, you will be warmly welcome.

May your inquiry be deep so that you abide in the Knowledge of the Self, the supreme purpose of life, and thus be ever happy and at peace.

Om Namah Sivaya

Ever yours in Truth,
Nome

[To the same seeker in response to another merssage:]

ॐ Dear . . . ,

Om Namo Bhagavate Sri Ramanaya
Namaste. The knowledge of your very Existence does
not depend on the mind and shines even when there is no
mind. Inquire at this depth.
Om Namah Sivaya

Ever yours in Truth,
Nome

[From a seeker, followed by Nome's response:]

April 23, 2013

Om Namo Bhagavate Sri Ramanaya
Namaste

Master Nome:
The immense gratitude for the teachings of Bhagavan Sri
Ramana Maharshi, made so clear by you, travel with me as I accom-
pany my wife for the impending death of her father. I miss SAT even
though what is here is there.
Master Nome you are deep in my heart!

In Devotion eternally
Om Namo Bhagavate Sri Ramanaya

ॐ Dear . . . ,

465

Om Namo Bhagavate Sri Ramanaya

Namaste. Thank you for your message and the messages from last week.

The deepest support that you can lovingly give to your wife is the steady, silent, inner abidance in the peace of the truth of the Self, which is unborn and imperishable. That which Sri Bhagavan graciously reveals, what he is, and that which truly all are dwells in your heart. The gratitude for such spiritual treasure makes it your own.

May you, with the fullness of devotion, ever abide in the Knowledge of the Self, realizing which the wise are free from sorrow, and thus remain as immortal, blissful Being.

Ever yours in Truth,
Nome

[A reply to a seeker:]

April 30, 2013

ॐ Dear . . . ,

Om Namo Bhagavate Sri Ramanaya

Namaste. Peace is of the nature of the Self. Happiness, also, is of the nature of the Self. One cannot truly expect something else to give her what is innately hers. Suffering is caused by such false suppositions. It is wise to thoroughly contemplate this, not only in reaction to some difficulty or loss, but to clearly guide the remainder of your life.

May you abide in the Knowledge of the Self, which is the eternal, perfect fullness.

Om Namah Sivaya

Ever yours in Truth,
Nome

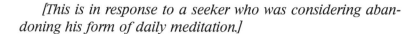

[This is in response to a seeker who was considering abandoning his form of daily meditation.]

May 1, 2013

ॐ Dear . . . ,

Om Namo Bhagavate Sri Ramanaya
Namaste. Thank you for your message.
You may wish to more deeply examine what meditation is before determining whether or not you will engage in it. If the misidentification with the body is abandoned, what becomes of your question? If the misconception that the senses can determine reality is relinquished, what becomes of your question? You may find it helpful to examine, with keen discrimination, what is truly meant by "inquiry," "silence," "Being," etc. If the misidentification with the mind dissolves, what becomes of all these ideas about them? If the objectifying tendency is absent and you truly inquire, Self-Knowledge will be self-evident.
I hope that you find the above helpful. May you, with profound inquiry, ever abide in the Knowledge of the Self, of the nature of Being-Consciousness-Bliss, and thus remain happy and at peace always.
Om Namah Sivaya

Ever yours in Truth,
Nome

[A devotee of Sri Ramana in India wrote:]

June 10, 2013

Dear sir,

Now my father is improving. At times he comes to know that something that hurts his mind is a thought, he could not come out of it.

Could you kindly suggest,
Thanks

[Nome's reply:]

ॐ Dear . . . ,

Om Namo Bhagavate Sri Ramanaya

Namaste. Thank you for your message.

Thoughts are not real. If one inquires for whom they are, this is realized.

Thoughts do not declare their own existence. Who is it that assumes that they exist?

Thoughts do not intrinsically have any importance. Who is it that gives them undue emphasis and assumes that they are valid?

Thoughts unexamined, confused with reality and identity, seem to veil the innate happiness, and thereby one suffers.

Meditating on what is indicated here, with Sri Bhagavan's Grace, happiness, identity, and reality shine clearly free of confusion, as One, and that is the Self.

Ever yours in Sri Bhagavan,
Nome

[A seeker wrote with these questions:]

June 18, 2013

Does one have to completely withdraw from the physical life? It seems that the masters, including you, live very simple lives, and it would seem to be easier to live the enlightened life.

I'm wondering how one who is employed, owns a home, has car payments, etc. does that and remains unattached. I'm reminded of Jesus who said to one of his want-to-be disciples, "to follow me you must sell all of your possessions." Without distractions it's easier to do than with. I pray all is well with you and yours.

[Here is Nome's reply.]

ॐ Dear . . . ,

Om Namo Bhagavate Sri Ramanaya

Namaste. Thank you for your message and for your kind donation to SAT.

One should withdraw from the ignorance of misidentification with the body and the false notion of being the performer of action, regardless of the activities in which the body is engaged.

The root of detachment is the certainty of knowledge about the source and nature of happiness.

Freedom from the concept of "my" is renunciation of possessions, and freedom from the notion of "I" is liberation from all of the imagined bondage.

Distraction is in the mind, and tracing the mind to its source to know its true nature is wise.

May your inquiry be deep, so that you always abide in the true Knowledge of the Self, which is neither active nor inactive, in which there is neither an ego nor a world, and for which there is no false supposition of being a body, and thereby are ever at peace.

Om Namah Sivaya

Ever yours in Truth,
Nome

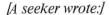

[A seeker wrote:]

June 23, 2013

Dear Master Nome,

This week I have been finishing up your book *Self-Knowledge.* Again, it is truly clarifying.

I had read the chapter on the nature of the Unborn, and it really stuck with me. During my sitting meditations and continuous inquiry, the unmanifest nature of my self still appears like a witness in relation to the appearance of the phenomenal/objective body and world.

As I understand it from your teachings, so long as the nondual self appears to be in relation to some phenomenal existence/world, it will seem like an observer. When there is no attention on the phenomenal world, that observer/witness realizes itself as simply the unborn and abides in and as sat-chit-ananda.

My question is: In order to help facilitate that shift, would you recommend absolute detachment toward that which appears as manifest? What else might you suggest?

As always, your insight is truly appreciated.

In devotion,

ॐ Dear . . . ,

Om Namo Bhagavate Sri Ramanaya

Namaste. Thank you for your message.

Absolute detachment, in essence, is true Knowledge. Thus, the Maharshi equates vairagya with jnana. Such absolute detachment is not only complete clarity regarding the source and nature of happiness and abidance as the forever-unaffected witness, which is of the nature of Consciousness, but the realization that there is neither an objective world nor an individual to experience such. Therefore, it is wise to deeply and thoroughly inquire. For whom is the manifestation? For whom is the appearance? In and for the Self, there is the Self alone. That is the sole-existent Reality. Inquire, "Who am I?"

Om Namah Sivaya

Ever yours in Truth,
Nome

[This aspirant was on a return visit to her native India.]

June 30, 2013

Namsate. Dear Nome and Sasvati,

I have a question on bhakti and Bliss. After coming to Kerala, I went to a lot of temples. When I see the God's idol in temples, there is no bhakti, no bliss, feel numb bodily, and I just stay in front of the God with no emotions. It has happened to me before also, but this time bodily I feel that a lot. There are also a lot of satsangs and events going on at [name omitted]'s house. I am having trouble focusing on the events spiritually. Be it at the temple or at home where there are spiritual events, this body does not get the happiness that I am doing something or attending a spiritual event.

I know spirituality is within. For some reason, I do not get that same happiness that I get at SAT temple, when I attend a spiritual event or pooja or do the chanting. In India, it is totally different for me. There is a lack of spiritual focus. What should I work on?

Is it just me or does the presence of Nome (my guru) for me make a big difference? Is it that my mind is set in a way that "bliss is only at some spiritual places"? How should I focus? Please help.

Yesterday we went to see [name omitted]'s uncle who is Ramana devotee. It was a good satsang.

Hope to see you soon.
Namo Ramana,

ॐ Dear . . . ,

471

Om Namo Bhagavate Sri Ramanaya

Namaste. Thank you for your message.

The source of bliss is the Self. Indeed, bliss is of the very nature of the Self. It is transcendent of bodily sensations and of emotions, which are a form of thought. It is to be found within.

Similarly, bhakti transcends the sensations and even the emotions that you may now associate with it. The source of bhakti is within, and, therefore, always available, no matter where in the world the body may be.

The satsangs, temples, etc., connected with one's Guru and such are naturally experienced with the deepest bhava, which is dissolution in the infinite and eternal. When you visit other temples, etc., remain keenly aware of the Existence of the Sadguru within, and He will reveal His omnipresence, as God, even as expressed in the form of the murti, temple, satsang, etc. There is no place where the Self is not. Realizing this, steady happiness is yours.

Reflection on your experience in India could serve to prompt you to turn inward more strongly and to experience what is at the SAT temple more consistently.

Please convey blessings to [name omitted].

May your heart blossom in the bliss of parabhakti.
Om Namah Sivaya

Ever yours in Truth,
Nome

[From a devotee of Sri Ramana in India:]

August 20, 2013

Though the fear, thought, has no value, it affects the body with pain. How can one overcome these things?

ॐ Dear . . . ,

Om Namo Bhagavate Sri Ramanaya
Namaste. Thank you for your message.

Fear is composed of thought. The Self, free from thought, is free from fear. Pain pertains to the body. The Self, transcendent of the body, is free from pain.

Where duality appears, there can be fear. In non-dual Self-Knowledge, there is fearlessness, because of the absence of misidentification with the body, the mind, or as an ego.

By Self-inquiry, which reveals the Knowledge of your true Existence, you realize the imperishable nature of your Existence, which is also your happiness. Similarly, by immersing yourself in devotion to Sri Bhagavan, seeking refuge in that One alone, you rise above thought, and fear dissolves.

Ever yours in Sri Bhagavan,
Nome

[An aspirant asked for an explanation of a verse in the Supplement to the Forty Verses on Reality (Saddarsanam, the Revelation of Truth)*]*

August 20, 2013

Om Namo Bhagavate Sri Ramanaya

Master Nome
Namaste

Please shed light on the following from *Ulladu Narpadu:*
Anubandam

30. Like one to whom a tale is told while his thoughts are far away, the mind which is free of attachment is inactive while it acts. But the mind immersed in attachments is active, though it does not act, like the sleeper lying motionless here, (but) who in his dream climbs a hill and tumbles down it.

In Devotion,

[Here is Nome's response.]

ॐ Dear . . . ,

Om Namo Bhagavate Sri Ramanaya

Namaste. Here is another translation, which appears in the 1979 edition of *Collected Works of Ramana Maharshi:*

The mind whose impressions (vasanas) have been destroyed is not engaged in activity even when it performs actions; it is like those who listen to a story absent-mindedly. The mind which is crowded with them is engaged in activity even when it does not perform actions; it is like one who, while lying still (in sleep), climbs a hill and falls into a pit in his dream.

Vasanas may be understood as the tendencies of the mind that are rooted in misidentification. Upon the destruction of such ignorant tendencies, the immovable Self alone remains, though, to an onlooker, it may appear that there is a body engaged in action. Thus, the analogy of someone appearing to listen to a story although his mind is not engaged in such at all.

Even if bodily desisting from actions, the mind that is filled with such tendencies is immersed in illusion. Although the Self alone is real, such a mind engages in imagination as in the dream analogy, confusing the experiences thereof with reality and deludedly thinks of oneself as if immersed in such.

Om Namah Sivaya

Ever yours in Truth,
Nome

[From the same aspirant:]

September 4, 2013

Om Namo Bhagavate Sri Ramanaya
Namaste
Master Nome:

During the just concluded retreat, you stated, in response to a question, something to the effect of exerting more effort if you have more effort to exert. My questions now are: who is it that exerts the effort? What is complete surrender? How do effort and surrender interplay or balance?
In loving devotion,
Om Namo Bhagavate Sri Ramanaya

[Here is the reply.]

ॐ Dear . . . ,

Om Namo Bhagavate Sri Ramanaya
Namaste. The inquiry regarding who applies effort is a wise application of effort. Likewise is surrender. Just as is so with inquiry, surrender is complete in the absolute nonexistence of the ego.
Om Namah Sivaya

Ever yours in Truth,
Nome

[In the course of a message dated October 31, 2013, a devotee of Sri Ramana in India wrote: Can I control my worrying mind by recollecting the letter by Bhagawan to his mother, "The ordainer controls the fate of souls..."? This is Nome's reply.]

475

ॐ Dear . . . ,

Om Namo Bhagavate Sri Ramanaya
Namaste. Thank you for your message.

Yes, diving deep into that instruction bestowed by Sri Bhagavan will remove all worry. That instruction concludes with, "the best course is to remain silent." He also reveals "silence is that in which no 'I' arises." So, relying on His Grace, which carries all, inquiring deeply or surrendering completely so as to abide in the egoless state, is liberation from all anxious thought.

The worry that appears in your mind is neither based on the Truth nor helpful to what you are endeavoring to accomplish. It consists of superfluous thought. Therefore, wisely adhere to the Maharshi's instructions, and you will remain happy and at peace.

Om Namah Sivaya

Ever yours in Sri Bhagavan,
Nome

[A seeker in France wrote:]

November 9, 2013

Dear Nome,

This experience of the heart at the right side: some disciples say it has no meaning or value. Of course, it is not at all the final experience. One must go beyond, deeper and deeper. I have this experience since the age of 20 (I am 65).

Any comment?
Om Ramana!

ॐ Dear . . . ,

Om Namo Bhagavate Sri Ramanaya
Namaste. Thank you for your message.
If you would inquire for whom the experience appears,
making your vision nonobjective, you would find the
absolute Existence of the Self, which is location-less, bodiless, imperceptible and inconceivable, and eternal. That
may be regarded as the true significance of the Heart. By
His Grace, with adherence to the spiritual instruction He
has bestowed, one is certain to abide in the Self, as the Self,
and thus remain in blissful peace.
Om Namah Sivaya

Ever yours in Truth,
Nome

November 11, 2013

ॐ Dear . . . ,

Om Namo Bhagavate Sri Ramanaya
Namaste. Thank you for your message.
The idea of "here" consists of the illusory combination
of existence and sense perception in relation to a body. You
are not the body. Existence alone is real. The belief in sense
perception is delusive. In deep dreamless sleep, there is no
notion of "here." Yet you still exist. Regard only that as real
which exists always, without any interruption for eternity.

Regard only the real as your Self. What is the case for "here" also holds true for the idea of "now." The Self is timeless and space-less.

If you inquire as to who should stay in or abide as "I am," the one Self without a second, without any alternative, will know itself as it is.

Your second question concerns pradakshina. What does it matter how other people may or may not approach this? If you know that such should be approached with deep devotion and an inward turned mind, that suffices. After all, your aim should be Self-Realization and absorption in that to which you are devoted. The formulation of opinions about other people and things does not serve a useful spiritual purpose. You may wish to look at the *Song of Ribhu* or *Nirguna Manasa Puja* for a profound understanding of pradakshina and other similar practices of worship.

May you ever abide in the Self, as the Self, of the nature of Being-Consciousness-Bliss, and thus remain ever happy and at peace.

Om Namah Sivaya

Ever yours in Truth,
Nome

[A reply to a seeker:]

November 22, 2013

ॐ Dear . . . ,

Om Namo Bhagavate Sri Ramanaya
Namaste. Thank you for your message.

The truth is that there is only the one infinite Consciousness, which changelessly exists forever, and you are that alone. Realizing this, the possibility of even the least illusion is no more.

If it ever appears otherwise to you, inquire to know the Self, and thus remain free and at peace.

Om Namah Sivaya

Ever yours in Truth,
Nome

[A reply to another message from the same seeker who wrote on November 11th. The questions can be inferred from answers.]

November 24, 2013

ॐ Dear . . . ,

Om Namo Bhagavate Sri Ramanaya

Namaste. Thank you for your message. Due to the Truth Revealed Retreat at the SAT Temple, this is the first opportunity to reply to you.

You may wish to read the previous response again. What is stated therein about reality and about sense perception applies to these present questions of yours, as well.

The waking state experiences are the content of the waking state of mind. Such is similar to a dream state of mind. To mistake the content of a mode of mind to be the reality is a basic definition of ignorance. Self-inquiry consists of true knowledge, and its focus is nonobjective in nature. The practice of actual Self-inquiry should be as consistent, deep, intense, and continuous as you wish your happiness and freedom to be.

The question about "relaxation" etc. is based upon the notion that the ego actually exists and that modes or moods of the mind are relevant to Self-Realization, which is not at all true.

You may find it very beneficial to read the actual teachings of Sri Bhagavan (*Who am I?, Saddarsanam,*

Talks, etc.) and other Vedanta literature (teachings of Ribhu, Adi Sankara, etc.). You may also find it useful to read and listen to what is available on the SAT website (www.SATRamana.org).

I hope that you find the above helpful.
Om Namah Sivaya

Ever yours in Truth,
Nome

[A response to a seeker.]

November 26, 2013

ॐ Dear . . . ,

Om Namo Bhagavate Sri Ramanaya
Namaste. Thank you for your generous donation to SAT and for your kind offering to Dakshina. May the revelation of the Truth of the Self ever shine within you as your natural state of absolute Knowledge. In such true Knowledge, may you ever abide transcendent of the body, its attributes and activities, free and ever in bliss. Abiding in the Self, as the Self, the Being-Consciousness that is One without a second, you will thus remain ever at peace.

Ever yours in Truth,
Nome

[The seeker's reply to the above response.]

November 26, 2013

Thank you Nome!!!

You are Grace manifest as a teacher who abides in and as the teaching. You are my guiding light. In the light of your instruction and example, all doubts are dissolved and questions answered. The Truth is revealed every time I listen to you speak. I can think of no greater blessing than to bathe in the teaching that reveals the Truth from a teacher who is what he reveals.

Thank you again and again,

Love ,

[This message was from a family member of a devotee of Sri Ramana in India. Nome's succinct reply follows.]

December 20, 2013

Dear sir,

My father had been to Ramanasraman on 20th. Usually when he goes, he sees all the devotee friends with enthusiasm, but he did not see like that. He used to run in the entire ashram and also take part in serving Narayana seva and also serve in the dining hall. He is not enthusiastic and avoids. He knows "There is nothing," but he has not got his "Be" stage back. Could you come to my father's rescue?

December 20, 2013

ॐ Dear . . . ,

Om Namo Bhagavate Sri Ramanaya
Namaste. Sri Bhagavan's Grace is always present. Your father has only to recognize this truth to be at peace.
Om Namah Sivaya

Ever yours in Sri Bhagavan,
Nome

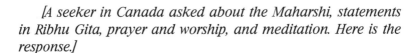

[A seeker in Canada asked about the Maharshi, statements in Ribhu Gita, prayer and worship, and meditation. Here is the response.]

December 20, 2013

ॐ Dear . . . ,

Om Namo Bhagavate Sri Ramanaya
Namaste. Thank you for your message.

You have fairly well answered your own questions pertaining to prayer, worship, etc., in the second paragraph of your message.

To clearly, correctly understand the meaning of the passages of *Ribhu Gita* and the state of the Maharshi, it is imperative for you to transcend the misidentification with the body. If you remain with the misidentification with the body, confusion, perplexity, and doubts in the mind are sure to arise due to the misinterpretation based on actions. If the misidentification with the body is abandoned by profound Self-inquiry, you transcend the action orientation of the mind, and the true significance of these passages etc., becomes clear.

Meditation ought to be upon the nature of the meditator, which is Self-inquiry. Concentration on respiration may lead to temporary calmness of mind, but, being an objective process, cannot result in Self-Knowledge. Similarly, modes of the mind such as "doing nothing" and "just trying to be," which leave the ego-notion unexamined and assumed, do not yield Self-Realization. There is no substitute for actual Self-inquiry. It alone does not include the illusion that one is trying to transcend.

Far more important than the amount of time the body is in a particular posture, such as seated, is the inner depth of meditation.

For the Self, which is eternally undifferentiated Being-Consciousness-Bliss, there are not two states of meditation and non-meditation. It is wise to intensely strive to realize this Self, which is Brahman. As Realization consists of Self-Knowledge, how else is it to be revealed except by the continuous, profound inquiry to know the Self, "Who am I?"

May you ever abide in That, as That, which is worshipped in the hearts of all, which illumines the meditations of all, and which, indeed, alone is the Self, the One without a second.

Ever yours in Truth,
Nome

[The Canadian seeker asked about his observation of his desires, aversions, and emotions. This is the reply.]

December 22, 2013

ॐ Dear . . . ,

Om Namo Bhagavate Sri Ramanaya

Namaste. Observing the emotions, desires, and aversions, etc., be sure to discern the actual thoughts that constitute them and the misidentifications that are the basis of those thoughts. The inquiry, "Who am I?" destroys the misidentifications, including their root, which is the ego-notion or assumption of individuality.

Om Namah Sivaya

Ever yours in Truth,
Nome

[A seeker questioned about sadhana and silence. Here is the response.]

483

January 3, 2014

ॐ Dear . . . ,

Om Namo Bhagavate Sri Ramanaya
Namaste. Thank you for your message.

The silence of the primordial Guru Dakshinamurti, of Sri Bhagavan, and of other such sages is of the nature of eternal, absolute Being. Sri Ramana declares it to be that in which no "I" arises. In that in which no "I" is ever born, no world is ever created. It is certainly free of any mental mode and transcends both activity and quietude of the mind.

Actual Self-inquiry consists of Knowledge, which is innately thought-transcendent. The nature of this nonobjective Knowledge is Consciousness, which is egoless and infinite.

As long as there seems to be a world, an "appearance," a "reaction," a "thought," a decision to inquire or not, a sankalpa (fixed idea, volition, concept, desire) to "abide" or to do otherwise, or someone for whom these pertain, it would be wise to deeply inquire.

The keen discrimination of the eternal and the transitory, the immutable and the changeful, may be helpful for making your approach nonobjective.

Om Namah Sivaya

Ever yours in Truth,
Nome

[The next day, the same seeker asked about nonobjective inquiry. This is the response.]

January 4, 2014

ॐ Dear . . . ,

Om Namo Bhagavate Sri Ramanaya
Namaste. Discern even more clearly. That which is

484

objective is not the Self, and the non-Self is unreal. Thoughts, inclusive of those that you refer to as "reactions," are objective; there is no such thing as a nonobjective thought. Silence, Self-Knowledge, which is abidance as the Reality, Brahman, is that in which thought and all of the differentiation imagined in thought do not exist. To view such as a mode or state of mind experienced by an individual, who is the root imagination, is only to conceive a thought of such, which cannot be the Reality, the Self, itself.

When, by constant, profound inquiry, the false assumption of "I" ceases, that which appeared as the inquiry is found to be the perpetual, nonobjective Knowledge. The end is the means. Inquire into the nature of the inquirer. The Self is one alone.

Om Namah Sivaya

Ever yours in Truth,
Nome

[A seeker in the UK requested clarity regarding several questions he had concerning death, karma, and how he wished to help his recently deceased father. The questions can be inferred from the replies given here.]

January 5, 2014

ॐ Dear . . . ,

Om Namo Bhagavate Sri Ramanaya
Namaste. Thank you for your message.
Clarity is by knowledge. The answers to your questions are different according to the perspectives assumed in the mind or if the orientation is that of transcendent Knowledge. If the perspective is discrete, distinct entities (vyasti), the jiva-s possess their separate karmas, which each

485

jiva must individually resolve. If the perspective is a collective aggregate (samasti), there is a connection or mingling of the jiva-s and their respective karmas. In either case, the distribution of the fruition of karma is said to be by Isvara, and the different perspectives are comparable to various views conceived within a dream. In transcendent, true Knowledge of the Self, "the jiva is Brahman alone, not another," jivo brahmaiva naparah (Adi Sankaracarya). This is the Knowledge of Reality, which alone constitutes Liberation. It is this that is revealed by Advaita Vedanta, Bhagavan Sri Ramana Maharshi, and other sages. In this Knowledge of the Self, which is Brahman, there is neither creation nor destruction, neither birth nor death, no one for whom there could be karma, no karma, and no results of karma. The Self, which alone exists (kaivalyam), is the only existence there really is, the only self that actually exists. The Realization of the eternal, infinite Self is complete, permanent freedom from all suffering, grief, the three kinds of karma, etc., and is unending peace.

In light of what is mentioned above, here are succinct answers to your particular questions.

1) According to one perspective, each jiva's karma is distinct, and the living person cannot assume the karma of the deceased. According to the other perspective, there is no such sharp division, and there are means, rituals, etc., said to affect that karma. The truth is, because the Self is not a body and not the individual ego, there are no distinctions such as life and death, you and he, etc. Inquire for whom is life, for whom is his death, for whom is karma, for whom is papa, who is he, and who are you?

2) According to one perspective, the pains undergone by the body, during life and in dying, serve to diminish the karma. According to another perspective, there is not necessarily a connection between the pains of the body and the karma adhering to the jiva. In truth, the Self is neither a body nor a jiva. The Self is untouched by karma, unassociated with a body, and not tainted by the body's experiences

of pleasures and pains. Inquire, "For whom are the pains? If I am not the body, who am I?"

3) The rewards of being honest and kind are primarily of a spiritual nature, and these are thus to be treasured. The material circumstances and bodily ease or hardship do not measure or reflect that which is of spiritual value. Suffering is equated with pain only by those who misidentify the Self with the body. Without such misidentification, though the body may still feel pain, one does not suffer.

4) Whatever spiritual practice is done, not a drop of it goes in vain. Seeing to your own Self-Realization, or Liberation, is the way for the liberation of all. Since you already know, as you mentioned, that the world is an illusion, inquiry that reveals the unreality of the individual and the reality of the Self will readily show you how this is so.

5) Communication between the living and the dead may be possible, though I cannot recommend anyone to accomplish this for you. If, though, you turn within to know the Self that you really are and that is the very Being of your father, you will not merely communicate, but you will be him, as the one, immortal, absolute Self.

6) Offerings for a Siva Temple, giving to and doing good for others, etc., are of tremendous spiritual benefit. There are no boundaries for such benefit. Adhere to that which is true, good, and beautiful, and all will benefit from the results of such.

Though these answers may not be precisely what you had in mind when you posed the questions, it is hoped that you find them helpful. Deep meditation upon their significance would be wise, if the perfection of the clarity of the Knowledge of the Self, the Reality, is that which you seek.

May you ever abide in That, as That, which is unborn and immortal.

Om Namah Sivaya

Ever yours in Truth,
Nome

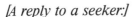

[A reply to a seeker:]

January 10, 2014

ॐ Dear . . . ,

Om Namo Bhagavate Sri Ramanaya
Namaste. Thank you for your message.

Deeper understanding and bliss are indications of being on the right path. Be certain to keep your discrimination, the inquiry, upon the real nature of the Self. The destruction of misidentification by Self-inquiry is for the purpose of the revelation of the true nature of the Self.

Emphasis on a "now" moment is not necessarily wise, for time is unreal, and the "now" is an objective conception. The conception of a "now" moment usually includes misidentification with the body and the senses and the ignorant belief in an external, existent world. Moreover, there is not the least trace of a "now" moment in deep sleep, but you still exist. This existence is ever the same. Know yourself as the Existence, and be free from the delusion of supposing that you are what is thought. If even the thought of "I" is not true or you, how could any other thought be true? The imperceptible and inconceivable Self is alone the reality and your identity. In this Realization is eternal, silent bliss.

Om Namah Sivaya

Ever yours in Truth,
Nome

[A reply to a seeker who asked about silence:]

January 16, 2014

ॐ Dear . . . ,

Om Namo Bhagavate Sri Ramanaya
Namaste.
Absolute silence, mauna, is that in which no ego "I" appears. This is the "state," actually the very nature, of being That, the Self, which is pure Being as it truly is and in which nothing else has ever come to exist. This is the silence of Dakshinamurti, Sri Bhagavan, and described in *Self-Knowledge.* The words of Self-Realized sages should be recognized as undifferentiated from the silence.
If you abide free of the least trace of misidentification, such is true mauna.
The best explanation of silence is silence, itself.
Om Namah Sivaya

Ever yours in Truth,
Nome

[This is the response to a seeker who asked about attention and constant inquiry.]

January 25, 2014

ॐ Dear . . . ,

Om Namo Bhagavate Sri Ramanaya
Namaste. Thank you for your message.
Even when the mind's attention is very much concentrated on a task or is involved in learning, you still know that you exist, though there may not be a thought about it.

489

At the depth of the knowledge of existence, the inquiry can be continuous.

Learning thus presents no obstacle to Self-inquiry. Be certain not to misidentify with thought or to regard thought and its content as real.

Om Namah Sivaya

Ever yours in Truth,
Nome

[A seeker asked questions about Self-inquiry and the mind in relation to a passage in the book Who am I?. *Here is the reply.]*

February 8, 2014

ॐ Dear . . . ,

Om Namo Bhagavate Sri Ramanaya
Namaste. Thank you for your message.

That which appears as an embodied individual is known as a mind. It is not your true identity. Your true identity is the Self, of the nature of formless Being-Consciousness-Bliss. The assumption of "I," which is but a bare supposition born of imagination, cannot stand alone but depends on some form, such as the body, in order to have even the appearance of some existence. By the term "subtle body" is meant a transmigrating entity, and "soul" indicates the spirit or Self with the superimposition of false individuality. If one persistently inquires into the nature of the mind, it subsides because it has no true existence, and only pure Consciousness remains.

Similarly, if one inquires into the nature or source of the "I," which in delusion appears as if an embodied individual, he finds the Heart, which means the quintessence of Being. Absolute Being is alone truly the source of the "I" and mind, and they cannot exist apart from That. In truth, they are not real, and the Self alone exists.

If one constantly contemplates the significance of "I," one abides as what the "I" truly is, which is the Self. Because all ideas depend on the "I" notion, liberation from the false individuality is freedom from all thought.

The inquiry, "Who am I?" is directed toward the nonobjective knowledge of yourself. Your existence is only one. In illusion, the same Self appears as if a mind or as if an individualized existence. By inquiry, the illusion is dispelled, and the very same existence remains as it truly is. This is Self-Knowledge. The knower is only one and of the nature of unalloyed Consciousness. The mind is not a second knower. The Self is undivided and is free of illusory differentiation such as higher and lower.

So, inquire, and thus abide in happiness and peace.
Om Namah Sivaya

Every yours in Truth,
Nome

[The reply to a seeker who wrote about an experience of bliss.]

February 9, 2014

ॐ Dear . . . ,

Om Namo Bhagavate Sri Ramanaya
Namaste. Thank you for your message.

Bliss shines upon, and proportionate to, the diminishing of the ego notion. Continue to make your approach nonobjective. In truth, the ego does not exist, and that which does not exist is not capable of doing anything.

Inquiry reveals the Self to be absolute Being alone. For the sake of the fullness of immortal bliss, joyfully discern and eliminate misidentification. When ignorance is seen to be only ignorance and nothing more, it ceases forever. Nothing is as fascinating as the Self, and no worldly pleasure can compare to the inner bliss of Self-Knowledge. Inquire deeply and continuously so that there is steady abidance in the Self, as the Self.

Om Namah Sivaya

Ever yours in Truth,
Nome

[The answer to further questions from a seeker regarding Who am I?*]*

February 12, 2014

ॐ Dear . . . ,

Om Namo Bhagavate Sri Ramanaya

Namaste. It is the nature of the "I" that asks, "Am I looking in truth or in thought?" that is the focus of the inquiry.

The entire world, inclusive of the examples mentioned by you, is in the mind. Thoughts constitute the mind. Thoughts neither know themselves nor declare their own existence. You know them or say that they are. What is the nature of this "you"?

Yesterday's response to you explains the Heart. The Self, which is God, is infinite, omnipresent, and location-less, for your true nature is bodiless.

To discern from where the sense of reality, or identity, derives, questioning within, "For whom is this? Who am I?" is the tracing to which Sri Bhagavan alludes.

Om Namah Sivaya

Ever yours in Truth,
Nome

[A reply to the same seeker who mentioned that he thought of himself as dense in his attempt to understand Self-inquiry.]

February 15, 2014

ॐ Dear . . . ,

Om Namo Bhagavate Sri Ramanaya

Namaste. You are not dense. The mind is so accustomed to the objectifying outlook that, when told to inquire and know yourself, you overlook the nature of the inquirer or yourself and attempt to know the Self as if it were apart from you as an objective topic of study. Self-inquiry is nonobjective knowledge.

The Self is only one and has no parts. Your Existence is absolutely singular. This is true regardless of whether you mistakenly conceive of yourself as an individualized "I" or know yourself as the Self you really are. So, there is no choice to be made, for there are not multiple selves or parts of yourself. Multiplicity is only in thought. You are not a thought. Seek to know the knower who is unknown by any thought.

Similarly, Consciousness is the only knower, and the mind is not a second knower. True Knowledge is in and of the sole Existence-Consciousness.

You may find it helpful to read *Self-Knowledge* and *Saddarsanam and an Inquiry into the Revelation of Truth and Oneself.*

Om Namah Sivaya

Ever yours in Truth,
Nome

[A reply to a seeker:]

February 24, 2014

ॐ Dear . . . ,

Om Namo Bhagavate Sri Ramanaya
Namaste. Thank you for your message.

It is good that you have an interest in Siva, who is understood according to the depth of the devotee. As you view yourself, so you view Siva.

Yes, the names have deep significance.

One who, with a heart full of devotion, remains awake to the Truth of the Self and free from the dreams of illusion, beyond the three states, absorbed in the auspicious, abides as Consciousness inherent in which is the power to destroy all ignorance and illusion and remains as the residual Absolute Being, finds perfectly full Bliss in the eternal, self-luminous great night of Siva (Mahasivaratri).

Om Namah Sivaya

Ever yours in Truth,
Nome

[In answer to a few questions about Self-inquiry:]

February 24, 2014

ॐ Dear . . . ,

Om Namo Bhagavate Sri Ramanaya

Namaste. Thank you for your message.

Regardless of whatever thought appears, be intent upon the knowledge of the Self. Trace your sense of identity to its source, which cannot be a thought.

The Self does not come from anywhere. It is ever existent.

All, including the mind, are not separate from the Self, but the Self is undivided and without parts.

Who is it that would follow a thought? Find out his nature. You are not a thought and cannot be determined by thought. You are thus inconceivable. Who are you?

Om Namah Sivaya

Ever yours in Truth,
Nome

[A seeker from Canada asked if it is necessary for him to worship the Gods and was perplexed about the relevance of such prayer to the Knowledge of the Supreme Brahman. This is Nome's reply:]

March 14, 2014

ॐ Dear . . . ,

Om Namo Bhagavate Sri Ramanaya

Namaste. Thank you for your message.

You need not be concerned about the Gods. They can take care of themselves; you should inwardly inquire and truly know yourself.

God or Gods appear according to the view of the perceiver (worshiper, meditator, etc.). Similar is the case in regards to Brahman. To know Brahman as Brahman is, know the Self. To know the Self, inquire "Who am I?" For inquiring to realize the Self, you have the grace of all the Gods and God.

As the grace is ever present, dive within and realize the Self, Brahman, which is the One without a second, and thus abide free, happy, and at peace always.

Om Namah Sivaya

Ever yours in Truth,
Nome

[This is a response to a seeker who asked about siddhis, the mind's sakti, and inquiry.]

April 8, 2014

ॐ Dear . . . ,

Om Namo Bhagavate Sri Ramanaya

Namaste. Thank you for your message. I am glad to know that the retreat was so beneficial for you.

Two terms should be distinguished: sakti and siddhi. Sakti means power. Siddhi means accomplishment, attainment, or established, and is sometimes used as a term to describe miraculous powers.

In *Who Am I?*, Sri Bhagavan says that the mind is a sakti of the Self, and it is, perhaps, this statement and commentary upon it that you recall.

Regardless of the term employed to describe it, the mind cannot know the nonobjective Self. Indeed, the mind has no knowing power of its own whatsoever. The power to know is rooted in Consciousness. Consciousness is the Self, and this Self is what you truly are. The Self alone is eternal, and that which is eternal is alone truly important. By profound inquiry, liberate yourself from any tendency to misidentify with that which is transitory, unimportant, or objective. In such freedom is found the perfectly full happiness that you have always actually desired.

Om Namah Sivaya

Ever yours in Truth,
Nome

[A devotee of Sri Ramana expressed his suffering due to unwanted thoughts. This is the reply:]

May 11, 2014

ॐ Dear . . . ,

Om Namo Bhagavate Sri Ramanaya

Namaste. Thank you for your message.

Relying upon Bhagavan's Grace, remaining steeped in devotion to Him, you certainly can cross over the mire of delusive thoughts and be at peace. If you discern the misidentifications that form the basis of those delusive thoughts and inquire so that you no longer create or adhere to those false definitions, you will abide as the bodiless, thought-transcendent, true Self, full of bliss.

Om Namah Sivaya

Ever yours in Sri Bhagavan,
Nome

*[The seeker wrote describing how his mind was disquieted
and that he was no longer enthralled with the reading of scriptures. This is the response:)*

May 23, 2014

ॐ Dear . . . ,

Om Namo Bhagavate Sri Ramanaya

Namaste. Thank you for your message. This response
will remain brief lest it meet with the same fate in your
mind as the scriptures did.

If approached clearly and humbly so as to be absorbed
in that which is ineffable and inconceivable, the sacred
books become a means of darshan of those who spoke or
wrote them, and the Truth thus revealed is of perpetual fascination.

Om Namah Sivaya

Ever yours in Truth,
Nome

*[A seeker from Denmark said that he knew of multiple ways
of Self-Inquiry and wished to know which of them would be
best for him. This is Nome's reply:]*

June 11, 2014

ॐ Dear . . . ,

Om Namo Bhagavate Sri Ramanaya

Namaste. Thank you for your message.

That which is most important in the spiritual practice of Self-inquiry is to actually inquire. The focus should be entirely upon your very Existence, questing within in a nonobjective manner.

Trace the sense of identity, of "I," to its source. For whom do thoughts appear and disappear? For whom are the patterns of the mind, the sensations related to the body, etc.? Inquire to know the nature of the inquirer.

May your inquiry be deep so that you ever abide in and as the Self that you truly are, which is of the nature of bodiless, mind-transcendent, egoless, ever peaceful Being-Consciousness-Bliss, infinite and eternal, and thus remain always happy and free.

Om Namah Sivaya

Ever yours in Truth,
Nome

[The same seeker wrote again.]

Just to be totally clear about the practice, do you mean that I should have my focus on the pure Existence that is in the space between and after thought patterns, or just simply on the feeling that I exist? Or the sense of self, and then follow this sense of self into its very nature?

With love,

[Here is the reply:]

499

ॐ Dear . . . ,

Om Namo Bhagavate Sri Ramanaya;

Namaste. It would be wisest to know the nature of the one who considers and thinks of these various ways. If this is realized by nonobjective inquiry, only the Self is found to exist and no individual to imagine anything else.

Om Namah Sivaya

Ever yours in Truth,
Nome

[The next two messages are from the same seeker:]

July 12, 2014

Dear Nome,
    Thank you so much for your reply, and I will continue to do the practice of self-inquiry, until I am fully establised in the Self forever.

    Om Namah Sivaya
    With love,

Dear Nome
    Namaste

    Thank you again so much.
    I have seen the one who inquires about these practices to come out of the nothingness or Being only to go back into that nothingness again. The one in me who thinks about these practices is not a permanent thing. The awareness that looks at the thinker is, though. The one who thinks about these practices comes out of that awareness also. So, it must be of the same nature as the awareness itself and therefore not a separate being.
    Please correct me if I am wrong.
    This way of seing things has the power to dissolve the ego (the

500

thinker), but it does not yet leave me in permanent peace, because there is obviously still a me in this body. Why is that? Should I just continue to see the thinker as awareness/Being instead of a separate being until everything is dissolved, or should I go about this practice in another way?

Thank you again for being here, and I really hope it's okay, that I ask you all these questions.

With love,

[Here is Nome's response:]

July 12, 2014

ॐ Dear . . . ,

Om Namo Bhagavate Sri Ramanaya

Namaste. Are there two selves, that one could come out of another? The Self is only one and is forever unmodified. If your experience seems otherwise, inquire into who conceives such differentiation, and the individuality, being unreal, will vanish.

Similarly, the misidentification with the body should be completely abandoned, for such is the basis of much ignorance. Free of misidentification as an ego and with a body, one abides in the natural state of blissful immortality.

Om Namah Sivaya

Ever yours in Truth,
Nome

[From the same seeker:]
July 17, 2014

Dear Nome

Namaste. I think I have come to realise where I went wrong in my inquiry. I have probably made it much more difficult than it actually is.

I have come to realise, that the source cannot be an object like a void or empty space. Tracing the I-thought back to the source simply means to put my attention back on the subject, the seer. In that, the I-thought vanishes, and pure Being is revealed.

Is that correct?

With love,

[Nome's reply:]

July 17, 2014

ॐ Dear . . . ,

Om Namo Bhagavate Sri Ramanaya

Namaste. This is clearer. Be certain that the inquiry consists of nonobjective Knowledge and not mere mental attention. The former transcends all thought, modes of mind, and the three states of mind. It is eternal. The latter is a transitory mode confined to the waking state of mind.

You may find it beneficial to read *Self-Knowledge, Saddarsanam, Song of Ribhu,* etc.

May you ever abide in and as the self-existent, self-knowing Self and thus remain in immortal bliss.

Om Namah Sivaya

Ever yours in Truth,
Nome

[A seeker wrote:]

July 28, 2014

Sri Nome

My question is: what is the attitude with which one should study *Ribhu Gita?* I do self enquiry and understand the difference between affirmations and actual self enquiry.

But when I study *Ribhu Gita,* affirmative and negative statements automatically create a mesmerizing I am Brahman bhava in me.

Should I continue to study *Ribhu Gita* with affirmation approach?

If not, please elaborate how to do self-enquiry and, at the same time, read *Ribhu Gita?* Because in self-enquiry one's entire attention goes to the inner feeling of "I."

Namaskarams.

[The response:]

ॐ Dear . . . ,

Om Namo Bhagavate Sri Ramanaya

Namaste. Thank you for your message.

In the "I am Brahman" bhava, it is the Knowledge-essence that is important and not the word or thought form. The Knowledge-essence is transcendent of words, thoughts, and modes or states of mind. It is of an eternal nature. Sri Bhagavan says that what is not eternal is not worth seeking. For Self-Realization, the means and the end must be of an identical nature, for, otherwise, dualism will be imagined. Self-inquiry is of the same Knowledge-essence; the end is itself the means. Just as Self-inquiry is not a form of thought, affirmative or negative, likewise is it transcendent of mental attention, which is not eternal and does not transcend the three states of mind. Beyond thought, modes, and states of mind is the pure Consciousness in which differentiation is impossible. There is the innate Knowledge of the Self, there is the place of profound inquiry, and there is the deep comprehension of what Ribhu graciously reveals. Therefore, in actual, experiential practice, there is no difficulty in reading *Ribhu Gita* and inquiring to know the Self simultaneously.

May you ever abide in That, as That, of the nature of undivided Being-Consciousness-Bliss, the one Self that alone exists eternally, and thus remain at peace always.

Om Namah Sivaya

Ever yours in Truth,
Nome

Index

Opinions, from others: 51,
193-194, 300, 311, 401
Opinions, one's own: 59,
193-194, 209, 221, 233,
460, 478
Opinions, about other
seekers: 156

P
Pain: 72, 98, 164-166, 173,
217, 246, 254, 278, 415,
419, 473, 486-487
Para: 326
Parabrahman: 99, 190-191,
202-204
Parabhakti: 243
Past life: 332-333, 338-339
Peace: throughout
Pedantic: 221
Perseverance: 34, 63, 169,
172, 211, 371, 403, 451
Practice: throughout
Praise: 57, 252, 353, 395
Prana: 66, 206, 224, 453
Pranayama: 165, 280, 329-
330
Prarabdha Karma: 59, 132,
162-163, 455
Prasad: 174
Prayer: 437, 482
Predetermination: 185
Presence: throughout
Puja: 44, 106-107, 140-
141, 376

R
Ramana Maharshi, Sri:
throughout
Regret: 237, 293
Reincarnation: 52, 360

Rejection: 89, 173, 184,
210, 300
Relationships: 171, 183
Renunciation: 10, 45, 441-
442, 469
Repression: 159
Reputation: 173, 300
Ribhu: throughout
Ridicule, for being spiritual:
36, 310-311
Ridiculing others: 156
RMCL, Ramana Maharshi
Center for Learning: 95,
143, 256, 350

S
Sacred Ash: 138, 174, 448
Saddarshanam: 79, 140
Sadguru: 31, 53, 84, 101,
144, 157, 163, 180, 193,
199, 221, 321, 444, 459,
472
Sadhana: 57, 59, 116, 135,
305, 438-439, 448, 452,
457, 483
Sadness: 189, 207, 220,
376-377
Sage, female: 134, 200-202
Sahaja: 58, 120, 130, 188,
334
Sahaja Samadhi: 54, 58,
211
Samadhi: 43, 54, 57-60,
187-188, 211, 334, 429,
445, 454
Samskaras: 360
Sanatana Dharma: 42
Satsang: 54, 160
Sattvic diet: 224-225
Security, in the world: 337

ॐ

Other SAT Publications available are:

~The Song of Ribhu (The English Translation of The Tamil Ribhu Gita)

~The Ribhu Gita (The English Translation of The Sanskrit Ribhu Gita)

~A Bouquet of Nondual Texts

~Origin of Spiritual Instruction

~Essence of Enquiry

~Self-Knowledge

~Self-Realization

~Timeless Presence

~Svatmanirupanam, The True Definition of One's Own Self

~The Four Requisites for Realization and Self-Inquiry

~Nirvana Satkam, Six Verses on Nirvana

~Nirguna Manasa Puja, Worship of the Attributeless One in the Mind

~Saddarsanam and An Inquiry into the Revelation of Truth and Oneself

~Advaita Devatam, God of Nonduality

~Essence of Spiritual Instruction

~The Quintessence of True Being

For a complete list of books on Advaita Vedanta and the Teachings of Sri Ramana Maharshi, please contact the publisher:

SAT Temple
Society of Abidance in Truth
1834 Ocean Street, Santa Cruz, California 95060
(831) 425-7287
www.SATRamana.org
sat@cruzio.com

512